I0124338

Goldfrey Holden Pike

Ancient meeting-houses

Memorial pictures of Non-conformity in old London

Goldfrey Holden Pike

Ancient meeting-houses
Memorial pictures of Non-conformity in old London

ISBN/EAN: 9783337150631

Printed in Europe, USA, Canada, Australia, Japan

Cover: Foto ©Andreas Hilbeck / pixelio.de

More available books at **www.hansebooks.com**

ANCIENT MEETING-HOUSES;

OR,

MEMORIAL PICTURES

OF

NONCONFORMITY IN OLD LONDON.

BY

GODFREY HOLDEN PIKE.

"HE IS THE VICTOR WHO TO TRUTH DOTH YIELD."

LONDON:
PASSMORE & ALABASTER 18, PATERNOSTER ROW.
S. W. PARTRIDGE & Co., 9, PATERNOSTER ROW.
MDCCCLXX.

TO THE

PASTORS, OFFICE-BEARERS, & CONGREGATIONS

OF

THE THREE DENOMINATIONS

OF

PROTESTANT DISSENTERS.

THE present volume is dedicated to you with all confidence as to the respect you cherish for the principles it illustrates, and the esteem in which you
hold the sainted men whose lives it records. A review of the severe conflicts, and of the heroic exer-
tions of the fathers in the faith, it is sent forth as
an affectionate memorial of their loyalty to conscience, their fidelity to revealed truth, and of their
sublime steadfastness amid difficulty and suffering.
It thus seeks to extend the pure fame of those
worthy confessors who so nobly defended the principles of civil and religious liberty when fiercely
assailed by the corrupt forces of tyranny and priestcraft; to whom, therefore, under Divine Providence,
the present generation must trace its priceless ad-

vantages. An endeavour is also made to do honour to those nonconforming worthies of the eighteenth century upon whom devolved the grave responsibilities which arose out of the moral victories of an earlier period. The reader will learn something of the patience, courage, and cheerfulness with which the Dissenters in the old City toiled while carrying on the work of Christ—a work now happily expanded into the unexampled evangelistic efforts of the present era. By a faithful examination of original manuscripts and other standard authorities, it has been sought to preserve accurate memories of the rapidly disappearing sanctuaries of old London; and thus, in some degree, to perpetuate the influence of those centres of religious life. The book is circulated with the hope that it may strengthen the love of freedom which so eminently distinguished the pastors, officers, and members of the Churches in less peaceful times, thus leading to a yet wider diffusion and a more manifest triumph of the Spirit of Liberty.

G. H. P.

Enfield, March, 1870.

CONTENTS.

CHAPTER I.

DEVONSHIRE SQUARE.

Introductory—Allusion to the Baptist in Hudibras—Jasper Fisher—First planting of the Society in Devonshire-square —WILLIAM KIFFEN and his biographers—Early troubles and conversion—Secedes from the Established Church— Joins the "Independents" under John Lathorp, and commences preaching—His marriage—Is imprisoned—Other troubles—Enters into the Dutch trade—His rapid rise— Ecclesiastical condition of England on the eve of the civil wars—Kiffen an officer in the Parliamentary army—Baptismal controversies—"Gangrene" Edwards—The custom of anointing—New troubles—Alleged plot to murder the King —A missing MS—Domestic sorrows—The Hewling tragedy —Battle of Sedgemoor—The "bloody" assizes—Reaction of public opinion—Kiffen is called to Court—Made an alderman—Secedes from the church—His liberality—Death and character—THOMAS PATIENT—Dies of the plague in 1665— Is succeeded by DANIEL DYKE—His death—The ancient discipline at Devonshire-square—RICHARD ADAMS—His persecution—Succeeds Kiffen—Disputes about psalmody— MARK KEY—Sir G. and Lady Page—Dr. SAYER RUDD—His church removes to Devonshire-square—Disagreement with the people—Libelled by Ivimey—Removes to Maze-pond—

GEORGE BRAITHWAITE—Early life and conversion—Becomes a Baptist, and commences his ministry—Unpopularity of his treatise against public-houses—Accession at Devonshire-square—Quarrel between that church and the Society at Maze-pond—His last days and death—JOHN STEVENS—Charges against him—Division in the church—Some particulars of his life—WALTER RICHARDS—His brief pastorate and resignation—JOHN MACGOWAN—Early life—Talents as a writer—Death—TIMOTHY THOMAS—His disadvantages—Genial nature—Death—The future of Devonshire-square.

PAGE 1

CHAPTER II.

PINNERS' HALL.

Ancient associations of the site—The hall is leased by the Nonconformists--ANTHONY PALMER--His troubles--Removes to London—Works with G. Fownes—Death—RICHARD WAVEL—Sufferings — The Merchants' Lecture — Sabbatarian Baptists—Dr. Watts and his people in Pinners' Hall —JEREMIAH HUNT—His talents—Friendship with Collins and Lord Barrington—JAMES FOSTER—His early days—Removal to London—Visits Lord Kilmarnock—Foster and his eulogists—His popularity and defective teaching—CALEB FLEMING—Early life—Becomes a Socinian partisan—Extinction of the church. . . . . PAGE 61

CHAPTER III.

CROSBY HALL.

Early history of the premises—The hall is leased by the Presbyterians—THOMAS WATSON—His devotion and industry —Death—STEPHEN CHARNOCKE—His ancestor "Rosicrucian" —Early life of Stephen—Settles in Dublin—Returns to London and serves under Watson at Crosby Hall—Works—Last resting-place—False story about him—SAMUEL SLATER—

The lecturers at Crosby Hall—BENJAMIN GROSVENOR—A *protégé* of Keach—Secedes from the Baptists—Great prosperity of the church under his pastorate—Retires—Society becomes extinct. . . . . : . . . . . . PAGE 79

CHAPTER IV.

THE OLD JEWRY.

The site named after the Jews—Sufferings of its early inhabitants—Description of the old meeting-house—EDMUND CALAMY—SAMUEL BORFET—JOHN SHOWER—Early training —He travels over Europe—Rome in the seventeenth century—Travelling adventures—Returns to England in 1687— His engagement at Silver-street under John Howe—Removes to Cripplegate—Erection of the Old Jewry Meeting-house— Correspondence with Lord Oxford on the Occasional Conformity Bill—The promoters of that measure—Robert Harley, Earl of Oxford—Shower's last days—TIMOTHY ROGERS— A strange story belonging to the Old Jewry, *note*—"A broken vessel"—JOSEPH BENNETT—His early trials—SIMON BROWNE—Shepton Mallet his birth-place, *see note*—Settles at Portsmouth—Removes to London, 1716—Extraordinary hallucination—He retires to Shepton Mallett—Continues his studies—Describes his own case, *see note*—Behaviour in company—His works—Cause of the delusion—Death and character—THOMAS LEAVESLEY—His unpopularity—SAMUEL CHANDLER—His education and college companions—Settlement at Peckham—Is engaged on a lectureship at the Old Jewry—Removes to London—Popery and the Pretender— The Gentleman's Magazine and the Dissenters—Romanist disputes—Chandler's zeal against the papacy—His action in the Rebellion year, 1745—His great success—Mary Chandler —DR. MILES—His singular industry—RICHARD PRICE— Early discipline—Removes to London—Settles at Newington-green—His book on Civil Liberty—Admirers and detractors —Doctrinal views—Death of friends—Centenary sermon on the Revolution—Death—THOMAS AMORY—Not popular—An archdeacon is invited to assume the pastorate—NATHANIEL WHITE—ABRAHAM REES—His vast industry in preparing his Encyclopaedia—His popularity and professorship at Hoxton—Last days of the Old Jewry Meeting-house— New chapel in Jewin-street—Death of Dr. Rees—DAVID DAVIDSON—Discouraging state of the congregation—The pastor resigns — Extinction of the society — Reflections PAGE 95

CHAPTER V.

THE SABBATARIAN BAPTISTS IN OLD LONDON.

Old Cripplegate—Curriers' Hall—FRANCIS BAMPFIELD— His provincial experience—Removal to London—Persecuted —Scene in Pinners' Hall in 1683—The pastor's arrest and death in Newgate—EDWARD STENNETT—His residence at Wallingford—The Castle and its privileges serve the cause of Nonconformity—A plot defeated—Pastorate at Pinners' Hall —Death—Abingdon—JOSEPH STENNETT—Early industry— Aids the Revolution—Becomes pastor of the Sabbatarians— A politician—Marries a French Protestant—Effects of revoking the Edict of Nantes—Tunbridge Wells in 1700—Stennett's popularity as an author—Many of his pieces lost—Dissenters and the war of the Spanish Succession—Treaty of Utrecht— The Ministry court the Dissenters—Stennett's reply—Last days and death—EDWARD TOWNSHEND—THOMAS WHITE-WOOD—ROBERT BURNSIDE—His early days—Singularities— Some account of his denomination, note—Death—Mill-yard, Goodman's-fields—The records not accessible—Whitechapel in the olden time—Petticoat-lane under James I.—Who was Goodman?—The Wilson MSS.—Founding of the Mill-yard Society—The people's peculiarities—The Fifth Monarchists

—JOHN JAMES—His arrest and trial—Prison experience—
An enthusiast in life but brave in death—Execution—His
character—JOHN SAVAGE—JOHN MAULDEN—ROBERT CORN-
WAITE—DANIEL NOBLE—WILLIAM SLATER—Places occupied
by the Sabbatarians—Their character—Other societies which
have settled at Mill-yard, *note.* . . . . . . PAGE 159

CHAPTER VI.

BURY STREET, ST. MARY AXE.

The old chapel still standing—Ancient associations of the
neighbourhood—Founding of the church—JOSEPH CARYL—
Early life—Conduct in the civil wars—Appreciated by Cromwell—Great industry—Death—WILLIAM BEARMAN—His
charities—JOHN HOWE—Libelled by Wood—The Owen
family—Early tutors—Enters the Church Establishment—
Removes to London—Coggeshall—Owen and the Long Parliament—Removes to Oxford—Wood's libels—Writes against
popery, *note*—Savoy Conference—Returns to London—Widely
esteemed—Death and character—ROBERT FERGUSON—A
plotter and a renegade—DAVID CLARKSON—Works—ISAAC
LOEFFS—ISAAC CHAUNCY—EDWARD TERRY—ISAAC WATTS
—His family—Early life—Tutors—Returns to Southampton
—Stoke Newington—The Hartopp family—First sermon—
T. Gunston—Illness—The church's solicitude—The Abneys
—Theobalds—Watts and the Unitarians—Songs for children
—1719—Watts and Bradbury—The times he lived in—The
clergy and the Jacobites—State of the common people—"The
good old times"—Strange number of suicides—Watts and
the Gentleman's Magazine—Poetical prizes—Sylvanus Urban
and his staff, *note*—Blair's "Grave"—Watts and his associates—Frequent illness—The Countess of Huntingdon and
Dr. Watts—Unhandsome behaviour of certain relatives—
Last days and death—SAMUEL PRICE—MEREDITH TOWNS-

HEND — SAMUEL MORTON SAVAGE — Tutor of Hoxton
College — Life-work — Death — THOMAS BECK — Removal
of the church to Founders' Hall, and thence to Bethnal-
green. . . . . PAGE 208

CHAPTER VII.

LITTLE CARTER LANE.

Ancient associations of the vicinity—Wilson's description
of the chapel—MATTHEW SYLVESTER—Life, work, and character—RICHARD BAXTER—Kidderminster in the olden time
—Baxter's early life—Education—Condition of rural districts
in his youth—Conversion—Early industry—Goes to Court—
Great physical weakness—Commencement of his ministry at
Dudley—Precursors of civil war—Abuses in the Church—
Baxter and Kidderminster—Great benevolence—Civil war—
Rough usage of Puritans—Coventry in the war time—Baxter
in the army—Polemical disputes—The COVENANT—The Restoration—Dissatisfaction of Nonconformists—A Court adventure—The Act of Uniformity—Black Bartholomew—Condition of the Dissenters—Margaret Baxter—Her family—
Baxter and the Charltons—A charmer—Marriage—Margaret
as a wife—Her death—Rumours of plots—Dissenters and
their friends—London in the Plague time—Acton—Great
love of the populace for him—Imprisonment—The Exchequer closed—Persecution—State of affairs in 1672—Indicted for calumny—Account of the trial—Last days—
Closing reflections—EDMUND CALAMY—Family connexions
—Home in Aldermanbury—School days—Visits to imprisoned Puritans—London and the great frost of 1684—
James II. proclaimed—Two remarkable incidents, note—
English travels—Andover—Oxford—Bristol—Hoxton-square
—Caution of the Nonconformists—Calamy's visit to the Uni-

versity press—French prophets—Account of ejected ministers —Walker and his collectors—Some of his heroes not martyrs —Calamy's last days and death—SAMUEL STEPHENS—Samuel Wright — JEREMIAH BURROUGHS — THOMAS NEWMAN — EDWARD PICKARD—JOHN TAILOR—JOHN FULLER, &c.— Last days of the old chapel—Closing reflections. PAGE 265

CHAPTER VIII.

THE KING'S WEIGH-HOUSE.

East-cheap in the olden time—The original King's Weigh-house—Planting of the Church—SAMUEL SLATER—THOMAS KENTISH—JOHN KNOWLES—Persecuted by Laud—Quakers and " Steeple-houses "—His great zeal—THOMAS REYNOLDS —Called from Silver-street to the Weigh-house—Early life— Return to London—Settles in East-cheap—JABEZ EARLE and JAMES READ, his assistants—Differences with the latter— Unkindness of brethren—Death—Psalmody disputes—Non-conformity after the Revolution—The latter event largely promoted by the Dissenters—Magnanimity of WILLIAM III. —English liberty preserved by the Puritans—Opposition of Liberals to Comprehension and Why—The Jacobitical clergy—Anglican encroachments—Their effect—Jacobitism its own enemy—Party writers—Apostasy of Nottingham— —The Schism Bill—Anti-Nonconformist riots—A clergyman hanged—Lingering love of Puritan customs—The old Dis-senters and Christmas-day—Accession of George I.—The King insulted in the Churches—Seditious pamphlets—The old Dissenters and their Sunday services—The Bangorian controversy — Renegades — A meeting in Dr. Williams's Library—Test and Corporation Acts—Methodism—Tithes and their opponents—Alehouses—The old newspapers and their readers—Ministers' stipends—SAMUEL SANDERSON— Removes to Bedford—Dr. WILLIAM LANGFORD—Early life—

Life-work—Death—SAMUEL PALMER—EDWARD VENNOR—
Dr. SAMUEL WILTON—Settles at Tooting—His charity—
Successful labours—Early death—JOHN CLAYTON—Birth
and education—Apprenticed to a chemist—Introduction to
the Countess of Huntingdon—Trevecca College in the days
of George III.—An unpleasant adventure—Clayton becomes
a Dissenter—Acquaintance with Sir H. Trelawney—
Introduction to the Weigh-house—Ordination—A Tory in
politics—Marriage—His life at home—His preaching—
Death. . . . . PAGE 333

CHAPTER IX.

SALTERS' HALL.

The Company of Salters —Their halls—The Church planted
—RICHARD MAYO—Kingston—Whitechapel—Popularity—
Great industry—NATHANIEL TAYLOR—Student life—A hard
student—Character— Ministers born in 1662 — WILLIAM
TONG—Early life—Temptation—Ministry at Chester—Plants
a church at Knutsford—Removes to Salters' Hall—Industry
—One of Henry's continuators—Death—The disputes of
1719—Arianism in the West—The ministers of Exeter—
Half-yearly synods—Circulation of pamphlets—The "peace"
meeting at Salters' Hall—Scene in the hall—Subscribers and
Nonsubscribers—Curious Tracts—Both parties appeal to the
public—Clark, the publisher—JOHN NEWMAN—SAMUEL
NEWMAN — Early death — JOHN BARKER — Settlement at
Hackney — Retires to Epsom — Becomes associated with
Salters' Hall—Doddridge—Last days—FRANCIS SPILSBURY
—Early bereavement—Strange cause of his settling in
London—Life-work—Death—HUGH FARMER—Student life
under Doddridge—Removes to Walthamstow—Mr. Coward
and his household régime—Settles with the Snells—Popularity
—A London lecturer—HUGH WORTHINGTON—Early days at

Leicester—Removes to London—Success in the City—Unexpected death—The last days of Salters' Hall. . . PAGE 376

CHAPTER X.

FOOTPRINTS OF THE BAPTISTS IN OLD LONDON.

Old chapels which have disappeared—Crutched Friars—PAUL HOBSON—Mark-lane—The Baptists in Turners' Hall—RICHARD ALLEN—Moral bravery and rough experience—Barbican—GEORGE KEITH—JOSEPH JACOB—Presides over a "reformed church" in Thames-street and in Southwark—Character of his followers—WILLIAM COLLINS—EBENEZER WILSON—THOMAS DEWHURST—Wesley and Turners' Hall—Our fathers' mistaken notions as to the size of London—Gracechurch-street—DU VEIL—Conversion—Searches for truth—Joins the Baptists—A pastor commits suicide—Lampoons on Nonconformists—Replies—Great St. Helen's—East-cheap—JOHN NOBLE—Life and character—State of London in 1731—SAMUEL WILSON—SAMUEL DEW—Last days of East-cheap meeting—Tallow-chandlers' Hall—Thomas-street — Joiners' Hall — JOHN HARRIS — JOSEPH MAISTERS — Tastes persecution—Pinners' Hall — THOMAS RICHARDSON—CLENDON DAWKES—Huguenot settlers in London—Petty Franco named after them—WILLIAM COLLINS—Simple Faith—Zeal—Death—NEHEMIAH COX—A learned shoemaker — Puzzles his judges — THOMAS HARRISON—White's-alley—Laying on of hands—The Commonwealth era and its pamphlets—Libels on the Baptists—Petition to Parliament—Satires on religion—An example, *note*—Houndsditch—HENRY DANVERS—Libelled by Macaulay—A prolific author — Governor of Stafford—Enemies—A politician and a patriot—A "calumnious" tract—Escapes to Holland—Is advertised for, *note*—The authorities for depreciating his character—Dr. Calamy and Echard, *note*—Macaulay's asper-

sions unfounded—Other assertions disproved—Inferences—
Baptists prosper under Cromwell—More libellous squibs—
Clerkenwell and its old gate—JOHN YOXLEY—Dr. WILLIAM
RUSSEL—The Old Jewry—JEREMIAH IVES—Disputes with
a Romanist—Basinghall-street—JOSEPH TAYLOR—Dr. WIL-
LIAMS'S LIBRARY — Redcross-street — THOMAS CRANER —
AUGUSTUS CLARKE—THOMAS MABBOTT—Aldermanbury—
Brewers' Hall, *note*—Closing reflections . . . PAGE 412

Chapter I.

DEVONSHIRE SQUARE.

AMONG the many associations inseparably connected with old London, those clustering around the Dissenting Churches of the seventeenth and eighteenth centuries are pre-eminently interesting. Truly, in many instances, these ancient buildings have passed away; and it is equally true that the principal ones which remain are appointed to destruction. While traversing the city and its boundaries how many hallowed spots are discovered—hallowed through once having been the resting-places of Religion, and the scenes of the labours of men of whom the ages they adorned were so often unworthy. Our curiosity respecting these places is no ordinary curiosity, although the sites may now be serving for commonplace merchants' warerooms. How vainly we regret that there did not arise, at least a century ago, some Nonconformist STOW or MAITLAND to hand down facts and traditions now irrecoverably lost. During the last century the Dissenters' chapels were more numerous than may be imagined. On account of altered circumstances they have disappeared. The

1

churches of the Establishment, on the contrary, remain, as under the voluntary principle they never
could have remained, to witness week after week
services conducted for the benefit of heedless walls
and empty pews. While, however, most of the
chapels of London proper have yielded to the action
of time, several remain intact; and with one of these
—Devonshire Square—we open the present volume.

In the third part of Hudibras a couplet occurs
which modern readers will find obscure:

> *That represents no part of the nation,*
> *But Fisher's Folly congregation.*

In a sumptuous edition of Butler's poem, published
some seventy years ago, the annotator fails to make
clear the reference alluded to. He thought the poet
pointed at Quakerism; and, therefore, our editor
may never have heard of William Kiffen. If such
was the case, Mr. Nash resembled a late reviewer,
who only recently, and for the first time, became
acquainted with the name of Thomas Shillitoe. The
lines, however, are apparently simply a parallel
which the author drew between the Long Parliament and the Baptist Assembly "neer Devonshire
Square." The distich, moreover, would seem to
refer to that period of our national history when,
in 1641, the King, on returning from Scotland to
Hampton Court, found discontent prevailing in
London and anarchy in Ireland—a crisis which
sufficed to prompt the after-famous Remonstrance

of the Commons, who, with a strong military guard about their house, were debating the state of the nation. But we are informed by the editor alluded to, "here is an equivoque on the word *represent.* It means either to stand in the place of and be substituted by others, or to resemble and be like them. In the first sense, the members they should pack would represent their constituents, but in the latter sense only a meeting of enthusiastic sectaries." From such an allusion the inference is fairly drawn that, prior even to the outbreak of the Civil Wars, the Baptists presided over by Kiffen were a notable society.

There lived in London three hundred years ago, a goldsmith of the name of Jasper Fisher. Vanity, it would seem, was this old citizen's besetting sin; and therefore a principal aim of his existence was to outshine his neighbours in splendour of living. Truly enough, our goldsmith's susceptible nature may have received a bias from the fact of uniting in his own individuality a worker in the precious metals, a justice of the peace, and a clerk in Chancery. Any man, who by fortune or accident, found himself so conspicuously raised above the vulgar, would naturally set down a little ostentation to the score of self-respect. It probably happened so with Jasper Fisher. Whatever his illusion may have been, it prompted the erection of a sumptuous mansion not very many yards from the Bishop's Gate; and this house was one of the finest homes which the old city then contained. The spaciousness of the premises, the fine

1 *

apartments and costly fittings, together with the
luxuriant gardens, often became the theme of conversation among thrifty freemen, as they chatted
away their evening hours. In those distant days a
simpler speech and living prevailed. In a way most
quaintly graphic, old Fuller tells us how, "a she
citizen" once became persuaded that malt was spun;
for the fair damsel, upon collecting her thoughts,
remembered having noticed the threads. The little
things of life, moreover, attracted more attention
than they do in these faster times. It necessarily
happened that a man's movements were narrowly
watched when his neighbours' intellect, from sheer
lack of proper food, could so ill-afford to let others'
business alone. Thus the rearing of four celebrated
mansions was commemorated in what the burgo-
masters considered most respectable rhyme—

> *Kirkebie's Castle, and Fisher's Folly,*
> *Spinola's Pleasure, and Megsie's Glory.*

The owner of the second-named house earned some
well-merited contempt by assuming a position which
his means were inadequate to maintain. Eventually
Master Fisher became involved in debt ; and doubtless his pecuniary difficulties obliged him to dispose
of this fair estate, which soon after passed into the
hands of several consecutive owners, among whom
stands out conspicuously the ancient name of DE
VERE. During the time that the mansion was
occupied by the Oxford family, the honour of a visit

was received from Queen Elizabeth, her Majesty being then presented with some perfumed gloves— the first imported into Great Britain. William, Earl of Oxford, died at this residence in the summer of 1628. His name appears in the list of parish bene- factors—a list not uninteresting, since one bene- volent lady has left funds in trust for an annual reunion of parson and flock. The property next descended to the Cavendishes, and has ever since been associated with their title.

Long prior to the date in question the Cavendishes were connected with Bishopsgate; for a Lady Caven- dish was interred in the Church a hundred years earlier.

The Society in Devonshire Square, London, is one of the most ancient Dissenting interests in England. The year of its first planting cannot be exactly stated, but the documents in the possession of the Church date from the reign of Charles the First. The people who obtained the original deed appear to have migrated from Wapping after seceding from the Church there, on a disagreement about the question of open communion. This probably occurred about the year 1638. Whether the retiring party coalesced with others already established, or whether they themselves were the sole nucleus of the new founda- tion, it is not easy to ascertain. The original title- deed is still preserved, and this is written in Norman- French, the legal jargon of the times, a jargon which no ingenuity can decipher, if we only except the ingenuity of an adept who may have mastered so peculiar a philological puzzle. William Kiffen is the first minister of whom we have notice; but from such a fact it may not be inferred that the pastor had no predecessors. The Church whence he and his followers withdrew, was founded in the beginning of the century. They were called INDEPENDENTS—a term which simply included evangelical Dissenters whose opinions upon baptism and discipline were various.

As regards William Kiffen, if there are desiderata in religious literature, a good biography of this merchant Baptist may fairly be reckoned one of them. Neither of the two we possess does justice to its subject. That by Orme is the best; and, strangely enough, he was prompted to write by the supposition that Bridgenorth, in Peveril of the Peak, was a caricature of the redoubtable Kiffen. The account by Ivimey, published some few years later, supplies no addition to our knowledge. The book is merely a reproduction of Kiffen's autobiography, unskilfully broken up and interspersed with useless observations, which perplex the reader by obscuring the narrative.

Our main source of information respecting this remarkable man is a manuscript which he chiefly composed himself; that part detailing the Hewling tragedy having been written by Hannah, the sister of the unfortunate youths, and included in the Western Martyrology of 1689.

The Kiffen family was originally of the Principality, the name in Welsh denoting *a borderer.* William, who was born in London, in the year 1616, found himself bereaved of parents and friends by that dreadful plague visitation which nine years later cut down a third part of the City populace. The lad himself was attacked and prostrated by the scourge; and, contrary to all expectation, recovered. A short time after these disasters, William was apprenticed to a brewer, and while in that situation, many humiliating circumstances added bitterness to his bereavement.* The mental depression and disgust experienced rendered his surroundings so intoler-

---

* Kiffen's master was that "great trouble-world and hodgepodge of religion," as Wood styles him, John Lilburne. He must indeed have been rarely gifted in the art of vexing civil governments, for he proved himself alike an enemy to kingly tyranny and to Cromwell's rule. Earth discovered no resting-place for his fiercely-turbulent spirit. When illegally punished by the Star Chamber for an alleged promotion of sedition, he made the pillory a platform from which to anathematise bishops and other episcopal malignants. At the same time he threw his books among the crowd. Like a true hero, he endured for three years the horrors inseparable from a loathsome confinement; and from his prison sent forth a political essay. It was even supposed he set the gaol on fire for the purpose of making an escape. After the Long Parliament had released him, Lilburne fought the Royalists at Edgehill. At the battle of Brentford he was captured, carried to the King's head-quarters at Oxford, and accused of High Treason. The Commons obtained his release by threatening their opponents with retaliation if they

able, that he resolved he would forsake the hated employment. To accomplish this resolution he arose one morning betimes, and left his master's house. While despondingly wandering through the old City, some persons were observed entering a church, and these young Kiffen listlessly followed, to find one of those early services proceeding which were so common in the Puritan era. To the young

proceeded with such a trial. Friends now triumphantly welcomed Lilburne back to London, and presented him with a testimonial of £300. About this conjuncture in the national crisis this zealot laid aside his sword to resume his pen. An extreme hostility to the Presbyterian regimen formed the principal reason for so doing. His many libels, however, proved so troublesome that Cromwell found the author a lodging in Newgate, whence he was afterwards removed to the Tower. His next adventure was to undergo a trial for treason. The jury found him Not Guilty, and to celebrate this acquittal Lilburne ordered a commemorative medal. He continued to pursue a most eccentric career till the Parliament condemned him to fine and imprisonment, which, however, he escaped by a flight into Holland. On returning to London in 1653 Lilburne was again seized, thrown into Newgate, tried, and once more acquitted. Eventually he joined the Quakers, and lived out his remaining days at Eltham. He died in 1657 when only in the thirty-ninth year of his age. One who knew him had an opinion about this old Puritan soldier and controversialist which apparently approximated nearer to truth than many of his contemporaries would have cared to admit; and this opinion was, that even if the world were emptied of all save John Lilburne, Lilburne would quarrel with John, and John with Lilburne.

auditor the sermon was composed of strange sounds;
very words in season, for the preacher forcibly
explained the relationship between masters and
servants, and thereby unconsciously persuaded the
boy to return to the forsaken brewhouse. Next followed conversion. From Kiffen's own account of
this process, some correct notions are derived of the
fiery ordeal of spiritual torture which he endured.
His terror-striking visions were doubtless partly
occasioned by a lively imagination. The happiness,
however, which attended the succeeding calm, more
than repaid for all such buffetings; and henceforth,
Kiffen's life was characterised by a pastoral industry
and dauntless courage which the enemy could
neither damp nor dismay.

Hitherto, young Kiffen had remained a consistent
member of the Anglican Church; but the Laudian
persecution became the means of inspiring a change
of sentiment. With a heathen ferocity, "the little
bishop" was driving from England her most Christian inhabitants; and, by a savage intolerance, was
alienating others. Our sharp-witted apprentice ex-
amined for himself the disputed questions of doctrine
and discipline, till conscience bade him join the persecuted section. Such was the process by which
worldly men in Christian offices expelled the
noblest spirits from a Church commonly extolled
as a shelter for all. The earnestness which animated such youthful Puritans is somewhat interesting. Kiffen, with a number of kindred natures,

habitually attended the six-o'clock-in-the-morning lectures, and the hour preceding each service was devoted to common instruction and prayer.

Being now a recognised Puritan, Kiffen found a pastor in John Lathorp, whose Church of *Independents* was among the earliest foundations of Nonconformity in London. The members congregated at unstated hours and in various places ; for Laud, by his introduction of " thorough," was endeavouring to lower Religion and Conscience to his own contemptible standard. While working for such an end, the prelate was becoming quite an adept at whipping, fining, and mutilation. Royal smiles and the approval of his own mean capacities, encouraged the bishop to persevere. John Lathorp and thirty of his people, by seeking a home in the New World, sought an escape from their enemies' fury. Kiffen, however, remained, and probably about this date inaugurated his ministerial labours. He had no sooner entered upon such a path than he found his action entailed much difficulty and self-denial, which would probably have been fatal to a preacher of less courageous faith. In such wretched times the ignorant populace never questioned the righteousness of a bishop's example. The insults of the rabble, therefore, were necessarily borne in addition to the opposition of their more knowing preceptors. On one occasion, when our young evangelist was about leaving the meeting-room, a rough and cowardly company who had congregated about the door, supplemented their coarse epithets. with a shower of stones. Such an adventure was. not one calculated to ruffle a Puritan's breast; and it was probably mentioned only for the sake of introducing its result. A year later a messenger appeared from a person in dying circumstances, who requested Kiffen's immediate attendance. The sufferer turned out to be a blacksmith, and the identical man who had thrown the stone. The poor creature who was utterly prostrate, and little more than a skeleton, earnestly craved forgiveness.. He confessed, moreover, that his flesh had wasted. since the fatal day whereon he had publicly ridi-culed the preacher.

Kiffen's act of "taking a suitable yokefellow" was almost simultaneous with another step of scarcely less importance as regarded himself— the adoption of Baptist principles. Five years. before, for similar reasons, some persons seceded from the Church with which he communed, to. establish themselves at Wapping, where Kiffen now joined them.

The young evangelist found his way beset by many troubles which, however, were bravely en-countered. He was suddenly seized while preaching in Southwark, and thrown into prison. Among the gaol society was a man who regarded him with unaccountable hatred; and the murder of Kiffen was planned by this mysterious enemy. The man so poisoned his fellow-prisoners' minds, that a

number of them, prompted by murderous motives,
abruptly entered the pastor's apartment during the
calm of a Sabbath evening, and while he was enjoying a brief visit from his family.   The hospitable
reception which the ruffians received fairly astonished them, and completely won them over.
Indeed, many minutes did not elapse ere the lately
intended victim interfered in order to shield his
accuser from injury.   The man's unseemly violence,
however, daily strengthened.   He reiterated his
charges of treason; and by such means contrived
to prolong the confinement of his innocent victim.
Circumstances at length occasioned the committal
to the Tower of Judge Mallet, who was Kiffen's
enemy also, and the latter became set at liberty.

   When in his twenty-fourth year, disease again
attacked and prostrated the young preacher.   A
number of relatives considered his restoration as
improbable, and therefore made the calamity an
opportunity for appropriating as much of the family
property as could be secured.   The invalid, as may
be supposed, grievously suffered by these dishonest
dealings.   While lying in a forlorn condition, his
case was pronounced hopeless by the surgeon who
attended him.   An abler physician was providentially
consulted, who immediately manifested so strong a
predilection for his patient, that he paid him incessant
attention, and Kiffen eventually recovered.   He was
nevertheless woefully reduced, both in natural vigour
and worldly substance.   He was therefore anxious

as well as grateful when the time came for rewarding his benefactor; but the good doctor checked every misgiving by only accepting a single crown, although, by his generous attention, he had neglected other interests.

After these troubles Kiffen undertook a trading expedition into Holland. He was assisted by a co-religionist, a young man as poor as himself. Their business was pre-eminently successful, and the merchant-divine soon found his circumstances daily growing easier. His resources were destined to increase, till, on account of his wealth and influence, he came to be regarded as the Metropolitan of the Baptist denomination, and till his authority was recognised by Baptists throughout the British Isles.

We may, in some degree, realise what England's condition was religiously, and of what the endeavours to extirpate dissent consisted, by examining the Reports prepared by the Archbishop of Canterbury for the use of Charles the First. As regards our present purpose, these documents have a special interest, on account of the glimpses they afford into the every-day life of districts through which Kiffen and Patient travelled, during their propagandist tour. In 1634, both Ashford and Maidstone were considerable centres of Nonconformist influence. Scarcely beyond the shadow of Canterbury Cathedral, a few Dutch Protestants were wont to assemble. These people were regarded with an evil eye, ordered to abandon their Church state, forego their meetings, and conform to the Rubric. Nonconformity also widely prevailed in Bedford. Lincoln is represented as having descended to a condition still more abject, for in Lincoln one Johnson, a Baptist, habitually preached; and to the Archbishop's sincere regret, crowds of admirers accepted his plain instructions. The populace even preferred his unlettered Gospel harangues to the sermons of the drunken clergy, who, as the Metropolitan admits, abounded in the diocese. All endeavours to suppress the meetings were not only contemptible failures, they manifestly aided in promoting their influence. In 1637, several Puritan preachers were captured in Kent. The principal was scarcely secured ere he "slipt out of prison," and recommenced with redoubled zeal his evangelising labours. Such intrepidity reaped an abundant reward, even when, as in the present instance, the subject of it was recommitted to gaol by the Court of High Commission. The Archbishop, however, was depressed by other trials that more excite our sympathy. He suspended an obstinate schoolmaster for refusing to conform, to take the oath of allegiance, or to introduce his rustic students to any knowledge, save orthodox theology. With such a leaven working, it was found that even Canterbury people were weaned from Anglicanism, although the lights of the Church were about to enforce a strict conformity. In the diocese of London, thirty clergymen were summoned before the Bishop's Chancellor to answer for a deviation from the Rubric, or for the then lighter offence, drunkenness. In the see of Norwich certain towns had dwindled away till the Church, the Manor House, and some miscellaneous ruins, were about all the relics remaining of former prosperity. In one, if not in more instances, the squire had appropriated for a storehouse the deserted aisles of the village sanctuary. Parishes were occasionally found destitute of ministers, and with churches gradually becoming ruinous. When such was the case, the people worshipped with their neighbours, and escaped the payment of tithes. An instance for illustration occurred at Lanwood, near Newmarket. In that town the church remained neglected till the roof fell in; yet only by forthwith selling the bells for old metal, did the authorities manifest any concern. The condition of burial-grounds in rural districts, as also in towns, was no less dangerous than disgraceful. In some places inn-keepers' signs were erected amid the graves; and the churchyard at Edmundsbury is reported to the King, as having a public-house in its centre. In some situations on the east coast, the sea threatened with common destruction both the churches and the homes of the people. But the crowning perplexity which, in those days, most sorely tried our bishops, was a matter of readmitting to communion some persons who had escaped from the prisons of Morocco, but who, to preserve their lives, had renounced their Christian faith. The prelates held long consultations, ere their conflicting counsels planned an escape from this unparalleled dilemma. When at length a form of readmission was agreed on, it was exactly registered for the weal of posterity, who would not be likely, while grappling with an identical difficulty, to discuss it with similar wisdom.

The share taken by Kiffen in the Civil Wars, and their attendant political troubles, was probably greater than we have any account of. We find that both he and Benjamin Hewling the elder, were officers in the Parliamentary army. Kiffen's military prowess, however, did not prevent his becoming a Trier of ministerial candidates. In addition to such engagements, he travelled about England, in company with Thomas Patient, specially to defend and expound the tenet of Believers' Baptism. These efforts put forth by one of Kiffen's character and standing in commercial society, were pre-eminently successful, if the effect produced, may be judged of the opposition encountered.

In 1642, the controversy between Baptists and Pædobaptists provoked some angry public discussions in London. The leading combatants were Kiffen and Dr. Featley. The latter, in his *Dippers Dipt*, has commemorated this passage-at-arms, and the public sufficiently appreciated his scurrilous book by raising its sale to a sixth edition in 1651. The curious even yet consult this quaintly-written farrago, but they only value it on account of the illustrations it yields of that fierce intolerance so common to the times. Kiffen and his people are alluded to as illiterate sots, belonging to a profane and blasphemous sect; and the judgments of heaven, likely to confound them, are fully prophesied. The libelled denomination replied to these malignant attacks by publishing a Confession of Faith, which, being signed by Kiffen and six others, appeared in 1644. By this publication the authors endeavoured to prove, that Baptists were neither Jesuits nor Polygamists; Adamites nor Epicures, nor even Phychopannychists—epithets, however, which through being freely applied, and industriously circulated, were commonly believed. By taking this defensible attitude, the Baptists awakened some amateur revilers. Upon the title-page of *The Anabaptists' Looking Glass*, printed in 1645, Kiffen is described as "the author and grand ring leader of that seduced sect." A more notable opponent was Thomas Edwards, the Presbyterian writer of Gangræna, a book wherein all are maligned outside the connexion of Thomas Edwards. In Presbyterianism the author discovered a sovereign panacea for the numberless troubles then vexing the Church. He alludes *en passant* to Kiffen as a mountebank; and to his people—who in fact were wealthy and influential—as a deluded rabble of servants and children, whose custom it was to assemble without the consent of either their masters or parents. The preaching of Edwards very nearly amounted to fanaticism. Such

2

an orator, it will be readily imagined, but rarely ascended the pulpit without denouncing those as Amalekites and scions of Jezebel's household, who disowned the Presbytery. Occasionally, to their own credit and our satisfaction, certain hearers would audibly dissent from the preacher's fiery declamation. Once a man vented his irrepressible indignation by calling out, "This rascally rogue deserves to be pulled out of the pulpit;" and immediately a responsive cry was heard, "Let's go and pull him out." Kiffen once addressed this formidable antagonist by a brief note, which, at the conclusion of his usual harangue against the sectaries, was handed up to Edwards in the pulpit of Christchurch, London. This letter was printed in the form of a handbill four inches square, and an original copy is yet carefully preserved.

The custom of anointing sick persons with oil, and accompanying the act with prayer for restoration, prevailed among the English Baptists until after the time of Queen Anne's accession. For such a purpose Kiffen visited Hanserd Knollys, and his health, we are told, was recovered. Another instance occurred of a female member of the congregation having been similarly waited on by her pastor and elder. She also recovered her strength, and public thanks were returned to God.

Thus years passed by. The Protector died. Troubles, national and personal, loomed in the distance. It could scarcely be expected that Kiffen, who united the earnest divine to the opulent merchant, would be allowed to pursue a course unnoticed or unmolested by the iniquitous government of the Restoration. Even before the return of the King the pastor found his trials begin. One night, just after bed-time, in February 1659, some soldiers forcibly entered his house, also that of Benjamin Hewling, and two others. The premises were overhauled and minutely searched—an outrage which was immediately followed by the issue of a libellous and seditious paper purporting to emanate from the congregational churches. Kiffen was arrested. He appealed to the Lord Mayor; printed the petition for general circulation, and so obtained his release. A few weeks subsequently, a squib appeared wherein the pastor was grossly caricatured, and his chapel referred to as New Bedlam. Even from such sources we learn that Kiffen filled a very eminent station.*

Only a few months after this an atrocious plot was planned having for its object the judicial murder of its victim, and the confiscation of his

* "After two or three conferences with Patience (Patient) and the devil, he was by instinct and revelation appointed to the work, and ordained Musty of all heretics and sectaries. But this was not without great heartburnings of other gifted brethren, who upon his assumption to the Pontificacy and Primacy began to separate and divide from the congregation, and to set up for themselves in their particular conventicles, intending to weaken Kiffen's design and party; but the wenches stuck close unto him, and he prevailed, as we see unto this day."—*Vide The Life and Approaching Death of William Kiffen*, 1659.

2 *

property. A treasonable letter, addressed by one Basset of Taunton to an accomplice of the name of Crabb in London, was discovered in the western mailbag. The writer referred to the recent decease of the Princess of Orange, and proceeded to speak of a plot ripe for explosion, when Kiffen's promised aid of arms and ammunition arrived. The sagacious merchant, however, pointed out how the conspirators had overshot their mark, by dating the paper several days earlier than the death of Her Royal Highness had really occurred, and thus he obtained his discharge.

Kiffen's free-trade sentiments were next the occasion of considerable trouble. Dangerous times had fallen upon England, and many through their days of difficulty and self-denial could have testified with Kiffen, that one trouble only came as the prelude to another. Our divine was required to give evidence before a Committee of the House of Commons, and in doing so spoke to the detriment of certain persons who were seeking by a royal licence to monopolise the cloth trade with Holland. The dismayed manufacturers in the west of England applied to their parliamentary representatives, whom they referred to Kiffen as a competent person to supply any information. The latter found himself scurrilously attacked, and charged with various crimes even before the King in Council. Fortunately a contrary effect was produced from that desired, and the maligned witness was raised in the King's esteem.

He even lived to obtain some influence over the government. A notable instance of his political power occurred when the fanatical magistrates of Aylesbury condemned twelve Nonconformists to death. Messengers were despatched to London, and Kiffen immediately obtained the Chancellor's interference. But notwithstanding all, the pastor was vexed by many trials fast following one upon the other.

The next surprise experienced was an arrest by the agents of the Duke of Buckingham, who accused their prisoner of planning the King's murder. In vain did the pastor express abhorrence at even the thoughts inspired by such atrocity, as affecting the meanest creature, much more as regarded his Majesty. During his dangerous affliction, Lady Ranelagh visited the captive, ministered to his comfort, and did much besides towards obtaining his release. Thankful for so welcome an issue, Kiffen hastened to Whitehall to express his gratitude. There, however, he encountered several enemies, and among others the Lord Chief Justice, who attempted to prove the truth of the late accusation. Escape was apparently impossible. On Clarendon's recommendation our divine petitioned the King to accept bail. Although he failed to obtain an interview with Charles, two substantial merchants appeared who were willing to stand as sureties, but the prisoner was told to depart about his business. Whether or not this absurd affair really inspired alarm, can never be known.

The monarch showed some temper over it, however, so at least declared the page who delivered to Kiffen his order of release.*

Kiffen's path was still beset by annoyances varying both in kind and in degree. He was ordered to appear before Justice Brown, to explain the manner in which he had lately spent his time. He was likewise required to prove, by satisfactory evidence, that "those people with whom he walked," at their church meetings and sabbath gatherings, did not lay schemes for the vexation of government. One witness actually testified that the society was a company of conspirators. Kiffen, however, obtained his release by showing that politics were no part of the congregational tenets. This episode was succeeded by a run of comparative quietness, broken at length by a party of soldiers paying the merchant-divine a visit at his residence in Austin Friars, for the purpose of overhauling and minutely inspecting the mansion. One searcher eagerly caught at a certain volume which lay temptingly exposed beneath a desk; but his cry of expectant surprise would neccessarily give place to disgust when the hoped-for treason turned out to be a well-thumbed copy of *Reynard the Fox.*

* The information of the plot to murder the king was given by one A. Bradley. "Lieutenant Colonel Kiffen said that the Scarlet Whore, the King, must be stabbed, and it could be easily done in his night-clothes." -*Vide Calendar of State Papers, Domestic Series,* 1662. Kiffen was also accused of saying he could command seven hundred men in the contemplated insurrection.

Crosby alludes to a trial of another complexion—a doubtful anecdote, yet probably true—to which Kiffen was subjected. Charles the Second once applied to him for a loan of £40,000. That sum being a larger one than the divine could afford to part with, the King was desired to accept as a present a quarter of the amount so graciously named. Kiffen, meanwhile, considered that by this gift a saving of £30,000 had been effected.

It is commonly supposed that a more particular account of himself and people was written by Kiffen. Such a work, did we possess it, would fill up a missing page in the history of the heroic period of Dissent. While wanting it, we must be content to borrow just what facts are available for the illustration of our narrative.

Kiffen's domestic sorrows were of themselves a severe discipline, and when considered as trials of faith, are found to have equalled in severity his more public troubles. Death struck down a son in 1679, and about the same time a daughter likewise died. One ailing son remained, and if possible to restore his departed vigour, he was sent on a sea voyage. The lad was provided with every comfort, and accompanied by a friend because of the dread entertained of Romish contamination. Notwithstanding these precautions a fanatical priest contrived to poison the youth at Venice. Mrs. Kiffen's death, in 1682, brought yet heavier trouble. Through good and evil report she had gladdened her husband's

heart, and had been for nearly half a century the
light of his city home.   The removal, therefore, of
such a companion could not fail to occasion great
and lasting sorrow.

But the old man's last days were especially
darkened by the untimely fate of his grandsons,
Benjamin and William Hewling.   About all the
trustworthy information respecting these young
heroes is included in their sister Hannah's account,
which now rare and valuable pamphlet was published
in 1689 and entitled *The Dying Speeches, Letters,
and Prayers of those eminent Protestants who suffered
in the West of England*.   The grandfather, in his
Autobiography, has copied the details without
alteration.   The good breeding of the youths, their
Christian mien and intellectual culture, awakened
admiration and respect in all who knew them. Their
violent death served the country in a way their
enemies little suspected.   The government by its
infamous policy unconsciously intensified in degree
that widely prevailing indignation and disgust which
gradually yet surely prepared the way for the
triumphant progress of the Revolution.   The father
of the Hewlings had been a merchant who had
principally concerned himself with the Turkish trade.
He died, however, before calamity overtook his
family, and ere "Jeffrey's campaign" had maddened
England, till even the hardened and profaned regarded
with a wholesome disgust both the wicked judge
and his contemptible master.   As the merchant's sons

belonged to a genteel and opulent family, they enjoyed the best education the times could afford. They were pursuing their studies in Holland when the expedition of Monmouth first attracted their attention. Inheriting a brave, adventurous temperament, they laid their books aside and joined the duke's supporters. They regarded the encroachments of Rome with hatred a Puritan rearing could alone have begotten, and therefore while taking the sword, they enthusiastically resolved to aid in reestablishing the throne, and in restoring the Protestant faith.

Landing with their leader, the brothers fought at the fatal battle of Sedgemoor. Our ancestors supposed that that dismal night would have ended differently, and so it would in all likelihood but for the unfortunate absence during a critical stage in the fight of the elder Hewling, who happened to be engaged in bringing up artillery from Minehead. This Benjamin possessed a military genius quite unique for his time of life. His modesty in private strangely contrasted with his intrepid courage in the emergencies of war. Hardship and peril, indeed, when duty prompted him to encounter them, were faced with a valorous bravery which awakened chivalrous memories, rather belonging to Richard Cœur De Lion. When all was lost the brothers put to sea, but contrary winds drove back their barque, and upon relanding they were taken, lodged in Exeter goal, and thence were brought to London a few days after. Their behaviour in captivity completely won the affection of the officials. The prisoners were nevertheless thrown into Newgate and loaded with irons. It was only by a determined perseverance against a host of difficulties, that the family could obtain the favour of an interview even with a turnkey present. The captives were ordered back to the west, there to take their trial, and during the journey to Dorchester they proved that their courage was sustained from a preternatural source; for not by undervaluing life, but by rising above the fear of death, they manifested the truest heroism of which human nature is capable. William, the younger brother, was condemned at Dorchester. The proceedings in either case were a complete mockery of justice. The contemptible Jeffreys only observed his usual custom when he insulted the prisoners, yet on this occasion his railings were supplemented by an outburst of extempore blackguardism, and he denounced, as only worthy of hanging, the grandfather Kiffen. On account of Jeffreys being a court confidant a peculiar meaning became attached to his language, and a belief gained currency among London Dissenters that the government only awaited an opportunity to effect the pastor's ruin and disperse his congregation.

On the day of their execution William Hewling and several others were taken from Dorchester to Lyme. The fruitful and sunny landscape—made glad on the summer morning by ripe cornfields and cyder orchards—well corresponded with the martyr's strange elation of spirits. To him the cheerful aspect apparently prefigured that perfect inheritance so soon to be realised, where all are gladdened by the presence of Christ.

Following Jeffreys' track of blood and death appeared an unpretending girl, who, though delicately nurtured and politely educated, endured through her sisterly love the round of horrors of the " Bloody Assizes." This was Hannah Hewling. The ordeal she underwent commenced at Dorchester, where she tenderly ministered to the comfort of her brother William. Having seen the grave close over William, Hannah wrote some consoling words to her stricken mother in London, and then hastened to Taunton to witness the completion of the tragedy which would fill her cup of misery. Causes identical with those which had supported one brother enabled the other to rejoice under corresponding circumstances. The sweetest season of his life, he declared, was that summer of 1685. His entire mien, amid such distressing surroundings, revealed a spirit submissive and forgiving, as well as a Christian ripeness not usually found in youth; and military men, not wont to weep, were heard frankly confessing that they were scarcely able to bear the spectacle. Even the horses which were used for drawing the condemned to the gallows, by refusing to stir for half an hour with their burden, appeared to sympathise with afflicted humanity. Thus was it that Hannah had her strength sustained through an ordeal sufficiently shocking to have shattered both mind and body. The maidens of the West, to the prayers they offered for their sister's support, added expressions of admiration ; and thus the young and the beautiful mourned in common at the open graves of the murdered youths. This protest against tyrannical cruelty, made in such a manner and at such a time, England has never forgotten. The seed was truly sown in tears, but when it germinated into full fruition, it brought confusion to the wicked by promoting the Revolution.

Meanwhile the afflicted family, as sufferers for the public good, would often be interceded for by Kiffen's congregation. The Hewlings, it must be remembered, made no recantation. They died as they had lived, believing Monmouth's cause to have been righteous, its failure a national calamity, and disastrous to the Protestant religion. Kiffen had vainly endeavoured to buy a reprieve by offering three thousand pounds to an influential commoner. When tidings of this reached the Chief Justice he became doubly anxious to see the sentence carried out, because he considered the money should have been offered to himself. Jeffreys was accused by his contemporaries of behaving to Miss Hewling with that coarseness which seemed inseparable from his degraded nature, but the truth of this is denied by Noble. Jeffreys, we are told, was expecting to inherit the fortune of a certain relative, and this person threatened to transfer the property to another unless strenuous endeavours were made to save the brothers. After such an explanation it is not difficult to believe that, for once, our historical savage may have conquered his repugnance to decency. He did use, so he averred, every means to avert the Hewlings' execution. The word, however, of such a man must ever be worthless. His atrocious career had so incapacitated him for anything but wickedness, that the distich of a contemporary poet was happily conceived :—

*With care this brat was reared, for fear it should
Grow tame, and degenerate into good.*

Two years after this western exploit of Jeffreys all was changed. The story has been too often told to need repetition how the iniquitous James attempted to serve his own Romanist faction by assuming for the moment a mask of toleration ; by which means he hoped, in his suicidal selfishness, to undermine the Protestant faith, or to destroy the Established Church by the agency of Dissent. Although numbers, and principally the Quakers, joyfully hailed the illusory Indulgence, the Nonconformists as a body were far too sagacious to be allured into the trap of the fawning tyrant. Among those honoured ones, who in England's extremity, refused the friendship of the common foe, such names appear as those of Kiffen, Howe, Bunyan and Baxter. Kiffen was so influential that the government regarded his alliance as of paramount importance, and he therefore received the royal command to appear at Whitehall. All this occurred while the revolutionary business was progressing of rescinding corporation charters; and, under the new arrangements for London, Kiffen was offered an alderman's gown. Noble, in his *History of The Protectorial House of Cromwell*, has told the story well, and Macaulay has drawn materials from the relation and used them with good effect :—" He— James—talked of his favour to the Dissenters in the court style of the season, and concluded by telling Mr. Kiffen he had put him down as an alderman in his new charter. 'Sire,' replied Mr. Kiffen, ' I am a very old man, and have withdrawn myself from all kind of business for some years past, and am incapable of doing any service in such an office, to your Majesty or the City ; besides Sire,' continued the old man, fixing his eyes steadfastly upon the King, while the tears ran down his cheeks, 'the death of my grandsons gave a wound to my heart which is still bleeding, and will never close but in the grave.' The King was deeply struck by the freedom and the spirit of this unexpected rebuke. A total silence ensued, while the galled countenance of James seemed to shrink from the horrid remembrance. In a minute or two, however, he recovered himself enough to say, ' Mr. Kiffen, I shall find a balsam for that sore,' and immediately turned about to a lord-in-waiting."

Notwithstanding his distaste for civic duties, the court duly appointed Kiffen an alderman, and acting on counsel's advice, he decided on serving against inclination, rather than risk the infliction of ruinous fines. The pastor's high commercial standing, and his great influence in Nonconformist circles, gave him ample power, had he chosen to exert it, to promote the designs of the Court. Had Kiffen adopted so degrading a policy, the sacrifice of his kinsmen would have had compensation in civic and county honours. Through nine months, however, he sustained the office of alderman for Cheap ward, and when the Corporation invited James to a grand banquet he contributed fifty pounds towards the expenses.

The closing portion of Kiffen's career remains obscure. About 1692, he had it would seem, some disagreement with his people which occasioned his resignation and withdrawal from the church.*

---

* About the era of the Revolution we find that Kiffen wrote a preface to The Prodigal's Return, a publication of which his friend, H. Hill, was the author. Hill was closely connected with the church at Devonshire Square, or as it is emphatically called "The Anabaptist congregation." In his younger days Hill rose to be printer to the government of the Commonwealth. Like many of his compeers, who were equally fortunate, he rose from an humble station—a Maidstone ropemaker. He took his first step upward by becoming servant to Harrison, by whom he was eventually placed in a printing establishment. Hill absconded from this employment to enlist in the Parliamentary army, and to fight in Cromwell's battles. His promotion, which was very rapid, commenced soon after. He was transferred from a foot regiment to one in the cavalry. About this conjuncture he declared for the independent regimen, and Cromwell appointed him his printer general. Hill produced most of the

A circumstance which occurred about this time will serve both to prove the pastor's benevolence, and to illustrate the times he lived in. He undertook the protection of a persecuted Huguenot family, by providing them a house well furnished, and liberally supplied with all necessaries including servants, the entire cost being paid by this generous Christian merchant.

Such was William Kiffen. He died on the 29th of December, 1701, having reached his 86th year. His remains were interred in Bunhill Fields. It would have been well had additional memorials descended to us of so active a Christian and of so eminent a man ; as it is, sufficient data remain from which to form a somewhat correct estimate of his character. He was orthodox according to the strict standard of the times, and the theological tenet which separated him from other contemporary worthies—Believers' Baptism—was embraced after

publications ordered by the Commons, including the proclamation for the King's arrest. At length an action for adultery was instituted against him, which entailed a fine of £260. On account of a lack of means the printer languished for a while in the Fleet, and it was from this prison the penitential book above alluded to was sent forth. This became the means of his re-admission to church fellowship, besides obtaining the appointment of "Printer to the Anabaptist congregation." A contemporary author thus alludes to Hill :—"At that time he was printer to Oliver the usurper. He became a zealous preacher among the Anabaptists, where he thumped the tub so furiously that he was much noted by the heads of that tribe, as Kiffen, Ives, King, &c."

a diligent study of the Scriptures, and a careful
examination of ecclesiastical history. Strong partisan
sympathies may have sometimes prompted an unwise
severity of language. Such transgressions, however,
must be excused, for they belong to the customs of a
ruder age, wherein ever threatening dangers attended
a conscientious walk. The man, if we fairly weigh
each trait of his character, manifestly appears to have
been a good man. Though not learned, and perhaps
overmuch addicted to controversy, he yet possessed
abilities of more than average merit. Thus was he
enabled during half a century, to proclaim the Gospel
he loved, and, maintaining a consistent walk in life,
he does not appear to have deviated by example from
the doctrines he expounded. Doubtless, therefore
Kiffen received in death the gift of Christ and the
approval of his heavenly Father.

The Kiffen family, it may be mentioned, became
nearly related to the Cromwells, in 1686, by Hannah
Hewling's marriage to the Protector's grandson,
Major Henry Cromwell. This lady survived her
husband about twenty years, and died in 1731, leaving
several children to imitate her virtue and Christian
heroism. *

The plague of 1665 proved a sore calamity to the

---

* Manuscript Records of the church at Devonshire Square;
Crosby's History of the English Baptists; Noble's Pro-
tectorial House of Cromwell; Orme's Life of Kiffen:
Edwards's Gangræna; Western Martyrology; Wilson's
History of the Dissenting Churches. Many tracts and broad-
sides of the period have been consulted also, but it is not

Church at Devonshire Square. From the manner in which his death is recorded, we infer that the scourge cut off Thomas Patient, Kiffen's co-pastor. He had only been ordained about a month when he died on July the 29th, and was buried on the day following. Although Patient occupied so prominent a denominational position, only little information can now be gathered respecting him. In his earlier days he had served a New England congregation, but while in this situation he renounced his Pædobaptist principles, and thereby incurred, it is said, the penalty of persecution from former allies. The convert closely followed the dictates of conscience, and even composed a small treatise, wherein he defended his newly-adopted sentiments. His name is also found among the Confessors of 1644.

Patient probably accompanied General Fleetwood into Ireland, and he is commonly regarded as the planter of the Church at Clough Keating, in Crosby's time a flourishing society of several hundred members. Among the political prosecutions preceding the Revolution, was a remarkable trial which befel these people. The minister and members being simultaneously accused of treason, were tried for their lives. The foreman of the jury, animated by the Laudian spirit, openly declared he would never leave the court until the whole company were condemned. As

necessary to enumerate them in order. The reports concerning the ecclesiastical condition of England may be seen in Rymer's Fœdera.

he entered the justice-room this man was stricken by death; and—perhaps through awe of so fearful a visitation of heaven—the eleven jurymen remaining acquitted the prisoners. We are mostly in the dark in reference to any advantages the Church in question derived from Patient's ministrations; for shortly after the Restoration he accepted the lectureship of Devonshire Square, and during the memorable summer of 1665, while the plague raged around the meeting house, he was solemnly inducted into his office. Hanserd Knollys and Kiffen were there to lay hands upon the head of the co-pastor, who, alas! a few days subsequently was "Discharged by Death from his work and office he being taken from the evil to come, and having rested from all his labours, leaving a blessed savour behind him of his great usefulness and sober conversation; this, his sudden removal being looked to be to his own great good and advantage, but the Church's sore loss. On this day he was carried to his grave accompanied by the members of this and other congregations, in a Christian, comely and decent manner." *

A successor to Thomas Patient was appointed in the person of Daniel Dyke, M.A., who as son of the Vicar of Epping, had enjoyed a University education. He was also in former days a chaplain in Cromwell's household, and likewise acted as one of the Protector's Triers. This divine held for a time the living of

* Church Book, 1665.

Hadham in Hertfordshire, and while there his prescience warned him of the ecclesiastical anarchy which would follow the Restoration. He resigned his cure, and is included among the ejected ministers, to whom he did not properly belong. Subsequently Dyke encountered a full share of persecution, yet so well did he weather the stormy period, that he never spent more than two consecutive nights in prison. After occupying the pulpit for several months our divine was chosen lecturer, and was set apart to his sacred calling by Kiffen and Hanserd Knollys, in February, 1668. The situation was held for twenty years, that period having been one of the roughest epochs in modern history. Dying in 1668, Dyke laid the arms of his warfare aside, when, before the dawn of a happier future, the churches' afflicting shade was passing from the land; and a more eminent Baptist, John Bunyan, that same year departing into rest, the two were in death divided by only a few paces in the burial-ground in Bunhill Fields.

It will not be out of place if we briefly refer to this ancient Society's discipline, revealing, as it does, some Nonconformist customs during the seventeenth and eighteenth centuries. The guiding text-book for daily life was the Bible. Members were expected strictly to adhere to its doctrine and directions. Any deviation from rectitude immediately awakening the warning voice of the Church, an inattention to which incurred the penalty of exclusion from communion. In the spring of 1644 a member was accused of the double offence of frequenting Bishopsgate Church, and of serving as Churchwarden. Persons were delegated to remonstrate with this erring brother, but because they remonstrated in vain he was cut off from fellowship. In 1666 the charms of a certain maiden captivated the heart of an imprudent swain, her inferior in social rank, and to ensure success in his suit, he falsely represented himself to be possessed of several hundred pounds. The youth attained his object, but when tidings of the subterfuge reached the ears of the Society, the offender was summoned and suspended from communion. In 1691 a young woman suffered excommunication Tor "keeping company with a parson of the Church of England." Another paid the like penalty for distributing £200 of her husband's money. Improper marriages were always discountenanced. In 1702 a female member was expelled on account of getting "unequally yoked." "We have ample evidence, that when Wesley inaugurated Methodism, the Baptist Churches very suspiciously regarded both the movement and its promoter. Members who assembled with the new sect in their public services were treated as disorderly. Some, whom the Arminian preachers had attracted, sought restoration to communion by confessing their errors. Yet exclusion for this offence, and for conforming, appears to have been very common. As regards Gifts, these old Puritans were very zealous encouragers of the earliest symptoms of ministerial ability, deeming themselves meanwhile the truest judges of its quality. In 1704, a youth addicted to talking, became desirous of assuming pastoral responsibilities. In strict accordance with Dissenting custom, he declaimed before the grave assembly, but the oratorical effort was entirely disapproved. Disdaining to act upon the advice given to discontinue his harangues— the lad continued, as opportunities occurred, to indulge in his ambitious platitudes. The indignant tribunal seeing its authority thus contemned, excluded him from fellowship, and only when he acknowledged having been "misled by Satan," did the offender gain re-admission. In the closing years of William's reign, the Church introduced the custom of appointing recognised visitors, and they were expected to render quarterly accounts of the general prosperity of individual members. It was usual for the necessitous poor to state their need in person, and occasionally such applicants received an amount representing a quarter's rent. Weekly allowances were likewise bestowed, and separate monthly subscriptions levied to meet these Christian demands.

Shortly after the Revolution, Richard Adams was appointed assistant-lecturer. He was the ejected minister of Humberstone in Leicestershire. On relinquishing his cure Adams continued to instruct as many of his late parishioners as chose to attend at his residence. A local "Justice" strenuously opposed this self-denying course, and allowed his respect for the man to be conquered by his hatred of Dissent. The persecution which the evangelist endured was, therefore, merely intended to counteract his influence. The country people, as did multitudes of their neighbours, continued to entertain for their former pastor much love and reverence. Unpaid fines accumulated, and the village officials could only be compelled by extreme pressure to seize the good man's property. Even when the goods were taken, it was found impossible to dispose of them, for none would buy them. Where such unexpected obstacles obstructed the smoother progress of the law, the magistrate summoned the divine into his presence sharply to rebuke him, but granted the unasked for permission to keep a school. Not long after, this enemy to the faith was taken, and the disease of which he died led the Dissenters to regard his death in the light of a special judgment.

How long Adams remained in this sphere after the removal of his opponent is uncertain ; that he shortly removed is probable, because some years prior to the Revolution he was a pastor in South London, whence in 1690, he removed to Devonshire Square. In the autumn of that year he was specially set apart, and the importance attached to the proceedings almost warrant the inference that they signified the admission of a convert to Believers' Baptism into the denomination. This ordination was one of the last occasions on which Hanserd Knollys and other eminent Puritan leaders were assembled together. Kiffen eventually withdrew from the pastorate, and Adams held the office till his death in 1716, though he was debarred .

by bodily infirmity in his latter years from frequently engaging in public ministrations.

About this period disputes arose among the
Dissenters concerning congregational psalmody.
Hitherto, the practice of singing had not been
customary; and the abettors of the innovation neces-
sarily worked with cautious timidity in the face of
a strong opposition from those who had been born
and were grown old under the ancient regimen.
But Isaac Watts was now a preacher at Pinners'
Hall, and a new chapel for the poet in Bury-street,
St. Mary Axe, was in course of erection. Watts
became a prominent advocate of the new movement,
as well as a writer of suitable pieces for singing.
As was the case with sister churches, the Society at
Devonshire Square was divided against itself; but the
contending sections wisely agreed to a compromise.
After the morning service, those who objected to "the
unchristian infection" retired, and they who remained
joined in singing one or more appropriate hymns.*

Mark Key, the succeeding pastor, assumed his
office as the turmoil was subsiding which the rising
for the Pretender had occasioned, and when society,
having recovered from the revolutionary shock and
having regained its wonted equilibrium, was settling
down once more to enjoy that common freedom
which, since the expulsion of the Stuarts, has been

---

* Manuscript Records of the Church; Crosby's History of
the English Baptists; Wilson's History of the Dissenting
Churches.

the heritage of Englishmen. The new minister was a
native of London, and being the son of poor parents,
had received but an indifferent education. His
friends were General Baptists, and, as early as 1691,
Mark had preached in Moorfields to a congregation
of that persuasion; but failing health four years
after obliged his resignation. In 1702 a change in
favour of Calvinism occurred in his sentiments; and
he was brought under the ministry of Richard Adams,
in whose pulpit a year later Key resumed his public
exercises. The intellectual endowments of this divine
were very considerable. His delivery was powerful
and impressive. On account of growing popularity
several attempts were made by various churches to
obtain his services, but the bond of union between
him and his people was of sufficient strength to prevent a removal. At first he was merely lecturer;
then, in 1706, he became fully recognised as the
aged pastor's regular assistant. At Mark Key's
ordination Adams placed his hands upon the head
of his younger brother and proclaimed aloud—" I
do declare by the authority of Christ and this Church
that my brother . . . is by the Church appointed
and ordained a joint elder, pastor, or overseer, with
myself over her." As already stated, Richard Adams
died in 1716, when the pastorate devolved on Mark
Key, who terminated his earthly career at Midsummer 1726. During his last years he was aided
by two members of the congregation, of whom little
is known beyond their names. These were John

Toms and Charles Bowler. Their signatures frequently occur in the Records—a circumstance proving them to have been active members of the Society. The first-named divided with the Non-subscribers at Salters' Hall in 1719.

It is unfortunate that so few particulars are to be obtained concerning the life-story of Mark Key— a man once famous for oratorical gifts. We are well informed, however, that honoured as were his efforts in life, the respect manifested for him in death far exceeded the ordinary expressions of bereavement; it also pleasingly illustrated that Christian sympathy which in an irreligious age could characterise minister and people—an age wherein the advent of better things, promised by the Revolution, was eclipsed by the dreary reign of George the First.*

In the early part of the eighteenth century a society from Pinners' Hall occupied the Chapel at Devonshire Square for one part of each Sabbath, and for this privilege allowed the sum of £10 a-year. At this time the Lady Dowager Page was connected with the congregation, and had a pew fitted up on either side of the pulpit for the convenience of herself and attendants. Sir Gregory and Lady Page were opulent and liberal Dissenters of the early Georgian era. The latter during her widowhood distributed her wealth with no grudging hand, and

* Manuscript Records of the Church at Devonshire Square; Crosby's History of the English Baptists; Wilson's History of the Dissenting Churches.

at her death bequeathed means for the succour of her poorer fellow-members. Lady Page was remarkable for the diligent attention she gave to religious literature. In the decline of life she suffered from a painful weakness. Her servants were wont to carry their mistress into the family pew in the old Chapel in Devonshire Square. Dame Mary died in March, 1730. Two sermons, an ode, and a funeral oration were published to commemorate her departure.

The members, meanwhile, keenly realised their widowed state as they looked upon the lifeless form of Mark Key, and evidence remains to prove how heartfelt was their mourning. On Thursday, June 30th, the Church assembled and sought divine direction. At a subsequent conference they decided on inviting Dr. Gifford, of Bristol, but circumstances prevented his immediate attendance in London, and he finally declined the proffered honour. While, however, the deacons were vainly endeavouring to conquer difficulties, matters were arranging themselves in a way quite unexpected. A Baptist Society then worshipped in Turners' Hall, and had statedly done so since the days of Charles the Second. At this date the pastor was Sayer Rudd, a town physician and an acceptable preacher, regarded by many as a suitable successor to Mark Key. It was likewise fairly represented that a union of the two communities would increase their common opportunities of doing good. The churches conferred together at Christmas, 1726, and were amalgamated six months afterwards. There remained but one obstacle to be surmounted. The company from Turners' Hall possessed an endowment only retainable so long as they preserved their separate state. This circumstance occasioned the invention of an unique device. In June, 1727, the people assembled to be addressed by John Toms, after which a unanimous vote dissolved their union. Sayer Rudd and his people from Turners' Hall now took full possession. A few minutes passed, and then the members of the late Society applied for Christian fellowship, and, on being received, the two assemblies became one. By an ingenious manœuvre they had fully protected themselves from future legal embarrassment.

Sayer Rudd retained his office till the spring of 1733, when a misunderstanding about a continental tour occasioned a separation. Rudd had privately determined to travel through France; his people were as firmly resolved that he should continue in England. The pastor effected his design; the people regarded the pulpit as forsaken. Resolutions were passed binding the members to stand by one another in their extremity. Only ordained ministers were permitted to dispense the Sacraments : preachers supplying the pulpit received a guinea a sermon; but only half that amount if from the country. John Rudd, the pastor's brother, had occasionally served in the pulpit; but prior to the disagreement he settled in the ministry at Wapping.

During his stay at Turners' Hall, Rudd proved himself a man of learning and ability. On his re-appearance in London, after having travelled through France, he consented to supply at Maze Pond: and all obstacles in the way of an amicable settlement were apparently removed, when some discovered, as they thought, defects in his doctrinal sentiments. The candidate, on an appointed occasion, plainly expressed his theological views, and, because the majority of his hearers detected Sabellianism, his further services were dispensed with. Rudd, nevertheless, drew after him an influential portion of the congregation, and one lady member, at her sole expense, provided an additional meeting-house, besides subscribing a hundred pounds a year towards its support. About this conjuncture Rudd was excluded from the ministerial conclave who assembled on Mondays at Blackwell's coffee-house. Two years after, death deprived the pastor of his able patron, Mrs. Ginns, and he conformed to the Rubric in 1742, for the purpose of accepting the living of Walmer. He also conducted a school at Deal, and died there in 1757. After the decease of Mrs. Ginns, her church in Southwark dwindled away, and eventually the chapel became one of John Wesley's preaching-stations. The young man who conducted the services gained a complete ascendancy over a large congregation, till he and his people imbibed such views of perfection as prompted them to exclude Wesley from their pure communion.

This occurred in 1763. Wesley engaged a neighbouring building, but his connection by this secession suffered a loss of six hundred members. The
chapel was successively occupied by the Primitive
Methodists and the Baptists.

However many or heinous Rudd's errors may
have been—and no attempt will be made to ex-
tenuate them—the manner in which he is treated by
Ivimey may justly be indignantly deprecated. It can
be clearly proved that the rough treatment Rudd experienced at Devonshire Square, sufficed to drive him
away. Although the Nonconformist ranks of those
days included so much that was admirable, it may
not, on the other hand, be denied that there were
among them ignorant, self-consequent persons, only
too ready to embrace opportunities of abusing
their liberty. At Devonshire Square they could not
tolerate the presence in their pulpit of a Pædobaptist. They were ready to quarrel with their pastor
when he purchased more books than they supposed
he required, and so needed a larger salary; or when
he indulged in too free language. Rudd found his situation become so uneasy, that in 1731, he addressed
a Latin letter to the Lord Chancellor, wherein he
asked for preferment in the Established Church,
although still objecting to the rite of infant
baptism; at another time he entertained some
thoughts of conforming to Quakerism. His motives
could not have been purely mercenary; for, had
he cared only for money, his desires would have

been satisfied by preaching Calvinistic doctrine, and remaining at Maze Pond. Ivimey thought otherwise: "He—*i.e.* Rudd—was a vain, conceited person," who "always prefixed M.D. to his name, and was called Dr. Rudd. From this circumstance, it does not follow that he ever understood medicine." It would be equally generous to reply: "A certain preacher compiled a Baptist history, and was called the *Reverend* Joseph Ivimey. Hence we are not to infer that he ever comprehended the Gospel." The fact is, Rudd has left behind him ample evidence of ability and scholarship. The pastor's *Certain Method to Know Disease* testifies to his knowledge of the Greek and Latin tongues; but of the existence even of this publication Ivimey was not cognisant, or he would have included it in the list he subjoins of the Doctor's works.

This interruption to the Society's prosperity was of nine months' duration, after which, by the happy choice of George Braithwaite, the Church filled the vacancy. This divine, then in his fifty-fourth year, besides being intellectually strong, had benefited by an extended experience as a Christian minister. His native place was Furnessfells, in Lancashire, and his family, who adhered to the Established Church, maintained a good position in the county; one of their number being a preacher of some eminence in the immediate neighbourhood. His parents intended that George should succeed his uncle in this living; and with this object in

view, he passed the preliminary stages of his education at the town grammar school. Thence he proceeded to the University, where by an industrious
application he won a degree. At this date the
death of a relative occasioned his recall home, and
he never returned to his college. Soon after Braithwaite's conversion to anti-pædobaptism occurred,
when he became ineligible for Anglican preferment.

In the year 1706 this young scholar settled in
London, and joined a company of Baptists who
assembled in Curriers' Hall. In such society his
cultivated talents attracted notice; and by acting
in unison with the people's desire, he allowed himself to be set apart with fasting and prayer to the
office of preaching. When the family discovered
that this scion of their House had arrived at such
determinations, they employed every art to allure
him back into the Anglican communion. As, however, conscience had led him in this direction, it
allowed of no yielding to temptation; for the report
is probably true that Braithwaite embraced antipædo-
baptist principles, while ignorant of the existence of
a Baptist denomination. Having finally determined
to embrace the ministerial profession, the young
evangelist felt constrained first to proclaim the
Gospel to his neighbours at Furnessfells. When a
very young man, he resolved and strangely vowed,
that should he ever enter the vineyard of Christ,
Furnessfells should first benefit by his Christian
endeavours. To accomplish this purpose he now

repaired thither, and upon a site chosen from his hereditary estate, erected a chapel. In this self-selected sphere Braithwaite successfully laboured, and to the character of a Christian gentleman united the attributes of a zealous pastor. There arose at length some difference of opinion between the latter and his people concerning open communion, and the dispute eventually led to a separation. This controversy at least served one good end: it further revealed the pastor's amiability and generous forbearance, for he presented the members with the chapel freehold as a parting gift of friendship and personal esteem.

The next scene of Braithwaite's Christian effort was Bridlington. While there he published a curious treatise against unnecessarily frequenting public-houses. In the days of George the Second, the pernicious custom complained of widely prevailed. Even respectable persons would assemble at the village hostelry to gossip away their evening hours. The publication of Braithwaite's book created an extensive ill-feeling, on account of which the author not only became unpopular, but uneasy in his situation. At that time numbers were found even among chapel-goers, who would thoroughly have agreed with Johnson in regarding a tavern parlour chair as the throne of temporal felicity. This occurrence led to the pastor's resignation, and his retirement from the vicinity. On returning to London, during the spring of 1734, he commenced

4

that occupancy, which continued through life, of the deserted pulpit of Sayer Rudd.

On Braithwaite's acceptance of the call to Devonshire Square, he was recognised by services which Dr. Gill and Samuel Wilson conducted. To the meagre account contained in a funeral sermon by the latter, we are chiefly indebted for the few particulars known about a life which doubtless abounded in interesting events and instructive lessons. Braithwaite is reported to have kept a diary during thirty years, and with great precision to have noted down numberless circumstances. This and many similar treasures of that era never saw the light.

The year 1744 was signalised by the fortunately rare occurrence of a public quarrel between the church at Devonshire Square and the sister society at Maze Pond, over which Edward Wallen presided. Aaron Spurrier.— an occasional preacher and a member at Devonshire Square — wrought much mischief by depreciating his pastor's labours and creating disunion, till his brethren severely censured his conduct. Spurrier then forsook his place in the assemblings, and on application was admitted to communion at Maze Pond. This reception of a suspended member was resented as an unprecedented affront, and as such was rebuked. In the City the indignation produced "An Appeal to the Baptist Churches in and around London." In this letter the Southwark people were accused of disorderly walking, a charge which prompted the issue of a counter-address, in turn to be immediately replied to by another statement from Devonshire Square. The dispute lasted several months, and became the occasion of some excitement among Dissenters in London. The upshot was that Spurrier surrendered, confessed his errors, and craved forgiveness. He afterwards statedly ministered to a Church at Lime-house, where he died in 1749. Dr. Gill, who preached Spurrier's funeral sermon, highly eulogised his character.

As the summer of 1748 advanced, Braithwaite's natural vigour gave place to weakness. To him, however, approaching death was but nearing "The Gate of Life ; " and in July he entered on his reward. During his last hours he selected the words " I have fought a good fight," from which he desired Samuel Wilson to preach a funeral sermon. The final scene of the pastor's course supplies a fine illustration of Christian triumph. Consolation derived from a complete trust in Christ, was supplemented by a clear testifying of conscience, that never knowingly, either for profit or for renown, had he deviated from rectitude. The Church's loss, after circumstances proved to be an unusually severe one. The members assembled at a special prayer-meeting, hung the chapel with black and voted the funeral expenses. It may be mentioned that Braithwaite's once ample resources were about exhausted some years prior to his decease; he even experienced the pressure of

4*

poverty. In 1746 the lease of some property owned by the Church in Moorfields expired, and this event probably narrowed the pastor's stipend. *

We turn to a gloomy page of the Society's history on parting from the pious Braithwaite. An attempt to bring Henry Lord from Bacup failing, John Stevens, a West-countryman, accepted the pastorate, being in the thirtieth year of his age. This occurred in the spring of 1750, after the young minister had served several months upon trial. During some following years great popularity attended his labours, so that in addition to his stated ministrations, he succeeded Dr. Gill in the Lectureship at Great Eastcheap. After this prosperity had lasted for or about ten years, it was suddenly ended by some blasting charges being preferred against his moral character, the impeachment being sustained by the testimony of several members who witnessed to his crimes. The majority nobly discharged their duty by ignominiously expelling from communion an intruder into the Church who had sullied her purity, and disgraced her mission. Nothing abashed, however, Stevens removed to Redcross-street, where he preached till his death in 1778. About ninety members, by whom of course he was regarded as innocent, fol-

* Manuscript Records of the Church; Samuel Wilson's Sermon on the Death of George Braithwaite; The Nation's Reproach, by G. Braithwaite; Wilson's History of the Dissenting Churches.

lowed him thither. This calamity, which very
severely tried the Society, arose from the usurpation
of the Christian office on the part of a wicked man.
During the six following years, only trifling addi-
tions were made to the Church.

When the disastrous division above mentioned
occurred, there was living in London a wealthy
lady of the name of Maisters, a Christian of un-
blemished character; but whose intellect, even then
tinged with insanity, was destined to fail her.
John Stevens, the expelled minister, who more
becomingly might have hidden his face in penitential seclusion, found in Mrs. Maisters a friend and
patron, and obtained from her a chapel in Redcross-
street, which she had reared at her own expense.

Stevens was a native of Exmouth, where his
parents filled nothing more than an humble station.
Before meddling with divinity, the lad tried his
skill both at ropemaking and agriculture. He was
first brought to a profession of religion by one of
Lady Huntingdon's agents. His next step was to
give his leisure hours to study. When he commenced to labour as a village evangelist, he achieved
a reputation for oratorical power very unusual
under similar circumstances. Such indeed was his
fame, that on first coming to London, his services
were valued by the Society at the Tabernacle in
Moorfields. Stevens likewise visited Scotland as an
itinerant preacher of her Ladyship's connexion.
Soon after returning from this tour he declared

himself a Baptist, and succeeded George Braithwaite at Devonshire Square. Ultimately, as already explained, the pastor's character and his prospects of further usefulness, were simultaneously annihilated by the dark charges preferred against him. The voluminous manuscript accounts extant too plainly prove the wicked man's guilt to allow any doubt to remain in the mind of an unbiassed reader, to whose lot the ordeal may fall of having to digest the details.*

Three years passed, and the community thus rent and impoverished, found no suitable leader. At length the choice of Walter Richards, a young man then living at Birmingham, carried with it some promise of a happier future. His brethren affectionately surrendered him, and just before Christmas 1762, he was ordained in London. The pastor's ministrations were unsuccessful. The people manifested dissatisfaction by shunning the chapel. By a minority, however, Richards was highly esteemed; but the insulting behaviour of others counteracted their support, and he resigned,—retired to Ireland, there probably to meet with better success, since he is referred to nearly fifty years later, as . still flourishing in the Emerald Isle.

To supply the pulpit so soon again vacant proved a difficult task. Richard Hutchings, a Northamptonshire minister, first attracted attention. The affectionate self-denial of his own people far exceeded

* Manuscript Records of the Church ; Wilson's History of the Dissenting Churches.

their poverty; and merely through considerations for their pastor's comfort, they urged him to seek a charge with ampler means. He visited Devonshire Square, but the call not being unanimous he declined accepting it.

Communications were next opened with John Macgowan, who was prevailed on to assume the responsibilities of the pastorate. A native of Edinburgh, and born in 1726, he merely received in youth an ordinary Scottish education, suitable for the weaving craft, his intended calling. In early life he embraced Wesleyanism, and when first religious impressions were deepened into real conversion, Macgowan promoted the Methodist movement by engaging as a preacher. Growing more Calvinistic his convictions led him into Independency; and by embracing the tenet of Believers' Baptism he eventually entered the Baptist denomination. Macgowan then settled at Bridgenorth, a situation which, through want of success, he resigned, and removed to London in 1766. After an introduction, he accepted a call to the pastorate at Devonshire Square, and in the following summer was publicly recognised in a service which Gill and Stennett conducted. The pastor continued to labour iu the old City till removed by death in 1780. He excelled in preaching and in writing, the fame he achieved by the *Dialogues of Devils* still surviving. A large number of contemporary readers justly appreciated the author's pieces, and during the present century they have been republished in a uniform edition. The first suggestion to write The Infernal Conference may have sprung from *Dialogues of the Dead,* a singular book printed in 1760.

Macgowan was constitutionally weak, and his strength was apparently unequal to that habitual application so indispensable in the ministerial profession. This will account for his oft-recurring mental cloudiness, and spiritual dejection. He was, nevertheless, a valuable minister; and often, by mere effort of will, would lay aside an ever present physical debility for the purpose of honouring Christ by building up his Church and comforting his people. A strong imagination, retentive memory, and large stores of general knowledge, rendered him an improving and attractive companion and a desirable counsellor. His farewell visit to Devonshire Square was an affecting occasion long remembered. It occurred on Sunday, November the 12th, 1780. Feeble by the weakness attending bodily decay, and suffering from the pains of impending dissolution, the pastor yet determined once again to dispense to his flock the commemorative Bread and Wine. To complete this pious resolve, to declare that he stood in his place for the last time, and to recommend Timothy Thomas for a successor, the strength of the dying man sufficed. On a quiet Sabbath evening a fortnight after, his spirit departed, to enter into rest.*

* Wallin's Sermon on the Death of John Macgowan; Introduction to Macgowan's Works; New Baptist Repository; Wilson's History of the Dissenting Churches.

Timothy Thomas—whose ministry some yet living will remember—is the last pastor of whom it will be necessary to speak particularly. The family were Welsh Dissenters, and the father of our subject held an honourable position in the ministry at Leominster. Thomas was born in 1753, and after receiving a second-rate education, was apprenticed to a carpenter. Wishing to attain increased proficiency, Thomas settled in London, and being employed by a member of Devonshire Square, he became connected with that Church. On manifesting an inclination for the Christian ministry, the young artisan found his way beset with difficulties. An extreme prejudice then prevailed against any literary training for the pastoral office; and Timothy Thomas was neither gifted nor educated. While perfectly conscious of his shortcomings and unpolished mien, he ventured on expressing a desire to enter Bristol Academy, but he received some contemptuous rebukes from many who maintained that a Christian's proper school was the Church, and his only teacher Christ. His elders, however, judged of his intellectual strength by listening to a sermon; they would only acknowledge the preacher to be possessed of " an infant's gift."

Timothy Thomas proceeded to Bristol, and there progressed as favourably as the disadvantages from which he suffered would allow. The tutors, Hugh Evans and his son Dr. Caleb, were able men, and it happened unfortunately for young Thomas that his pastor's decease in London occasioned a shortening of the allotted curriculum. The people quickly acted on Macgowan's dying counsel by despatching a message to Bristol to call on their fellow-member to return and minister to their need. On the Sabbath of Macgowan's death his *protegé* preached his first sermon at Devonshire Square, and during the following summer was fully installed. One small matter—widely separated from study—had obtained some attention at Bristol, a principal result being a transformation of the tutor's daughter into Mrs. Thomas.

The young minister's life prospects were now far from being unpromising, although certain drawbacks checked his prosperity. The invitation to the pastorate not having been unanimous, the minority were a source of vexation. Annoyances increased till, by acting on the advice of his brethren, the pastor resigned; and although not accepted, that resignation had the effect of restoring peace by compelling the withdrawal of the opposing forces. Troubles thus blowing over, life's happiness flowed on uninterruptedly through several succeeding years. In 1796 Thomas left his manse in Houndsditch to establish himself as a schoolmaster at Islington—a step which was immediately followed by the untimely death of Mrs. Thomas.

As he grew in years so Timothy Thomas increased in favour among his cotemporaries. The man's broad open countenance revealed his generous and honest nature. He very heartily loved the Baptist denomination, and laboured hard to promote its general well-being, besides faithfully distributing the *Regium Donum.* The heavy afflictions which overtook him in his declining years need not be particularly mentioned. The principal, a stroke of paralysis in 1824, disabled him from frequently preaching for ever after. The affection of his people, however, prevented their listening to any proposal concerning resignation. They preferred looking into Bristol College for an assistant; in their search they found Thomas Price. For the purpose of hearing his young colleague, and then of administering the Sacrament for the last time, Timothy Thomas attended the chapel on the first Sabbath of 1827. Illness debarred him from fulfilling the second part of this design. He was carried home to linger till the opening days of summer, when he too passed into that rest which so many of his predecessors already enjoyed.

Our sketch must now conclude. The recent and lamented death of Dr. Price might very properly have occasioned a reference to his career and to his connection with this ancient Church, had not the particulars of his life been already so widely diffused. A rebuilding of the meeting-house celebrated his accession to the pastorate, the present chapel having been opened by Mr. Binney, in 1829.

In our own day the name of John Howard Hinton has long been indissolubly associated with Devonshire Square. His term of office extended through twenty-seven years—from 1837 to 1863. On accepting their respected pastor's resignation, the Church secured the services of William Thomas Henderson, of Banbury, who then removed to London. He still retains his office, and the affection of the people, to whom his ministrations are peculiarly acceptable.

The Metropolitan Railway Company being about to extend their line to Tower Hill, the site of Devonshire Square Chapel will be required. The Church will thus become necessitated to forsake a spot which many sacred and ancient associations have endeared to Nonconformists. As in all things, Providence is to be trusted, so in this matter likewise. Out of present difficulties good will doubtless arise, and in a new sphere—wherever that may be—we may fervently trust that the connection between pastor and flock may remain unbroken through many prosperous years.

Some eminent thinkers have supposed that the saints enjoying eternal rest are acquainted with and interested in terrestrial affairs. If this be so, then Kiffen, Braithwaite, Macgowan, and a multitude more, are witnesses to the removal of this old Christian landmark from the spot they loved so well, and so greatly frequented. While this may be truly so, our desire is that those who remain, by love and Christian harmony in action, may prove themselves good soldiers of the Church Militant, and descendants worthy of their noble predecessors.

Chapter II.

THERE came to London about the year 1580 a citizen
of Venice, of the name of Verselyn. Being skilled
in the art of glass-blowing, he became anxious to
establish a trade in the country of his adoption.
With this end in view he sought the countenance of
Elizabeth, and the Queen extended her patronage by
granting him a patent. With his newly-acquired
power the trader planted a factory near Old Broad-
street, in the City of London. The opposition of
the citizens to this innovation was determined and
persevering. Extraordinary representations were
made to Government of evil consequences likely to
follow the sanctioning of such an institution—*e.g.*,
sundry families already engaged in the glass trade
would be ruined; vast quantities of wood required
for other purposes would be consumed in the Vene-
tian's furnaces; and, worse than all, the customs
would suffer merely to enrich a contemptible
foreigner. Verselyn bravely weathered the storm
which his enemies raised, and probably sold more

glass on account of their opposition; for in after
years the business he founded was sufficiently prosperous for the overseer to resign his office, the heat,
he declared, being so excessive that he would soon
have melted away among those hot Venetians. The
site of Verselyn's manufactory was afterwards occupied by Pinners' Hall. The trade of this guild—
pin and needle-making—greatly suffered from foreign
competition. In the time of Charles the Second
this hall passed into the hands of the Nonconformists, who, besides founding a Christian Church
of the Independent order, established a Tuesday-
morning sermon—the once celebrated Merchants'
Lecture.

The first pastor at Pinners' Hall* was Anthony
Palmer, a divine, who through the religious dissen-
sions of the Commonwealth, sided with the Presbyterians, and subscribed the Covenant, but afterwards
joined the Independents. He rose in the estimation
of his party till preferred to the living of Bourton-
on-the-Water. Our libeller-general, Anthony Wood,
declares that Palmer "was all things to all men,
such was the mutability and vanity of the person."

* Several distinct societies were connected with Pinners'
Hall, but in our present sketch we must principally confine
ourselves to the Independent Church planted by Anthony
Palmer. The Glass-house, as it was called, was connected
with a society of Baptists in the time of Cromwell. Palmer
and Fownes, prior to their settlement at Broad-street, appear
to have preached in the house of one Savage, on London
Bridge.

According to the same authority, moreover, he became "Anabaptistically inclined."

The testimony of more credible witnesses to the integrity and religious zeal of Anthony Palmer cannot fairly be called in question. After studying at Oxford he settled at Bourton in 1649. Bourton was then an inconsiderable village of not more than seventy houses, containing three hundred and fifty inhabitants. Immediately after the Restoration the vigilant enmity of his foes followed the pastor to Bourton. He had been one of Cromwell's Triers; and to be especially hated by the country gentry was the penalty paid by those who had dared to prove the uselessness of bishops. As for Palmer, on being accused of plotting against the Government, he was literally driven from his living by the leading parishioners. He was also greatly harassed by the malicious spite of his enemies. In April, 1660, a military party invaded his private residence under a pretence of searching for arms, but really for purposes of plunder and outrage. Such were the things which made up the routine of a Nonconformist's life two hundred years ago. Strange reports were sometimes current of judgments which overtook the persecutors. One of Palmer's detractors, so people said, had been visited by death, while another was smitten by a strange disease.

Palmer removed to London in 1662. After preaching for a time in a private house, he settled at Pinners' Hall, where, to quote the words of the Oxford

historian, " he carried on the trade of conventicling
to the last," and "was buried in the phanatical
burial-ground joining to Old Bedlam, near to Moorfields by London."* The truth is, that Palmer's
efforts to promote the advancement of peace and
righteousnesss were only terminated by death. For
long after, the Church held his name in honour; but
the Royalists left nothing undone and unsaid which
by saying and doing they could blacken his character.†

Palmer was assisted by the able and devoted
George Fownes, who, on embracing Baptist principles, resigned the cure of High Wycombe during
the ascendancy of Cromwell. The times changed,
and Fownes encountered the harshest treatment;
his chief opponent being a local magistrate of the
name of Wroth. Ultimately the pastor was driven
to London by the troubles of the times, and there
undertook a lecture at Lothbury, and thence removed
into Pinners' Hall. After the death of Anthony
Palmer, Fownes settled at Broadmead, Bristol, to
which Church and City his history properly belongs.
At Bristol he proved himself a worthy successor
of the noble Hardcastle. A relentless persecution
brought him to a premature grave; but although
he died under them, he never quailed before his
trials. As usual in those days, the enemy-in-chief

* Bunhill Fields.
† Athenæ Oxonienses; Nonconformists' Memorial;
Ackyn's History of Gloucestershire; History of the Dis-
senting Churches; Crosby's History of the English Baptists.

to any evangelising efforts was the bishop of the diocese. Such shepherds were not ashamed to re-sort to every manœuvre which promised to harass Nonconformists. Witnesses were suborned who said Fownes had broken the peace of a certain place; but it transpired that he and his horse on their peaceful travels had been the only rioters. He found himself continually under arrest. To walk upon the King's highway, or to stand up amid his people, was to risk a sudden seizure. During three years he lay in the gaol of Bristol, and not until 1685 was that freedom awarded which belongs to "The noble army of martyrs."

The spirit of persecution continued to predomi-nate after Palmer's decease. His afflicted church anxiously sought a suitable successor to his arduous duties. The necessary qualities were found in Richard Wavell, whom the little band now chose for their leader. He was a native of the Isle of Wight, and during the Civil Wars his father had espoused the side of the Royalists. Wavel had been previously tempted to conform by liberal offers of preferment, but he now agreed to risk comfort and freedom if the people would as openly hazard their money. Each party exactly fulfilled this heroic contract. The pastor fearlessly discharged his duties, and his followers cheerfully bore the expenses entailed by frequent legal embarrassments. Several services were regularly conducted on the Sabbath, although the utmost caution had to be observed—a course of action especially praiseworthy when, as in this instance, alluring paths to affluence had been nobly eschewed.   This good man held his ground against the sophistries of the tempter and the attacks of persecution, and remained with the people of his choice long after the iniquitous Stuarts had forfeited the crown their reign disgraced.   At one period Wavell possessed a valuable friend in the person of the Lord Mayor, Sir Harry Tulse, who helped him through many trying seasons.   Once it fell to the lot of Sir Harry to apologise for the term "gentleman," coupled by a thoughtless indictment writer with Wavell's name, and at which the sitting magistrate, as he thought, reasonably quibbled.   At another time Tulse detained a principal witness against Wavell in conversation till the completion of the trial.   Such troubles, however, being ended by the Revolution, Wavell lived on till the year 1705, loving his work, and doing it well.   When the dawning appeared of approaching repose, he laid aside the arms of his warfare with visible joy.   His place was never properly supplied, for from the period of his death we date the earliest symptoms of decay in the church at Pinners' Hall."*

It is manifest by the eminent names associated with it, that Pinners' Hall in the times we write of, was a chief centre of Nonconformist influence.

* Nonconformists' Memorial; History of the Dissenting Churches, &c. For an account of Townes see Crosby, and more particularly the Broadmead Records.

From a union of Independent and Presbyterian
Ministers in 1672, sprang the Merchants' Lecture,
the first preachers of which were men with characters
closely approaching the apostolic standard.   Dr.
Manton, leading the way, was supported by Owen,
Bates, Baxter, and others.   Unfortunately, the tie
which united this illustrious galaxy was sufficiently
weak to be broken by the discussion of some
doctrinal tenets.   Baxter's first sermon in the course
awakened an anti-Arminian outcry throughout London ; but the malcontents were sharply rebuked by
Manton, and also by the lecturer himself in a broadside called " An Appeal to the Light."   Thus for the
time was the threatened breach prevented.   In a
few years, when some of the original lecturers lay in
their graves, disputes again arose to breed division
between the two denominations, so that a rival
lectureship was instituted at Salters' Hall.   These
Tuesday services grew into real attractions, and
hearers from the outskirts were wont to return at
mid-day to their suburban homes, well repaid for a
toilsome walk by having listened to some distinguished preacher.

The old hall was likewise used in Puritan times
by a congregation of Seventh Day Baptists.   Francis
Bampfield, their pastor, being persecuted to death,
ended his sufferings in Newgate in 1684.   A
metrical broadside, commemorating his sufferings,
makes him say :—

> " I spent in prison more than twice five years."

5*

The people's sense of bereavement is thus expressed :—

> " Shall we pine for want of living bread ;
> Or shall our hungry souls with husks be fed ?
> O, Heaven forbid it ; give us not dross for gold ;
> Let younger prophets still succeed the old."

The society of Independents which leased the hall met only in the morning; and consequently other congregations were allowed to assemble during other parts of the day. Dr. Watts and his people enjoyed such a privilege till their removal, in 1708, to a newly erected meeting-house in Bury-street, St. Mary Axe. At other periods, by special arrangements, various churches were permitted to use the room. Wavell's successor, Dr. Hunt, introduced the practice of preaching twice on the Sabbath ; but even then the General Baptists occupied the building in the afternoon. When the lease expired in 1778, the Independent society was dissolved. The hall next became leased to Anthony Crole for twenty-one years, who during that space, ministered to a flourishing congregation. Eventually he removed to Founders' Hall, where he continued till his decease. Finally Pinners' Hall was taken down, and no traces now remain of a structure interesting because so intimately associated with the history of Nonconformity.

From 1707, till his death in 1744, the pulpit was occupied by Jeremiah Hunt. His election was an unfortunate procedure, for it marked the fatal first

step towards a declension in doctrine and prosperity.
Born in 1678, young Hunt at two years of age lost
his father. He was originally intended for trade,
but his mother encouraged a ruling inclination which
prompted his studying for the Christian ministry—
a course he followed successively at London, Edinburgh, and Leyden. Being a laborious student, he
especially excelled in a knowledge of Hebrew and
Oriental lore. While staying in Holland, moreover,
he attained to that oratorical fluency which he ever
after displayed. So manifest indeed were his powers
of extempore speaking that he occasionally trans-
gressed the warning of the hour-glass, "without," as
Dr. Lardner says, "any discernible confusion or disagreeable tautology." Dr. Hunt's first settlement ·
was at Tunstead, near Norwich. Thence, in 1710,
he removed to London, and continued till his death
at Pinners' Hall.

In London, Jeremiah Hunt won a reputation for
genius and learning, and from a Scotch university
received the diploma of doctor of divinity. As a
preacher he was characterised by many singularities.
On the consecutive Sabbath mornings of several years
he selected texts from the Book of Proverbs. His
custom was thoroughly to work out his subject, and
this he often did without making notes. So good a ·
judge as Dr. Lardner classed the pastor at Pinners'
Hall among model preachers, although the results of
his labours prove him to have been very unsuccessful. We can in some degree realise the estimation

in which contemporaries held Dr. Hunt by some lines on the Nonconformists of London, written by one of the "advanced" party for the *Gentleman's Magazine* in 1736—the author having probably been the abandoned Richard Savage :—

> " With soundest judgment and with nicest skill,
> The learned Hunt explains his Master's will;,
> So just his meaning, and his sense so true,
> He only pleases the discerning few."[*]

There are some almost incredible stories testifying to the strength of the Doctor's memory. He had the reputation of never forgetting sermons after once delivering them ; according to his own confession to Dr. Lardner, he believed that nearly all the discourses he had preached could be recalled. In one notable instance a lecture, given fourteen years before, was reproduced with scarcely a verbal variation from the original.

At this date a principal member at Pinners' Hall was Viscount Barrington, whose eminent station and ability enabled him to exercise an extensive influence among Nonconformists. His lordship had already attained to some celebrity by writing in defence of the

---

[*] A parody on this poem soon afterwards appeared, and the author portrayed Dr. Hunt in less brilliant, though possibly truer colours, *e.g.*:

> " The busy Hunt, with little skill,
> Takes mighty pains to extol his own freewill ;
> So dull his meaning, and his action too,
> He really pleases but a very few."

principles professed by himself and by his brethren.
Dr. Fleming communicated to the editors of the
Biographia Britannica some particulars of the
friendship which existed between Dr. Hunt, Lord
Barrington, and the freethinker, Anthony Collins.
At the Viscount's seat in Essex these friends were
wont to meet; and they made a point of gratifying
their critical taste by introducing a Greek Testament
with the dessert. One day Collins so far committed
himself as to express some admiration of the character of St. Paul. While in a magnanimous mood,
the infidel admitted that the Apostle was at the least
" a man of sense and a gentleman." Collins further
confessed that, he would have believed in miracles
had Paul himself laid claim to miraculous power.
An immediate reference to such a circumstance
having occurred in the apostle's life, confounded
the unwary deist, and he soon after withdrew from
the company.*

The eminent orator James Foster next succeeded
at Pinners' Hall, and continued to occupy the pulpit
till his death in 1753. Being a native of Exeter he
was educated in that city; and his first tutor at the
Grammar School became so delighted with the genius
and learning of his *protégé*, that he openly boasted
of him about the town. Foster continued his studies
in a Nonconformist academy at Exeter, where his

* Lardner's Sermon on the Death of Dr. Hunt ; Biographia
Britannica ; Gentleman's Magazine, vol. vi. ; History of the
Dissenting Churches.

abilities and kindly nature exalted him into high favour. He won the friendship of Dr. Conybeare, Bishop of Bristol, and conscience alone, it would seem, debarred young Foster from taking a foremost position in the Established Church. His public ministry began in 1718, in the midst of that controversy respecting subscription to theological doctrines which, arising in the West, reached a climax of violence at Salters' Hall in the following spring. Unfortunately for his good influence and reputation, Foster imbibed the sentiments of Pierce, who originated the dispute, and was thus never popular in the western counties. He wandered from place to place without affording his hearers any satisfaction; at one time the eloquent preacher, with a yearly stipend of fifteen pounds, simultaneously ministered to two congregations in the neighbourhood of the Mendip Hills. So unacceptable indeed were Foster's earlier endeavours, that to relinquish his profession in favour of trade appeared a manifest duty; and he only escaped the glove craft by accepting a chaplaincy in a gentleman's family. This change of fortune was shortly succeeded by a call to London, whither he removed, and settled in Barbican with Jeremiah Burroughs; thence, on the death of Dr. Hunt, he removed to Pinners' Hall. After settling there, Foster's great abilities were appreciated to a degree beyond the most sanguine anticipation.

Foster possessed every attribute requisite for attaining popularity. He was a correct scholar, and a

good critic; he inherited large stores of miscellaneous
knowledge, all available at command. He possessed
a voice of great compass, which he controlled with consummate art; and this contributed in no small degree
to the successful working of his other powers. His
elocution was admired by the best judges, including
Johnson; and although surpassed in pronunciation
by Watts, the most fastidious were never offended by
his delivery. Whether in their lowest key, or otherwise in the peroration, his tones rang clearly throughout the building. One thing effected by these accomplishments was the attraction of large numbers
of women to the chapel—a crowning triumph of
genius; so at least thought Foster's contemporaries.

In 1746 Foster frequently visited Lord Kilmarnock during that nobleman's confinement in the
Tower previously to his execution—the penalty he
paid for having actively shared in the rising for the
Young Pretender. While admitting his treason, the
prisoner confessed that his crimes had been occasioned by the demands of extravagant and dissolute
habits. Hope of retrieving his decayed fortunes, he
said, allured him into joining the desperate adventure for Charles Edward. Foster drew up an account of the imprisonment and death of Kilmarnock,
but was so lastingly affected by the Earl's untimely
fate, that, till the close of life, the dark impression
never could be effaced from his kindly nature.

Many eulogies on the oratorical powers of Foster
are still extant, having mostly appeared in the

Gentleman's Magazine. His popularity surpassed that
of all contemporary Nonconformists, and therefore,
at various times, Sylvanus Urban contributed some
fitting mites to the common flattery, *e.g.* :

> " But see the accomplished orator appear,
>   Refined his language, and his reason clear;
>   Thou, Foster, only hast the pleasing art
>   At once to charm the ear and mend the heart."

> " In him (great modern miracle) we see
>   A priest from avarice and ambition free ;
>   Thee, honest Dissenters, we with pride may own
>   Our Tillotson, and Rome her Fenelon."

> " Truth stands by thee displayed to mortal sight
>   In naked majesty supremely bright ;
>   While from thy arm her darts unerring fly,
>   And folly, vice, and superstition die."

One section of the press depreciated the doctor's
work and character. In the *Weekly Miscellany* of
June the 7th, 1735, he is depicted as a "teacher of
false doctrine ; a spreader of sentiments injurious to
Scripture and the cause of Christianity."

Foster's contemporaries accounted for his popularity by tracing its origin to an eminent physician,
who, on being driven by stress of weather into Pinners' Hall, was favourably impressed by the preacher's
powers, and in consequence made him a subject of
eulogy throughout his connexion. This absurd
accounting for success gained sufficient currency to
be widely credited. If we accept it as truth, how

happily has England changed ! Preachers of to-day
may be congratulated, since modern intelligence so
quickly appreciates merit. The necessity for Dissent
to seek constituents in Belgravia, or in any way to
be beholden to the good offices of a fashionable
physician, has completely passed away.

Considering the religious apathy of the period,
Foster's fame appears to have been somewhat singular, if not unparalleled. The then unusual number
of two thousand persons subscribed for his work on
Natural Religion ; and but for this success—such
was the author's liberality—he would have died in
poverty. Among the number of Foster's eminent
admirers appears the name of Alexander Pope, who
seems to have been an occasional hearer. In his
Epilogue to the Satires, the poet has bequeathed
us a graceful tribute to the preacher's power :—

> " Let modest Foster, if he will, excel
> Ten Metropolitans in preaching well."

Such praise awakened the ire of the High Church
party. The principles of that party made it appear
too extraordinary to be probable, or even possible,
that a dissenting teacher, in an old room originally
dedicated to pins and needles, should show talents
then vainly sought among George the Second's
bishops. Anglican spleen was fittingly expressed
by Warburton's sneering note on the above couplet,
which, as an insult to taste and sense, is scarcely
worthy of quotation.

Other celebrated hearers, however, besides Pope, crowded to the feet of Dr. Foster. During his Sabbath-evening lectureship at the Old Jewry, the attractive force of his eloquence drew to the chapel the wits, the courtiers, clergymen, and freethinkers of the town. Whiston, the translator of Josephus, on seceding from the Establishment, became Foster's disciple. Nevertheless, there were certain observers who dared to speak the reverse of compliment— *e.g.* :—

> " But see the bold Socinian now appear,
> Full fraught with pride, but void of fear ;
> For Foster truly has the running art
> To please the ear, but leaves one in the dark."

Such having been the character of Dr. Foster, it need occasion no regret that his influence has not been lasting. Let us rather grieve that one who to great intellectual powers added other endearing qualities, yet forsook the light of the Cross and the teachings of Paul for the lifeless dogmas of Socinus.*

The last pastor of the old Independent church, Pinners' Hall, was Caleb Fleming, a native of Nottingham, and born at the end of the seventeenth century. He received his early education in the neighbourhood of his home, but had no intention

---

* Funeral Sermons for Dr. Foster by Caleb Fleming and Charles Bulkley ; Protestant Dissenters' Magazine ; Gentleman's Magazine, vols. v. and xxiii. ; History of the Dissenting Churches.

of following the course he did till, on removing to London, he extended his studies, and commenced preaching. In 1738 he accepted the pastorate at Bartholomew Close; and, while stationed there, he occasionally assisted Dr. Foster, at whose death Fleming and his people removed to Pinners' Hall. There our divine laboured on until infirmities common to age compelled his retirement. After the pastor's decease, in 1778, the Society was dissolved. Fleming and Lardner maintained a close friendship; the two having found great delight in corresponding on doctrinal and historical themes, although their homes in Hoxton Square were only separated by a few paces. Fleming was unfortunately a strong Socinian partisan; and it is therefore well that his publications, sixty in number, are now forgotten, being chiefly met with in the remote nooks of our public libraries. The doctor's extreme hostility to the orthodox faith caused many even of his own party to shun his acquaintance; yet ample proof remains that he suffered in worldly matters for conscience sake. His principles prompted him to abandon prospects which opened before him of Church preferment. A portrait of Fleming will be found in Dr. Williams's Library; but the features are not those of a man who possessed a happy disposition.

Thus, the end of this church in Pinners' Hall was not worthy of its opening promise. In tracing the history of Nonconformity, it invariably follows that, so far as churches have receded from those central truths of the Gospel—Christ's divinity and atonement—so far has the power to accomplish their mission diminished. It is not always easy to discover when heresies in a given society first made their appearance, or what the causes were which led to the introduction of pastors of a lower theological standard. The history of Pinners' Hall is the story of a religious degeneracy hardly to be paralleled in the annals of Dissent.*

* Palmer's Sermon on the Death of Dr. Fleming ; History of the Dissenting Churches, &c.

Chapter III.

CROSBY HALL.

CROSBY HALL, as the finest remaining specimen of the domestic architecture of old London, has seen changes, humiliating and otherwise, since the days in which it was forsaken by its lordly possessors and the Nonconformists. By turn it has served as a packing-shed and a wine-cellar. About seventy years ago a tradesman of the former calling used it for a workshop; and posterity has witnessed how pipes of claret and Sauterne can desecrate the time-honoured pavement. The hall is now a dining establishment; but as the premises have been offered for sale, some reasonable fear may be entertained respecting this interesting relic, which, if permanently secured, might properly be transformed into a library and reading-room for the City of London.

Crosby Hall, as it now exists, is a portion of a sumptuous mansion erected by Sir John Crosbie in 1470. The present room was known as Richard the Third's Chapel, that tyrant having once been lodged there for a few nights, on which occasion some of his villanies were planned. Originally the house was the most lofty of London private residences, and to the citizens of a ruder age it was doubtless an object of prominent interest. The site was bought of Alice Ashfield, the Prioress of Saint Helen's. About five years only did Sir John Crosbie survive the completion of his mansion. Subsequently the property passed out of his family. Years later the house was inhabited by Sir Thomas More. In Elizabeth's reign the apartments served as a lodging for some foreign ambassadors, and occasionally for a lord mayor. On the accession of James the First, the French ambassador, with a grand retinue, occupied the place, imparting to the chambers a magnificence such as had seldom or never been equalled within their walls. About 1640 it fell into the hands of Sir John Langham, afterwards to be destroyed by a calamitous fire; but the Hall, escaping unscathed, was converted into a meeting-house of the Presbyterian denomination.

Thus Crosby Hall was destined to become associated with other and nobler objects. When, in 1672, Charles the Second proclaimed his Indulgence, the premises were hired by Thomas Watson, the ejected minister of St. Stephen's, Walbrook, who gathered upon the spot a flourishing congregation. Watson owed much to the patronage of Sir John Langham, the owner of the property, for Sir John in those rough days was a staunch friend of Nonconformists. As a pastor, Watson was laborious and conscientious. Previously to the opening of Crosby Hall he had habitually preached as opportunities were afforded, either in private or otherwise. The pastor's conscience was sufficiently tender, and he believed apparently in the divine right of kings, for after siding with Charles, through the Civil Wars, he brought trouble upon himself by mixing with certain conspirators who sought to anticipate the Restoration by bringing in the exiled heir. Watson was one among other divines whom Cromwell, on account of this business, imprisoned in the Tower. One of the number—Christopher Love—was executed for traitorous practices; and supposing so terrible an example would act as a salutary warning, the government released the remaining prisoners. Watson enjoyed a good reputation for scholarship, and was besides an able preacher. He indulged in authorship to the great admiration of a wide circle of readers. Many of his works were composed during the period of enforced silence, and one of them, Heaven Taken by Storm, was instrumental in the conversion of Colonel Gardiner. He also composed A Body of Divinity, the same being contained in a folio of one hundred and seventy-six sermons on the Assembly's Shorter Catechism. He moreover possessed, even for Puritan times, an uncommon gift in prayer. At one service he had for an auditor Bishop Richardson, who was agreeably surprised at the fervour and beauty with which the pastor prayed. At the conclusion of the service

6

the prelate followed Watson home for the double
purpose of expressing gratification and of begging a
copy of what he had heard. "Alas!" exclaimed the
pastor, "that is what I cannot give; for it was no
studied thing, but uttered as God enabled me from
the abundance of my heart and affection." The
bishop expressed great astonishment at finding a
man who could thus intercede with heaven without
a book.

Watson continued pastor at Crosby Hall until the
failing of his natural vigour compelled him to resign.
He spent life's closing years in rural retirement,
and lived to see the Revolution consummated, and
those principles of freedom in the ascendant for
which he had so greatly suffered. He died in his
study, while engaged in prayer, in 1689.

A more illustrious man associated with Crosby
Hall was Stephen Charnocke, whom the Christian
world agrees to honour as a luminous star in the
Puritan galaxy. The Charnockes were a family of
ancient and respectable standing in the county of
Lancaster. In the olden time one of their number
was distinguished by the *sobriquet* of Rosicrucian
Charnocke, and during the sixteenth century this
singular character attained some celebrity as an
alchemist. He once determined on exploring England in quest of that knowledge which he deemed
so indispensable to one of his absurd profession.
While accomplishing these studious peregrinations he
stayed for a season at Oxford, but soon after he settled

in Salisbury, where he allied himself to a celebrated chemical investigator. A chemist or alchemist, as he existed in the days of Elizabeth, was a being very widely differing from any known species of the modern pharmaceutist. He was a creature whom the vulgar regarded with awe and the literate with curiosity. He commonly passed his days and nights within the precincts of two apartments. In one of his rooms he hurriedly swallowed his food, and took, in restless snatches, what little sleep his excited brain permitted him to enjoy. In his working room he was continually engaged among crucibles, furnaces, salts, and the mysterious *lapis philosophorum.* Occasionally these disciples of the philosophers' stone stooped from their lofty pursuits to the degradation of authorship, but unfortunately for this later age, their directions about reducing baser metals into golden ingots of a hundredweight each are usually written in a professional jargon unintelligible to common people. Like his compeers, Rosicrucian Charnocke not only laboured at his fires, but composed several treatises, and a portion of his literary effusions was dedicated to Queen Elizabeth. He once tolerated a slight interruption in his studies, and in the interim married Mistress Agnes Norden, of Bristol. His last days were spent in the neighbourhood of Bridgwater. Our old alchemist is found to have burnt himself out, but profiting by experience he contrived a laboratory of fireproof construction—a highly necessary precaution, if we consider

6*

that his little sleeping-room adjoined. Rosicrucian
Charnocke died in 1581, and lies in the churchyard
at Otterhampton.

Stephen Charnocke, the justly celebrated author
of the Discourses on the Existence and Attributes
of God, was the son of a lawyer in the City of
London, and born in 1628, not far from the spot
so intimately associated with his name and labours.
He was entered at Emanuel College, Cambridge, and
there studied under Archbishop Sancroft. At an
uncertain period, during the last years of Charles
the First, Charnocke was engaged as a preacher in
Southwark. In 1649 he relinquished his charge
and removed to Oxford. While there his splendid
endowments won the high favour of the Presbyterians, who elected him proctor of the University,
or, as Anthony Wood sneeringly puts it, he was
"then taken notice of by the godly party for his
singular gifts." When we consider how high he
ranked among the Puritans it will appear extremely
singular that the particulars of his life should be so
scanty, the last five years of which were spent with
Watson at Crosby Hall. Charnocke's friend, John
Gunter, is commonly supposed to have prepared some
additional memoirs now not known to be in existence. Our author himself wrote an account of his
conversion and early career, but unfortunately these
papers, with his entire library, perished in the Fire
of London.

On leaving Oxford, in 1656, Charnocke visited

Ireland, to reside for some years with Sir Harry Cromwell, in Dublin Castle, meantime receiving a salary of £200 a-year. The Lord-lieutenant was also accompanied by a number of eminent divines, so that in such a sphere, and among such associates, Charnocke was encompassed by pleasant surroundings. His stated labours agreed both with his capacities and predilections. His lectures in the cathedral, and in the old church of Saint Wesburgh, were thoroughly appreciated, and encomiums on the preacher came from persons of all parties. His lively fancy and graceful delivery set off his great powers to the best advantage. Persons to whom the elevated piety which animated the orator would have been but small attraction, were drawn as by an irresistible charm around him. These useful and happy labours were interrupted by the Restoration. After finally quitting Dublin, Charnocke passed fifteen years either in travelling or in studious seclusion.

In 1675 Watson obtained the assistance of Charnocke. After settling at Crosby Square the latter took up his residence with a glazier's family in Whitechapel, and in an apartment of this tradesman's house wrought out those profound discourses on the Attributes of God which have made their author's name dear and familiar to students wherever the language in which they were spoken is known: Few, surely, will be able to renew their acquaintance with Crosby Hall without feeling an additional interest in the structure which once resounded with the living voice of the preacher of these celebrated pieces.

Though only in his forty-seventh year when he engaged himself at Crosby Hall, Charnocke had grown prematurely old. Persons who remembered him as he appeared in Dublin, twenty years before, could scarcely recognise in Thomas Watson's assistant the original of their favourite orator. Because his memory had once proved treacherous he could not be prevailed on again to trust it; his sermons were consequently written at length. His weakened eyes rendered a glass a necessity, and this, in his nervous trembling hand, was doubly inconvenient. Notwithstanding these many drawbacks, Charnocke continued to be almost the idol of many admirers. Indeed, when we consider the position he held, we get a fair conception of this man's modesty, who, during his whole life, only published a single sermon. In his declining years he endeavoured to bring before his hearers a complete body of divinity; and he was busy with the discourses relating to the Attributes of God, when death ended his labours. His collected works were published by his executors, Edward Veal and Richard Adams; and the Christian community of the era of William and Mary was not slow in discovering our author's extraordinary merits, for a third edition appeared twenty-two years after his decease. On the 27th of July, 1680, death found Charnocke in the midst of his labours, but more than willing to respond to the summons.

Having throughout life set a notable example of
redeeming time, rest to his weary spirit was the
more welcome. A broadside of poems celebrated
his departure, an original copy of which is extant,
whence we learn how sincerely the people bemoaned
their loss, *e.g.* :—

> " O surely now great darkness doth draw on,
>   When God such shining stars as he calls home;
>   Methinks I could have rendered up my breath
>   To have saved him from grim conquering death."

His remains were carried from the house of
Richard Tymns, in Whitechapel, to Crosby Hall,
and thence to St. Michael's, Cornhill, where John
Johnson preached the funeral sermon. The coffin
was committed to the earth hard by the tower,
beneath the belfry of that fine old sanctuary. Many
tearful eyes, as they took a farewell glance of the
grave, proved the sincerity of the mourners' grief—
a grief well excused by the poet already quoted :—

> " Sure when such a Moses doth fall asleep
>   It is high time for Israel to weep."

Numbers are still attracted by the internal beauties
of St. Michael's, but how few of such visitors remember, while passing into the church, that they
are walking over the dust of Charnocke!

There is a story told, on the authority of Bishop
Parker, about Charnocke's having been engaged in a
conspiracy against the government of the Restoration.
One Presbyterian minister was hanged on account of

complicity in this affair, and one Charnock is mentioned as having been an accomplice. That this last
named was Stephen Charnocke is quite improbable,
for the conspirator appears to have been living some
years after our subject's decease.*

Samuel Slater, the successor of Charnocke, was a
son of the person of the same name who originated
the Weigh-house society. Educated at Cambridge
University he officiated during the Cromwellian era
in a parish church; but, on refusing to read the
Common Prayer, was ejected from his cure at the
Restoration. "The first place which was blessed
with his stated public labours was Nayland, in
Suffolk, and in that candlestick was this great Gospel
light first set up, where it spread and diffused light
and knowledge for several years, till removed to St.
Edmundsbury, in the same county." Slater's settlement in London took place about the time of the
King's proclamation of Indulgence, in 1672. His
accession to Crosby Hall was occasioned by the
removal hence of Stephen Charnocke, and his
pastorate continued until May, 1704, when he died
at a good old age, "like the gentle expiring of a
lamp that ceaseth to be fed."†

---

* Johnson's Sermon on the Death of Stephen Charnocke;
Athenæ Oxon, &c., &.

† Nonconformists' Memorial; History of the Dissenting
Churches; Daniel Alexander's Sermon on the Death of
Samuel Slater:—

"And now give me leave to throw in my mite of sorrow
into the common treasury, which (I doubt not) you will

From the time of this Society's formation to the date of its dissolution in 1769, the services were enjoyed of twelve ministers, including their assistants. Scarcely any particulars respecting some of these have survived. John Reynolds, one of the number, was stationed here at the time of the Revolution, having belonged to that minority which unwisely thanked the tyrannical James for the Indulgence of 1687. Reynolds died four years later, and if the eulogies pronounced upon him were not the offspring of too fond a partiality, the pastor was " A person of considerable abilities, a truly gracious humble Christian, a profitable preacher, an able catechist, and a faithful friend." Another assistant was Daniel Alexander. He stayed at Crosby Hall from 1693 till the death of his colleague in 1704. Some difficulty arose which caused his removal. At Armourers' Hall he officiated till his death in 1709.*

admit to be real and sincere ; and others will be inclined to believe when I have said that I had the honour and advantage to be assistant to him for near eleven years, in all which time not the least tincture of jealousy or suspicion obtained to hinder our usefulness or mutual confidence; but I was always treated by him with that unparalleled candour, condescension, affability, endearing kindness, and sincere respect which rendered my work in that relation much more pleasant and desirable than otherwise it would have been, as is now manifest from the quite contrary treatment I have met with since his death." *Daniel Alexander's Sermon on the Death of Samuel Slater.*

* Nonconformists' Memorial; Samuel Slater's Sermon on

Another eminent man connected with Crosby Hall for nearly half a century was Dr. Benjamin Grosvenor. His term of office extended from 1704 to 1749. The doctor's connections were respectable traders of the City of London. Benjamin, who was born on New Year's-day, 1675, from early youth "had a most awful sense of God upon his mind." During his early years, while one day passing through Gravel-lane, Southwark, he turned aside into the old chapel formerly standing there; he heard a sermon by one unknown to him, and whose name he could never afterwards discover. That discourse became the means of his conversion, and henceforth Grosvenor was remarkable for extraordinary seriousness. He manifested no predilection for the common pastimes of boys, but loved seclusion for purposes of reading and self-improvement. Reared in Southwark, under the pastorate of Benjamin Keach, that eminent divine and his Baptist connections were not slow to discover young Grosvenor's abilities. Through their advice and instrumentality he was placed in the academy of Timothy Jollie at Attercliffe, and trained for the Christian ministry. He was thus thrown into Pædo-baptist society, and on returning to Southwark he surprised his friends by appearing among them as a full-fledged Presbyterian. The Baptists, it is affirmed,

the Death of John Reynolds; History of the Dissenting Churches. Slater's discourse is a closely-printed quarto of thirty-two pages with scarcely a word of information respecting its subject.

behaved somewhat harshly to their former *protégé* on
account of this change of sentiments. Even if correct, the story will bring little discredit on the Baptists, for at that era a tendency to bigotry pervaded
all sections of the Christian Church.* After relinquishing Antipædobaptism, Grosvenor was approved
by the London Presbyterian examiners, and settled
with a charge in Southwark under Dr. Oldfield. The
lecturer shone in this sphere till endeavours were
made to bring him into the City. He was ultimately
appointed to conduct a lecture established at the Old
Jewry by some opulent citizens.

During the spring of 1704, shortly after Slater's
decease, Grosvenor acceded to the pastorate at Crosby
Hall, which his earnest and effective services sufficed
to crowd with a rich and influential congregation.
Soon after he lost his young wife, an amiable Christian, and daughter of Captain South, of Bethnal
Green, whose family were distinguished Nonconformists. The doctor composed some fine reflections
on his great trial. He married again in 1712. In
subsequent years he was severely troubled and perplexed by unmanageable sons.

* As regards the persecution of which Grosvenor's friends
complained, Crosby admits that " the church dealt plainly
with him," an expression which means excommunication.
Both Dr. Grosvenor and Crosby changed their sentiments
while young. The first, having been reared a Baptist, became
an eminent Presbyterian; and the other forsook the Pædobaptists to become the historian of his adopted denomination.
Posterity respects the conscientiousness of both.

The London citizens of those days being addicted to establishing lectureships, several were set up by the Nonconformists, and advanced to high appreciation. To sustain these institutions the services of the most able divines were secured, and among such Benjamin Grosvenor may be fairly classed. He is found to have been early engaged in the Weigh-house Psalmody Lecture, and also in the Merchants' Lectureship at Salters' Hall. In the last-named place, many years later, he and others chose Romanism for a theme on account of the apprehensions then prevalent of that curse overshadowing England, and centreing in the Young Pretender, who, though an exile, was still sanguine of regaining the throne of his ancestors.

The Church at Crosby Hall attained its zenith of popularity under the pastorate of Dr. Grosvenor and the able colleagues by whom he was assisted. Dr. Wright officiated for three years, and resigned in 1708, to succeed Matthew Sylvester at Blackfriars. Dr. Wright was followed by John Barker, who continued till the summer of 1714, when he took the place of Matthew Henry at Hackney. In Crosby Hall, moreover, laboured Clerk Oldsworth, of whom little more is known than that he divided with the Nonsubscribers at Salters' Hall in 1719, and died seven years later. Here also preached Edmund Calamy—the son of a more celebrated father—who resigned simultaneously with his colleague in 1749.

On the completion of the first half of the eighteenth century Dr. Grosvenor entered into that seclusion of studious ease so well earned by a laborious career of nearly fifty years' duration. His evening of life he devoted to reading, and thereby attained to what appeared a universal acquaintance with contemporary literature. He attended at Bunhill Fields on the day of Watts's funeral. After the poet's coffin was lowered into the grave a friend exclaimed, " Well, Dr. Grosvenor, you have seen the last of Dr. Watts, and you will soon follow; what think you of death?" "Think of it? Why, when death comes I shall smile upon death if God smile upon me." During his last days Grosvenor was an intense sufferer, till death severed his mortal chains on the last Sabbath morning of August, 1758. He has left us twenty-seven separate publications.*

It is probable that Dr. Grosvenor retained his pulpit longer than prudence dictated, for when he relinquished the duties of active life the church had lost its former prosperity. The efforts of Dr. Hodge, who succeeded, to revive the dwindling interest were unavailing. He resigned after twelve years' perseverance in labour. Very little is known about this pastor's life, but we have an affecting account of a calamity which overtook his son. Young Hodge was at Daventry Academy preparing for the

* John Barker's Sermon on the Death of Dr. Grosvenor; Crosby's History of the English Baptists; History of the Dissenting Churches.

Christian ministry. On the occasion of a fire in the town he hastened to the scene of action, and under the influence of excitement exerted himself till excessively fatigued and soaked with water. A slow fever succeeded, to be quickly followed by death. Just prior to his departure, while walking in a neighbouring graveyard, the youth pointed out the spot where he desired to be buried.

Richard Jones, of Cambridge, followed Dr. Hodge, but his utmost endeavours to revive prosperity were unsuccessful. A few years later the lease of Crosby Hall expired, and because the members were too few to warrant a renewal a dissolution took place. A solemn scene, therefore, was witnessed within the ancient hall on the first day of October, 1769. The congregation then being assembled for the last time heard a sermon suitable to the occasion. The bread and wine were dispensed, after which the members separated to be, we trust, ere this reunited in the church of the First-born in the Land of Promise.

Thus just a hundred years ago did Richard Jones bid adieu to Crosby Hall. Subsequently he settled at Peckham, where he continued for a lengthened period. The old hall grows in interest the better we become acquainted with its history, and with the great and good men who laboured in it—men who, by laying their talents at the foot of the Cross, glorified God and benefited their fellows.

Chapter IV.

THE OLD JEWRY.

WHENEVER we visit the Old Jewry imagination crowds the spot with people and scenes of other days—those actors for good or for evil whose life-deeds still live in history. This suburb or Jews' garden of Old London derives its name from the Israelitish inhabitants, with whom it was anciently a favourite retreat. Within its precincts flourished a synagogue—the earliest erected in Great Britain. Henry the Fourth's principal palace in the Old Jewry was a building of unknown date, which, according to Maitland, occupied the site of demolished Jewish houses. In this neighbourhood a remnant of the chosen people congregated, while our fathers regarded them with superstitious hatred engendered by their rejection of Christ and their love of usury. In those days a trifling affront, if from a Jew, sufficed to rouse the fiercest passions of so-called Christians. The infuriated populace were ever ready to redress a compeer's real or imagined wrong. The local annals abundantly illustrate this proposition. The parish church of St. Mary Cole formerly stood at the corner facing Cheapside. Within this sanctuary, on the ninth of November, 1261, a Jew and a Christian disagreed about some trifling matter, and proceeding to fight over their difference, the Hebrew wounded his antagonist. News of the quarrel quickly spread through the city. Armed persons from all directions gathered upon the spot, by whom the Jew was hunted down and murdered. Actuated more by desire for plunder than by religious zeal, the inhabitants next proceeded to massacre the inhabitants. Three years later the Old Jewry presented a scene even yet more melancholy. It happened during Palm Sunday week, 1264, that a Jew quarrelled with one of his debtors —a citizen who owed him twenty shillings. A revengeful mob immediately assembled and slew five hundred inhabitants of the colony, besides robbing the houses and destroying the synagogue. The Government suppressed the meeting-house after this manifestation of popular vengeance. It was subsequently occupied by a fraternity of begging friars, who endeavoured to win popular sympathy by a pious austerity which prompted them to sup on the diet of hogs and to clothe themselves in sackcloth. In the succeeding reign of Edward the First the entire Hebrew race was banished from the land by a royal edict, and nearly four hundred years elapsed ere Jews were again allowed to settle in Britain, and they never returned to the vicinity so intimately associated with their history.* This interesting ground, however, was early occupied by the Non-conformists. In Puritan times Jeremiah Ives gathered here a congregation of Baptists, of whom only scanty memorials remain.

The Presbyterians erected their church in the Old Jewry during the opening years of the eighteenth century, and throughout that century it remained one of the most considerable places of worship in England belonging to their denomination. Carefully shielded from the street, it stood in Meeting-house Court—the only trace now remaining of this once celebrated building. On entering the passage the visitor obtained a side view of what was an extensive and substantial structure. With its two large central bow-windows, one over the other, and four smaller ones on either side, the Dissenters of the days of Queen Anne thought the exterior handsome and imposing. The interior occupied an area of two thousand six hundred square feet. There were three galleries, furnished with seats five or six deep, the whole having been fitted up in a style of great elegance. The meeting-house dated its origin from the

* A bill for the Jews' naturalisation passed in 1653; yet so loud was the popular clamour against its provisions, that it was shortly after repealed. The Rabbi Manasseh Ben Israel visited London in 1655; and from this date some would reckon the modern history of the race in England. The Jews, however, did not really return until after the Restoration, and when they came again amongst us, they did so apparently with neither permission nor hindrance.

year 1701; but the Society was founded forty years
before, by Edmund Calamy, the ejected minister of
Moreton, in Essex.*

  Although Calamy's disposition was modestly shy,
he fearlessly adhered to the principles inculcated in
his father's house, and in the church at Alderman-

___

* He was son of Edmund Calamy, the Puritan vicar of
Aldermanbury, London. It will reveal the kind of home in
which the founder of this great church spent his youth if we
devote this note to his father's career. The elder Calamy
was a London citizen, and born in the year 1600. After
completing his education at Cambridge University, he accepted a chaplaincy under Felton, Bishop of Ely. A little later
he settled at Edmundsbury, whence he was driven by his
diocesan for refusing to read the Book of Sports. When
installed into the living of Aldermanbury, in 1639, Calamy
at once achieved a high reputation. As many as twenty
carriages conveyed their aristocratic owners to the weekly
lecture. The old Puritan never seems to have manifested
the least ambition. His straightforward conscientiousness
prompted him either to reprove Cromwell, or publicly to
reproach Monck, while the latter was present. He lived to
repent of the zeal with which he had promoted the Restoration;
for, on coming into power, the party he had befriended shut
him up in Newgate for preaching. The excitement his imprisonment occasioned is scarcely paralleled in the annals of
Puritan persecution. Broadsides of doggrel were plentifully circulated, either for the purpose of extolling him as a
martyr, or of denouncing him as the blackest character among
Newgate thieves. Dr. Wild, of Cripplegate, who defended
Calamy, dealt out some equivocal compliments to bishops in
general:—

> " I can behold them take into their gills
>   A dose of churches as men swallow pills."

bury. The old Puritan acted as his son's tutor, till in due time Edmund was entered at Cambridge University. During his youth he acquired extensive stores of knowledge, besides making himself singular by the liberal views he entertained concerning toleration. He successively took the degrees of B.A. and

Wild cares for none of the riches of these men who are striving to climb by steeples to heaven. He envies Calamy his imprisonment, and would count it happiness if he might but keep his cell-door. If any imagined that Newgate could sully Calamy's fame they are likened to one,

> " Who thinks reproach or injustice is done,
> By an eclipse to the unspotted sun."

The poet proceeds:—

> "Thanks to the bishop and his good Lord Mayor,
> Who have turned the den of thieves into a house of prayer."

Complaint is then made of another tyrant, Bishop Gout, who had extended his diocese to the person of Dr. Wild:—

> " Now, sir, you find our sufferings do agree,
> One bishop's clapt up you, another me."

A scurrilous rejoinder to Wild was immediately put in circulation. Meantime, the traffic in Newgate-street was inconveniently obstructed by the coaches of Calamy's visitors. A certain Romanist lady, who only by great difficulty had been enabled to ride past the prison, represented to the King what a bad influence was being exercised by such a state of affairs, and Calamy was soon after released. He did not long survive the Great Fire. A few months after that event he was driven through ruined London. The desolate spectacle so completely shocked his nervous system that, on reaching home, he retired to his chamber, whence he was destined never to come forth again alive.

7*

M.A. On leaving college,, after having been approved by Richard Cromwell's commissioners, he was installed into the living of Moreton. He manifested a strong love of retirement; but gave sufficient attention to politics to side with the promoters of the Restoration, and, as a sequel to his endeavours, encountered much hard treatment when the restorers of monarchy triumphed.

On retiring to London, Calamy settled at Aldermanbury, and, in an apartment of his house, ministered to a congregation of Nonconformists. This practice he continued till the proclamation of Indulgence in 1672, when the people removed to Cripplegate, and occupied Curriers' Hall. Thence the church was driven by fresh persecution, and during the remainder of Calamy's pastorate the members met with caution as occasion made it necessary. The pastor was exceedingly fortunate in escaping apprehension, although closely watched by enemies. Malignant opposition could neither check his industry nor repress his moral bravery. Throughout his comparatively brief career, spiritual zeal was superior to a sickly constitution. His kindly temper and moderation were also conspicuous. He refused the Covenant while preferring the Presbyterian order. Incessant application, an indifference to worldly wealth, or even to the necessary comforts of life, aided in undermining the pastor's health, and consumption ended his useful life in May, 1685, in the fiftieth year of his age. A constitutional timidity never allowed him to favour the world with one single specimen of literary skill.*

Calamy was succeeded by Samuel Borfet, the ejected minister of High Laver, in Essex. This divine was likewise of a weakly constitution, and his infirmities reacted upon his mind till they produced seasons of severe spiritual dejection. At times he found it impossible to fulfil the ordinary duties of life. He and Janeway were fellow-students at Cambridge University, and, as is seldom the case, an early attachment ripened into a lifelong friendship. In one instance only did Borfet commit himself in print, by writing a recommendatory letter for the preface of Janeway's Memoirs. He encountered a large share of persecution, and settled in London after having been roughly used at Maidstone, where he had endeavoured to plant a church. He parted from his country flock with much sorrow, for his amiable mien and pastoral ability commanded the esteem of all who knew him. After coming to the metropolis frequent gloom clouded his soul, and a preternatural terror oppressed him when he contemplated his eternal prospects. Such misgivings were happily superseded by peaceful assurance, in the possession of which he died soon after the Revolution.†

* Nonconformists' Memorial; Neal's History of the Puritans; Wilson's Dissenting Churches; David's Nonconformity in Essex; Calamy's Autobiography. The eminent Dr. Calamy was the eldest son of the above.

† Nonconformists' Memorial; David's Nonconformity in Essex.

John Shower, who during the reigns of William and Anne was among the most eminent of London divines, next succeeded, in 1691, the chapel being then in Jewin-street. He came of a good family, and was born at Exeter, in 1657. He and three other sons were dependents upon a widowed mother. These were all handsomely started in the world, and one of them, Sir Bartholomew Shower, attained to eminence at the Bar, and in the Senate.

During the severe winter of 1716, William Tong, the pastor at Salters' Hall, busied himself in writing the life of his friend, and his scarce old volume is now the main source whence modern biographers of Shower must draw information.

The mother, Dorcas Shower, acting on the advice of her brother, a neighbouring Nonconformist divine, trained John for his uncle's profession, being encouraged to do so by the lad's superior capacities. When he had obtained his grammar learning he removed from Exeter to the academy of Matthew Warren, at Taunton, a kind of scholarly hero, who then incurred much personal risk by superintending a theological seminary. His institution was one of the earliest of its kind. To Matthew Warren and Richard Frankland, therefore, the honour belongs of having originated a plan of education upon English ground, which embraces to-day an extensive system of collegiate training.*

* "The learned and reverend Mr. Warren, who for many years, and with great success, kept up a private academy, as

That her sons might enjoy yet greater advantages, Mrs. Shower removed to Newington-green, near London, about the year 1674. There John had Dr. Manton for a friend, and Charles Morton for a tutor. Having reached his twentieth year, young Shower delighted his distinguished connections by delivering his maiden sermon in an old meeting-house long since demolished.* He at once became unusually popular. "He had," says his biographer, " lively affections, a grave and serious behaviour, great freedom of expression, and chose the most awful and affecting subjects : it was impossible for him to lie concealed in this great city, where there were very many of the first rank that adhered to the Dissenting way in that time of restraint, and some

the reverend and very learned Mr. Frankland did in the north of England; and I think those two venerable men were the first that ran the risque of much trouble and per-secution, that they might train up a rising generation of ministers in those principles and ways which they them-selves had suffered for, as really believing them to be most agreeable to the Word of God."—*Tong's Life of Shower.*

* This was situated in Hand-alley, Bishopsgate, and the pastor was Thomas Vincent. The chapel was commodious and well fitted up with roomy pews, benches, and three galleries. After the Great Fire the parish authorities forci-bly appropriated the premises for the services of the Estab-lishment; and not until the churches were rebuilt did Vincent recover his pulpit. Dr. Williams, the founder of the Library, was likewise a minister here. In 1720 a site for a new meet-ing-house was obtained in Broad-street, when the old one was taken down, and some houses erected upon the spot.

of them with much more affection and zeal than they have since discovered in a long term of liberty."

In Tong's opinion, the Papists had been the chief promoters of the Nonconformist persecutions, for Protestantism was thus attacked at its least pro- tected point. On the supposed discovery of the Plot, in 1678, this spirit, if it really existed, was rudely checked. The Dissenters were not suspected of any complicity in this business, but, on the con- trary, they rose in favour, and some of the harsh restrictions imposed by their enemies were relaxed. In the year named, when greater freedom of worship was established, a kind of merchants' lecture was instituted at a coffee-house in Change-alley, and the services attracted a rich congregation, Shower being one of the preachers. For a while he divided his time between his City congregation and another at Westminster. He was not regularly ordained, how- ever, until Christmas, 1679.

But Nonconformist life in England was daily becoming rougher. Shower, therefore, consented to leave trouble behind, and to make the tour of Europe, with Samuel Barnardiston, a gentleman of fortune, and son-in-law of Dr. Goodwin. Setting out in 1683, the travellers passed through Paris to Lyons, and thence to Geneva. The details of their adventures are valuable because illustrative of every- day life in that distant era. The summer was chiefly spent at Geneva, and the time spared from social pleasures was often devoted to the collection of valuable books and curiosities. Later in the season the travellers proceeded into the papal dominions, but found it necessary to exercise the strictest caution, whether in regard to speech, or in avoiding the malignant infections which the miserable inhabitants exhaled who roamed about the wild and undrained wastes.* During the continuance of the

* The party passed through Naples *en route* for Rome. An extract from the description of the tourists' doings in the former city will serve as a specimen of biography-writing 150 years ago :—

" Mr. Shower and his Friends were much delighted with the curiosities particular to this place, namely the *Grott Lucullus*, which is a road of considerable length, cut with immense labour through the bottom of a high hill, at a little distance from the Town, for a shorter and more easie reciprocal Passage, and the pleasant Hill *Pauselippo*, covered with Trees of various Kinds and famous for the Tomb of *Virgil*, who, as Tradition reports, was buried there. Mr. Shower and his friends were pleased with the extensive and charming prospect which this Eminence affords. Turning their faces to the South, they saw with pleasure the Bay of Naples spread beneath, and ships under sail making to the port, or coming from it; beyond the bay rises high in the Air, Mount *Vesuvious*, vomiting from its hollow Peak Clouds of Smoake and cynders; on the Right Hand they viewed the Isles of *Ischa* and *Caprea*, on the Left the beautiful City of *Naples*, stretching across the Shoar towards this place. They were informed that the Gentlemen and Ladies during the hottest seasons, constantly in their pleasure Boats pass hither from the City in the Evening to breath the refreshing Air, as those of *London* spend the evenings in the Ring of Hyde Park. Mr. Shower was no less pleased to visit the antiqui-

summer heats, Rome was a pestilential focus, the atmosphere of which, in a radius of thirty miles, was not safe to sleep in. During cooler weather the travellers ventured into the city, and, as distinguished Englishmen, were well received, and, besides other attentions, obtained free passes to the theatres. Prudence, however, soon dictated an abrupt exit from Rome, for one hardened Briton had refused to kneel

ties of *Baiae* near this place, particularly the Vapour Baths of the ancient *Romans*, and the Fish Ponds of *Julius Cæsar*; in another place he was surprised with the sight of Zoephotara, famous for its stores of brimstone whore, as he was amazed to observe, that when he rode on Level Ground that was bare of Grass, it shook under his Feet at every Step, and if pierced with the point of his sword, that it let forth Smoak and hot Vapours; so he viewed with Admiration the hot and yellow mouth of the Volcano, that glow'd in the sides of the rising ground which emcompasses the Place. He was informed that frequent Bellowings under Ground, heaving earthquakes, and terrible eruptions of melted Minerals happened here; and that not many years before so vast a Heap was raised, carried through the Air, and let down at about a mile distant, that it formed a new Hill now called *Montagna Nuova*. Mr. Shower, accompanied by his fellow travellers, was so curious and hardy as to visit the top of the famous burning Hill *Vesuvious*, whose Head is a towering Heap of Cynders, difficult to ascend. Approaching near the wide and smoaking Mouth, to gratify his curiosity he trod on Lakes of Sulphur, unform'd Oar and hot Cynders, and heard a terrible noise issuing from the Bowels of the burning Mountain. From this scene of horror he was relieved by another of as great pleasure, when looking Eastward he had a different view of *Campania Felix*, the Garden of Italy, and beheld a wide and fruitful plain covered with beautiful cities."—*Tong's Life of Shower*.

when the Host was elevated. The party began to attract an attention unpleasantly dangerous, and their perplexity was probably enhanced by a disrespect for the Pope's slipper which another Briton had previously shown. On being warned of danger by a friend, Shower and his party wisely retreated from the capital. The young scholar thought he discovered by observation that the revocation of the Édict of Nantes was planned by the French and English Courts, in order to ensure papal supremacy, as a prelude to the establishment of arbitrary power. The ruling despots imagined they could accomplish their designs by first annihilating the Huguenots, and secondly, by repressing English Nonconformity. If this be true, the plot was a promising one. But the Dissenters' sufferings were the darkness preceding a happier dawn, although at James the Second's accession their ministers risked insult and peril by openly walking the streets of London.

Meantime, Shower and his party were meeting with some strange adventures in Switzerland and Germany. Once, for example, they resolved on spending a night at sea, in a small sailing-boat. On the morning following, they were thrown into a fever of consternation by discovering that their captain had slept till the frail barque had drifted far from land, "in the turbulent Adriatique Sea." After experiencing some unsettling apprehensions of pirates and of a watery grave, the party safely reached an hospitable haven. They returned to England shortly prior to the Revolution, and Shower resumed his lecture in Exchange-alley. He must have found his procedure attended by much personal risk, and ere long he again retreated to the Continent, attended by Howe and several others.*

When the insane policy of the Court—which, if not dictated by Jesuits, was prompted by the King's popish predilections—had turned the scale of public opinion, and rendered necessary, as James imagined, the Indulgence of 1687, the Dissenters freely opened their chapels, and completed many new erections. At that crisis Shower was comfortably settled at Rotterdam. His powers were well appreciated; and had he chosen, he might have accepted a still richer cure in the Dutch capital. When, how-

---

* William Tong thus describes the state of London society in 1685:—"For some time before a popish prince ascended the Throne, and popish councils so far prevailed, that it was not safe for a Dissenting minister to be seen in the streets of London; many of them were thrown into common gaols. Their meetings, which for some years they held by connivance, were every where suppressed. They chose in some places to meet in the night, in small numbers, rather than be wholly destitute of the worship of God, in that way of administration which they thought most comformable to his Word. The civil liberties of the people of England met with a violent shock at the same time. Some of the best blood that ever ran in English veins was then spilt as water upon the ground; juries were packed, false witnesses suborned, corrupt judges upon the bench, and mercenary lawyers encouraged at the Bar, with noisy insolence to hunt down the true friends of the English Constitution."—*Life of Shower.*

ever, the church in Silver-street, London, earnestly
desired his return, he thought well to comply.   He
only continued about a year in the congenial society
of Howe and his people, for when affliction disabled
Samuel Borfet, Shower was called to the pastorate,
many, with some reason, arguing that no *single* pulpit   Χ
should retain a HOWE and a SHOWER.   As for John
Howe, he valued his colleague, and " was loath to
part with him."   Indeed, the polite and wealthy
assembly in Silver-street had become accustomed to
their lecturer's peculiarity—his love for the mysterious and the sublime.*   They showed some indignation at this turn of affairs, but notwithstanding,
Shower deemed it a duty to station himself at Cripplegate.   The sequel proved the wisdom of his decision, as the prosperity of the church immediately
revived, and a removal to a more commodious building in Jewin-street soon became necessary.   When
at length this latter place grew too narrow for the
congregation, the meeting-house in the Old Jewry
was erected ; there Shower continued to sustain his
usefulness and popularity till overtaken by decay of
natural vigour.

The funds requisite for providing the church in
the Old Jewry were readily raised by the opulent
merchants and well-to-do shopkeepers who, as admirers of Shower, made up his congregation, and

* "They (Shower's sermons) chiefly relate to earthquakes,
and other awful and great events, as he had a talent for
pathetic writing."—*Noble's Continuation of Granger.*

whose homes for the most part were within the City
boundary.   The pastor laboured for a length of time
without any abatement of power, although he bore
some severe domestic afflictions.   Immediately after
removing to Curriers' Hall death took his youthful
wife.   In the year of settlement at the Old Jewry
his second wife likewise died.   In 1706, during a
visit to Epsom, he was himself suddenly prostrated
by fever.   At this crisis the Christian community
were intensely anxious that Shower's life should be
prolonged.   Day after day many such wended their
course up the Old Jewry to attend the frequent
prayer-meetings held on the pastor's behalf.

There is one interesting passage in Shower's life
to which Tong does not even allude, although it
merited a passing notice.   In 1711 he wrote a protest* against the Occasional Conformity Bill, which

* See a letter by Shower with a reply by Swift in Scott's
edition of the dean's works. According to Sir Walter, Shower's
letter "was written by the dissenters in the extremity of
their despair." This epistle and the "caustic and acrimonious
answer" are subjoined for the satisfaction of the reader.

MY LORD,—   *London, Dec. 20th*, 1711.
Though there be little reason to expect your lordship
should interpose in favour of the Dissenters, who have been
so shamefully abandoned, sold and sacrificed, by their professed friends; the attempt is, however, so glorious in all its
views, tendencies and prospects, that if it be not too late, I
would most humbly beg your lordship not to be immovable
as to that matter. The fatal consequences of that bill cannot be
expressed; I dread to think of some of them, and shall as
much rejoice, with many thousands, if you may be instru-

he transmitted to the Lord Treasurer Oxford. This letter and the reply it evoked from his Lordship's secretary, Jonathan Swift, are extant, and serve to show with what temper Dissenters were regarded in high quarters during the Augustan age, and by such an unprincipled and profligate writer as Lemuel Gul-

mental to prevent it. May Heaven direct you in this, and all your great affairs for the public good of your country, I am, my honoured lord, your most obedient servant,—JOHN SHOWER." The next day, the following reply to the above was received. "Dec. 21st 1711. Reverend Sir,—Had not a painful distemper confined me, I had desired the favour of seeing you some time since, and should have spoken very plainly to you, as I shall whenever I see you. I have long foretold that the Dissenters must be saved whether they will or not; they resist even restraining grace; and would almost convince me that the notion of man's being a mechanism is true in every part. To see men moved as puppets, with rage for their interest, with envy acting against their own interest, having men's persons in admiration; not only those of their own body, who certainly are the first who pretend to consummate wisdom and deep policy, yet have shown that they know not the common affairs of this nation, but are dwellers in thick clay. They are epicurian in art, Puritans in profession, politicians in concert, and a prey and laughing-stock to the church and synagogue of the libertines in whom they have trusted, and to whose infallibility they have sold themselves and their congregations. All they have done, or can do, shall never make me their enemy. I pity poor deluded creatures that have for seventeen years been acting against all their principles, and the liberty of this nation, without leaving so much salt as to keep the body of them sweet; for there has not been one good bill, during that term of years, which they have not opposed in the House of Com-

liver. A quarrel had through many previous years
been in progress between the Tories and their hereditary foes, the Nonconformists. The former were deeply
tainted by Jacobitical sympathies, while our fathers
were strenuous promoters of the Protestant succession. The Anglican party began to regard meeting-

mons; contrary to the practices of those very few Dissenters
which were in the Parliament in King Charles the Second's
time, who thereby united themselves to the country
gentlemen, the advantages of which they found many
years after. But now they have tested themselves with
those who have first denied our Saviour, and now have
sold them. I have written this only to show you that I
am ready to do anything that is practicable to save people
who are bargained for by their leaders, and given up by
their ministers. I say their *ministers*, because it is averred
and represented that the dissenting ministers have been consulted and are consenting to this bill. By what lies and arts
they are brought to this, I do not care to mention; but as to
myself, the engineers of this bill thought they had gained
a great advantage over me; finding I had stopped it in the
House of Commons, they thought to bring me to a fatal
dilemma, whether it did or did not pass. This would have
no influence over me, for I will act what I think to be
right, let there be the worst enemies in the world of one side
or other, I guess by your letter that you do not know that
the bill yesterday passed both Houses, the Lords having
agreed to the amends made by the Commons, so that there
is no room to do anything on that head. What remains is
to desire that the Dissenters may seriously think from whence
they are fallen, and do their first works, and recover their
reputation of sobriety, integrity, and love of their country,
which is the sincere and hearty prayer of, Reverend Sir, your
most faithful and most humble servant, OXFORD.

houses with increased antipathy now that the Revolution had brought the Act of Toleration. A small thing sufficed to excite their spleen or to occasion an unwonted stir among their ranks—*e.g.*, when a civic dignitary ordered the City symbol of justice to be borne before him into Pinners' Hall. The Occasional Conformity Bill originated with this party, and was their leading hobby through many succeeding sessions. Englishmen influenced by sentiments of barest justice, or even of common sense, condemned this measure as one likely to draw down only odium upon the Established Church. Messrs. St. John and Bromley, the two Commoners who fathered the Bill, were in all respects fitting tools for their work. Each represented a university. The first, by writing a book of travels, had so revealed his conceit and ignorance that out of pity the family stopped its circulation.* The measure in question was introduced during the session of 1702, and provided for the exemption of " Dissenters from such offices as cannot by law be executed without receiving the sacrament." By the Lower House it was immediately passed ; but the Lords, whose mien throughout more became them as Englishmen than did that of the Court or the Commons, proposed fourteen amendments. The majority

---

* Oxford once repaid St. John a grudge by reprinting an edition of this volume and circulating it among his morning callers. He could devise nothing more likely to effect his purpose.

of the Commons were chagrined at this miscarriage, but with the best grace they were able to command they agreed to hold a conference of both Houses. Accordingly a conference was convened, and the abettors of the measure adduced some far-fetched arguments in vindication of their action. If unchecked, Dissent would ultimately gain an ascendency in corporate towns, or even in the Parliament itself. Occasional conformity was to add hypocrisy to schism. The Nonconformists, moreover, only wanted power, and they would destroy the Established Church. Such sophistries chiefly emanated from the "October men" (fox-hunters), of whom the Commons' majority was largely composed. The better educated peers proceeded to answer the charges. The last they entirely denied. They pointed out the beneficial effects which sprang from the Act of Toleration. They demonstrated that harsh and unsettling laws would be improper, because dangerous, at so critical a season, for hardship would be imposed upon a large section of the population at home, while a corresponding disgust would be created abroad. Opposed by the Lords, the bishops, and the reasoning of Locke, the Tory scheme for the time was defeated.

In the reign of Anne a high churchman was usually supposed to sympathise with the Pretender, and to approve of Nonconformist persecution. In 1703 the Tories again pressed to the front with their pet measure. Two scribes were found to represent the faction in literature—one of whom was a

worthless Jacobite fanatic, while the other was
an unprincipled adventurer. One of the leading
supporters belonged to a family which had endeavoured legally to murder some Worcestershire Dissenters. Among the bishops, Burnet eloquently
denounced as infamous this attempt to annihilate
the liberties of a loyal class—an attempt made by
known enemies of the Constitution. One peer facetiously advised the tacking of the Pretender to the
Bill if their Lordships seriously intended passing it.
News, however, soon reached the City that the Tories
were once more defeated, and the intelligence brought
great joy and relief. Nothing daunted, the country
squires renewed the attack in the session of 1704.
Their movements were characterised by cautious
subtlety. Their rendezvous, the Vine Tavern, in
Long Acre, was nightly thronged by rural politicians,
who at heart were with the Pretender, and whose convictions were that heresy only abounded without the
Anglican pale. This enlightened conclave threatened
to tack the Bill to another which the Lords would
be unable to reject; but even in the Commons the
stratagem met with determined resistance, and was
finally abandoned. Out of the hundred and thirty-
four members who voted for it, fifty lost their seats
at the next election, and *tackers* became the oppro-
brious epithet by which the clique were known in
Liberal circles. Nevertheless, the Bill passed in its
separate form to the Upper House. Queen Anne
attended the debate, which ended as others of pre-

8*

ceding sessions had ended. In 1710, however, the Sacheverel riots acted as a stimulus to bigotry, so that the country party took fresh courage. A change of ministers likewise occurred. Robert Harley, a Presbyterian, "sacrificed religious principles to his political views" till he betrayed his former friends, and won the earldom of Oxford. Harley belonged to a Nonconformist family which had sided with the Parliament in the Civil Wars, and as a renegade he earned the contempt of the three denominations, when the iniquitous measure at length was carried. Time, as it so often does, brought retribution, for in the succeeding reign the obnoxious measure was repealed, Oxford impeached, and committed to the Tower.

Shower accounted it a great happiness that he lived to witness the triumph of the Protestant Succession. During his declining years the pastor, in search of health, removed from one locality to another. At one time we find him benefiting by the air of Epping, at another drinking the waters of Tunbridge Wells. Last of all, he retired to Stoke Newington, there to make one in a circle of which he and Watts were distinguished ornaments. In June, 1715, Shower entered into rest, leaving behind him twenty-three separate publications, one of which, *The Mourner's Companion*, gracefully commemorates the loss of his wife.

The assistant lecturer from 1691 to 1708, was Timothy Rogers, son of the ejected minister of

Croglin, Cumberland.* Timothy early manifested serious predilections, joined to talents of a high order. He prosecuted his studies in the north

* Timothy Rogers was born at Barnard Castle. His father, after his ejectment, officiated as a Dissenting minister, and as such was sorely harassed by a neighbouring High Church justice, Sir Richard Cradock. This magistrate prided himself on the faithful rigour with which he enforced the statutes against Nonconformists, and he truly used every device to hunt them into prison. He once hired two spies, commissioned them to attend Rogers' meeting, and take down the names of the persons composing the congregation. This business the obsequious agents accomplished to the letter. The sequel was, that the pastor and a number more were cited to appear at the Hall. The little band duly attended; but, as will easily be imagined, harboured many misgivings. While waiting to be called before their persecutor, they attracted the notice of the squire's granddaughter, who was a child of about seven years. Rogers inherited a nature which children found very attractive; and in the present instance a strong friendship immediately sprang up between the little girl and the venerable-looking gentleman. On account of the illness of a witness and his consequent absence, the party were dismissed, yet were commanded to reappear when required. On the day of their second appearance at the Hall they were of course all committed. The justice, in his satisfaction at so auspicious a result, proceeded to make out the mittimus. Rogers had not forgotten his little acquaintance. The child came flitting across the hall, and gladly accepted a present of sweets which the pastor had brought her. The grandfather, it seems, had over-indulged the little miss, till she, in her waywardness, insisted upon having all she desired. She had once pierced her arm and endangered her life on account of having received a denial. The established custom was, therefore, to refuse her nothing. "What are you here for,

of England, but completed his curriculum under Edward Veale, of Wapping—a tutor who then industriously applied himself to the work of preparing

sir?" she asked Rogers. "I believe," he answered, "your grandfather is going to send me and my friends to gaol." "Why?" continued the child; "what have you done?" "Why, I did nothing but preach at such a place, and they did nothing but hear me." "But my grandfather shan't send you to gaol." "Aye, but my dear, I believe he is now making out our mittimus to send us all there." She hastened to the library-door, and after vigorously kicking till admitted, called out, "What are you going to do with my good old gentleman in the hall?"" That is nothing to you, go about your business," exclaimed the magistrate. "But I won't!" passionately replied this juvenile vixen: "He tells me that you are going to send him and his friends to gaol; and if you do send them, I'll drown myself in the horsepond; I will, indeed!" Her determined manner so alarmed the old man, that he gave way. He proceeded into the hall, and addressing the prisoners, said: "I had made out your mittimus, to send you to gaol as you deserve, but at my granddaughter's request I drop the prosecution, and set you all at liberty." The prisoners expressed their gratitude without acknowledging any guilt. As for Rogers, he placed his hand upon the head of his benefactress, and exclaimed, "God bless you, my dear child! May the blessing of that God whose cause you did now plead, though as yet you know Him not, be upon you in life, at death, and to all eternity!"

In Queen Anne's reign there resided in London a Mrs. Tooly. Like some others of her class, she customarily entertained at her table the Nonconformist ministers of the town. It was on one of these occasions that the Old Jewry lecturer, Timothy Rogers, related the above passage from his father's history. When the story was finished, Mrs. Tooly astonished the company by remarking: "And are you that Mr. Rogers's

young men for the Christian ministry. Rogers began his public life at a week-evening lecture in Crosby Hall, which he and Thomas Kentish jointly

son? Well, long as I have been acquainted with you, I never knew that before. And now I will tell you something which you do not know: I am the very little girl your dear father blessed in the manner you have related, and it made an impression upon me which I can never forget." Thomas Bradbury, of Fetter-lane, who was present, expressed his surprise that the speaker had so effectually risen above the bias of education and early prejudices against Nonconformity. The lady then explained the reasons. After having inherited her grandfather's wealth, mental disquietude prevented her from deriving any satisfaction from it. She thought a visit to Bath would dispel her reigning gloom. During her sojourn in that gay city a certain apothecary attended her professionally, and being a Christian man, he got his patient to promise she would read a book which he would provide, for the book, he said, was an antidote to gloomy spirits. After repeatedly calling for the eagerly-expected treasure, the lady scarcely concealed her chagrin when presented with a New Testament. She acted, however, upon her promise, and perused the book; yet from such perusal gained no immediate benefit. Her next resolution was to try the effect of a London season. Lodgings were engaged for herself and maid in a fashionable quarter. Like all preceding experiments, this change likewise failed to relieve the mental burden. While in this state of mind she dreamed one Saturday evening about a chapel, a preacher, a text, and a sermon. So apparently real was the vision, that upon awaking she distinctly recollected the aspect of the meeting-house, the minister's features, and his text seemed yet to ring in her ears. The impression this occurrence made upon her mind was deep and lasting. The next morning being the Sabbath she set out, accompanied by her

sustained. His peace and continued usefulness were simultaneously interrupted by a strange spiritual gloom which darkened his mind with preternatural horror. His appetite declined, social enjoyment became impossible, because his tortured soul wandered into regions beyond the reach of human consolation—in "a land of darkness on which the sun never seemed to shine." During a temporary suspension of his affliction, Rogers published a treatise on Trouble of Mind. He also resumed his duties at

servant, with the determination to discover if such a place as the one dreamed of existed. The travellers walked eastward, and after a diligent but unsuccessful search, they found themselves at one o'clock in Cheapside. They dined, and then recommenced their wanderings. As they approached the Old Jewry, they observed that numbers of persons were turning down the street. This crowd turned out to be the afternoon congregation at the Presbyterian Meeting-house. The strangers followed them, and turned with them up Meeting-house-court. The lady was startled at the first view of the chapel. "This is the very place," she cried, "I saw in my dream." Immediately after entering and taking seats, the pastor, John Shower, took his place in the pulpit. "That is the very man I saw in my dream; and if every part of it hold true he will take for his text, Psalm cxvi. 7." The words sounded like a preternatural message when Shower read, "Return unto thy rest, O, my soul, for the Lord hath dealt bountifully with thee." Thus originated Mrs. Tooly's connection with the Old Jewry Meeting-house. Thus it was, moreover, that she simultaneously became a Christian and a Dissenter. The above narrative was well authenticated at the time by many eminent divines. A fuller relation was also prepared and published in a separate pamphlet.

Crosby Hall, which he probably again relinquished on accepting the lectureship at the Old Jewry. Shower greatly admired both the character and the ability of his colleague. A large congregation also held Rogers in high esteem. "He was," we are told, "a man of a most heavenly temper." His sad depression returned with unabated force in 1707, and rendered his resignation necessary. He received a life pension from his people. He retired, it is supposed, to Wantage, in Berkshire, where he occasionally assisted his brethren of the district; but he continued to regard himself "as a lamp despised, a broken vessel, and a dead man out of mind." Rogers died at the age of seventy, in 1729.*

Another of Shower's assistant's, Joseph Bennett, belonged to a family which through several generations nobly defended truth and conscience. His father's name is among those of the Sussex ejected ministers. This old confessor afforded his son a careful training; he placed him with Thomas Goldham, a brother Nonconformist, who after Bartholomew-tide, 166?, set up a school at Burwash. Thence young Bennett removed to the academy of Charles Morton, at Newington-green—a tutor whose ability and attention the pupil never after failed to acknowledge.

After leaving Stoke Newington, Bennett saw a gloomy prospect spreading before him as he looked abroad in search of employment. His family was

* Nonconformists' Memorial; History of the Dissenting Churches. Rogers published several works.

poor, and his class despised. Having no funds at command, he might still have secured a competence by violating conscience had he chosen to conform. In such a strait, with threatening poverty on one side, and beguiling temptations on the other, he sat down, once for all to examine the basis of Nonconformity, and he arose from the investigation with those great principles strengthened which he learned at his father's hearth and in Morton's class; he had no resources, however, other than trust in God.

Providence wonderfully opened his way. He obtained a tutorship in the family of Dr. Singleton, the ejected head-master of Rugby School; and when the Revolution lessened or removed the grievances of Dissenters, Bennett sought that labour which he considered his peculiar work. He engaged himself to a suburban congregation, and, in 1694, was ordained, with six others, at Little St. Helen's. He subsequently accepted a lectureship at Stoke Newington under "good old Mr. William Wickens," who died in 1699. Bennett was called from this rural retreat to the Old Jewry on account of the loss of Timothy Rogers. He passed an uneventful life, yet laboured with satisfactory success till the period of his death in 1726. For the space of forty years he lived the valued friend of Edmund Calamy, and the doctor paid him a last mark of respect by improving his departure in a funeral sermon.*

* Dr. Calamy's Sermon on the Death of Joseph Bennett; History of the Dissenting Churches.

A more remarkable man is seldom encountered than Shower's successor, Simon Browne, who was born in 1680, at Shepton Mallet, Somerset.* For the particulars extant respecting him we are mainly indebted to Anthony Atkey, whose affectionate reverence for his subject pervades the funeral sermon he has bequeathed to posterity. The Brownes were very respectably connected, and having been intended for the Nonconformist pulpit, Simon was

* This interesting old town, which is situated five miles east of Wells, was early occupied by the Nonconformists. The rector, David Calderwood, was among the two thousand confessors of 1662. Either the tourist or the antiquary will find the vicinity full of attractiveness, and the neighbourhood is rich in historical associations. *Mallet* was anciently appended to Shepton, because its possessors were of that name. Some centuries ago there were placed in the church two interesting effigies. They are supposed to represent two of the Mallet family, who were members of the Society of Knights Templars, and as such accompanied the crusades. At an early date Shepton was also associated with Christianity in Britain. In the year 709 an Irish convert, named Indractus, here encountered death, as he and a hundred fellow pilgrims were journeying homeward from Rome. A certain robber, called Hona, supposing the party to be laden with wealth, attacked them while sleeping, and after slaying the whole number, he buried them in a neighbouring pit. At Shepton, moreover, Walter Charleton, the Court physician during the reigns of the First and Second Charles, was born. The Revolution, which happened in his old age, appears to have reduced him to poverty. He was the author of a curious work wherein he maintains that Stonehenge originated with the Danes. Here may be mentioned a very remarkable occurrence that created some little consternation in Shepton

early placed under John Cumming, the Shepton Presbyterian minister. On completing his preparatory course, he studied university learning with John More, an eminent theologian, at Bridgewater. Even in early life, Brown's talents were very conspicuous. Before attaining his majority he served in various pulpits; and such were his ability and grave demeanour that the most judicious readily excused his early practice on account of the profit they derived from his discourses.

In due course Browne settled at Portsmouth, where the Nonconformist society was as respectable as any then existing in the provinces. A strong attachment sprang up between pastor and people; and our divine had sustained several years' local popularity when called to the Old Jewry to supply the place of Shower. For seven more years in his metropolitan pulpit he sustained his reputation. Then a domestic crisis occurred; death deprived him of his wife and only

during the year 1763. There was then living in the town an old military pensioner, who worked at the tailoring trade. In the decline of life he was overtaken by illness, and was in consequence confined to the house. A sister, well-nigh as poor and as old as himself, was his only attendant; they both mainly depended upon charity for daily necessaries. In warm weather the invalid was occasionally carried downstairs that he might enjoy a change of scene and air. About sunset one evening the woman for a short time left her brother alone, and upon returning home found only his empty chair. In vain did the townspeople scour the neighbourhood in search of the old soldier, and to this day his fate is a mystery.

son, and from that shock Browne never recovered. Sorrow produced a mental disorder, accompanied by an hallucination of a very singular nature, so singular, indeed, as to need a psychologist in any degree to explain it.

During his stay at Portsmouth the pastor won some literary laurels. The Caveat Against Evil Company appeared in 1706, and was a piece pronounced by Dr. Williams and other eminent judges, to be the finest performance which they had seen of its class. This was followed, in 1709, by The Character of a True Christian. In this work the importance of governing the thoughts is forcibly argued. After his settlement at the Old Jewry, in 1716, Browne continued with unabated perseverance to pursue his favourite studies. In 1720 he published his Hymns and Spiritual Songs. This volume includes nearly three hundred separate pieces, a dissertation on the practice of psalmody, and a set of engraved tunes, several of which the accomplished author himself composed.

When the delusion referred to took possession of the pastor's mind, one grand idea ruled his action. Providence, he supposed, had gradually drawn the soul from his body. He consequently imagined himself a pitiable wreck—a creature incapable of intellectual effort, because he had lost "the thinking substance." He discontinued all pastoral duties; and, as he was now wholly animal, religious exercises were also relinquished. He desired that friends

would not offer prayer on his behalf, for he had
ceased to be, he declared, a moral agent. A dark
melancholy supplemented these illusions. At one time
the case appeared nearly hopeless, and relatives even
feared an attempt at self-destruction. As months
wore on, however, Browne became somewhat calmer;
but after he settled quietly down, he continued for
the remainder of his days to be insane on the point
in question. He supposed himself beholding all
things with the ken of an animal, and perfectly
to resemble a parrot in speech. When persons
accepted his words as intelligent utterances, or
recognised his gaze as not meaningless, they gave
offence by seeming to doubt his veracity. He often
took great pains to demonstrate the reality of his
affliction, and on such occasions his behaviour showed
how keenly incredulity annoyed him. When some
would reason with him to prove all an hallucination,
Browne invariably showed signs of uneasiness.

Thus disabled, the pastor retired to Shepton
Mallet, where he soon gave convincing evidence,
that, instead of having suffered annihilation, his
mental capacity had really grown stronger, while his
imagination was capable of taking higher flights.
He was still a valuable acquisition to any company
caring for intelligent converse. He continued to
reason ably and clearly, and showed in conversation
an extensive acquaintance with science and general
literature. He applied himself to study with un-
flagging perseverance, and published several valuable

treatises. Indeed, he may be said to have accomplished prodigious mental feats, for he produced poetical pieces, translated the classics, and composed a spelling-book, a grammar, and a lexicon.* Once,

* Prior to his leaving London, Browne addressed the following remarkable letter to a ministerial friend. It has been several times published, e.g., in the Gentleman's Magazine for 1762, in the Biographia Britannica, &c. "Reverend Sir,—I doubt not you have been earnest with God on my behalf since you left the city, who expressed so much tender concern for me while you were in it. I wish I could write anything to you that might turn your compassion into thanksgiving, and your prayers into praises. But, alas! nothing of that kind is to be expected from one who has lived a life of defiance to God, under a Christian profession and a sacred character; and now through his just displeasure is in the most forlorn state a man can be on earth, perfectly empty of all thought, reflection, or consideration, destitute—entirely destitute of all knowledge of God and Christ, and of his own soul, and the things both of time and eternity, being unable to look backward or forward, or inward or outward, or upward or downward, having no conviction of sin or duty, no capacity of reviewing his conduct, or looking forward with expectation of either good or evil, and, in a word, without any principles of religion or even of reason, and without the common sentiments or affections of human nature; insensible even to the good things of life, incapable of tasting any present enjoyment, or expecting future ones; dead to his children, friends, and country, having no interest, either bodily or spiritual, temporal to value or mind, but converted into a mere beast, than can relish nothing but present bodily enjoyments, without tasting them by anticipation or recollection. This is my true condition: thus am I thrown down from my excellency. Because I had not, God has taken away the things that I had. Indeed, I have not those horrors on my

when absorbed in these literary occupations, a curious
visitor, peeping in at the study door, enquired what
he was doing. "I am doing nothing," Browne
quickly replied, "that requires a reasonable soul; I
am making a dictionary; but, you know, thanks
should be returned to God for everything, and therefore for dictionary makers." At another time, while
sitting at table, some one pressed him to say the
grace; he uneasily hesitated, but at length exclaimed
with much emotion, "Most merciful and Almighty

mind to which you were a witness; I am grown more calm,
because more insensible, and every day since you saw me
has this insensibility been growing upon me, nor can it be
removed without a miracle of grace, and for this grace I
cannot pray, having lost all sight of God, and tenderness of
soul towards Him. Such an instance of divine displeasure
the world hardly ever saw, much less one recovered by divine
grace out of such a condition. I doubt whether you have
room to pray; but if you think you have, I doubt not
but you will be fervent at the throne of grace in your re-
quests. But I am so changed that I must first be made a
man before I can become a Christian; having now none of
that knowledge, or common sentiments on which a saving
change must be founded. I am entirely incapable of any
business in life, and must quit my present station, and think,
as soon as I can, to be retiring into my own country, there
to spend out the wretched remains of a miserable life, which
I am continually prompted to destroy. I thought you would
be willing to hear from me, and though you cannot be pleased
with the account, I am obliged to give you a true one, and
beg an interest in your prayers, which will turn to your own
account if it avails nothing towards the salvation of the
wretched and wicked sinner who would yet, if he was able,
be your friend and servant,—SIMON BROWNE."

God, let Thy Spirit, which moved upon the face of the waters, when there was no light, descend upon me, that from this darkness there may rise up a man to praise Thee." At dinner, on another occasion, under similar circumstances, he said: "O Lord, I am nothing. I ask nothing, and I want nothing; but bless these good creatures to those who are about to receive them." After retiring to Shepton his illusions never checked his singular industry. At one time fancy prompted the translation of a classical author: but it led him at another time to make verses for children. He composed a Scriptural History, and a commentary on Paul's Epistles. "With great labour," says Anthony Atkey, "he also amassed together, in a short compass, all the themes of the Greek and Latin tongues, and compiled likewise a dictionary to each of these works, in order to render the learning of both those languages more easy and compendious." Neither these nor several minor pieces were ever published, yet such as are curious enough, and have the opportunity, may inspect for themselves in the British Museum several manuscripts by Simon Browne.

While thus multifariously employed, time only strengthened our author's hallucination. The Defence of the Religion of Nature and the Christian Revelation he dedicated to the Queen, on account of its being, as he imagined, a literary curiosity emanating from a THING, once mortal. The book, which he would have thus madly introduced to the

9

world was hailed by scholars as one of the best produced by the controversy with Woolston and the freethinkers.* Marvellous as such an halluci- nation will necessarily appear, it was not entirely without precedent. In the autumn of 1743, one Lewis Kennedy, a gardener employed by the Bedford family, committed suicide under a similar delusion to that which affected Simon Browne.

Although the probable cause of the pastor's affliction has been described, his contemporaries, on this mysterious subject, held various opinions. Dr. Ashworth, in a lecture on the Passions, delivered

* " Of all the extraordinary things that have been tendered to your royal hands, since your first happy arrival in Britain, it may be boldly said, what now bespeaks your Majesty's ac- ceptance is the chief. Not in itself; it is a trifle unworthy your exalted rank, and what will hardly prove an entertaining amusement to one of your Majesty's deep penetration, exact judgment, and fine taste. But on account of the author, who is the first being of the kind, and yet without a name. He was once a man, and of some little name, but no worth, as his present unparalleled case makes but too manifest; for, by the immediate hand of an avenging God, his very thinking substance has, for more than seven years, been continually wasting away, till it is wholly perished out of him, if it be not utterly come to nothing. None, no not the least remembrance of its very ruins remains, not the shadow of an idea is left ; nor any sense, so much as one single one, perfect or imperfect, whole or diminished, ever did appear to a mind within him, or was perceived by it. Such a present from such *a thing*, however worthless in itself, may not be wholly unacceptable to your Majesty, the author being such as history cannot parallel ; and if the fact, which is real, and

before the students at Daventry Academy, affirmed that sudden fright was the primary cause of Browne's hallucination. The latter and a companion were one day travelling together, when a highwayman suddenly demanded their money; and the man threatened violence unless his demands were instantly complied with. Browne sprang at, the robber, and after a short struggle upon the ground disarmed him, and held him down with a deadly gripe until assistance arrived from a neighbouring town. On the officer's arrival, Browne released his hold of the enemy's throat, but was horror-stricken when a lifeless body lay before him. That dearly-purchased victory unbalanced his nervous system, and originated his strange illusions. It has now become impossible either to disprove or to establish the truth of this explanation.

The private character of Simon Browne was amiable and attractive. His researches had been multitudinous, and on scientific and literary themes he was competent to converse with freedom and judgment. His general knowledge was extensive and correct. After returning to his native town he worked on in melancholy seclusion, until inces-

no fiction nor wrong conceit, obtain credit, it must be regarded as the most memorable, and indeed astonishing event in the reign of George II., that a tract composed by such a thing was presented to the illustrious Caroline."—*Vide the suppressed dedication to The Religion of Nature and the Christian Revelation.*

9*

sant application produced a mortification which
ended his life. When in 1725, all hopes of cure
were abandoned, a successor at the Old Jewry was
appointed, while a present of £300 was transmitted
to the disabled pastor. Browne died in 1732,
in his fifty-second year, and rests in the chapel at
Shepton Mallet.*

The constitution of the church in the Old Jewry
made it sometimes difficult to effect a pastoral
settlement. Members and subscribers voted in
common, a proportion of two-thirds being requisite
to render an election valid. When Browne retired,
several endeavours to secure a suitable successor
failed. Dr. Wright, of Blackfriars, and John
Warren, of Coventry, were both ineffectually sought.
An unanimous invitation, however, brought a well-
known divine — Thomas Leavesly — to London.
Since the year 1700 he had presided over a
country charge at Little Baddow, in Essex. His
predecessor was John Oakes, the ejected minister
of Boreham, whom the Barringtons had protected.
The congregation soon became an important one
in the district named; and among such rural surroundings the character and habits of Leavesly
were formed. It happened, therefore, notwithstanding his private worth and amiable disposition,
that an unchaste style and homely illustration,

* Atkey's Funeral Sermon for Simon Browne ; Biographia Britannica; Protestant Dissenters' Magazine; Browne's
Hymns and Spiritual Songs; Wilson's Dissenting Churches.

which sufficed to instruct and edify Essex agriculturalists, proved entirely unpalatable to the refined assembly at the Old Jewry. Leavesly, in consequence, was not popular, although, till his death in 1737, he worked on, highly esteemed by his colleague and by his hearers.

A very celebrated divine and author of the eighteenth century was Samuel Chandler, who succeeded Joseph Bennett at the Old Jewry in 1726. His family was of the West of England; and one relative, a Taunton trader, bravely suffered for conscience' sake in the troubles preceding the Revolution. Henry Chandler, our subject's father, officiated during many years in the Nonconformist ministry at Hungerford, whence he removed to Bath. In the former town Samuel was born in 1693.

In the reign of Queen Anne there flourished at Bridgwater a Presbyterian divine—John Moore— whose services as a trainer of youth were highly approved by educated Dissenters. At a proper age young Chandler was placed with this tutor. Thence he removed into the academy of Samuel Jones at Tewkesbury. While a student, Chandler enjoyed the daily companionship of Joseph Butler—the future author of the Analogy—and Thomas Secker, who afterwards rose to the archiepiscopate of Canterbury. Happily neither time nor circumstances destroyed the friendship begun in youth, for it flourished till the last amid the vicissitudes of life.

When Chandler left Tewkesbury, in his twenty-first year, he commenced his way in the world, and in 1716 settled at Peckham over a Presbyterian congregation. During those years of inexperience he embarked a large sum—his wife's dowry—in the wild speculations preceding the crisis of 1720; and on the collapse of the South Sea Bubble the Chandlers shared the common ruin. In some measure to repair this reverse, a bookselling business was established at the Cross Keys, in the Poultry. His adopted profession brought him into close companionship with the celebrated printer, William Bowyer; and he and Chandler were wont to walk together to the Mitre in Fleet-street to attend the meetings of the Society of Antiquaries.*

Soon after Chandler's settlement at Peckham a lecture was founded at the Old Jewry for the object of examining the basis of Christian belief, the appointed preachers being Chandler and Dr. Lardner. This course was discontinued, and followed by another series by Chandler only. His sermons were highly appreciated, and were eventually published as a vindication of the Christian religion. Archbishop Wake perused the volume while ignorant of the author's station, and expressed some surprise on finding such learning and ability emanating from a bookseller. The prelate addressed the pastor by

* In after years these meetings were held at a house in Chancery-lane. Since 1780 the Society has had apartments in Somerset House.

letter, and ventured an opinion that such talents would be better employed in writing books than in selling them. If it did not obtain a Scotch diploma, the work placed Chandler in a position to obtain one had he so desired ; but an honour so equivocal he lightly valued, " because so many blockheads have been made doctors." The distinction of doctor of divinity, however, was ultimately accepted during a visit to Scotland with the Earl of Findlater. His City lectures were also instrumental in effecting Chandler's removal to London, although he continued to preach at Peckham once on the Sabbath until 1729. His abilities produced results even yet more unexpected, for offers of Anglican preferment reached him only to be unwaveringly declined. In many distinguished circles regrets were plentiful, that so able a writer should be a Nonconformist.

In 1735 the nation grew excited about a supposed spread of popery, closely connected with which was the future rebellion in favour of the Pretender. Taking advantage of the occasion, the Dissenters established a lecture at Salters' Hall, and a number of eminent ministers were engaged to expose the falsities of Romanism. The lectures of Chandler created much interest, and awakened a controversy on the subject in hand, for while denouncing Rome, our orator dealt some heavy blows at the English Establishment. This he effected by pointing out that a blind subjection to priestcraft is the soul and essence of popery. He moreover saw no reason why

similar means should not be used for the propaga-
tion of truth as the Jesuits resorted to for dissemi-
nating error.

In the *Gentleman's Magazine* for this year will be
found several allusions to the anti-papal divines at
Salters' Hall. Indeed, among his poetical essays for
February, Mr. Urban has a piece directly relating to
the subject in hand, *e.g.* :—

" What thanks are due to Neal, and to the rough handler
Of all *divines*, and of all *Churches*, *Chandler!*
Ye demagogues, 'tis commendably done
T' unmask the *whore of Babylon:*
In *Salters'* Hall to sacrifice the Beast,
And with a *roasted Pope* the rabble feast."

The other lecturers followed in Chandler's wake,
and the newspapers accused them of attacking the
Anglican regimen. Rusticus, however, proceeded to
ask :—

" We mourn Rome's superstition daily growing;
But is not to your schism that evil owing?
Is not the *worship* of the *man* of *sin*
Promoted by contempt of discipline ? "

It is not easy to realise either the need or the
value of such services against popery as our fathers
encouraged, and we certainly cannot realise the interest these endeavours excited, unless we understand
that alarm with which Rome and her *protégé*, the
Pretender, were regarded. Not only did lecturers
deliver their harangues, disputes were arranged
between Protestant divines and Catholic priests.

Smaller conflicts came off before tavern bars and among coffee-house groups. One day in the winter of 1734–5, a Romanist preacher was seen walking up Cornhill, and on reaching the Pope's Head tavern, he entered, and began freely conversing with the assembled company. He complained of some charges against his order, made by the Hackney pastor, John Barker, at Salters' Hall. Persons present defended the ground taken up by the Nonconformist, and the upshot was that arrangements were made for a verbal combat at the Bell tavern, Nicholas-lane, a discussion at which Dr. Hunt, of Pinners' Hall, and Samuel Chandler, were present. Dr. Hunt volunteered an argument two hours long against transubstantiation, and he aptly concluded by declaring he would talk no longer. The two divines probably retired with those pleasurable emotions which are only begotten by intellectual conquest. Their chagrin, therefore, must have been considerable on finding that intelligence had travelled to the Continent of a victory over the Protestant leaders in London. Indignant and mortified, Chandler hastily sent forth An Authentic Account of the Late Discussion. The sermons preached at Salters' Hall were likewise published in two volumes.

Dr. Chandler well understood the pernicious tendency of Romish superstition. Zeal in checking the enemy's encroachments prompted him to translate Limborch's History of the Inquisition, which he prefaced with an able dissertation. A sharp controversy was awakened by this publication, and after several pamphlets had appeared on both sides, it was followed by the History of Persecution. Chandler's pen was also actively employed in 1736, when the Dissenters endeavoured to promote a repeal of the Corporation and Test Acts. These and other literary labours raised up many opponents. Two rival poets presented the town with their effusions, and their lines reveal the conflicting sympathies which animated the citizens, *e.g.* :—

> "In Chandler's solid well-composed discourse,
> What wondrous energy, what mighty force!
> Still friend to Truth, and strict to Reason's rules,
> He scorns the censures of unthinking fools."

How differently thought the parodist :—

> "In Chandler's frothy ill-composed discourse,
> There's nothing found of energy or force;
> Still friend to Arius and blind Reason's rules,
> He seeks the praises of unthinking fools."

During the season of political turmoil in 1745, ten editions of his Great Britain's Memorial Against the Pretender were scattered abroad to produce a marked and salutary effect among the people. The doctor promoted the discomfiture of the Jacobite faction by depicting the results likely to follow a wider prevalence of popery. This he accomplished by illustrating his arguments with descriptions of the Huguenots' persecution after the revocation of the Edict of Nantes.

Chandler's Old Jewry pastorate was a forty years' story of prosperity. Loved by his people, and universally respected, he was also admired by a wide circle of distinguished friends. The rapid promotion of his early companion, Thomas Secker, occasioned certain Dissenters to harbour some groundless hopes of a Comprehension. To this subject Doddridge alluded when he congratulated the bishop on his translation to Oxford, and spoke of " reconciliation." " Doctor," replied our Tewkesbury student, " my sentiments concerning these matters are different from yours." Such a rebuff dispelled for the time all delusion about Comprehension. Nevertheless, in the year 1748, Chandler conferred with the bishops of Norwich and Salisbury on this subject. He even visited Archbishop Herring, who very handsomely received him, and spoke of the proposed scheme as "a very good thing ; he wished it with all his heart; and the rather because this was a time which called upon all good men to unite against the infidelity and immorality which threatened universal ruin, and added, he was encouraged to hope, from the piety, learning, and moderation of many Dissenters, that this was a proper time to make the attempt." "But, may it please your Grace," interrupted his Lordship of Norwich—who in a recent charge had affirmed, " The leaders of the Rebellion (1745) were Presbyterians,"—" Mr. Chandler says, ' the Articles must be altered into the words of Scripture.' " " And why not ? " continued Dr. Herring, " it is the imperti-

nences of men thrusting their own words into
Articles, instead of the words of God, which have
occasioned most of the divisions in the Christian
Church from the beginning to this day."

Throughout his long career Chandler was as guiltless as most men of absurdities. The temperate
regimen which he necessarily imposed on himself
was not wholly profitless, for in many ways it promoted a healthiness of body and mind. Vegetarians,
therefore, are welcome to Chandler's case as an illustration of their principles, for he had to deny himself, and subsist chiefly on vegetable diet in order to
counteract a singular predisposition to fever. As
to the absurdities, one deserves special mention. In
a funeral sermon on the death of George the Second,
he extravagantly eulogised the King, and drew
parallels between the Psalmist and our old German
prince. Chandler's acumen discovered that the two
rulers resembled each other in character, and that they
had reigned an equal number of years. This discourse
acted as a provocation to Grub-street, having been
answered by a scurrilous attack on the Psalmist himself. To the profane audacity of a literary hack,
posterity is partly indebted for our author's Critical
History of the Life of David.

Mention may just be made of Mary Chandler, the
doctor's deformed sister, who early relinquished every
hope of happiness apart from a single life. Nevertheless, she wisely determined to cultivate her mental
faculties, in order that literary accomplishments

might outweigh her life misfortune. On settling
at Bath, Mary divided her days between millinery
and poetry, and her literary efforts won the commendation of Pope. Eventually, when she grew as attractive as she had originally determined to be, a
gentleman who had seen her, travelled a hundred
miles for the purpose of seeking her hand in marriage. His suit was unsuccessful. Mary remained
in maidenhood, to die, at the age of fifty-eight, in
1745.

When, in May, 1764, Chandler entered on his
reward, the whole body of Dissenters sustained the
loss of a champion. His remains were interred in
Bunhill-fields. At the subsequent sale of the doctor's
library some valuable manuscripts were disposed of.
An interleaved Bible containing a great number of
notes, is yet preserved in Dr. Williams's Library. A
copy of Bowyer's Conjectures upon the New Testament, with the margin written on, was vainly searched
for in later years by Mr. Nichols, of *The Gentleman's
Magazine.**

We have again and again visited the spot in the
Old Jewry which its old meeting-house once occupied, and have realised on such occasions those
emotions which are awakened by time's ceaseless

* Biographia Britannica; Chandler's Sermons edited by
Amory; Nicholls' Literary Anecdotes of the Eighteenth
Century; Authentic Account of the Late Debates in Nicholas
Lane; History of the Dissenting Churches, Maitland's and
Pennant's Histories of London, &c.

changes. Imagination recalls those distant days when the most gifted divines were alone deemed worthy of preaching in that famous pulpit. Yet, alas! who among the splendid congregation is now remembered, when even the names of the pastors are well-nigh forgotten?

Dr. Chandler enjoyed the services of several able assistants. Dr. Miles, of Tooting, succeeded Thomas Leavesly. By enormous industry the doctor repaired a deficient youthful training, and won an extensive acquaintance with classical and general literature. He was elected a member of the Royal Society, and occupied a first place among his accomplished com-peers. His literary industry was singular in the extreme, for it frequently prompted him to com-mence his daily labour at two in the morning. His sermons were commonly written out, and were the result of incessant application. At his death his study was so abundantly furnished with manuscripts that Dr. Furneaux considered a parallel case had never occurred of a divine's having produced such piles of papers. Although he inherited neither a stout con-stitution nor a strong voice, Dr. Miles preached twice each Sabbath during a period of thirty years, and declined several invitations to settle entirely in London. He lived to be sixty-five, and died in 1763.*

In 1744 Richard Price, then a young man, by accepting the lectureship at the Old Jewry, rose to

* Dr. Furneaux's Sermon on the Death of Dr. Miles, &c.

immediate popularity. Dr. Chandler was even accused of jealousy, because he advised his colleague to show more modesty and less energy. Young Price soon after resigned. His subsequent course was a mixture of sadness and prosperity. From the hereditary faith of his fathers, he lapsed into Arianism, a change from which he was apparently widely removed when, absorbed by the way in Butler's reasonings, he returned to his college across the snow-covered Breconshire hills. The life-story of Richard Price, who, on coming to London, rose from being a barber's lodger in Pudding-lane, to an influential position among the best society, is fraught with interest. At different times he was stationed at Newington Green, Poor Jewry-lane, Edmonton, and Hackney. For twenty years his wife was an invalid, and the doctor himself had long been a sufferer, when he died in 1791.

Tynton, in Glamorganshire, claims the honour of being the birthplace of Richard Price. The family was strictly orthodox; and the father on one occasion snatched a volume of Clark's sermons from his son's hand, to throw it upon the fire, choosing so to manifest his horror of Arianism. The extreme rigour of the parental rule, it may be feared, prejudiced Richard's susceptible mind against the tenets thus harshly supported. Richard received his early instruction from a dissenting minister at Neath. Thence he removed to Pertwyn, where he studied under Samuel Jones. Having completed his grammar learning, he went to Talgarth College, of which Vavasor Griffith was president. In 1739 his father died, when Price found that that father's eccentricity of temper had diverted from him a proper share in the family estate: one brother being endowed with the whole at the expense of all other dependants. At this conjuncture, Richard had an uncle settled in London—an assistant of Dr. Watts. By acting on the advice of this relative, he removed from Wales to the capital; and the events of the road from Cardiff to London, aptly illustrate student life in the days of George the Second. Etiquette, it seems, obliged the richer brother to provide a carriage to Cardiff; but when landed in that convenient seaport, Richard was left to shift for himself, with scarcely anything more substantial than commonplace good wishes to aid his journey. A lady travelling to Bristol fortunately overtook him, and judging him to be a youth of gentlemanly birth and polished mien, offered him a seat in her carriage. From Bristol to his destination in London, the means of transit was one of those broad-wheeled waggons which then traversed England in all directions. On settling in the metropólis, Price perseveringly applied himself to study, under the celebrated professor Eames. A too ardent pursuit of knowledge, and some inconveniences inseparable from a barber's saloon, ere long prostrated the young aspirant, and rendered the air of his native Cambria an indispensable restorative. After spending a season in Wales, he returned to London and completed his curriculum. Through the succeeding thirteen years he held a chaplaincy at Stoke Newington. Both his patron and his uncle died almost simultaneously ; and, inheriting a legacy from each, Richard found himself in easier circumstances.

From youth upward, Price had manifested an ability to think for himself on theological and ethical questions. The too independent opinions, it may be feared, which he formed, greatly irritated his father ; and the uncle at Bury-street declared he would prefer seeing his nephew transformed into a pig, to having him lapse into a heterodox dissenter. Nevertheless, Price advanced in so-called liberality of sentiment ; and while he never reached Socinianism*, he may fairly be classed among Arian preachers. At the age of thirty-two he married, and settled in Hackney. His lady belonged to an unfortunate but numerous class, whose wealth had taken wings amid the mad speculations of 1720. After two years' sojourn at Hackney, Price resigned, preferring the Church at Newington Green. He now began those literary pursuits which rendered his name a household word both in the British Isles and in the American colonies. His first ethical work brought him into acquaintance with David Hume ; and the two occasionally dined together at Cadell's publishing

---

* I hope it will not be thought that I ever use this term offensively. I use it, as Priestly does also, as the opposite of Calvinism.

10

house in the Strand. Hume professed not a little surprise at the theological broadness of his courteous opponent; and the celebrated sceptic found some pleasure in sometimes passing a quiet day at the Newington manse.

When the pastor entered on his new sphere at Newington-green the congregation had declined in numerical strength and in purity of doctrine. For such degeneracy it is always difficult to account ; and it becomes more difficult in the present instance, be- cause forty years earlier, during the disputes of 1719, the minister at Stoke Newington, Martin Tomkins, had been dismissed on account of theological defec- tion. That Price was animated by an honest desire, faithfully to fulfil the office of a Christian teacher, cannot justly be questioned ; for, while his tender treatment of a deistical antagonist almost amounted to effeminacy, his susceptible nature was troubled on account of the apathy of his own people. On one occasion, in particular, he was more than ordinarily discouraged. He exerted all his powers, mental and physical, in an endeavour to awaken his hearers to a just sense of the terrors attending a final judgment. His utmost efforts merely sufficed to lull them to sleep. Indeed, the Church was sleeping in the truest sense ; for when members died, or removed away, none came forward to fill their places. Price, therefore, entered on a more promising field at Hackney, still continuing to preach at Newington - green on Sabbath afternoons.

The admiration of Price's London friends prompted them to bestow upon him a very equivocal compliment. They purchased a diploma at Glasgow University, and dubbed their favourite Doctor of Divinity. Certain is it, that had Price himself suspected the manœuvre, he would have contemptuously declined so small a distinction.

In those days Hackney boasted of its literary and scientific circles, the prestige of which a few master-spirits sustained, as week by week they assembled to enjoy the social delights contributed by their common talents. A society likewise congregated at a city coffee-house, including Kippis, Priestley, and others of high attainments; yet none of his distinguished associates outshone Price in intellectual lustre and conversational power.

When the misunderstanding occurred between England and the American colonies, Price grew intensely anxious to preserve the friendly relation of the two peoples. When the quarrel progressed to an open rupture, in common with most Dissenters of that period, he sympathised with the settlers. The winter of 1775 was spent in preparing his celebrated treatise on Civil Liberty—a book which created a sensational interest then well-nigh without a parallel. The run upon the publisher was so extraordinary, that the printers were not able to keep pace with the demand. This wide dissemination of his sentiments stimulated many enemies into activity; the more distinguished of whom were the Archbishop of

10*

York, Wesley, and Edmund Burke, the last, in particular, having proved the weakness of his cause by violent invective. Calumniated by a crowd of detractors on the one side, and congratulated by countless admirers on the other, Price apparently experienced little either of elation or concern. As regarded the war, he observed a commendable caution, whether in speaking or in writing. He became, however, a leading representative of a great party, and, for the time, probably no living politician exerted a greater influence over the world's destinies. The Corporation of London presented him with the freedom of the City in a golden box. The effect his writings produced on society in the New World, doubtless hastened the Declaration of Independence. The first Congress invited the doctor to accept an office either of trust or honour under the new Republic. So widespread and so high an appreciation of his conscientious services in the cause of Liberty, further incensed his opponents, as was proved by their manifestations of rage and spite. Some denounced him as a traitor, and even threatened his life. Others represented him to be an abandoned profligate; but notwithstanding such attacks, Price, had he chosen, might have accepted a secretaryship under the premier, on the change of ministry in 1782. His actions were ever showing that his heart was uncorrupted by ambition. Though tempted to court the patronage of nobles, or to feel raised by their flattering attentions, he manfully repelled

the tempter. The allurements of worldly preferment
were far less attractive than a peaceful pursuit of
literary avocations.

Some additional interest was awakened among the
literati by the publication of Price's objections to the
leading Socinian tenets. This was an apparent endeavour to steer betwixt opposing schemes, and the
charitable inference may be fairly drawn, that the
author, after all, only slightly swerved from the
Baxterian standard. His views were zealously con-
troverted by Priestley and Lindsey—a fact which in
itself is a most auspicious omen in the author's
favour.

The flight of time brought to our divine what, as
we grow in years, we must each realise—that death
is continually severing terrestrial ties. Dr. Shipley,
of St. Asaph; Dr. Adams, of Pembroke College; and
John Howard in a distant country, all died, and their
vacant places naturally tended to depress the spirits
of their surviving friend. In 1787 Mrs. Price also
died. This loss, joined to that of so many early
companions, occasioned the pastor's removal from
Newington-green to Hackney, where his home would
have been only a melancholy one but for a sister's
tender superintendence. By the death of Benjamin
Franklin and John Howard the doctor was particularly affected. He received a last letter from the
philanthropist, written during his visit to the Moscow
hospitals.

Dr. Price was chosen to preach a centenary sermon

at the Old Jewry in celebration of the hundredth
anniversary of the ENGLISH REVOLUTION; and such
was his strain of patriotic eloquence, on this occasion,
that the audience could scarcely refrain from venting
their admiration by shouts of applause.   Very possibly both Price and his compeers too readily sympathised with the French politicians, many of whom
as their personal friends, were hospitably received
at Hackney.

Although Dr. Price was only for so short a time
connected with the Old Jewry, that brief connection
must be sufficient apology for having given the
above particulars of one who died as he had lived—
an honest man.   For some time he devoted a fifth of
his income to charitable uses, and few were found who
surpassed him in conscientious endeavours to act out
their teaching.   His death was accelerated by a cold
taken in Bunhill-fields while attending a funeral,
and he entered into rest during the spring of 1791.
The following lines commemorating his departure
were written by one of Price's friends, and are here
for the first time printed :—

> " See the freed soul, from earth's low cares removed,
>   Expatiates in the liberty he loved ;
>   And leaves the cruel shackles far behind.
>   See Sydney, Hampden, Locke, each patriot name
>   Dear to the friend of freedom and to fame.
>   O ! see them all in smiling triumph meet,
>   The dauntless friend of human kind to greet.
>   See humble Wren, too, urge his eager way,
>   To introduce his friend to perfect day.

Their shouts united shake the upper skies;
And as they lead him to receive the prize,
Lo angel warblers the full song sustain,
While choirs responsive catch the glowing strain,
And loudly hail him to that happier shore,
Where Burke can neither stab nor tyrants vex him more."

The interesting and pretty town of Taunton was the birthplace of Thomas Amory, whose name appears among the pastors at the Old Jewry. At Taunton, Nonconformity early throve in a congenial soil. Amory was born in 1701, at his father's house —a grocery establishment. The parents' circumstances enabled them to endow their son with every educational advantage; yet even in those days, after the Revolution had cleared the political horizon, the obstacles in a dissenting student's path were many and perplexing. A theological seminary was opened in Taunton by Stephen James and Henry Grove; but the Schism Bill obliged these professors to close their doors until the happy accession of the House of Hanover.

After being approved by his examiners, Amory returned to Taunton, where he was duly appreciated. For a time he was associated with the Presbyterian Church, but when his colleague refused to divide the stipend, an indignant section of the congregation provided another chapel. Although he secured an influential and happy position at Taunton, he resigned in 1759, and removed to the Old Jewry. His family benefited by many advantages peculiar to London, but the pastor himself never achieved any popularity in his more elevated station.   He succeeded Chandler in 1766, and found his hearers willing, for the sake of his learning and private worth, to overlook some defects—*e.g.*, a weak voice and heavy delivery.   He never inherited the happy knack of making learning attractive, and never raised himself into very high esteem.   In 1768 he followed Jabez Earle * in the Merchants' Lectureship at Salters' Hall, and died six years later. †

At this conjuncture the people took a remarkable, if not an unparalleled, course : they invited Archdeacon Blackburn to forsake the Anglican communion by taking their society under his charge.   "The writings of that eminent man upon the subject of religious liberty," says Wilson, " had coincided so fully with the fundamental principles of Protestant Dissenters, as to lead to a supposition that, upon a favourable opportunity, he would quit the Establish-

* He was in some respects a remarkable instance of longevity. He died in his chair during the year named at the age of ninety-two. He was a London minister of good position for nearly seventy years, and he preached on the last sabbath of his life. Throughout this protracted period he never experienced a day's illness, and he would probably have known pain only from hearsay and from books, had not a broken arm added to his knowledge in this direction. A favourite recreation in his latter years was to repeat lines by the hundred from Homer and Virgil.

† Dr. Flexman's Sermon on the Death of Dr. Amory; Biographia Britannica; History of the Dissenting Churches.

ment and join the Dissenters. This apprehension, however, proved ill-founded; for though the worthy archdeacon was far from being a good churchman, yet some *weighty* reasons induced him to decline the proposal."

Nathaniel White, who eventually succeeded, had studied under Dr. Doddridge, and was undergoing the Northampton curriculum when his amiable tutor died, in 1751. White removed with the academy to Daventry to continue his course under Dr. Ashworth. On leaving college, he immediately won a good position, and successively settled at Hinckley and at Leeds, but removed to London in 1766. He held a lectureship at Hackney, which he resigned after his assumption of office at the Old Jewry. His death occurred in 1783.

The last pastor at the old chapel was Abraham Rees, whose connections in the Principality were highly respectable. During the persecutions of the sixteenth century a member of his family suffered martyrdom. From infancy, Abraham was set apart for his sacred profession, and his earliest instruction was received in the neighbourhood of Llanbrynmair; thence he removed to Hoxton Academy, where he studied under Dr. Jennings. Rees there attained to great proficiency in various branches of literary knowledge. He was consequently appointed assistant tutor, and ultimately became the principal —a position he held for twenty-three years. Rees' first settlement was over a church in Southwark;

his removal thence to the Old Jewry, it was expected, would restore prosperity—an anticipation not wholly unfounded.

The life of Abraham Rees pre-eminently belongs to the history of literature, and his individual fame is chiefly based upon the Encyclopædia named after him—a work comprising forty-five volumes in quarto. The completion of so vast an undertaking necessitated twenty years of incessant labour—an ordeal which sufficed to impair the editor's health. If this work be admitted to be, what in fact it is, a continuation of Harris's Lexicon Technicum, it will then appear to be the first encyclopædia in the English language. John Harris was a mathematician who flourished in the reign of Anne, at his retreat in Amen-corner, beneath the shadow of St. Paul's. There he spent his days in writing for neighbouring booksellers: his spare hours were devoted to lecturing on scientific themes, and the company which benefited by his instructions met at the Marine Coffee House, Birchin-lane, "At six o'clock in the afternoon." In after years a revised edition of the author's dictionary was prepared by Ephraim Chambers, to be again improved by Dr. Rees, and published in four volumes folio, in 1786. This again formed the basis of that great monument of learning and industrious perseverance, REES' ENCYCLOPÆDIA, commenced at the beginning of the present century.

Notwithstanding the success it achieved, the En-

cyclopædia did not afford entire satisfaction. Dr.
Rees, his critics urged, lacked judgment by over-
crowding his pages with redundant matter. Not
only was the book cumbered with useless articles,
but those articles were oftentimes defective and erro-
neous. Dissertations properly belonging to one subject were inconveniently subdivided, greatly to the
bewilderment of enquiring students. In physical
and mathematical science the editor excelled, but his
philological attainments were not very highly rated,
and Kippis, it was generally supposed, surpassed
Rees in refinement of taste. That the latter, however, was a man of vast acquirements, the successful
conduct of his Encyclopædia amply testifies.

In the pulpit, Dr. Rees to a commanding presence
added a winning manner. Naturally, therefore, his
eminent position and valuable works brought him a
crop of honours. He was elected a Fellow of the
Royal Society; the University of Edinburgh created
him a Doctor of Divinity. In several offices of trust,
Rees rendered honourable and useful service. He
was a manager of the Presbyterian Fund and a dis-
tributor of the *Regium Donum*, which he frequently
supplemented by money placed at his disposal
by private beneficence. Twice during his long
life did Rees approach the Throne with addresses
from the Three Denominations. On the second
of these occasions the Dissenters congratulated
George the Fourth on his accession, and a lord-
in-waiting expressed regret that, on account of

principle, our doctor's loyalty could not be suitably rewarded.

Dr. Rees also distinguished himself as a college tutor. He and Drs. Savage and Kippis were the professors at Hoxton Academy, at the era of the collapse of that institution in 1785, a catastrophe doubtless hastened by the low standard of theology adopted by two of the professors. Rees and several others then combined to establish a college at Hackney, agreeably to the Arian scheme; but after a trial of two years or thereabout this endeavour likewise failed.

The opening years of the nineteenth century saw the last of this old meeting-house. In 1808 the lease expired, and an attempt to obtain a renewal was not successful. A site for another church was procured in Jewin-street, the memorial-stone of which was laid by Dr. Rees, who also opened the building in 1809.

Dr. Rees died at his house in Finsbury-square, in June 1825, at the age of eighty-two. Tall in stature, he had a countenance open and handsome, with a voice strong and musical. His genial nature, gentlemanly mien, and great attainments rendered him the valued friend of numerous distinguished members of the learned professions, many of whom followed him to his last resting-place in Bunhill-fields, the pall of the coffin being borne by six ministers of the Three Denominations.*

* Rees' Encyclopædia; Encyclopædia Londinenses; Gentleman's Magazine, vols. v and lxxxv ; Biblical Repository 1809 and 1825 ; Private Information.

David Davidson, the assistant and successor of Abraham Rees, and a graduate of Glasgow University, was the last pastor of this ancient society. When, in 1825, he removed from Dundalk in Ireland to Jewin-street, he already enjoyed the reputation of being an able scholar. Numbers considered him even superior to the great encyclopædist, whose endowment of voice, talent, and commanding exterior, sufficed to retain a popularity more lasting than most can enjoy. It would seem, however, that Rees held his office longer than prudence warranted. Numbers of his youthful hearers forsook the chapel, while the migration from city to suburb was on the increase. The pastor, in consequence, year by year, sorrowfully witnessed a diminution of his congregation. It has been supposed, that if the doctor had resigned earlier, the chapel would have remained his successors' inheritance; but from our standpoint, we think we discover a far more potent cause of decline; but as doctrinal controversy forms no part of the present design, we gladly waive particular reference to this vexed question.

Meanwhile the decrease in the congregation progressed, and the minister resigned his office. The trustees eventually disposed of the building to the Wesleyans, and a flourishing society of that persuasion still assembles within its walls. After retiring in 1840, the pastor never accepted another charge, but employed himself in various literary pursuits and other matters. In 1850 he sustained a paralytic stroke, and died at Epsom in December 1858.

Thus passed from the world this great society. Had the members retained that purity of doctrine so prized by Calamy and Shower, their descendants would probably to-day have been witnesses for Christ in the world. How many communities as ancient are still in existence, simply because their standard of faith has been preserved! What, could they have descried it, must have proved a well-spring of grief to the illustrious founders, is at least to posterity a lesson fraught with momentous truth—THE TENETS OF SOCINUS GENERATE DECAY.

Chapter V.

THE SABBATARIAN BAPTISTS IN OLD LONDON.

CRIPPLEGATE, as most persons are aware, derives its name from the cripples who anciently stationed themselves around its entrance for the purpose of soliciting alms. This gate, in all probability one of the four original inlets to London, stood upon the Roman Ermine-street, and dated its foundation from a dim antiquity. In the year 1010 the citizens saw its ponderous doors thrown open to admit into London the remains of a martyred king whose life and fate are commemorated in the church of Saint Edmund, Lombard-street. Once upon a time the neighbourhood of Cripplegate-without-the-Wall was a formidable bog and an eyesore to venturesome strollers, besides being sufficiently unhealthy to prompt various attempts on the part of the citizens to improve the surface by drawing off the stagnant pools. But engineering art in the Plantagenet era was scarcely equal to the converting of marsh into dry subsoil, and the area of Moorfields seems to have baffled all endeavours to improve it, by persisting in remaining a bog till the eve of the Reformation; about which time the watery supremacy was partially conquered by one more determined and expensive effort. The place gradually assumed the pleasant aspect of a recreation ground, and instead of pestilential pools spreading disease in the summer heat, or giving amusement to sliders and idlers when frozen in winter, the space was laid out with gravel walks, plots of grass, and beds of herbs, the whole being studded over with trees for shade and ornament. In a ruder age the inhabitants of Cripplegate drew their daily supplies of water from "a well with two buckets," and a neighbouring spring, the inheritance of a city monastery, gave a name to Monkwell-street. In this ward was situated The Swan with two Necks, the ancient rendezvous of northern carriers. With what spirit our fathers sought to protect life and property we learn from many a time-stained document, *e.g.* :— "There are to watch at Cripplegate and at several other stands in divers places of this ward every night a constable, a beadle, and forty watchmen." At a neighbouring chapel, The Hermitage-on-the-Wall, the officers of the Clothworkers' Guild were wont to meet at intervals of three months; on which occasions, as they marched to their pews, wigged and robed, they imparted to the congregation a hue of civic picturesqueness. Doubtless while engaging in the service, some thoughts intruded into these good traders' minds of the substantial fare which commonly followed. Be that as it may, the sermon over, these dons of clothworking piously distributed

twelvepence each to twenty-four old men and women,
the gift at Michaelmas having been supplemented by
" A frieze gown, a lockram shift, and a pair of winter
shoes." Such quaint customs retain a freshness of
interest long after the buildings they belonged to
have passed away. Both time and space would fail
us, however, were we to enumerate the events of
interest and the list of historical personages associated with this ancient parish and its noble sanctuary. The names of Milton, Cromwell, and a host
of others who were celebrated in divinity, politics,
and literature, readily suggest themselves. Nevertheless, from these we are constrained to turn aside, and
to make way to the court of old appropriated to
that "indifferent good building" styled Curriers'
Hall; the reason of our visitation being that this
place was anciently associated with a denomination
now nearly extinct in the metropolis—the Sabbatarian Baptists.

It will not come within our present design to
account in any way for the peculiar notions these
people professed in regard to the Sabbath; but as in
past times their ranks included some very eminent
names, a few reminiscences may not prove uninteresting. In the matter of the Sabbath only did
they differ from orthodox Baptists. Through one
portion of the last, and also of the present century,
the doors of the chapel at Devonshire-square were
opened on each Saturday morning to admit their congregation. The founder of this particular society was

Francis Bampfield, in whose lifetime the people used Pinners' Hall, but afterwards removed to Cripplegate. He is yet remembered as one of the most zealous and efficient of those confessors, who, during the iniquitous ascendancy of the Stuarts, testified unto death.

Bampfield came of a highly respectable family in the county of Devonshire. At the age of sixteen he proceeded to Oxford, and on completing his course at that university he was presented with a prebend's stall at Exeter, and afterwards with a country living, which he resigned in favour of Sherborne * in Dorsetshire, where, with an ardour rarely surpassed, he fulfilled the duties of his pastorate. His efficiency is partly accounted for by the fact of his having been prepared from early childhood for the Christian ministry.

* This old town—121 miles distant from the metropolis —was called by the Saxons Seiraburn, a name signifying *a clear spring*, and which old English writers spell in a variety of ways. The surrounding country was formerly the territory of the West Saxons, and constituted the immense diocese of Winchester. When the see was ultimately divided, Sherborne was made the seat of episcopal rule, and here the King created Aldhelm the first bishop. The last-named diocese included six counties, and extended to the Land's End. After the Conquest, the prelates removed their headquarters to Old Sarum. In Saxon times Sherborne boasted of an important monastery, which, at the Dissolution, was set down as worth £700 a-year. The Normans erected a castle in the town; but after standing for 600 years, this stronghold was stormed and demolished by Cromwell.

Bampfield's first rural charge yielded a stipend of £100 a-year; but, possessing private means, nearly equivalent to that amount, he distributed his entire salary in charity. At Sherborne he continued till the general secession of 1662. According to Crosby, it is doubtful if Bampfield ever relinquished his allegiance to Charles the First; for, says the Baptist historian, he " was zealous against Oliver's usurpation and the Parliament war." If it was so, the Government he had the unhappiness to live under was too eagerly pursuing passing pleasures to heed the sufferings of former friends, many of whom, apparently on account of having been friends, were the more relentlessly persecuted for Nonconformity. When the disputes broke out between King and Parliament Bampfield sided with the Royalists, and he harboured some conscientious scruples about paying such taxes as were imposed by the Commons. To Richard Baxter, it is supposed, the responsibility belongs of having diverted the pastor's sympathies into the channel of Parliamentary politics. As it occasionally happens under similar circumstances, the convert went far beyond what his preceptor would have sanctioned; for, on joining the Puritan party, he subscribed the Covenant—a procedure Baxter never sanctioned. At Sherborne, Bampfield laboured with indefatigable zeal, and although two centuries have rolled by since those troublous days, many readers will be interested, and even concerned to learn, that the evangelist's principal opponents

11*

were " Quakering witches," whom he appears to have successfully resisted. Indeed, that estimable authority, Anthony Wood, testifies " He (Bampfield) carried on the trade among the factious people till the Act of Uniformity cast him out." After the secession of Bartholomew's Day he was not permitted to pursue his course in Sherborne without tasting the discipline of the county gaol. For the crime of conducting family worship after the Puritan order, he was seized and summarily imprisoned; but the superior offence of "praying and preaching" in public entailed a confinement of eight years at Dorchester, where his presence proved a lasting blessing to many of his fellow prisoners. When, in 1675, he regained his liberty, he immediately engaged in itinerant preaching, undaunted by a severe experience. While passing through Dorchester he was again arrested, and confined for eighteen weeks at Salisbury, from which city he sent forth his little work, The Free Prisoner. On leaving Salisbury he retired to London, and finding the persecuting laws were less rigorously enforced, he gathered a church in Pinners' Hall in 1676.*

* Among the State Papers there is a letter which Bampfield addressed to the King, and of the supposed date of 1664. While denying several false reports respecting himself, the author testifies to his good affection and peaceableness during the late civil commotions. He avows an abhorrence of war and sedition, and an aversion to opposing such as are set up in authority. As regards his personal comfort, he confesses a willingness, if need be, to bear pain for conscience' sake; because, by unheeding that faithful monitor, a heavier

But troubles springing from the civil magistrate
were not lessened by a removal to London, for in
that city Bampfield was imprisoned during the last
year of his life. What character the pastor sustained, during his years of usefulness in the metropolis, we are enabled to learn from the testimony of
both enemies and friends. In ecclesiastical government he was notoriously given to change—a fickle-
mindedness supplying Wood with an opportunity
of venting those sneers which appear to have constituted a part of that historian's nature. Wood
was dumbfounded at this example of a Gentile
who preached sermons, besides publicly worshipping
God on Saturdays; and accordingly, Bampfield is
designated, "almost a complete Jew," and so "enthusiastical and canting, that he did almost craze
and distract many of his disciples by his amazing
and frightful discourses." While not attempting to
excuse this harsh judgment of an enemy, it may yet
be conceded that, in many respects Bampfield was a
sanguine enthusiast—an admission in no degree ex-
cusing the hard treatment he endured. He seems to
have regarded with strong disapproval all systems of

punishment is entailed than merely human inflictions, and
on that account he cannot relinquish preaching the Gospel.
He points out to Charles, what estimable advantages a king
possesses for benefiting others, and adjures him to make the
Bible his standard of government. By many of his contemporaries Bampfield was mistaken for a Quaker.—*Vide
Rolls' House MSS., Domestic Series, Charles II.*, vol. xcix.

human learning: he refused to countenance any
science other than the Bible supplied. He stoutly
maintained that, Scriptural knowledge alone was
sufficient for all temporal as well as all eternal purposes. He manifested a general dissatisfaction with
terrestrial affairs, and even wished to see the Roman
characters superseded by the Hebrew alphabet. A
survey of education afforded him still less comfort.
Youth were taught to reverence " Enthusiastic phan-
tasms, humane (human) magistralities, self-weaved
ratiocinations, forced extractions, indulged sensua-
tions, and unwitting scepticisms."

The various events of Bampfield's diversified life
strikingly reveal the roughness of those times, and
of the pastor's way in particular; besides illustrating
what was too often the experience of a dissenting
minister in the reign of Charles the Second.

We have now specially to refer to Saturday,
February 17th, 1682, the place being that sanctuarium of Nonconformity, Pinners' Hall. The congregation is not a large one, but every member is
genuine, as is sure to be the case in time of danger
and trial. The pastor, who is in his pulpit, is now
an old man, and in addition to the furrows of time,
he discovers some honourable scars of hard service.
Suddenly, and without warning, a company of armed
men enter the room, the leader exclaiming, " I have
a warrant from the Lord Mayor to disturb your
meeting." " I," replied Bampfield, " have a warrant
from Christ, who is Lord Maximus, to go on." This

brave or defiant mien, however, avails nothing. The preacher is ruthlessly pulled down from his desk, and, with six of his followers, arraigned at the bar of that impersonation of justice and patron of feasting, the Lord Mayor, who, with undissembled pleasure, fines the culprits ten pounds each. Other strange events were destined to characterise that memorable Saturday. In a short space the time arrives for afternoon meeting, for none of these veterans intend relinquishing their second service on account of their preceding experience. Anon, this service is speedily interrupted by the representatives of civic justice, and a scene ensues which perhaps is scarcely precedented in the history of Pinners' Hall. The occupants of the pews warmly remonstrate with the official intruders, until the latter, with abashed faces and apologetic tones, excuse their performance of duties which necessity alone compels them to discharge.

Although again arrested, Bampfield is immediately dismissed. He next openly proceeds to his own house, and there conducts the service which the law forbids his holding in the Pinmakers' Hall. On the morning of the following Saturday, the 24th of February, pastor and people are again molested, the former being dragged from his pulpit while in the act of prayer. Bible in hand, he is led captive through the City streets, testifying to the spectators that, for Christ's sake, he willingly surrenders liberty. According to their predilections, the citizens express sympathy or resentment. "A Christian Jew!" exclaims one party, while others as readily reply, "A martyr; see how he walks, with his Bible in his hand." Ultimately, the Lord Mayor commits him to gaol, and he is sentenced to imprisonment for life for refusing to swear allegiance to the King, although his principal crime was, doubtless, Nonconformity. On hearing the judgment of the Court, Bampfield essayed to speak, but could only evoke the reply of "Away with them!" We have only to follow the old confessor to Newgate, for there the dismal tragedy of his suffering is ended in February, 1683, at the age of seventy years. In those days, the Dissenters possessed a graveyard in the vicinity of Aldersgate, and thither, in the wintry morning, were conveyed the remains of Francis Bampfield, the ceremony of interment being attended by "a very great company of factious and schismatical people."*

Edward Stennett was in every respect a man superior to Francis Bampfield, whom he succeeded in or about 1686. It is to be regretted that the materials at disposal for making a sketch of his life are too scanty to do the subject justice, the memoir of his son Joseph being the principal source whence our facts and inferences have to be drawn. Very probably Edward was the first of his family to pro-

* Athenæ Oxonienses; Calendars of State Papers, Domestic Series, Charles II. ; Crosby's History of the English Baptists; Calamy's Account and Continuation; Wilson's History of the Dissenting Churches, &c.

fess the Baptist tenets, or even to embrace the Nonconformist regimen; for, on the breaking out of
civil war, his principles prompted an espousal of the
Parliamentary cause—a procedure which estranged
him from his nearest relations. Besides sorrow of
heart, this action ensured a large amount of temporal difficulty. He practised physic while discharging the functions of a Dissenting preacher.
His success in the medical profession far exceeded
his expectations, since he amassed sufficient means
to start his children handsomely in life.

After the Restoration, Stennett bravely shared the
common trouble, and in his turn suffered imprisonment for conscience' sake. Residing at Wallingford,
he had a home in some apartments of the castle in
that town, which then existed entire. This baronial
stronghold having been associated with the most remarkable portion of the pastor's life, we may venture
on a short digression to say a few words concerning it.

The Parliamentary borough of Wallingford, situated
about fifty miles from London, was anciently of some
importance, as is testified by the Roman ramparts
which may yet be traced, and by the antiquarian
relics occasionally discovered. In the year 1006
the town became a prey to Danish invaders. About
half a century later the castle was inhabited by
Wigod the Saxon, who, when the prestige of his
race declined at the battle of Hastings, conformed
to misfortune, and entertained the victorious William during his march to London, in 1066. A

Norman officer wedded Wigod's daughter, and on
this son-in-law's inheriting the castle, he superseded
the old pile by another more in sympathy with continental tastes. Amid the quarrels of hostile parties which characterised succeeding centuries, the
weather-beaten walls and towers went through some
hard service, now resisting, and anon succumbing to
the fury of maddened assailants. The middle of the
seventeenth century found the castle in a state of
decay, but the whole being speedily repaired, passed
into the hands of the Royalists, from whom it was
wrested by Fairfax, in 1646, to be utterly demolished in succeeding years.

At the Restoration era, as just stated, Edward
Stennett resided in the castle at Wallingford.
Among other privileges attached to this place, and
a remnant of feudal times, was this : no civil
functionary, ranking lower than a Lord Chief Justice,
could grant warrants of search, no matter how great
the emergency. Stennett resolved on taking advantage of a fact so auspicious, and, therefore, in spite
of squire and parson, he metamorphosed the hall of
kings and barons into a Nonconformist conventicle,
for the innovation could be effected with impunity,
if only ordinary caution were exercised to exclude
such undesirable society as common informers. The
consummation of the project supplied an apt illustration of the proverb, "An Englishman's house is
his castle." So uninterrupted a progress to Nonconformity, however, gave unspeakable annoyance to

those brave gentry, whose too liberal scheme of ethics embraced the rustic joviality of maypoles and village ale-houses.   As the resident magistrate cast many malicious glances at the proud gates of Wallingford Castle, his ire was stirred by the remembrance that, not by his puny authority could those venerable towers be humbled.   By false pretence or stratagem, various were the endeavours made to get an emissary admitted, for the Dissenters' keenness in scenting interlopers was every way worthy of and as provoking as their general mien and teaching.   In fact, the Nonconformists had literally encamped in the very midst of the enemy's territory, their citadel, meanwhile, wearing a front as boldly defiant as those mud ramparts described by Foster, which could be neither stormed by surprise nor reduced by perseverance.   But with "The Merry Monarch" gracing the throne, and willing hands to support a different order of things, it could not be tolerated that this centre of religious influence should continue to flourish.   The squire and parson alluded to convened a conference, whereat were debated certain grievances, but those of Wallingford in particular. Ultimately resolving to honour the maxim, "all is fair in love and war," they determined to effect, by questionable measures, what a fair and open procedure refused to accomplish.   The arts resorted to were suggested by purest knavery.   Witnesses were to be hired who, for a certain consideration, would supply the wanting testimony.   The parson, it is true, had openly expressed friendship for Stennett, because the physician had ably served him in his professional capacity without accepting fees. But now Dissent had to be repressed, and, if necessary, by the sacrifice of both principle and gratitude. The witnesses were duly marshalled, each having his appointed task, and as success appeared not unlikely to attend their manœuvres, Stennett took due precautions to thwart the conspiracy. The plotters were in high spirits. When the assizes came off at Newbury, even the presiding judge acted like a confederate; but on the morning of hearing some curious disasters discomfited the conspirators. A son of the judge, an Oxford student, who was to have shared the perjury, opportunely absconded with some strolling players. Both by his presence and by his lying testimony, the parson designed aiding the prosecution, but death suddenly disconcerted his plans. Sickness cut down one of the witnesses, accident prostrated another; at length, but one of any importance remained, and on him were fastened the dearest hopes of the party. This man was a gardener, whom the Stennetts had partially employed, and, although by them he had been very considerately treated, they had never ventured on admitting him into the hall at the hours of service. By bribes and by drink the better nature of this gardener was temporarily overcome, yet, prompted either by superstitious fear, in consequence of the strange turn events had taken, or by remorse for his ingratitude,

he disappointed his employers at the critical moment.
Instead of testifying against his master, he expressed
penitence for his individual wickedness. When,
therefore, he walked into court on the day of trial,
our physician found the course completely cleared,
and the proceedings against him were immediately
quashed.

After the death of Francis Bampfield, Stennett
succeeded to the pastorate at Pinners' Hall, but because he still continued to reside at Wallingford, he
only visited London at stated periods. He was
peculiarly happy in his family, his sons and only
daughter no less exemplifying the Christian graces,
than they did those intellectual accomplishments
which rendered them the charm of cultivated circles.
Benjamin and Joseph entered the Dissenting ministry, Jehudah succeeded his father in the practice of
physic, and honoured his Jewish name by publishing
a grammar of the Hebrew tongue at the age of nineteen. Miss Stennett discovered an aptness for learning equally worthy of her family, her knowledge of
the ancient tongues being such as members of her
sex only rarely achieve. The favoured sire of this
amiable galaxy just survived the triumph of Liberty
in the accession of William the Third, in 1689.
The pastor's remains rest with those of his lady, in
the town so closely associated with his life and
labours.*

* " Here lies an holy and an happy pair;
    As once in grace, they now in glory share;

Abingdon, in the county of Berkshire, is ranked among the most venerable of English towns, dating its foundations, as some imagine, from the days of the ancient Britons. The name, being of Saxon origin, signifies *the town of the abbey;* for at Abingdon in the olden time flourished one of the wealthiest of monasteries. The ancient borough records contain some interesting items—*e.g.,* here lived Offa, King of Mercia; and here an English prince, afterwards Henry the First, was educated. Not, however, on account of such matters do we make this allusion to Abingdon; but rather, because, in 1663, Abingdon was the birthplace of Joseph Stennett.

This divine—a son of the eminent physician alluded to above—spent his youth with his father at Wallingford. In early life he mastered Hebrew, French, and Italian in a manner to discover his remarkable philological capacities. Probably directed by his father, he also fulfilled the prodigious task of systematically studying the writings of the Christian Fathers; and by a diligent attention to these and to Scripture, his principles became early and firmly fixed. After honourably acquitting himself in the prepara-

> They dar'd to suffer, but they feared to sin,
> And meekly bore the cross, the crown to win ;
> So liv'd as not to be afraid to die,
> So dy'd as heirs of immortality.
>   Reader, attend : though dead, they speak to thee ;
>   Tread the same path, the same thine end shall be."
> *Vide Epitaph on Edward and Mary Stennett in Wallingford Churchyard.*

tory stages of his education, he left his parents' roof
to settle in London, in 1685—one of the most gloomy
and humiliating periods of our national history. At
that date, indeed, the friends of our constitution were
troubled, not so much by the death of a profligate ruler
as by the accession to the throne of his popish brother.
During the momentous five following years, when events
transpired, and triumphs were achieved, the blessing
of which we are yet enjoying, Stennett was quietly
located in the capital, earning his living as a common
tutor. A a young man he was a keen-sighted politician, who gladly lent his genius and wit to the
cause of the patriotic party. Many of the squibs
privately circulated by the Whigs were the offspring
of his versatile pen. In the Indulgence year—1637
—Dissenters would have been more extensively
allured by the specious bait but for Stennett's dexterity in versification—the means he employed to
expose the wily monarch's real design, meanwhile
taking care plentifully to strew the printed copies
among the Nonconformist assemblies. After the
happy accession of William the Third a collection
was made of this revolutionary literature; but having been published anonymously, it is now impossible to distinguish our author's handiwork.

On religious liberty being restored by the Revolution, Stennett earnestly turned his attention to what
he had long considered his legitimate work—the
Gospel ministry. At the outset of his course he
ably acquitted himself at an evening lecture set up

by the Baptists at Devonshire-square. It soon became evident that his learning, natural talents, and winning mien were sufficient to raise him into an enviable station among the Nonconformists; but to his cost, in a pecuniary point of view, his principles coincided with those of the Sabbatarians to whom he engaged himself, in 1690. Stennett's mastery of English would have eminently qualified him for successfully discharging the functions of the orator, had his vast knowledge and ready utterance been attended by a larger compass of voice. It having been otherwise ordained, one humble sphere constituted his lifelong pastorate. What a path of conscientious self-denial he trod is shown by the scantiness of his followers, and also by that poverty which prevented their raising anything considerable towards their pastor's support. Besides tending his regular charge, he very generally employed himself on the ordinary Sabbath. For a number of years he thus ministered to the General Baptists of Barbican—a station he relinquished, in consequence of a disagreement, in the last year of the seventeenth century.

Stennett sufficiently meddled with politics to prove his patriotism, and to lay bare his purely unselfish nature, as anyone may judge from his published pieces. Among those numerous addresses which, in 1698, congratulated the King on his escape from assassination, none were more heartily sincere in expressions of loyalty than the one which our author himself drew up and presented on behalf of the Baptist denomination. Other passages in Stennett's life are sad illustrations of that fierce animosity which then separated the English people from their neighbours of France. Several years prior to the date we write of—in the dark days when Louis the Fourteenth basely revoked the Edict of Nantes—a Huguenot trader, of the name of Gill, sought an asylum in England. He was accompanied by his two daughters—one of whom became Mrs. Stennett, while the other married Daniel Williams, the munificent founder of the library named after him. Threatened by imminent peril, Gill had hurriedly forsaken his native country, leaving property behind to the value of £12,000. Lord Preston, the ambassador of Charles the Second at Paris, was commissioned to represent the case fairly to Louis the Fourteenth; and that despot readily signed an instrument promising the restoration of the estate; but when the Revolution changed the aspect of English affairs, and for a base betrayer of his people's honour substituted A PRINCE OF ORANGE, passionately eager to humble the haughtiness of France, Louis found it inconvenient to remember his engagement. Nevertheless, it was supposed that some persons might venture across the Channel to investigate the probability of being able to reclaim the estate; and on account of his fluency in the French language, Stennett was adjudged the individual most likely to succeed in so hazardous a service. The latter, in his anxiety to serve his father-in-law, would have embarked for

12

France had not the counsel of more judicious friends occasioned the project's abandonment. It subsequently transpired that the pastor had escaped the hard usage of certain other Englishmen who, while travelling through French territory, were grossly maltreated.

In the year 1700 Stennett retired to Tunbridge Wells—then, as now, the fashionable resort of pleasure-seekers and invalids—to recruit his strength, which a dangerous illness had recently reduced. Although his modesty blinded him to the fact, he ingratiated himself in the good opinions of the distinguished company with whom he daily associated. Thus while benefiting on the one hand by relaxation from pastoral cares, by the pure atmosphere, and by drinking the waters; on the other hand, he materially widened the circle of his acquaintance. One of that circle, Mordecai Abbot—one of Stennett's most generous friends—as receiver-general of the customs, was a great favourite with William the Third. A genial and high-spirited Nonconformist, Abbot never missed either public or private opportunities of honouring the principles he professed. For Stennett he showed particular fondness—an attachment as warmly returned, as the epitaph on the abbot's grave survives to testify.* This gentleman and his amiable daughter

* " Just, prudent, pious Abbot's dust
  Has found a sleeping-place beneath this stone;
  Earth, in thy bosom hide thy precious trust,
  Till his departed spirit claim its own.
  How that returning soul will joy to see
  Her body as immortal and as blest as she!"

were prematurely and almost simultaneously removed
by death. Stennett so acutely realised the severity
of the loss that the shock threatened to impair his
constitution.

Meantime, Stennett's great learning and correct
judgment won general appreciation. While he
ranked as a principal leader of his denomination
in the capital, provincial admirers, and even those
in foreign climes, availed themselves of his wisdom
and impartiality when perplexed by cases of discipline or of disagreement. By reading his pieces,
whether in prose or verse, such persons in the distance naturally formed a high estimate of Stennett's
powers and personal character. As Baptists, they
had hailed with grateful delight their champion's
able and temperate rejoinder to Russen's True Picture of the Anabaptists. On the appearance of
Stennett's treatise many outsiders were found, who,
while not sympathising with the author's conclusions,
yet failed not to commend the wit, learning, and
good temper pervading his pages—virtues but poorly
cultivated by controvertists of the Augustan age.
Besides such services of the pen, the pastor proved
himself a formidable disputer, since Quakers and
Socinians, Nonjurors and Romanists, were made to
smart in succession. Had health and leisure been
awarded, he intended writing a complete and elabo-
rate history of the Baptist denomination—a work
posterity may regret the want of; for had it been
written, the succeeding century and a quarter would

not have seen the Baptists suffer as they did from the unskilful hands of incompetent historians.

His answer to Russen forms the fifth volume of Stennett's works in the edition of 1732. The first four volumes are chiefly sermons and poems, the sermons having been taken down in shorthand ; for, on account of his fluency in our language, the pastor never favoured written notes, but stored his memory with ideas rather than words. After his death many regretted the irrecoverable loss of numbers of very successful discourses, these not having been secured at the time of delivery in the manner described. In Nonconformist circles Stennett's poems were very popular, but many of these fugitive pieces, parted with in manuscript to private individuals, were lost for ever; while others, by not being inserted in the collected edition of their author's works, no less mournfully passed into oblivion.

During the war of the Spanish Succession, or those years of widespread carnage, of terror, of devastation, and of what are popularly called great victories, the national conscience would seem to have been seared, till even such a kindly nature as animated Stennett could attend with comparative complacency, and even with emotions of exultation, to narratives of wholesale destruction of life, and to evidence of misery's having extended her empire to the homes of unoffending peasants, provided such peasants were classed with papists, and were sufficiently unfortunate to live under Louis the Fourteenth.

The terror inspired throughout Europe by the encroaching ambition of the French king, must excuse that passion for war and hatred of France so characteristic of our fathers. The barbarous campaign of 1704 culminated in a double triumph— the capture of Gibraltar, and the magnificent victory of Marlborough at Blenheim. Hundreds of burning towns and villages, whence the luckless inhabitants were driven into neighbouring woods and fields, marked the track of the chivalrous allies. Anon, these preliminary manœuvres were followed by the defeat or the almost annihilation of the French at Blenheim. The pamphlet literature of the day yet testifies to the extravagant joy which the news occasioned throughout the nation: the pulpits of the Nonconformists resounded loudest with thanksgiving sermons. The discourse by Stennett was immediately printed, and eagerly read by admiring thousands. Some unknown person presented a copy to the Queen, and her Majesty showed her appreciation by ordering the author a gratuity from the privy purse— a procedure thought the more remarkable, because Anne in her most genial moments assumed an ungracious mien before Dissenters. As we read the sermon to-day, when the enthusiastic patriotism which inspired the preacher has subsided into sober history, this performance reflects honour on the head rather than on the heart of its author; for sooner than conceal the satisfaction, which the cutting off of prodigious numbers of human beings afforded, he exult-

ingly dilates upon the fact that the arms which
chiefly struck down myriads of papists, or drove them
panic-stricken into the Danube to be drowned, were
not those of Germany, but of Protestant England.*
None were found who more vehemently vindicated
the war than did the Dissenters; † for, in our fathers'
eyes, Louis the Fourteenth exactly personified what
is morally bad and politically contemptible. Stennett ably and largely shared in the doings of those
stirring times. The addresses to the throne and the

* "Our enemies have not only been conquered, but cut off
in prodigious numbers; many squadrons which escaped the
edge of the sword were precipitated into the Danube, and
drowned therein, as the Canaanites were in the river of
Kishon, and the Egyptians before in the Red Sea, and a
great number of battalions made prisoners of war; so that
a numerous and well-disciplined army was not only routed,
but, in a manner, totally ruined. . . . They so ordered
the matter that, when their army was broken, a great part
of it was so enclosed by the confederate forces, that it was
impossible for them to escape, and many others found no
other way of retreat than that of throwing themselves into
the Danube, leaving their camp and the spoil of it to the
conquerors; and that which ought to endear to us the
memory of this action, and to give a particular accent to our
thanksgivings, is, that the forces of the Protestant princes
and States, and more especially the English troops, had the
far greatest share in it, and consequently of the honour that
attends it."—*Vide Stennett's Thanksgiving Sermon for the
Victory at Hochstadt (Blenheim).*

† "And how much soever peace is to be desired, especially
after a long and expensive war, yet 'tis so very evident that,
'tis impossible for the balance of power in Europe to be pre-

petitions to Parliament which he assisted in drawing up, amply prove that the avocation of the divine sufficed not to engender an indifference to politics.

When the war at length drew to a close, Stennett assumed a somewhat conspicuous place among the notables of the memorable year 1713, when, betrayed by the renegade Harley, the Tories, and even by their Sovereign, the better part of the English people indignantly witnessed the signing of the disgraceful treaty at Utrecht. In such seasons of national humiliation, there is ever a sufficient number of sycophants forthcoming, who, only anxious about advancing their individual interests, satiate the ears of royalty with contemptible adulation. On this occasion the ranks of the parasites were more thickly peopled than the national credit for honesty could afford. The Whigs were now completely at bay. The Tories or Jacobites, to consummate their triumph, strenuously endeavoured to evoke congratulatory addresses from persons supposed to belong to neither of the great political parties. The ascendant faction tried the experiment of flattery on the Three Denominations, but to the Dissenters' honour, even

served, and the trade of the nation to be retrieved without reducing the exorbitant power of France to just limits, and restoring the crown of Spain to the house of Austria, that we think it much more eligible to bear the burden of a just and necessary war than weakly to fall into the obvious snare of a dishonourable and destructive peace."—*From a paper by Joseph Stennett, written for presentation to the honourable members for London, in* 1708.

the least sanguine were disappointed at the result.
The conditions of the treaty of Utrecht were eminently solacing to the pride of that exhausted and
bewildered tyrant, Louis the Fourteenth, because
more was surrendered to his rapacity than he would
have dared to demand, and the articles of peace rendered completely nugatory the enormous outlay of
treasure, life, and national reputation, which sustained
the sanguinary campaigns of the war of the Spanish
Succession.   In their united capacity, the Nonconformists contemptuously spurned the Tory advances,
but not losing hope, the latter imagined that, being
the smaller body, the Baptists would rejoice to bask
for a season in the sunshine of Court favour.   Four
peers were commissioned " to try what could be
done with the Baptists."   The leaders of the forlorn
hope staked their all on Joseph Stennett, now in the
last months of his life.   The pastor listened to promises of government favour and of royal protection,
but these could not estrange him from the conscientious procedure of the other denominations, *Neither
myself nor my brethren*, said he, *can ever be brought
to justify with their hands what their hearts disap-
prove, and no particular advantage to themselves can
ever counterbalance their regard for their country*.   An
answer as honourable to the Stennetts as it was
worthy of English Nonconformity.
     Stennett's high qualifications, natural and ac-
quired, would have rendered him a very desirable
trainer of others for the profession he so well

adorned himself, had not a multiplicity of business
and constitutional weakness forbidden his attempting such a scheme of education. Nevertheless, in
his closing years, several youths were lodged in his
house whose studies he partially directed.

That ardent pursuit of knowledge which characterised Stennett's early life, and which, indeed, he
never suffered to abate, is supposed to have weakened his fragile body, and ultimately to have cut
short his life and usefulness. In the early part of
1713, when symptoms of decay appeared, he was
only in his forty-ninth year. His weakness increased while the season advanced. The last discourse he preached was a funeral discourse for that
friend of the Stennetts, and the pastor at Little
Wild-street, John Piggott. In search of health,
Stennett now undertook a journey to Knaphill, but
it soon became apparent that he had only removed
to die. In his last hours, wife and children gathered
around his couch to receive the dying counsel of
their best earthly friend. A bystander, on enquiring
what feelings the pastor experienced in the near
prospect of life's awful change, received for answer,
" I rejoice in the God of my salvation." Many
attach peculiar value to the latest utterances of the
great and good; such persons will be edified to learn
that Stennett's last spoken words were PERFECTLY
SATISFIED. When his remains were carried to
Hickenden churchyard, the mournful ceremony of
interment attracted large concourses of people from

London and surrounding towns, who, by gathering
around Joseph Stennett's grave, paid a last tribute
of respect to the Christian, the philosopher, the poet,
and the divine.

The vacancy occasioned by the death of Joseph
Stennett remained unfilled for fourteen years—a fact
for which the fewness and poverty of the people
satisfactorily accounts. Of Edward Townshend, who
succeeded at or about Christmas, 1727, little or
nothing can be told, although his term of office extended to the year 1765. Thomas Whitewood followed two years later. After preaching but three
times Whitewood died, and several ministers—John
Macgowan, John Reynolds, Dr. Jenkins, William
Clarke, and John Rippon—successively served in
turn on Saturdays. At Midsummer, 1780, Robert
Burnside was called to the ministry, and in 1785 to
the pastorate ; he may therefore be said to have been
a London minister through a period of forty-six
years.

Being a native of Clerkenwell, Burnside was removed thence during infancy to Snowfields, Ber-
mondsey, and the home of those early days continued
to be his home for the remainder of life. Educated
successively at Merchant Taylors' School and Aberdeen University, he was a man of ripe scholarship, his
classical attainments, in particular, having been held
in sufficient repute to prompt several families of distinction to secure his services in tuition. Possessing,
moreover, a strong constitution, he scarcely expe-

rienced illness till the closing month of his life, if
we only make exception of that weakness of sight
and defective hearing by which he was permanently
afflicted. Notwithstanding all drawbacks, his manners
were affable, and his whole mien revealed the polished
gentleman.   By teaching, by authorship,* also by

* His principal work, published in 1825, is entitled, "Remarks on the Different Sentiments entertained in Christendom
relative to the Christian Sabbath." This is an octavo volume
of 354 pages. Besides serving as an illustration of our
author's style, the following extract will interest the reader:
"The Sabbatarians derive their appellation from the
peculiar tenet held by them concerning the scriptural weekly
Sabbath, as being the last day of the week *since* our Lord's
resurrection as well as *before* it.   They make their appearance in the history of the Church as early as their
Christian brethren who are of a different opinion from them
in this particular.   Their Sabbath is said by the historians
Socrates and Sozomon, to have been kept, in conjunction
with the first day, everywhere among the Christians, except
at Rome and Alexandria, for upwards of three centuries.
Accordingly, the seventh day and the first day are called
sisters by Gregory Nyssen. Strong remonstrances were made
against not keeping both days by St. Ignatius and others,
and penalties were ordered by the Councils of Tullo and
Laodicea to be inflicted on clergymen who did not observe
both days as festivals.   At length Constantine, the first ,
Christian emperor, issued a proclamation about A.D. 321, in
favour of the first day solely, which was followed by several
others similar to it. In consequence of these edicts, which
strictly enforced the observance of the first day without
making the smallest provision for the seventh day, that had
hitherto been on an equality with the other, the Sabbatarians, like all other religious bodies that found themselves

officiating at public services on the First day, he
found full employment for his time and diversified
talents; but by passing his days in bachelorhood, by
practising an extreme economy, and by divers eccentricities in private life, he occasioned many to mis-
interpret his actions and to misunderstand his motives.
Thus at his death an exaggerated report gained currency that, the late president of the four or five old
people, who then constituted the expiring society
of Sabbatarian Baptists, had amassed a fortune of
£40,000. If Burnside did evince some singular

aggrieved by imperial and ecclesiastical mandates, seem to
have retired into Abyssinia; for there, as Scaliger and Brerewood, the professor of astronomy inform us, they still
remained in the time of Queen Elizabeth. Whether they
returned to Europe soon after the decrees of Constantine
does not appear; but most probably, like many other bodies
of people who could not in conscience accede to all the
decisions of princes and councils on religious subjects, they
took refuge in the valleys of Piedmont. From there they
emerged, it would seem, about the beginning of the Reformation; since, according to Bishop White, history associates
them, in the time of Luther, with the people called Anabaptists,
in Germany. Their state in England during the seventeenth
century, was sufficiently important to draw the attention of
professors Brerewood and Wallis, who wrote against them;
as also did White, Bishop of Ely, by the direction of Laud,
Archbishop of Canterbury. There were Sabbatarians among
the refugees who came over to this country from France.
A century or two ago there were several congregations of
Sabbatarians in London, and also congregations of them in
many of the counties in England; but their state in this
country at present is very low. However, in the United

predilections, such failings were amply counter-
balanced by that amiability of disposition which
advanced him into the high esteem of the Three
Denominations; and his enviable capacity for improving social intercourse is proved by a number
of allegories he expressly composed for the enliven-
ment of the tea-table at a neighbouring ladies'
school.* After enjoying so lengthened a term of
uniform and uninterrupted health, our author at
length departed rather suddenly. On the first Saturday of May, 1826, he officiated as usual at Devon-

States of North America, whither some of them went
from England during the reigns of the Stuarts, they have
greatly increased within these few years. One of their
churches has 900 members. Another of them, in the year
1820, received an accession of 140 members in the space
seven months. Among their communities are two churches,
the foundations of which were laid by persons from Germany
and Scotland; from the former in 1720. With respect to
their religious principles, as far as is known, they have
always been, and still are, connected with that description
of Christians which in this country bears the name of
Protestant Dissenters, and more particularly with that
denomination of them called *Antipædobaptists*, or Baptists.
But they do not all hold the same doctrinal tenets, either
here or elsewhere, any more than the other descriptions
of Christians. Those to whom I belong (*i.e.*, Robert
Burnside) are styled *Particular* or *Calvinistic* Baptists. Their
creed may be found in the doctrinal articles of the Church of
England, and in the Assembly's Catechism."

* *Vide* "Tea Table Chat, or Religious Allegories told at
the Tea Table in a Seminary for Ladies." By Robert Burnside, 1820.

shire-square; what proved to be his last sermon
having been preached on the following day, at Mill-
yard, Southwark. On retiring from the latter service, the weakness of bodily decay rapidly overtook
him, and he died on the 19th of the month named.
During Burnside's continuance in office, few or no
accessions were made to the number of his followers.
Under the care of his successor, J. B. Shenston, this
little band assembled in Eldon-street, Finsbury,
and some scanty remnants of the denomination are
still to be found in Whitechapel. As an intimate
friend of his predecessor, Shenston published A
Tribute to the Memory of Robert Burnside. This
pamphlet drew forth some cutting animadversions,
which provoked its author to publish a defence of
his Sabbatarian sentiments: The Authority of
Jehovah asserted. " As Mr. Shenston now regards
the fourth commandment as his rule in regard to the
Sabbath," wrote the reviewer of the latter piece in
the *Baptist Magazine*, "He must of course enforce
its requirements on both his congregations. . . .
Did he ever consider that men are not at liberty to
keep two weekly days of rest; that it is as much
their duty to work six days as it is to worship God
on the Sabbath?" Written throughout in a caustic
strain, this article, and also the answer it elicited,
occasioned at the time an interesting stir. Indeed, as
regarded the review, one authority even hazarded the
opinion, that nothing so severe had previously appeared in the *Baptist Magazine*.

During the last summer (1869) some things found their way into the newspapers about an ancient society of Sabbatarians who perpetuate their quaint order by maintaining a scantily-attended meeting in Mill-yard, Goodman's-fields. As no account of these people has been forthcoming the remainder of this article will be devoted to their history.

It is only fair to state that the records of Mill-yard have never been easy of access, and had it not been for the discovery of some manuscript references to the old settlement and its unfashionable surroundings, what follows would not have been written. In treating of the general subject of Sabbatarians in London, the mistake should not be made of confounding these people with the society planted by Bampfield in Pinners' Hall. The two churches represent two distinct denominations. The followers of Bampfield and Stennett were Calvinists; their brethren in Whitechapel were Arminians. The latter are now understood to be in sympathy with Socinus.

In what are somewhat facetiously called the "good old times" the citizens called Whitechapel the Essex-road, their most excellent reason for so naming the thoroughfare being, that this Essex-road formed the highway into Essex. Although not then so crowded with traffic as now, Whitechapel was a main outlet from the capital, and the homes of its substantial inhabitants, lining the broad roadway,

overlooked a never-ending stream of vehicles constantly arriving from or departing for the eastern
counties. The Whitechapel of those days was enlivened by the presence of many hospitable hostelries,
some of which yet remaining are quaintly interesting. Numberless travellers, in these old inns have
experienced a pleasant introduction to London. The
hay-market is an ancient institution, as is likewise
the butchers' quarter. "They carry on a good
trade," observes one trusty chronicler, "and kill
excellent meat, lying so convenient to have their
cattle from Romford Market."

Early in the seventeenth century that Sabbath-
day's disgrace to London, Petticoat-lane, as an attractive semi-rural retreat, had it shady hedgerows
and stately elms. The house wherein John Strype
first saw the light, occupied a court in this lane,
which the inhabitants named after the famous historical collector. The same mansion was also once
occupied by Hans Jacobson, jeweller to James the
First. In the same locality stood the house of the
Spanish ambassador.

But we are concerned with Mill-yard, Goodman's-
fields. Who was Goodman, and when did he flourish? Questions curiosity may have often put without obtaining an answer. Goodman was a yeoman
of the Elizabethan era, whose sleek and healthy cows
grazed on smooth meadows surrounding his farm-
stead, the area of which is now covered by the
murky streets of the Minories. During his youth

the historian Stowe habitually called at Goodman's dairy for a halfpennyworth of milk, the quantity carried away for that humble coin having been three pints or a quart, according to the season. This pleasant inheritance, in natural course, descended to the younger Goodwin, who even at so early a date, and notwithstanding the laws made for repressing the growth of London, found he could secure larger profits by letting land for building than by the prosaic avocation of cow-keeping. In the times we write of the neighbourhood was a favourite retreat for fashionable and substantial people, on which account it appears to have been chosen as the site for a theatre.

Among the manuscripts of the late Walter Wilson, in Dr. Williams's Library, are some particulars of the Mill-yard Sabbatarians. Wilson, as is well known, industriously collected materials for Nonconformist history, and he would have laid posterity under yet greater obligation, had a more liberal encouragement been awarded his endeavours. Whatever he undertook, Wilson accomplished thoroughly, and Dissenters of all denominations will continue to hold his name in grateful remembrance.

The society in Mill-yard is of ancient foundation, its planting dating as far back as the reign of Charles the First. The history of the original meeting-house, which was destroyed by fire, may be possessed by the present occupants; but the people seem to be animated by an hereditary aversion to

13

communicating anything about their ancestors. An example of their caution occurred at the beginning of this present century, when the pastor, then in possession, denied Wilson access to the records. The historian was told that the church had existed for two hundred years, an improbable story, since such a reckoning would extend backward to the days of James the First. " He, *i.e.*, the pastor, is not disposed to communicate any particulars," says the manuscript, " and says there is nothing concerning his church that is at all material for the public to know." But Wilson, not to be completely balked, recovered from various quarters many facts belonging to the annals of these peculiar nonconformists.

Of the pastors of this church who preceded the Commonwealth, if there were such, no accounts survive. The first Arminian Sabbatarian preacher, about whom history breaks silence, is John James, a Whitechapel silk-weaver of humble origin. While of delicate constitution, necessity compelled his toiling to supply more mouths than he could conveniently feed; but notwithstanding he seems to have gladly borne the burden of ministering to some forty followers who congregated in the chapel in Bulstrake-alley. His public discourses proved the preacher to be far gone in enthusiasm if not in fanaticism. From these failings sprang his future troubles. About a year after the Restoration, the authorities learned that the preaching mechanic boldly proclaimed the dreaded, because highly dangerous, tenets of the Fifth Monarchists. Only a few months before, the citizens had been extremely terrified by a band of these mad sectaries, who, with flaunting banner and scriptural watchwords, emerged from their meeting, indiscriminately to shoot or otherwise to maim unoffending passengers, and all by way of inaugurating that theocracy they for long had predicted. We shall scarcely be suspected of unduly sympathising with the Government of the Restoration; but it is idle and unfair to blame that Government for repressing zealots who regarded no life sacred when its sacrifice furthered their extravagant designs, and who read the Bible as a political text-book until they lost sight of the spiritual significance of its peaceful precepts. Ecclesiastical historians, however, follow one upon the other in a well-beaten track, accusing Charles and his administration with persecution in regard to their treatment of these people, meanwhile forgetting how Cromwell—as zealously as ever did the Stuarts—by spies and by the law, shielded himself from zealots whose crotchets were dangerous because subversive of all earthly rule. It is a questionable procedure to paint the worst of kings in hues too black to be believed. Charles, for example, issued a proclamation against these uncompromising enthusiasts; and so far from regarding that document as "a characteristic specimen of Stuart knavery and audacity," as does a late

13*

Baptist historian, it seems to have been demanded by reason and necessity.

The poor weaver, John James, was doubtless sufficiently harmless, and would have pursued a useful way had he not adopted sentiments peculiar to a sect whose strange doings and worse threatenings struck with dismay their brethren of the Baptist denomination, no less than they did all other parties. Nevertheless, we cannot doubt that James had many enemies, whose action may have been prompted by mercenary or revengeful motives. However this may have been, one Tipler, a journeyman pipemaker, volunteered information of the sedition which, as he averred, made part of the weekly teachings, and which were uttered sufficiently loud for the pipemakers to hear while following their daily business. One objection remained in James's favour : Tipler was " a scandalous idle fellow," and no justice would receive his unsupported testimony. A neighbour then appeared to make good the accusation, and the justices supposed they were but consulting public safety by maintaining due surveillance over the assemblings of Bulstrake-alley. On the afternoon of Saturday, the 19th of October, 1661, a magistrate and an attendant visited the service. The magistrate's servant ordered James to leave the pulpit, while accusing him of treason ; and on his unheeding the interruption, the preacher was dragged from his desk amid great uproar.

It now remained to tender to the entire society

the oath of allegiance. The congregation, instead of being allowed to depart, were despatched in companies of seven to a tavern near at hand ; thence, if they declined the oaths, to be remitted to Newgate.

That this was not the first occasion of James's arrest transpires in his examination by the lieutenant of the Tower. The prisoner confessed having previously appeared before their worships, when the bench very civilly treated him, and cautioned him about exercising for the future a more sober circumspection. He admitted his sympathy with the Fifth Monarchists, the Bench meanwhile indulging in some merriment, and exclaiming, " Now we have it from himself." Some things adduced as telling against the pastor were trifling and ludicrous. He had accommodated a lodger, for example, who annoyed the neighbourhood by practising on a war-trumpet, and now it was argued that James used the instrument in question for the purpose of attaining perfection against the day of a contemplated insurrection. Thus the court ended the sitting of that autumn day with —" Take this man, be careful of him, and commit him close prisoner to Newgate."

When the trial came on in Westminster Hall the charge against James had nothing to do with religion. He was arraigned " for preaching maliciously and traitorously against the life and safety of our sovereign lord the king, and against the peace and government of the whole realm." However unjustly he may have suffered, it is only fair to remember that James was not condemned for religious teaching, but for treason against the State. The jury, it has been supposed, were unfavourably biassed, for a mysterious message received by the pastor while confined in the King's Bench before his trial, advised an objection to certain "pickt men" who were summoned. If the prisoner adopted the advice volunteered, and purified the jury-box of the obnoxious persons, there is less reason for supposing he had an unfair trial as trials went in those days. Although condemned to death, James till the last stoutly maintained the reasonableness of his political principles. On the last Sabbath of his life he addressed a small company of friends in the yard of Newgate, when he as bitterly denounced the rule of Cromwell as he did that of other earthly governors.

Some facts belonging to the imprisonment of this remarkable man are humiliating revelations of the England of the Restoration. While the prisons in their loathsomeness resembled literal lazarettos, the delinquencies of prison officials were in terrible keeping with the iniquitous dens they superintended. The prisoners were as miserable as disease and filth could make them. The warders were grasping, heartless, and unsympathising. In the person of James a culprit was delivered into their charge whose woes in his highest prosperity might have provoked the compassion of generous hearts. By hard, prolonged, and painful effort he had barely supplied the wants of his numerous family. But no such considerations affected men grown callous by prison associations. This man, whose drudgery at his daily business usually reacted on his system till it deprived him of sleep, was not used worse than myriads of others, when on being delivered to the officials of Newgate he became a prey to their avarice. They stole his clothes, and worried him out of sums of money, varying from one to sixteen shillings—prisoners' fees, and fees which officials, whether of high or low position, were not ashamed to exact at the expense of starving families.

But another trial—and one infinitely more shocking to posterity—fell to the lot of this unfortunate Fifth Monarchist. On the day preceding his execution the hangman visited his lodging and demanded twenty pounds, "that he might be favourable to him at his death." His victim being too poor to raise so large a sum, this literal "scum of the earth" reduced his desires to ten pounds; and anon, on coming down to five pounds, the wretched bribe-seeker threatened to "torture him exceeding" if so reasonable a consideration were not forthcoming. Stripped of his clothing and robbed of his money, James could only consign himself to the miscreant's mercy.

If in his daily life he had favoured an extravagant enthusiasm, James in his last days displayed much Christian heroism. Seldom has death more completely lost his sting. The charms of life were outshone by the superior lustre of unfading realities.

Visitors thronged his apartment to witness the triumph of his faith. On the last evening of his life he exultingly observed to some friends who were present, "I sup with you to-night; but you would be glad to sup with me to-morrow." Nevertheless, he endured temptations. Dark seasons occurred when the flesh quailed, and when even *his* brave heart trembled before the ordeal through which he was passing. After perspiring with agony through such a season, he would rise, declare the trial past, and express that "joy and peace unutterable" which possessed his spirit.

Even more affecting was the farewell he took of his wife. After Mrs. James had unsuccessfully petitioned the King in person to pardon her husband, they separated in the strongest hope of being eternally reunited; and thus, by the grace of God, were "as willing to part as ever they were to come together."

Then came the end. James was taken from Newgate on Wednesday, the 26th of November, to be dragged on a hurdle to Tyburn, through the mud and water of the sloppy and ill-paved streets. "The sheriff and hangman were so civil to him in his execution as to suffer him to be dead before he was cut down." According to the repulsive custom of the time, his limbs were exhibited on the city gates, and his head exposed on a pole to the denizens of White-chapel. If a misguided, James was at least an honest man; and, if he may not be classed among the martyrs of the Church, for the sake of what was sterling in his character he deserves to be remembered with respect. If not a martyr, he was at least a victim of those stirring times in which his lot was cast.*

John Savage, who died in 1726, presided for a great number of years over these Sabbatarians. During his pastorate the removal from Bulstrake-alley to Mill-yard occurred. This divine is stated to have been the grandfather of Dr. Savage.

Savage enjoyed the assistance of an able lecturer in the person of John Maulden, who, prior to the Revolution, keenly suffered from steadfastly adhering to the principles of Nonconformity. Refusing to discontinue preaching, and being unable to pay the ruinous fines of twenty pounds a month, he was arrested and thrown into Clerkenwell gaol, his goods, meanwhile, being sold by his persecutors. At Clerkenwell he passed his days among common felons, but remaining himself uncontaminated, he became to his rough associates a rare exemplar of Christian patience. His history shows that even the wretched government of the Stuarts could experience momentary shame at the scandal in-

* " The Speech and Declaration of John James, a weaver in the pressyard at Newgate, on Sunday last, to the Fifth Monarchists, &c., 1661." " A Narrative of the apprehending, commitment and execution of John James, who suffered at Tiburne, November the 26th, 1661, &c." See also the Calendars of State Papers, Domestic Series, 1661; and Crosby's History of the English Baptists.

separably connected with the incarceration in noisome dungeons of men whom God had appointed to dispense His gospel. Thus it happened in the case of Maulden and others that criminals' quarters were exchanged for more comfortable accommodation. On regaining his liberty Maulden settled with the Baptists of East Smithfield, who, on account of the dangers attending the holding of public services, assembled in private households. After the Revolution this society erected a chapel in Goodman's-fields. The pastor, however, did not for long share this freedom and prosperity, for, accepting office under John Savage, he continued with the Sabbatarians till released by death in 1714. He is the author of several published pieces.

Robert Cornwaite, the successor of Savage, was a native of Bolton, and born in 1696. His father dying early, and the family being large, Robert contributed to their support by establishing a school. He also proved his capacity to think for himself by setting his kindred the example of seceding from the National Church in favour of Presbyterianism, and thence, by another step, he joined the Baptists. On assuming pastoral responsibilities he stayed with his first charge at Boston about twelve months. The encouragement he met with to work among Dissenters was not of the warmest kind, and, had not conscience dictated his principles, his opportunities were ample to have retreated from an unattractive path into the more comfortable parterre of the

Anglican Church. He appears to have shown a changeable temperament, but after once forming his opinions he would zealously defend them. On settling in London he became attracted by, and then interested in, the controversy regarding the Sabbath, ' the result being his conversion to the sentiments of the Sabbatarians. Succeeding in 1726 at Mill-yard, he there laboured till his death. He was a man of great literary activity, and wrote in defence of the distinguishing tenet of his denomination, having been honoured by the opposition of Samuel Wright and Caleb Fleming. "His death was sudden, but previously to it he had expressed a complete and absolute resignation with respect to the length and shortness of his life." Of one Peter Russell, an assistant of Cornwaite, and who was stationed over this church in 1730, no memorials have survived.*

Daniel Noble was set apart for the ministry at Mill-yard in the autumn of 1755, and remained till his death in 1783, meantime holding another charge at Barbican.

Noble was born at Whitechapel in 1729. After being grounded in grammar learning by a local tutor, the pastor Cornwaite directed his education. He appears to have been no ordinary school-boy, for he differed from his companions in so far, that he loved to burden his memory with longer lessons than either his elders or prudence prescribed. His

* Daniel Noble's Sermon on the death of R. Cornwaite; Protestant Dissenters' Magazine, vol. vi.

strange predilections would draw from his tutor the
impatient exclamation, "Get you gone; have I no
other boys to hear but you?" From his childhood
upward, Noble enjoyed a training worthy of his
abilities, his parents from the first having intended
him for the Nonconformist ministry. After passing
his boyhood in London, he removed to Kendal, and
studied under Dr. Rotheram, thence removing to
Glasgow University. On returning to London in
1752, he succeeded in due course at Mill-yard, and
also established a school at Peckham. But teaching
and divinity were not the only objects of Noble's
pursuit. Loving literary activity, his experience in
authorship commenced in his sixteenth year, or in
1745, when he wrote against the Young Pretender
in a Letter to the People of England. In maturer
years he started a periodical called The Library,
which only lived till its thirteenth issue. Dr.
Jeffreys, who survived Noble about three days,
prepared a funeral sermon for his friend, but died
before he could deliver it; and, although he pro-
nounces a high eulogy on his character, it is not
more extravagant than justice demanded. That he
was able and learned, Noble's lifework is sufficient
proof. He may also have been eccentric; for
whether so or not he called his children by eccentric
names, his three daughters having been distinguished
one from the other by Experience, Eusebia, and Serena.*

* Dr. Jeffreys' Sermon on the death of Daniel Noble;
Protestant Dissenters' Magazine, vol. v.

William Slater succeeded Noble, and died in August 1719. He was followed by his grandson W. H. Black. The church at Mill-yard still exists; but any further allusion to its modern upholders will not be expected in this place.

We must take our farewell of the Sabbatarian Baptists. On the formation of Bampfield's Society in March, 1675, they had a meeting-place in the old chapel at Devonshire-square. Thence they removed to Pinners' Hall; thence to Broad-street; thence to Curriers' Hall, Cripplegate; thence to Red-cross-street, and so back again to Devonshire-square. From Devonshire-square we trace them to Finsbury, there to lose sight of them, as we are unable to identify them with the little church in Whitechapel.

The regard these people showed for the seventh day entailed a self-denial too burdensome, or at the least, an inconvenience too oft repeated, to allow of their attracting adherents in any considerable numbers after the subsiding of Puritan enthusiasm. That they could act with straightforward conscientiousness, it were easy to prove; since to adduce but one example, the father of Burnside on embracing Sabbatarian views, unhesitatingly sacrificed a lucrative business to principle. Thus, while unable to sympathise with them in all things, we honour the memory of these singular people as the memory of good Christians and honest citizens deserves to be honoured; and gladly add this

chapter of their history to our annals of Nonconformity in London.*

* From time immemorial it has been customary with those
observing the seventh to allow others to assemble in their
chapels on the first day. In the year 1700 the Presbyterians
settled at Mill-yard. Their pastor was Samuel Harris,
formerly of Canterbury, who seceded from a charge
at Wapping in consequence of some change of sentiment,
the nature of which we do not understand. According to
Wilson's manuscript he proved an acceptable preacher, and,
as a Calvinist, divided with the Subscribers at Salters'
Hall in 1719. As Harris grew in years, his secluded habits
and singular bearing lost him many friends and led to the
decrease of the congregation. He had several lecturers, but
"does not appear to have agreed with any of them," says
Wilson. The assistants alluded to were John Lewis, John
Shuttlewood, Samuel Stockwell, and another of the name of
Clark. The first retired from a meeting in Ropemakers'-
alley, in consequence of disagreeing with his people. The
second served at Mill-yard till 1711. The third, after coming to a misunderstanding with his superior, settled at
Redcross-street. The fourth came from Potter's Pury, and
retired from the ministry in 1730. Harris was succeeded by
Joseph Waite, formerly of Saffron Walden and Romford.
" When he came to London he was advanced in years, and
yet a preacher of no small courage and boldness." Without
any pretensions to scholarship or culture, he kept up the
congregation. In or about 1741, the Presbyterians left Mill-
yard and the chapel was occupied on the first day by a
society of Baptists, who paid £10 annually for the accommodation. These enjoyed sufficient prosperity to remove twenty-
two years later into premises of their own in Church-street
Whitechapel. Mathew Rudmall, who came from a neighbouring chapel in Virginia-street, held the pastorate till his
death in 1756. He was followed by John Brittain, an

uneducated tradesman. After itinerating for a time about
the south of London he was regularly ordained. He laboured
very zealously by ministering to his own large congregation,
and by setting up two lectureships which he partly sustained.
His election at Mill-yard occasioned division; but notwithstanding some discontent he had numerous followers, being
in fact "extremely popular." An anecdote told of Brittain
strikingly shows how deficient in common knowledge even
popular ministers might be in the Georgian era. One day
Brittain and a friend crossed Moorfields for the purpose of
hearing the great orator, who in those days preached in the
Tabernacle, named after him. An expression in Whitfield's
sermon—"Some people are as ignorant of religion as they
are of algebra"—supplied a topic of conversation during the
walk home to dinner. "Aye," enquired Brittain, with
laudible curiosity, "what language *is* algebra?"

We may also notice, "A small society of Particular Baptists," who favoured Mill-yard with their presence. John Mat-
lock, "not a very honourable character," preached here. He
left for America, and we lose sight of him. Thomas Thomas, a
native of Aberdeen, was also connected with this society.
He studied at Bristol under Hugh and Caleb Evans. Leaving college in 1780, he settled at Pershore, there to be
rendered uncomfortable by disputes and dissatisfaction. On
visiting London, in 1787, he settled at Mill-yard, where he
stayed till his death in 1808. During his pastorate the chapel
was destroyed by fire and rebuilt, but remained without its
first day frequenters till August 1805, when the Independents reopened the first day services.

Chapter VI.

BURY STREET, SAINT MARY AXE.

Probably few only of the sightseers who occasionally spend a week in London, are ever found turning down Bury-street, Saint Mary Axe, to visit the quaint chapel, which through so many years of interest was associated with the honoured name of Watts. Nevertheless, in the locality specified the sanctuary may be found, but degenerated into a merchant's wareroom. The venerable pile will by no means strike its visitors as being ornamental. The plainest of brick walls with openings for the plainest of leaded windows, were what our chapel-building fathers thought proper for a house of prayer. Their chapels, moreover, were so erected from choice rather than necessity, or were so in numbers of instances; for the society under notice was one of the richest in London of the Independent regimen.

As we walk up this London street, many things belonging to the past will flit across the memory. In the olden time, when Popery was dominant, the abbots of Edmund's-bury inherited a town residence in this vicinity. Prior to the confiscation of the monasteries, at the dawn of the Reformation, the site of Bury-street meeting-house was occupied by the Priory of the Holy Trinity, founded by Matilda, Queen of Henry the First. After the King had confirmed the gift, the house became extremely wealthy, and consequently strongly provoked the initiatory attack, when in 1531, Henry the Eighth decided on demolition. He who chiefly benefited by the unfortunate monks' change of fortune was Sir Thomas Audley, successively Speaker of the House of Commons, and Lord Chancellor. This gentleman came into possession of the estate, and after taking down a portion of the mansion, he converted the remainder into his town residence, and there died during the reign of Mary. Holbein the painter likewise died of plague in this house, in 1554, after having enjoyed the patronage of Henry the Eighth, and that of the Norfolk family. Henry had delighted to honour the artist; for a king, here-marked, could in a single day make twenty nobles, but never a single artist. The daughter of Sir Thomas Audley married one of the Howards, and after the dukedom of Norfolk, therefore, one part of the neighbourhood we are concerned with is called Duke's-place. It was in the days of Queen Anne that the dissenting congregation, then assembling on Sabbath afternoons at Pinners' Hall, prevailed on one Charles Great to lease them a portion of his garden at a ground-rent of twenty pounds,

14

upon which site they erected the chapel still extant.

During the reign of William the Third the congregation assembled at a private house in Mark-lane, but in the summer of 1704 they removed to Pinners' Hall. Four years later the building in Bury-street was provided at a cost of £650. This chapel, which in happier days had three galleries, was opened by Thomas Bradbury, in October 1708. At that date the congregation ranked highly among Nonconformists, many of its members having belonged to families of title or distinction.

The founder of this important church was Joseph Caryl, the ejected minister of St. Simon Magnus, London-bridge. He was born in 1602, and trained at Oxford University. His descent was genteel, and to the polished manners of good breeding, he added the art and subtlety of the accomplished disputant. In his twenty-fifth year, when national troubles loomed in the distance, Caryl took holy orders, and commenced his pulpit exercises in the vicinity of Exeter College. As he grew in years the preacher became "puritanically inclined," but obtained the lectureship at Lincoln's-inn. Amid the social and political confusion engendered by the Civil Wars, Caryl continued an uncompromising adherent to the cause of Freedom; and accordingly he frequently officiated before the Long Parliament. About this conjuncture he obtained the living of St. Simon Magnus, and in that situation found employment on several state occasions. He attended the commissioners at Newcastle, who there waited on Charles the First, in 1646. In the Athenæ Oxonienses we are entertained with an anecdote concerning this journey. The King, as all know, treated Presbyters themselves with high contempt, as he did their preaching. He one day refused to delay his dinner while one of them invoked a blessing. During their stay at Holmby House, in Northamptonshire, Caryl and his companion, Stephen Marshall, offered to officiate before his Majesty, but were of course denied the honour. The King, it seems, also preferred saying grace himself—a piece of presumption which Marshal once thought well to rebuke :— "While he was long in forming his chaps, as the manner was among the saints, and making ugly faces, his Majesty said grace himself, and was fallen on his meat, and had eaten up some part of his dinner before Marshall had ended the blessing." Caryl, Wood has deigned to inform us, "was not so impudent." He likewise attended the King at Newport, in the Isle of Wight, and was appointed to the melancholy office of chaplain on the fatal 30th January, 1649 ; but his services were declined, as were also those of his colleague, Philip Nye.

During the Commonwealth, Caryl rose into high favour, as his numerous printed sermons preached before the Parliament on special occasions testify. In 1650 he attended Cromwell in the Scottish campaign, and after returning to London was ap-

14*

pointed a ministerial Trier. Through those momentous
years Caryl may too often have descended from his
high vocation to political interference, but his every-
day life never ceased to discover the laborious and
popular minister. The near prospect of the Stuarts'
return, however, prompted a renewal of his political
activity ; yet, while he conferred with Monk on the
state of the nation, we do not find that he opposed
the King's restoration. After the consummation of
the last-named event, Caryl retired to his charge of
St. Simon Magnus, of which he was finally deprived
by the Act of Uniformity.

The daily life of this old divine is said to have
been a fair acting out of his sermons. Of his literary
abilities and enormous industry he has left us the
most substantial evidences ; indeed, his stupendous
Exposition of the Book of Job, in twelve volumes
quarto, is one of the marvels of English literature.
Probably only the author and the abridger ever
perused this book throughout, which since the day
of its being ushered into the world has resisted the
witticism of ironical pleasantry. Nevertheless, this
Exposition is a great work, and its intrinsic worth
is fitly represented by its material bulk. It is the
best commentary extant on the patience of Job, and
a complete study of it will be found "a very sufficient exercise for the virtue of patience, which it
was chiefly intended to inculcate and improve."
Only little in addition to the above can be told of
this able Puritan. He died at his house in Bury-

street, in February, 1672, and several published
poems commemorate his departure. At the crisis
of death the pastor requested his friends to withdraw, so that his soul might pass away in solitude.
He then raised his hands, apparently to signalise his
triumphant departure. *

Another learned divine and able preacher connected with this society was William Bearman, the
ejected minister of St. Thomas's, Southwark. After
relinquishing his cure he retired to Hoxton-square
—a classical spot to Nonconformists. Being possessed of considerable wealth, he escaped that ordeal
of poverty which so heavily pressed upon others.
His naturally benevolent disposition prompted him
to become his own almoner. Eight almshouses were
erected and endowed in the rear of his residence.
Through a wicket-gate, opening from his private
grounds, this benefactor was wont to pass into a
kind of little chapel, where he habitually met his
pensioners, either to advise with them or to impart
religious instruction. The topographist Maitland,
rather sneeringly refers to this institution, because
the endownent, as he supposed, consisted merely of
a quantity of coals; but had further enquiry been
made he would have discovered an endowment in
money. Thus Bearman in life manifested extraordinary benevolence, and at death bequeathed the

* Athenæ Oxonienses; Nonconformists' Memorial;
Calamy's Account and Continuation; Wilson's Dissenting
Churches.

whole of his estate for the benefit of Nonconformity.*

The year 1673 was a gloomy era in the annals of Nonconformity. It witnessed the revocation of that famous Indulgence which, only a few months prior, the King had proclaimed, but the rescinding of which the Londoners celebrated with shoutings and bonfires. In this year, while the sun of that great Puritan author, Joseph Caryl, was setting, his people in Leadenhall-street were looking towards a still brighter luminary of the Christian Church, John Owen, or as his admirers with some reason style him, the "prince of modern divines."

Considering of whom he wrote, the account of Owen by Anthony Wood, is probably as wilful a piece of historical slander as the range of literature affords. He was a very consistent maintainer of the dogma, that kings are incapable of error, and are therefore not to be resisted. Our unamiable historian is so absurdly loyal, that he will not even deign to allow a distinction between wanton rebellion and a reasonable opposition to tyranny. At random, he accuses persons of perjury whose action in life was in strict accordance with the requirements of honesty and patriotism. By acting on Wood's morality, those fellows of universities who swore allegiance to Charles, must have proved themselves traitors to the State had they observed the strict letter of their

* Calamy's Account; Maitland's History of London; Wilson's History of the Dissenting Churches.

oath. Adherence to a king who himself becomes recklessly lawless, may not be extolled as loyalty.

The above remarks have been suggested by the malicious spleen of Anthony Wood, as discovered in his article on Dr Owen, in the Athenæ Oxonienses. It is perfectly obvious to those who are correctly acquainted with the story of his life, that Owen's conduct in espousing the popular cause, was conscientious, reasonable, and patriotic.

The family of Owen lays claim to some ancient importance in the Principality of Wales, although the father of our subject was an Oxfordshire schoolmaster, and only occupied an humble station. He was sufficiently fortunate, however, to get installed into the vicarage of Steadham, in the county named, and in that village his son John was born in 1616.

John's earliest tutor was Edward Sylvester, who during the reign of the first James, grounded youths in grammar learning in the parish of All Saints, Oxford. Having progressed through the curriculum of this old schoolmaster, the young scholar matriculated at Queen's College, and while there, proved himself possessed of more industry than prudence by frequently allowing himself but four hours' sleep.

At this early date his assiduous application was not prompted by religious enthusiasm. He was animated by no purer motives than those which are commonly found to urge on ambitious youth to fame and fortune. To young Owen's unformed judgment, the arena of politics wore a face as attractive as the fairer field of theology.

Having made sufficient progress in his studies, Owen at length decided for the Christian ministry, and took orders as prescribed by the *régime* of the Established Church. It is yet doubtful if Owen would ever have made a good Anglican, even had he lived in more peaceful times. Before he completed his university course, the lad was shocked by the procedure of Laud, who, with that dominant spirit so characteristic of his nature, introduced into colleges many strange innovations, provoking the more conscientious students to revolt, although others, less scrupulous, conformed to the times. Because conscience forbade compliance, Owen, was pointed at as a Puritan, and the annoyances of the situation ultimately obliged him to resign his fellowship. After leaving Oxford he was for a time enveloped in the gloomy clouds of religious doubt. It was about this conjuncture, that he subscribed to the Covenant, and so far honoured the Presbyterian order. His religious principles were probably fixed at an early date; and from the original basis of his faith he does not appear to have swerved when he declared for Independency. As already explained, when civil war broke out, he zealously espoused the cause of the Parliament. It was natural and orderly that such a divine should rise to high favour while Cromwell was in the ascendant. There is no ground for doubting the purity of those motives which prompted

him to follow the path described, for thereby Owen
forfeited an estate from his uncle, which as a
" Loyalist" he would have inherited.

On removing to London, Owen made his home
in Charterhouse-square. At this date his confidence
in Christ had not carried him to that triumphant
peace subsequently possessed, and, under Providence,
he became indebted to an unknown friend for the
dispelling of his prevailing gloom. He strolled
away one Sabbath morning into Aldermanbury,
thinking to hear the Puritan rector, Edmund
Calamy. On that particular day a stranger preached,
whom Owen could never afterwards discover, and
whose name he could not even learn. That sermon
marked a turning-point in the life of our divine, by
inaugurating a reign of peace in his soul.

The alarm of discord between King and Parliament was now distracting the nation; and one of
Owen's vast ability was certain greatly to influence
whichever side he supported, and to be a general
favourite with his compeers of corresponding sentiment. Accordingly when, in 1642, he published
the Display of Arminianism, that work became
instrumental in advancing the author to the living
of Fordham, in Essex. The vicar of Fordham had
lately been sequestered by the Committee of Inspec-
tion; and when the superseded pastor died, another
person was installed into the vicarage, so that Owen,
in consequence, transferred himself to " that nest of
faction called Coggeshall." Coggeshall, therefore,

traces back to Owen its heritage of Nonconformity. How effectually the pastor laboured, the
extensive congregation he raised abundantly testified : the weekly auditory numbered two thousand
persons.

Owen was frequently appointed to preach before
the Parliament; and it was after one of these
exercises, in 1646, that he first encountered
Cromwell. "Sir," cried the lieutenant-general,
"you are the person I must be acquainted with."
"That," returned the divine, with ready wit, "will be
more to my advantage than yours." The friendship,
thus auspiciously begun, between these remarkable
men, continued unruffled till the Protector's death.
When Cromwell entered on his campaign in Ireland
he insisted on having the company of Owen. The
latter hesitated, as he cast towards Coggeshall some
looks of lingering fondness, and thought how unwill-
ingly his people would part with him. A temporary
separation, however, of a year and a half, seems only
to have strengthened their bond of union. When
his term of office expired Owen gladly re-embarked
for England and Coggeshall, where his people welcomed him with joyful manifestations. So great,
indeed, was Cromwell's admiration of Owen, that
the general was apparently averse from travelling
without the divine. The latter was requested to
attend the forces ordered into Scotland, and on discovering a reluctance again to forsake his people, an
order of Parliament compelled both him and Caryl to

assume the chaplaincy. After a painful absence of several months the pastor returned to Coggeshall.

In the spring of 1651 the eminent services of Owen were recognised by his being presented with the deanery of Christ Church, Oxford. By delegation, moreover, from Oliver Cromwell, he discharged the duties of the chancellorship, and was eventually elected vice-chancellor. During a short period the Doctor even sat in Parliament as the University member. Anthony Wood has bequeathed us a ludicrous caricature of this grave senator, author and preacher, in a description of him as he appeared about the streets of Oxford during those prosperous years. He cocked his hat, we are told, and powdered his hair, wore Spanish-leather boots with lawn tops and gaudy ribbons, by which means he aped the mien of younger coxcombs. We are further informed, *en passant*, by this audacious libeller, that Owen was a perjured time-server, a hypocrite, and a blasphemer. Such a lying farrago can scarcely produce other effect than that of awakening for its concocter our contemptuous derision. However fantastically Owen may have arrayed himself, while in the University city he was assuredly distinguished by a large-hearted charity which commanded the esteem of other denominations.

At Oxford, Owen led a laborious life both as regards preaching and writing. He thus progressed till 1657, and in that year Richard Cromwell deprived him of the vice-chancellorship. Subse-

quently, when this same Richard rose to his brief
protectorate, " the Doctor," says Calamy, " was cast
out of his deanery;" but, according to Wood, " St.
Mary's pulpit was cleared of him." Owen was a
victim, it would seem, of Presbyterian influence. He
is reported by the Oxford historian to have exclaimed,
" I have built seats at St. Mary's, let the Doctor find
auditors ; for I will preach at St. Peter's-in-the-
East." The matter resolves itself into this plain
truth : Owen decided on preaching elsewhere, and
his congregation chose to follow him.*

* What may be termed the minutiæ of Owen's diversified
career, plainly reveals the narrow-mindedness and petty
jealousy of the Anglican party during the intoxication of
their regained ascendancy. In 1662, for example, a Fran-
ciscan monk issued a work in which he extolled the Roman
communion as the only refuge of peace from the religious
distractions of the times. Somewhat alarmed at this book's
rapid dissemination, his friends prevailed upon Owen to produce an answer. This the Doctor eventually accomplished,
but the friar sent back an angry rejoinder. To this Owen
again replied. While in manuscript, the last-named piece was
laid before the licensing bishops, who were staggered by two
prominent blemishes, e.g., the apostle Peter throughout this
work was mentioned as *Peter* simply without the prefix of
Saint ; and the author, moreover, further endeavoured to demonstrate that the great apostle named was never at Rome.
The Secretary of State, however, peremptorily interfered, or
otherwise, by such contemptible quibbles as these would the
ecclesiastical noodles of the Restoration have suppressed
the offspring of a master mind. Another churchman, in his
imagined superiority, refused to concede to Owen the title of
Reverend. " I do give him notice," wrote the Doctor, " that

Dr. Owen made a principal figure at the Savoy Conference. His sun of prosperity was clouded for the time by the removal of his great patron, Cromwell. The Doctor, in consequence, retired from Oxford and settled at Stadham, his native town, where he possessed an estate. In this retirement he laboured on for the extension of Christian truth, till, at the Restoration, the county militia finally dispersed his congregation. It appears from sundry documents among the State Papers, and particularly from a letter by Dr. Lamplough, dated Oxford, January, 1661, that the excesses of Venner in London were made an excuse for oppressing Dissenters in provincial districts. The soldiers were busily employed each Sabbath morning in breaking up the worshipping assemblies of Independents, Baptists, and Quakers, not a few of whom found temporary homes in prison cells. * Even the house of Owen was not sacred against the attacks of these fanatical cavaliers, who were then striving to get

I have very little valued it since I have considered the saying ┼ of Luther, *Religion was never endangered, except among the most reverends.*"

* Intelligence reached Whitechapel from Plymouth, that ˎ the authorities there were on the watch against an expected insurrection of the Baptists, who had for a pastor the future martyr, Abraham Cheare. Forty or more of the church members were simultaneously seized and imprisoned, because they refused to bind themselves not to take up arms against the Government. *Vide Calendars of State Papers*, 1661 *to* 1664, etc.

the Presbyters included in the order against conventicles. Meanwhile, our author was slandered by
lying informers, who represented at Whitehall that
he and Dr. Goodwin, especially, were dangerous.
persons. The chief ground for supposing them such
was their refusal to wear the surplice, although in
former times they had been wont to "wear velvet
cassocks, and receive from five to seven hundred a
year." Fortunately, Owen found a powerful protector in the Earl of Oxford : thus, while true bills.
were issued against him for convening unlawful
assemblies, he is not found to have suffered any
particular injury. Nevertheless, he sought an
asylum in London, where, in laborious seclusion, he
applied himself to literature, and, as opportunities
were offered, to preaching. Even in those days of
gloomy misgiving the Government did not entirely
neglect him. Clarendon remained his friend; and
had Owen chosen to conform he might have inherited rich preferment. At or about this con-
jecture, while religious troubles were thickening
around, Owen was looking towards the American
shore, or the plains of Holland ; for at either destination his services were eagerly sought, and substantial rewards in return were offered. " The wind,"
says Anthony Wood, " was never in a right point for
a voyage."

After the desolation of London by fire and death,
when Dissent enjoyed a term of comparative freedom,
Owen gathered a congregation in the city which

many persons of distinction supported and attended.
A fierce spirit of persecution was again awakened in
1670, and, in that year, a weighty paper written by
Owen was laid before the House of Lords. The
author's eloquent arguments and appeals were not sufficient to obstruct the progress of the infamous Conventicle Act. Then came days of anguish to many little
able to bear the ordeal. The Indulgence of 1672
allowed a short-lived respite, which extended into
the following year; and, amid the gloomy trouble
which came with its revocation, Owen succeeded
Caryl, at the old meeting-house in Leadenhall-
street.

Such was the amiable mien of our divine, that
numbers among the nobility deemed themselves
honoured by sharing his friendship. Even the king
and the "marble-hearted" James both professed for
him a generous esteem. On a certain day, during
a visit to Tunbridge Wells, Charles, it is said,
favoured Owen with an interview, in the course of
which he expressed a predilection for freedom of
worship; and, apparently, while repenting for the
moment of wrongs inflicted, handed his visitor a
thousand guineas for distribution among the suffering Dissenters. Thus this great divine, in his
own immediate circle, and far beyond it, was immensely popular. He occasionally found some
pleasurable days of relaxation at the seat of Lord
Wharton, of Woburn, a nobleman, who, by a Christian hospitality, loved to gladden the hearts of Non-

conformist fugitives. Throughout the Protestant world of the Continent the fame of Owen, if possible, was even more extraordinary than in England. Numbers of scholars, who with delightful profit had perused his Latin pieces, commenced grappling with the difficulties of English grammar, in order to achieve the power of studying Owen in his native language. Others, prompted by even higher enthusiasm, crossed the sea, visited the pastor, and doubtless returned to their native marshes with emotions of elated satisfaction.

Through one period of his busy and eventful life Owen resided at Kensington. His means were sufficiently easy to allow of his keeping a coach, in which he was more than once stopped on the highway by agents of the Government—a fact which illustrates the roughness of these times. In his sixtieth year the Doctor was bereaved of his wife. He again married, having for his second companion a rich young widow, with whom he retired to Ealing, a pleasant vicinity, where, according to Wood, he "took all occasions to enjoy all the comfortable importances of this life."

Thus lived John Owen, and he died at length in his sixty-seventh year, in August, 1683. After taking into account his incomparable qualifications of intellect and advantages of person, his mastery over his passions, his persevering industry, his tolerant spirit, and, more than all, his genuine piety, vast learning, and abundant works—now the inheritance of the church—we may cordially subscribe an opinion another has pronounced, that Owen is at once the Prince, the Oracle, the METROPOLITAN of Independency.*

Among the early lecturers of this society appears the name of that arch plotter Robert Ferguson. The historian Echard has bequeathed us a word portrait of this old Presbyterian: "A tall, lean man, dark brown hair, a great Roman nose, thin jaw'd, bent in face, speaks in the Scotch tone, a sharp piercing eye, stoops a little in the shoulders, he hath a shuffling gait that differs from all men, wears his periwig over his eyes, about forty-five years of age." Ferguson was ejected by the Act of Uniformity from the living of Godsmersham, Kent. On leaving his cure he immediately commenced a system of plotting which, till the period of his death, fifty-two years later, he never wholly relinquished. The Government determined on securing him, and, accordingly, directions were transmitted from Whitehall for assisting the agents in accomplishing their object. This occurred in January, 1662–3, at which time he was supposed to be one of Dr. Calamy's pensioners; for the late Aldermanbury pastor, so people said, had funds entrusted to him wherewith to

* The authorities to which I am principally indebted for the facts of Owen's life are—A. Wood, in his Athenæ Oxonienses; the Calendars of State Papers, Domestic Series, Charles II; Granger's Biographical History of England ; Wilson's History of the Dissenting Churches, etc.

15

relieve Nonconformist fugitives.   Be this as it may,
Ferguson was "committed close prisoner to the
gate-house for treasonable practices."   After several
weeks' confinement the prisoner petitioned for "examination or speedy trial," and also that his relatives
might be permitted to carry him supplies.   He had
never done aught, he averred, to injure the King's
interest, and therefore he was released on giving
bail for £300, to return to his home at Tottenham
High-cross.

   Although Ferguson had a chief hand in the Rye
House Plot, his action was apparently winked at by
the Government, till many considered him a Court
spy.   He likewise superintended a secret press, and
he loved to have it supposed that he himself composed what he so prodigally dispersed, such was his
vanity, being "a very empty man."   During the
period of his service under Doctor Owen, Ferguson
lived at Islington, where he conducted an academy,
but at length his numerous plottings against those
in power brought him into imminent danger, and
he fled the country.   While a fugitive he won the
esteem of Shaftesbury and his party.   His next
exploit was to return to England as a zealous promoter of Monmouth's ill-fated expedition.   Ferguson
wrote the absurd manifesto put forth by that unfortunate duke, who during his last moments complained of the villainy of his late accomplice.   After
this rising was subdued, Ferguson contrived to escape
to Holland.   He again appeared in England, in

1688, among the supporters of William of Orange, and he was amply rewarded for his services by the new Government. Plotting being his natural element, he felt constrained to join the Jacobite faction. This extraordinary character died in 1714, and in neglected obscurity. Among his Nonconformist contemporaries he bore a disreputable character. Neither Burnet nor Calamy regarded him as anything better than a political renegade, a time-server, and a hypocrite.*

David Clarkson was another of that noble band who sacrificed comfort and even income for conscience sake. On relinquishing his pulpit at Mortlake, in Surrey, in 1662, this staunch old Independent retired into studious solitude—a life towards which his predilections inclined. His seclusion, however, was interrupted, in 1686, by his acceptance of the lectureship under Dr. Owen. In the double capacity of author and preacher, Clarkson was successful and industrious. He had this favourite saying, " The blood of the soul runs out in wasted time." Both Owen and Baxter have portrayed his character, but neither has supplied any details of the pastor's labours, and, in consequence, scarcely anything is known respecting him. Baxter tells us

* Calendar of State Papers, Domestic Series, 1662-3; Oldmoxon's, Echard's and Macaulay's Histories of England; Calamy's Account and Continuation; Grey's Secret History of the Rye House Plot; Sprat's True Account; Burnet's History of His own Time, &c.

he was "a divine of extraordinary worth, for solid judgment, healing moderate principles, acquaintance with the Fathers, great ministerial abilities, and a godly upright life."

As master of Clare Hall, Cambridge, Clarkson in his younger days instructed the youthful Tillotson. It is much to be regretted that only such fragmentary memorials are procurable of one who ranked so highly in his day as a writer and pulpit orator—a celebrity which time has scarcely diminished. Ten years after our author's decease his works were collected in folio—" Printed for Thomas Parkhurst at the Bible and Three Crowns, at the lower end of Cheapside." The only engraved portrait extant of this author is the one accompanying this edition. The countenance is full, and pleasingly intelligent, and from beneath a close-fitting cap his abundant ringlets reach to the shoulders. A new edition of Clarkson's writings has been issued, with a memoir by Dr. Miller, who, however, has not been able to add anything new to the few particulars already known of his subject, who died in 1686.*

Another assistant of Dr. Owen, Isaac Loeffs—a fellow of Peter-house, Cambridge—was the ejected minister of Shenley, Hertfordshire. He settled in London, and accepted a lectureship at St. Simon

* Calamy's Account and Continuation; Clarkson's Works, ed. 1696 ; Ditto, Nichol's Puritan Divines ; Granger's Biog. Hist. of Eng.; Wilson's History of the Dissenting Churches.

Magnus, of which the Act of Uniformity deprived him. His connection with this church then commenced, and eventually he succeeded Clarkson in the pastorate, but only survived till July, 1689.

Isaac Chauncy, for convenience' sake, may be numbered seventh among the early pastors of this society. He was the ejected minister of Woodborough, in Wiltshire. His father, in the days of the first Charles, was minister at Ware. He refused to read the Book of Sports, and on that account provoked the opposition of Laud. Being of a timid disposition, the vicar quailed before his persecutors when confronting them in the Court of High Commission, and consequently confessed to having been in error in regard to certain matters— as kneeling at the altar, &c.—which surrender of principle he so bitterly bemoaned that he withdrew to New England, and even expressed repentance in his will. He died in 1671, leaving six sons, for whom he chose Hebrew names. Isaac, our present subject, studied medicine and divinity in an academy conducted by his father, and at an English university. The family predilections were for the Independent order ; and after being deprived of his cure by the Act of Uniformity, Isaac is found to have settled at Andover. While there persecution obliged him to relinquish his pastorate and to follow the practice of medicine. When, in 1687, the political atmosphere showed signs of clearing, and the opposition to Dissent became relaxed, Chauncy associated himself with the church in Mark-lane. The four-teen years of his pastorate which followed were years of discouragement and decline, and he, therefore, resigned his charge in March, 1701. As a preacher he was never popular, having too frequently dwelt on themes which his people deemed unsuitable to their necessities. He was likewise a zealous de-fender of Dr. Crisp, and attacked with some asperity the opinions of Dr. Williams, the founder of the library in Redcross-street.

An assistant of Dr. Chauncy was Edward Terry, the ejected minister of Great Greenford, Middlesex. Among other adventures, the father of this divine spent two years at the Court of the great Mogul. His son, with whom we are now concerned, studied at Oxford, and for a time was engaged as a tutor in that town. In the year preceding the Bartholomew ejectment he succeeded to his father's sphere, but how he spent his time between the secession of 1662 and the Revolution is not known. In 1688 he accepted a lectureship under Dr. Chauncy, and remained at his post until disabled by infirmity. He died at a good old age in March, 1716, after a long afflicting confinement.*

The old town of Southampton, or Suth-Hamtun, as the Saxons, who founded the castle, called it, is remarkable on account of these following events :—

* Athenæ Oxonienses; Granger's Biog. Hist. of Eng.; Calamy's Account and Continuation; Nonconformists' Memorial; Wilson's Dissenting Churches.

It was there Canute rebuked his flatterers; and it was there that Isaac Watts was born in July, 1674.

The family of Watts was highly respectable, and figured among the more considerable sufferers for conscience' sake amid the abounding persecution of the Restoration. Thomas Watts, the poet's grandfather, in the capacity of a naval captain, was an active servant of the Commonwealth Government; and by his comrades was generally respected as a man of knowledge and taste. An anecdote is told which strikingly illustrates the old sailor's bravery under any dangerous emergency. During his sojourn in the East Indies he one day found himself pursued by a tiger. Being near a river he ran into the stream—an example immediately followed by the ferocious enemy. A close encounter ensued, in which Watts secured the victory by seizing the animal's head and forcing it under water till life was extinct. This veteran eventually lost his life by the explosion of his vessel while engaged in the war against Holland. His wife long survived him, and constantly manifested a laudable desire for the weal of her grandson Isaac; and the latter, till the verge of life, held her memory in just veneration.

Isaac Watts, the poet's father, was a Southampton schoolmaster of established repute, and the fame of his attainments and aptness to communicate knowledge had travelled across the seas, till families in the British colonies were wont to send their children to the mother country, in order that they might enjoy his tuition.

Among the two thousand confessors of the Anglican Bartholomew-tide, there are two honoured names closely connected with Southampton—Nathaniel Robinson, and Giles Say; the one of All Saints', and the other of Saint Michael's. The families of these ejected ministers were intimately acquainted with the family of Watts, and their attachment was continued to the next generation, as Samuel Say, a son of the above, and an eminent Dissenting minister of the last century, was one of the poet's most valued friends.

During the era of persecution under Charles the Second, Giles Say and the elder Watts were the foremost defenders of freedom of worship in Southampton, and the former became a licensed teacher at the proclamation of Indulgence in 1672. When, in the year following, that Declaration was revoked, to appease the violence of the Commons, and to inaugurate a new reign of persecution, both the elder Watts and Say were confined in the county gaol. To this period, therefore, belongs the anecdote of the poet's mother having been occasionally observed sitting upon a stone without the prison, suckling her son. His enemies kept a most vigilant eye upon the movements of the elder Watts, and he was frequently imprisoned. He became obliged to lead an exile life in London, whence he habitually despatched to his family those excellent precepts

which circumstances debarred him from enforcing by
example. In connection with this excellent man, a
curious story is told of a stonemason who sought his
advice under peculiar circumstances. The man
having purchased the materials of an old house in
the town, one night strangely dreamed, that while
taking the premises down, a stone—which really
was in the building—fell and killed him. "I am
not," said Watts, on hearing the circumstance, " for
paying any great regard to dreams, nor yet for utterly
slighting them. If there is such a stone in the
building as you saw in your dream, my advice to you
is to take great care to keep far enough off from
it." Whether the man purposely slighted this
sensible counsel, or whether he neglected it by in-
advertence, cannot be determined; but the stone
fell and killed him, in strict accordance with his
night vision.

Young Watts received his early education under
the care of John Pinhorne, the rector of All Saints',
Southampton. Thence, in 1690, he removed to
London to study divinity under Thomas Rowe, the
pastor at Girdlers' Hall, where the poet was received
into Christian communion. Those were, indeed,
momentous times. The late king was actively employed in sowing in Ireland the seeds of discord and
sedition. At home by their factious quarrels, Whigs
and Tories were working for the undoing of the
Revolution, till the patriotic William, disheartened
and weary, was declaring his intention of relinquish-

ing the hopeless task of reconciliation, by retiring to his native Holland.

Under Thomas Rowe, Isaac rapidly progressed, and gratified his tutor by manifesting tokens of future usefulness. Those years were a pleasant season, and it is scarcely strange that Rowe was ever after remembered by Watts as a model professor. Rowe was a celibate, and his example, it would seem, prejudiced Watts against married tutors, as was evinced by the advice he offered Doddridge on the occasion of the founding of the Kibworth Academy. Certain it is that, Thomas Rowe turned out some scholars of future eminence; but to affirm that his success at all resulted from his untrammelled social condition, would be ungallant in the extreme. Neal, the historian, and other celebrities were fellow-students with Watts, and in the poet's journal this entry is found: —"Aug. 5, 1705. Mr. Rowe, my tutor, died." The good man was one day riding through the City, and on nearing the Monument a fit seized him, and he fell from his horse and died.

During the four years of Watts's college curriculum, many great events of English history were in course of accomplishment. It was pre-eminently an era of war. Ireland was completely distracted until a truce was effected by the Peace of Limerick. On the Continent, the Herculean efforts of our general King were being exerted against the common enemy, Louis the Fourteenth. The youthful Watts must have given some attention to such occurrences as the siege of

Londonderry, the battles of Landen and La Hogue, the massacre of Glencoe, or on the side of Peace, the founding of the Bank of England, and a thousand other things which happened while he was quietly storing up his University learning. The poet, we know, was always patriotic, and the remains of his early days prove him to have been no less painstaking and laborious as a student. He was not even dismayed at the enormous application entailed by abridging such authors as he or his tutor deemed worthy of so particular a regard. Through life, indeed, he habitually interleaved the books he perused, and wrote notes on their margin.

In the early part of 1694 Watts completed his college course, and retired from the household of Thomas Rowe. He now proved his classical proficiency by complimenting his early tutor, John Pinhorne, in some Latin verses. A Dr. Speed, moreover, of Southampton, offered to place the young poet at one of the universities, but the articles of subscription contained sufficient excuse for rejecting the temptation. From this date, till nearly the end of 1696, he lived in seclusion beneath his father's roof, and assiduously applied himself to the study of literature, or, as Dr. Gibbons says, " to reading, meditation, and prayer "—an expression not to be too literally understood in the case of so young a man. Only scanty particulars of this quiet period in the poet's life are now obtainable, although it was the period in which many of his Hymns were written.

The story has been often told, how the poverty of expression and want of poetical fire, discoverable in the pieces then popular among Dissenting congregations, were so " little to the gust of Mr. Watts," that he complained to his father, who counselled him to "try and do better." Isaac accordingly did better, until his efforts sufficed to fill a volume. While thus employed, in the autumn of 1696, he was invited by Sir John Hartopp, of Stoke Newington, to remove into his family in the double capacity of tutor and chaplain.

At that date Stoke Newington was entirely rural, and had been one of those suburbs where tradesmen's tokens were allowed during the seventeenth century. What the village was a hundred years earlier the parish register of the days of Elizabeth will help us to form an opinion. During certain specified years only a single baptism in each occurred, while in other years no marriages at all took place, or only one ; and it was the same with burials. In the old Manor House, then situated near the church, but taken down after the Revolution, tradition says the Princess Elizabeth was occasionally concealed. Some aged persons who were living a century ago were wont to tell of an ancient tower—a relic of this mansion—which they remembered having seen in their youth. Even in 1793 Stoke Newington contained only 200 houses.

This rural suburb was the scene of Watts's entrance upon the world. The Hartopps, with whom he was now intimately connected, were an old Leicestershire family of established repute who had ably promoted the cause of freedom during the troublous era of civil war. Sir John had formerly attended the ministrations of Owen at the old meeting in Leadenhall-street, and as an intense admirer of that divine, he supplied some important manuscripts when the Doctor's works were collected in 1721. The Hartopps were closely associated with the leading families of the Commonwealth, and even with the Protector himself. They were conspicuous sufferers for conscience' sake in the succeeding persecution. They intermarried with the Fleetwoods, who were residents at Stoke Newington. General Fleetwood's wife was Ireton's widow and Cromwell's daughter. The Nonconformity of either family was of the most uncompromising type, and both had been molested in common by the military agents of the now banished Stuarts. The character of Sir John is portrayed by Watts in highly flattering colours.

Watts preached his first sermon in July, 1698, and was immediately afterwards elected to the lectureship at Mark-lane, under Dr. Chauncy. The poet's entrance upon the ministry was attended by a dangerous illness of several months' duration. Dr. Chauncy ultimately resigned, and upon a momentous day in the annals of England—March the 8th, 1702, when the spirit of William III. was passing away—Watts accepted the pastoral office.

An affliction of another complexion was the death of Lady Abney's brother, Thomas Gunston, and Watts's bosom friend. This gentleman was about rearing a sumptuous mansion at Stoke Newington, when his days were suddenly ended, and his departure was commemorated in a poem by Watts. The Gunstons were likewise decided Nonconformists, who had ably served the Puritans in their season of need.

In the summer of 1702, after a pleasant visit to Southampton, Watts was again prostrated by illness, which disabled him for a lengthened period. Then the time came round for leaving the home of the Hartopps, and his next residence was with "Mr. Thomas Hollis, in the Minories." Whether in the erection of chapels, schools, or almshouses, this last-named gentleman was a generous benefactor to the Nonconformists. Watts prolonged his stay with the Hollis family till the end of 1710—a dismal period in our religious annals; for the Establishment was threatened by the inroads of Jacobitism, and a latitudinarian sophistry, while Nonconformity was endangered by rival Arian and Antinomian schemes. During a portion of the time in question the poet's constitutional weakness obliged a partial or total abstinence from the burden of study; and from this date he appears to have provided himself with an amanuensis. The people at Bury-street discovered a laudable solicitude for their pastor's comfort and welfare by appointing Samuel Price to the lectureship,

in 1703—a year made for ever memorable by the
great and unparalleled storm which swept over and
desolated England. In 1705 Watts published his
Lyrics, and, two years later, the Hymns, the copyright of the last having been disposed of for ten
guineas. The year which gave these spiritual songs
to the Church saw the Union completed between
England and Scotland, and the religious world somewhat perplexed by the fantastic pretensions to inspiration of the sect called French Prophets. About
Christmas, 1710, the poet removed from the home
of his friend Hollis, and "went to live with Mr.
Bowes." This same year he begun to use a horse,
and within the space of a few weeks rode no less
than eight hundred miles, including a journey to
Southampton. Although the Hymns appeared thus
early, the version of the Psalms did not follow till
1719, in which year four thousand copies were sold.
While, therefore, the Hymns are the offspring of the
poet's youthful genius, the Psalms must be regarded
as the work of his maturer days. The circulation of
these sacred pieces has far exceeded the bounds of
human comprehension, though, as a separate book,
their sale is now on the decline.

After separating from the Hollis family, Watts
probably remained in his new quarters about
two years. He was again laid low by fever and
nervous affection, to remain in a weakened condition
for a long and weary season, and never really
throughout life, perfectly to recover his wasted

vigour.   The church at Bury-street showed their sympathy, first, by promoting Samuel Price to the ex-pastorate, and again by observing certain days of special prayer on the poet's behalf.   It was also at or about this date that Sir Thomas Abney invited Watts to spend a week at Theobalds, where his family mansion adjoined the royal estate.   As all know, the author's visit to Sir Thomas only ended with his life—a space of six and thirty years.   For such a student and reader of nature the refined homes of the Abneys at Stoke Newington and Theobalds, with their spacious pleasure gardens, were congenial retreats.   Some seventy years ago the poet's favourite summerhouse at the latter place, standing on the edge of some artificial water, was pointed out as the retreat where many of his versions of the psalms were composed.   The society of the neighbourhood included Richard Cromwell, between whom and Watts an unbroken friendship was sustained.

The Abneys were an ancient Derbyshire family, whose original home was at Willesby.   Thomas, the patron of Dr. Watts, was born there in 1639, and lost his mother early in life.   In the wars which immediately ensued, the Abneys were considerable sufferers on account of their espousing the cause of freedom.   Thomas was educated at Loughborough, and, during his schoolboy days, benefited by the virtuous solicitude of an aunt, and the adoption of her instructions appears to have not a little conduced to his after success.   Eventually he embarked upon

the world as a London tradesman, to become sheriff
in 1693, alderman of Vintry-ward in the year following, and lord mayor in 1700, when the honour
of knighthood was conferred by William the Third.
An anecdote is told of Sir Thomas's retiring from
dinner—or "supper," as it was then more appro-
priately called—on the night of his installation, for
the purpose of conducting family prayer.   To his
high credit, he won the hatred of City Jacobites by
strenuously promoting the politics of the Revolution.
The faction in question was especially chagrined by
a patriotic address transmitted to the King from the
Common Council, while the former was engaged in
the continental wars—an action which some supposed to be worth more than a million of money to
the Protestant interest, because provincial corpora-
tions, by following in the wake of the capital, aided
the Pretender's abjuration and the establishment
of the Hanover Line.   The language of Jeremiah
Smith, however, who preached Sir Thomas's funeral
sermon, may not be exempted from the charge of
extravagance when he proceeds to eulogise his subject by making him the foremost promoter of the
Protestant succession.

The   pastor's   continued   weakness   necessitated
his continuance in the country air of Theobalds,
and prompted the Abneys to offer him a perma-
nent home.   Only a week's existence in the London atmosphere sufficed to provoke unfavourable
symptoms.   Watts sought to make amends for his

16

pastoral inability by means of the press. In 1720
he published The Art of Reading and Writing English—written for the use of the Misses Abney, but
published to celebrate the opening of the Cheshunt
Charity School, which the family founded. A volume
of sermons, dedicated to the church at Bury-street,
shortly followed. At length he again essayed to
preach, but found himself reduced by weakness to
a pitiable condition. He frequently retired from the
pulpit to a darkened room, where, in utter prostration, he would await the partial recovery of his
excited nerves.

As Dr. Watts is known to most persons more by
his Hymns than aught beside, there is something to
be said about the endeavours made by Unitarians to
class the poet's name among their supporters. The
chief offenders are Belsham and Mrs. Barbauld. The
former, in his Memoirs of Lindsay, has done his
best to glorify his party at the expense of Watts's
reputation. The Hymns are represented as having
been written at an age of unformed judgment; and,
on account of having disposed of the copyright, the
author was debarred from making amendments. The
book was circulated, we are therefore expected to
believe, with sentiments the writer would gladly
have altered "if he had been permitted by the
proprietors of the copyright, who knew their own
interest too well to admit the proposed improvement." For the correctness of so astounding a
statement, we have Belsham's unsupported testi-

mony, which we are assuredly not prepared to accept when it turns the balance against the honesty of Watts. It is true that a correspondence took place on the subject of doxologies between our author and an Arian minister, Martin Tomkins; but the letters will abundantly prove the poet to have remained sufficiently sound not to desire the slightest alteration in the sentiments of his published works.

It has become fashionable to speak of Watts's poems for children as his most humble endeavour; yet it may be fairly questioned if any one of the author's works has enjoyed a more extensive influence for good. It is quite impossible to form an estimate of what may be the salutary effect of religious principles instilled into the juvenile understanding by means of beautiful couplets, so well adapted to captivate the heart. No wonder the work achieved immediate popularity, or that large editions only increased the demand for what the present age has seen dispersed by millions. In regard to Mrs. Barbauld, before mentioned, we would have the procedure to be held in abhorrence, which has tampered with the handiwork of a dead author, by making him the apparent exponent of doctrine, such as his life condemned. In an edition of the Songs for Children, printed in 1785, we are informed that the editor has undertaken to alter "some particular doctrines and phrases, which (Watts's) better judgment would probably have

16*

corrected or expunged." What a labyrinth of curiosities is the literary world! Bunyan may be encountered in a Puseyite guise; and Watts must rest contentedly while his matchless juvenile couplets are metamorphosed into Arian doggrel!

We have grown thoroughly accustomed to the poet's numbers, and are consequently unable to realise the delight by which they were hailed when heard for the first time. In one of his letters, Doddridge has testified to the almost magical effect upon a rural congregation of

" Give me the wings of faith to rise," &c.

Emotion would scarcely allow of the singing of the lines ; and, on enquiry, Watts was found to be the daily entertainer of such poor persons. "What if Dr. Watts should come to Northampton?" exclaimed one. "The very sight of him would be like an ordinance to me," was the reply of another. "I mention the thing," wrote Doddridge, "just as it was, and am persuaded it is but a natural specimen of what often occurs amongst a multitude of Christians who never saw your face."

In 1719 disputes about subscribing to articles of faith distracted the Three Denominations, and bred divisions which many subsequent years sufficed not to heal. With the laudable desire of restoring union, Watts wrote on such mysteries enshadowing the Godhead as are wisely hidden from the ken of humanity. He incautiously advanced opinions which

were readily misinterpreted by Bradbury, of New-
court, Carey-street, the arch-champion of the Subscribing party. The latter would, even in the pulpit,
whether at his own chapel or at Pinners' Hall, descend to the use of defamatory language. " Jesus, ,
the searcher of hearts, knows," replied Watts, to
some reiterated charges of Socinianism, " with what
daily labour and study, and with what constant addresses to the Throne of Grace, I seek to support
the doctrine of His Deity as well as you, and to
defend it in the best manner I am capable of."
Bradbury and Watts had formerly preserved the
closest friendship; but the former was now bitterly
incensed against the poet, and even spoke contemptuously of his Hymns as " garblings, mang-
lings, and transformings." He once startled a clerk,
in the act of giving one out, by telling him, in sten-
torian tones, to " let us have none of Mr. Watts's
Whims." It is painful, even at this distance of
time, to mark the differences which could separate
such excellent divines. Bradbury was well meaning, but excessively bold, and his conduct was not
always tempered by prudence. He has earned our
gratitude, however, by the intense zeal with which
he promoted the establishment of the Hanoverian
Succession, an action which ensured him the bitter
hatred of contemporary Jacobites. The Government
of Queen Anne, it was reported, proffered him a
bishopric by way of pacification, and, as may be
supposed, the bribe was contemptuously declined

This old Independent was also a master at smart
repartee. At a certain crisis of the debate on the
Trinity at Salters' Hall, hisses were more than
usually abundant, which prompted Bradbury de-
fiantly to call out, " It is not wonderful that the
seed of the serpent should hiss." The pamphlets
which emanated from his pen are characteristic of
an eager controvertist of the early Georgian era.
To Bradbury an opponent was "a sawcy villain,"
" a blaspheming wretch," or "a sorry buffoon." The
more amiable and timid Watts was quite outmatched
by this determined disputant. Bradbury headed
the Nonconformist deputation which congratulated
George the First on his accession to the throne.
" Pray, sir," asked a nobleman, alluding to the
sombre-looking cloaks then worn by Dissenting
ministers, " is this a funeral procession ? " " Yes,
my lord," was the response ; " it is the funeral of
the Schism Bill, and the resurrection of Liberty."
He was sometimes disagreeably sarcastic. Watts
was one day addressing a company of ministers at
Dr. Williams's Library, when his voice showed
symptoms of weakness : " Brother Watts," cried
Bradbury, " shall I speak ⁻for you ? " " Brother
Bradbury," returned the poet, " you have often
spoken *against* me."

 It will not be necessary to apologise for detailing
here some stray impressions of the times of Watts,
gathered form such scattered sources as the pamphlets
and periodicals of the era. During the reign of Anne,

the Established Church was notoriously Jacobitical, and proved an obstinate and serious obstacle to the Protestant Succession. The Jacobite faction, when favoured by opportunities, even transformed the parochial schools into political seminaries, in which the youth of England were corrupted by the instillation of traitorous sentiments. This dangerous and intolerant party was characterised by "a bigoted zeal for the word Church," and a hatred of Nonconformity. Historians have scarcely revealed to what extent our country is indebted to hearts so loyal to the House of Hanover as Watts, Bradbury, Shower, and a multitude more, whose names should not be forgotten; and but for whose united action against a treacherous conspiracy, the present Royal Line would probably never have inherited the throne.

In those days the extreme party in religion and politics endeavoured to make even the commotion of the elements redound to the prosperity of the cause uppermost in their affection. A contemporary writer tells us, that if it thundered, snowed or rained, it thundered, snowed and rained for the Church. So firmly persuaded were many, of heaven's vindicating their cause, that they imagined the regiments would be frozen to death while marching northward to suppress the Pretender's insurrection. Of what the teaching dealt out to the humbler classes too often consisted the following will aid us to form an estimate. In the autumn of 1710, a boy belonging to a rural parish was killed by lightning. His parents were Dissenters, and therefore when news of the catastrophe came to the vicarage, the pastor exclaimed, "It is what I always foretold, that that boy would come to a dismal end: he went constantly to a fanatical conventicle." Strangely enough, during the same storm, another person was visited by the like misfortune. This man had not only been an uncompromising Churchman; he had ever been the most active in erecting maypoles, and directing village pastimes. The vicar listened to the sad narration and then ejaculated, "It is appointed unto all men once to die." "What a pity it is," says a contemporary author, "that neither the clouds, nor the sun, nor the moon, nor the stars, nor anything above them, can be brought to favour the cause of the Church."

It is not easy to imagine the influence produced among the peasantry by unprincipled Jacobites. The whole strength of the party was exerted to create a prejudice against the family of Brunswick; and no sin was committed, they taught, by killing an enemy to the House of Stuart. The Hanoverians were portrayed as literal cannibals. George the First was a miserable being who had eaten up his offspring, the Prince of Wales only excepted, and rural boors were circumstantially acquainted with the reasons of that exception. The clergy are depicted as being "blasphemously loyal," and preaching up the Queen to losing sight of Christ. After the Sacheverel riots it was by no means an uncommon occurrence for Anne to be surrounded

during her progresses by crowds of the lower
orders shouting, " God bless your Majesty and
the Church : we hope your Majesty is for Dr.
Sacheverel." Such popular enthusiasm has been
pronounced " a salutary attachment." While we
may admit, however, that it is better for the
ignorant populace to be nominally attached to a
religious establishment than to show no signs of
religion at all, it is no favourable testimony to the
utility of the State connection that, such blind
attachment could only manifest itself in an era of
gross darkness. The poor people were carefully
tutored in politics, while not possessing the ability
to read their Bibles. A gentleman who travelled
into Somersetshire, during the reign of George the
First, found the clergy there insulting the King by
preaching against foreign intruders. In the Rebellion of 1715, these reverend traitors were constrained to draw some equivocal distinctions. A
foreigner, it was then maintained, if he came to *save*
the Church was worthy of succour. Brave accounts
were propagated of the Pretender's noble mien and
the gallant bearing of his splendid retinue, his
high-spirited and handsome cavaliers. The western
maidens even despaired of their charms ever winning
the notice of such pure-eyed and unselfish heroes.
" Will such outlandish men," one Venus enquired,
" marry with us poor English folk ? " The clergy
consigned Dissenters in general to the Gehenna of
schism; but were not unreasonably reproached by

the opposite party with going there first themselves to say who were coming.

It was pre-eminently an age of pluralities—of luxury among the clergy on the one hand, and of hard work allied to poverty on the other. In the days of George the First there lived a certain vicar, whose life-experience illustrated this proposition. Once a year he travelled down to his country cure, visited his curate, and paid him an annual dole. On such occasions the pastor was not averse from preaching a sermon, in the course of which he would humbly depict himself as the Lord's ambassador. Sleeping in church, on one of these occasions, were two boors, both possessed of some native wit, and each better competent to digest material than mental fare. Presently one awoke, and caught a sentence which prompted him to nudge his still unconscious friend with, " Tom, do it hear ? " " Aye, what ? " snored Tom. " He says as how he's the Lord's hambassador." " I think he's more likely the Lord's receiver-general," returned the now awakened Tom, " for he never comes but to take money."

The common people, during the first half of the century, were in a state of ignorance bordering on barbarism. The farmers at once imagined they scented witchcraft when their cattle or children were ailing. Old women, whose crimes against society were represented by their years and ugly features, if only suspected, would be suddenly arrested by indignant neighbours, to be weighed

against a folio Bible, which if they outweighed,
well; but aught otherwise was evidence of guilt.
A whole hamlet would sometimes rise, assemble at
the door of some decrepid dame, to drag her,
perhaps, from her bed, and throw her into the
nearest pond: if she sank, well: if she swam, she
was a witch. Both men and women were thus
summarily disciplined by being sometimes beaten,
and sometimes branded.

Most elderly persons are strongly inclined to regard the times as having degenerated since the days
of their youth. The explanation of such a delusion
is not difficult. The subjects of it can no longer
sympathise with the predilections of their youthful
contemporaries; and are, in consequence, disposed
to regard as folly even such harmless pleasures and
pursuits as they themselves were wont to appreciate.
In George the Second's days a goodly number complained of the altered times, as they fondly called to
remembrance an era when an Englishman's breakfast
consisted of ale, ham, and sirloin; and his dinner of
plain joints, plainly dressed by gentlewomen, who
were superior economists and housewives to the degenerate daughters of their tenants' descendants. As
regards the moral condition of the capital, a contemporary wrote: " Riches are merit; an estate learning;
and South Sea Stock wit. Want is the only folly,
and poverty the only vice." The number of footpads
about the City was inconveniently great; and prudent
persons considered it unsafe to travel the town after

ten in the evening. Aristocratic journalists, who were possibly the ancestors of Saturday reviewers, were extending their patronage to the Bible—such patronage probably being a more subtle form of enmity. We find the Bible spoken of as a book embodying "A great deal of morality and good sense," and therefore worthy of respectful treatment from gentlemen and scholars. Indeed the religious and political state of the nation, at this conjuncture, was gloomy to a degree which cannot now be contemplated without awakening the saddest emotions.

It is remarkable that during certain years of the reign of George the First, a strange number of suicides occurred, and were prompted, as was supposed, by the ruin attending the wild speculations of 1720. In one year—1725—a hundred and seventy-six persons were found dead in London alone, the majority of whom were self-murdered. Hence the origin of Watts's sermon against so detestable a crime, the salutary maxims of which were useful to many. The discourse on the death of George the First is not free from the blemish of overdrawn eulogy; yet the elation engendered by the triumph of the Protestant Succession must excuse that Nonconformist failing. At the same time, by a graceful ode, the poet celebrated the accession of George the Second. In the year ensuing, Watts was created Doctor of Divinity by the Universities of Edinburgh and Aberdeen. It was also about this date that the ministers of the Three Denominations first formed themselves into a Body, to act in concert upon public questions. Their original rendezvous was the George Inn, Ironmonger-lane. Members of the Association necessarily lived within a ten miles' radius of London.

Watts's literary fame was now extending throughout the civilised world. In America he early became a favourite, and, according to Neal, a volume of his Hymns was among the earliest printed at Harvard-college press.

At the era of Sylvanus Urban's entrance upon the world of letters, Watts was enjoying one of the most active and happy seasons of his life. In the summer of 1733 he was gladdened for a season by the company of Doddridge at Theobalds. In that year was likewise published the volume of the Bury-street Discourses, delivered and published at the expense of Mr. Coward, nine of which were by Dr. Watts. It does not, however, come within our present compass to detail the long list of our author's publications, nor to venture any critical opinion upon their merits.

In 1735 the Gentleman's Magazine was in the fifth year of its existence. Hitherto Edward Cave' the projector and editor, had made his venture merely a faithful chronicle of contemporary events and opinion. He now sought to extend its influence by inserting original articles of a high standard of literary excellence, for which premiums as large as £50 were offered. With the utmost good humour

Watts allowed himself to be pressed into the service of adjudication. It is both amusing and interesting to witness the acute disappointment which such laudable endeavours brought home to Mr. Urban. The more eminent among the *literati* turned scornfully aside from the arena of competition. The liberal editor found he had completely misjudged the world, for the geniuses of that un-reading age so far rated their gifts above the golden allurement that they vented their contempt by ridiculing those whose notions of literary decorum were less a source of trouble, *e.g.* :—

> "The Psalmist to a cave for refuge fled,
> And vagrants followed him for want of bread.
> Ye highly gifted bards, would you with plenty dwell ?
> Fly to that best of Caves in Clerkenwell."

Although the competitors bore names of no repute in the republic of letters, the pieces sent in were of considerable merit. The impartiality with which Watts fulfilled the duties of his somewhat thankless office afforded ample satisfaction to all concerned.* Indeed, the critical acumen of Watts was held in

* Concerning the Gentleman's Magazine, Cave, it would seem, for years previously, entertained an idea of one day commencing a periodical digest of the proceedings in Parliament, though the scheme had not been encouraged by any advisers to whom he had mentioned it. At this date Parliament was extremely zealous in protecting its privileges, and regarded the slightest intrusion upon its privacy as a gross affront. The publication of the wished-for intelligence,

high veneration, and his judgment was relied upon
by the most eminent persons. He perused Blair's
poem, The Grave, before the author would venture
on publication. " I have a letter from the Doctor,"
wrote Blair to a friend, "signifying his approbation
of the piece in a manner most obliging. A great
deal less from him would have done me no small
honour. But, at the same time, he mentions to me

therefore, was beset both by difficulty and danger. During
the term of an engagement in the Post-office, Cave had contrived to be a kind of editors' news-agent. From the coach-
guards he procured copies of the provincial journals, and sold
their fresh intelligence to the London offices; while by
similar means he transmitted into the country the gossip of
the town coffee-houses. This would chiefly consist of
extracts from manuscript parliamentary reports, which were
previously prepared for the public rooms, before newspapers
were allowed to publish the speeches. As early as 1728, Cave
was arrested by the Serjeant-at-Arms for supplying the
Gloucester Journal with this description of news, and
suffered several days' imprisonment for the offence. When
at length the Gentleman's Magazine was launched, the aim
of its projector was merely to make the work a reflection of
public opinion. The early volumes contain little besides
articles culled from the Craftsman, Fog's Journal, The
Universal Spectator, The Free Briton, The Daily Advertiser,
and others. That such an undertaking should at once succeed
and attract the attention of the learned world is perhaps
a little remarkable. The circulation of 10,000 a month then
attained, was a fact which of itself sufficed to render the old
Gate an important object. In 1736 the long-cherished design
of publishing the debates was attempted. The narration of
the difficulties which had to be overcome sounds incredible
to modern ears. As a perliminary step, it was indispen-

that he had offered it to two booksellers of his own
acquaintance, who, he tells me, did not care to run
the risk of publication." Such glimpses no less reveal the poet's amiable bearing than the extreme
depression of the literary market. Of the many
critical or moral sayings which occurred in the
course of Watts's social life only a few have descended to us ; but these scanty remnants make us
regret that such mental gold-dust was not preserved
in larger quantities. Thus we find him evincing a

sable that the doorkeepers of the House should be handsomely bribed. On this being done, the editor and his party
were admitted secretly, and took hasty notes of what was
spoken. After they retired, the report would be amended at
a tavern. The materials thus obtained were collectively
handed over to a competent scribe, upon whom it devolved
to manufacture, from such odds and ends, a debate more
ingenious than ingenuous, which, on being distributed the
country over, was gravely regarded as genuine by rural
squires and London politicians. All proceeded smoothly for
nearly two years, when, in the spring of 1738, an interruption occurred by a threatening resolution passing the
Commons, which denounced as an indignity offered to themselves any publication of their august proceedings. Thus
warned, Mr. Urban showed himself not devoid of the genius
which eludes a danger and still pursues its object. From
this date the speeches were given as emanating from the
" Senate of Lilliput ; " and the further precaution was
observed of substituting the name of his nephew for his own
upon the cover of the Magazine. Shortly after, Guthrie,
who had hitherto prepared these papers, was dismissed to
make way for the rising star, Samuel Johnson, by whom
they were continued for two or three years longer.

correct taste in art by dilating upon Raphael's cartoon of Paul Preaching at Athens. "I will tell you," one day cried Watts, when fascinated by the painter's genius, "what the Apostle is saying:—BEHOLD, HE COMES." At another time he declared he would rather be the author of Baxter's Call to the Unconverted than of Paradise Lost. Night Thoughts, he imagined, had "too much of the darkness of night in them." He ever showed a generous sympathy with young ministers and their early hardships. On behalf of such beginners he advocated a procedure which would now find but little favour. He thought young preachers should be allowed to repeat the sermon of another on one part of the Sabbath, and so reduce their labour to the composition of one weekly discourse.

Among the eminent persons who, in those days, were the *élite* of Nonconformity, and the associates of Watts, the name must be mentioned of John Shute, Viscount· Barrington, a celebrated lay Dissenter of the century, who occupied a considerable position on account of the works he published, and the political influence he exercised. He was undergoing a preparation for the Bar when the Whig ministry of Queen Anne invited him to use his authority with the Presbyterians in favour of the Union with Scotland. That Union was eventually effected about the date of the removal of Watts's congregation to the chapel in Bury-street. Shute was rewarded with the Commissionership of Customs,

a post he surrendered on the accession of the Tories
to power in 1711.   From a Berkshire gentleman,
John Wildman, Mr. Shute inherited considerable
wealth, bequeathed to him merely through personal
esteem.   He afterwards enjoyed the patrimony of a
relative, Francis Barrington, when he assumed the
family name, and was created a Viscount by George
the First.

While strength and health permitted him, Watts
unflaggingly pursued his industrious course, even in
declining years.   He was now, however, continually
interrupted by the inroads of disease and nervous
affection ; and sometimes only half-an-hour's exertion in the pulpit would suffice to overpower him.
In 1743 he was again confined to his chamber by
his constitutional malady, which was aggravated by
an oft-recurring inability to sleep through several
consecutive nights.   To this period does the anecdote belong which Toplady communicated to the
Gospel Magazine in 1776.   The Countess of
Huntingdon was one day visiting at Abney House,
and on approaching Watts, the Doctor exclaimed,
" Your ladyship is come to see me on a very
remarkable day."   " Why is this day so remarkable ?" enquired the amiable visitor.   " This very
day thirty years," continued the poet, " I came to
the house of my good friend, Sir Thomas Abney,
intending to spend but a single week, and I have
extended my visit to the length of thirty years."
Lady Abney, who was standing near, with a rarely

equalled readiness of generous wit, replied, "Sir, what you term a long thirty years' visit I consider as the shortest my family ever received."

We now come to the closing years of this great man's life, which it is saddening to find were troubled by the unhandsome behaviour of certain relatives, whose offences are described as "most marvellous, infamous, enormous wickedness." The offenders were Richard Watts, and a person of the name of Brackstone. The shock sustained by his nervous system well-nigh reduced the poet to a state of stupefaction; and his life would actually have been endangered but for the watchful solicitude of Lady Abney, who, with true feminine dexterity, kept the enemy at a becoming distance, and her chaplain in ignorance of his machinations. Dr. Doddridge travelled from Bath to see his venerable friend, and found him in a lamentable state of physical and mental prostration. The sight of the most loved or familiar face failed to arouse him, and, in reply to enquiries as to how he fared, he would say, "Waiting God's leave to die." Some malicious reports gained currency that the poet had at last lapsed into insanity; and such rumours were aided by the relatives above referred to, although totally unfounded. The last two years of Watts's life were nevertheless years of quiet retirement and cessation from labour. Among his last visitors were Jabez Erle, Joseph Stennett, and Mr. Onslow, Speaker of the House of Commons. These one day rode to

17*

260 ANCIENT MEETING HOUSES.

Abney House on a farewell visit to the poet and
Christian philosopher. Then came life's closing
days, in which the Doctor was constantly attended
by his faithful amanuensis, Joseph Parker. With
sleepless assiduity did Parker watch by his master's
dying couch. While easing the posture, or moisten-
ing the lips of the sinking sage, he would exclaim,
"You have taught us how to live, sir, and now you
are teaching us how to die." Thus, after passing a
life of eminent usefulness, died the amiable Isaac
Watts, on Friday, November the 25th, 1748.*

Of Samuel Price, Dr. Watts's colleague, through
a very lengthened period, scarcely any particulars
can be supplied, beyond the fact that, he was laid to
rest in Bunhill-fields, after having been engaged in
the ministry at Bury-street during the space of fifty-
three years. "He was," we are told, "a man of
sound and solid sense, a judicious, useful preacher,
and eminent for his gift in prayer. He possessed
great sagacity, was very able, faithful, and ready to
advise and communicate his mind in serviceable
hints and cautions to his friends. His disposition
was friendly and peaceable, and he laid himself out

---

* The chief sources of information respecting Dr. Watts,
are the Memoirs of the Poet, by Johnson, Southey, Gibbons,
and Milner, and also the account prefixed to the quarto
edition of his works. For many of the facts embodied in the
above, I am indebted to various pamphlets and periodicals
of the era; Robinson's History of Stoke Newington; the
Biographia Britannica, &c.

to do good, in which he much delighted. He was highly esteemed by his excellent friend, Dr. Watts, who in his will styles him ' his faithful friend and companion in the labours of the ministry,' and mentions a legacy he bequeaths him ' as only a small testimony of his great affection for him on account of his services of love during the many harmonious years of their fellowship in the work of the Gospel.'" He died in April, 1756.

An assistant of Samuel Price was Meredith Townshend. He removed from the church in Bury-street to Hull, and thence to Stoke Newington. His respectable talents and stainless character won him a moderate share of popularity, and the esteem of a wide circle of acquaintances.

The colleague and successor of Samuel Price was Samuel Morton Savage, whose family originally belonged to the county of York, and was connected with the noble house of Rivers. The Savages were nearly related, moreover, to Dr. Boulter, the Irish Primate ; and, under the Archbishop's distinguished patronage, young Morton would have entered the Established Church, had not his sympathies gone strongly with the cause of the Dissenters, and made him determine to cast in his lot with them. The lad spent most of his youthful days with " Mr. Toulmin, an eminent apothecary in Old Gravel-lane, Wapping." For a time he lived without any fixed plan or purpose. At length he resolved on communicating with Dr. Watts, to whom he fully explained his literary and ministerial predilections. Watts discovered in Savage some shining abilities, and from that date the poet made it his business to aid his *protégé* in realising his desires. For a tutor Savage had John Eames, and eventually became an assistant in the academy under the succeeding professor, Dr. Jennings. When the college was ultimately removed to Hoxton, Morton Savage filled the divinity chair, having for his colleagues Drs. Rees and Kippis. Dr. Savage engaged himself at Bury-street as early as 1742, and in 1756 acceded to the pastorate on the death of Samuel Price. He continued in the ministry till the end of 1787, having two years prior resigned his connection with the academy. In addition to his regular duties, Dr. Savage served on several lectureships, and was foremost among the agitators who demanded the repeal of the Test Act. As an acknowledgment of his worth and service in the cause of truth, the University of Aberdeen conferred upon him the distinction of Doctor of Divinity. Like too many of his class, our author, in his earlier days, injured his health by midnight studies. His death was at length occasioned by a throat affection, which obstructed the passage of nourishment beyond a drop at once. He died of sheer starvation, after having grown so emaciated that the bones protruded, and occasioned a soreness of the skin. Yet, notwithstanding so sharp an affliction, he continued in a resigned and happy frame of mind, and enjoyed the satisfaction of offering up the family prayer of his household on the Sabbath preceding his death, although necessarily held in his chair. The Doctor breathed his last in April, 1791, and was long remembered in the circle of his acquaintance as an able, divine, and Christian gentleman.*

Dr. Savage was succeeded by Thomas Beck, a native of Southwark, and born in 1755. His parents apprenticed him to trade without harbouring the notion that he would ever adopt the ministerial profession. Young Beck's predilections were of a serious kind, and by following the Wesleyan preachers he became a local preacher himself, and in that department of Christian work grew extremely popular. According to his early intentions he was to have studied at the Countess of Huntingdon's College, at Trevecca—a design which was never accomplished, and he never enjoyed the advantage attending a theological curriculum. He first settled in the ministry at Wapping, where he remained a year, after which he became closely associated with the people at Whitfield's Tabernacle. For a while he preached in this connection, next removing to Gravesend, there to continue for nine years. At Gravesend he published his only printed piece, if we except his poetical works. In 1788 he removed to Bury-street, but found himself unable to restore a departed prosperity.

* Toulmin's Life of Savage; Wilson's Dissenting Churches.

Nevertheless, he displayed some spirit in fulfilling what he deemed to be his duty; for he erected a chapel in his private garden at Deptford for the use of his poorer neighbours. The pastor was also one of the projectors of the Evangelical Magazine. He resigned his pulpit about 1820, and was succeeded by Mr. Mummery. Three years later the members forsook their ancient meeting-house, and settled in Founders' Hall. Thence they finally removed to Bethnal-green, and the Rev. Isaac Vale Mummery, a son of the former pastor, is the present minister. This gentleman has our congratulations, seeing he has become so worthily associated with that splendid Nonconformist galaxy, which, by the writings of OWEN, CLARKSON and WATTS, will shed its refulgence over unborn generations.

Chapter VII.

LITTLE CARTER LANE.

CARTER-LANE, Doctors'-commons, is overshadowed by St. Paul's. A visit to this spot occasions some quaint associations of the cathedral and its vicinity to crowd into the mind. Here, for example, it is supposed a demolished church of the Christian Britons testified to the fury of the Diocletian persecution. Here also was reared, at amazing cost, that fair structure which, covering four acres of land, fell a prey to the flames of 1666. In the olden time the bishop's palace standing close to the church was linked with some important events in English history; and the hum and rattle of the modern street need not prevent the old scenes from rising in our imagination. Thus we seem to behold that ill-fated child, Edward the Fifth, pass in at the great hall door just prior to his death in the Tower. In the same manner we witness the first meeting of Catherine of Arragon and Prince Arthur, which took place in one of these apartments. Perhaps of higher consequence still is a lead-covered pulpit we discry in the distance; for Paul's-cross occupies a prominent place in the annals

of England and of the Reformation. But such archæological minutiæ must give place to the object of our
visit—the Meeting-house in Carter-lane.

Many readers will remember the old chapel. "The
meeting-house in Carter-lane," says Wilson, "is a
large, substantial brick building, of a square form,
and contains three galleries of very considerable
dimensions. The inside is finished with remarkable
neatness, and in point of workmanship is scarcely
equalled by any place of worship among the Dissenters in London. The sombre appearance it ex-
hibits, arising partly from the colour of the pews and
galleries, immediately arrests the attention, and appears much better suited to the solemnity of divine
worship than the theatrical style of decoration
adopted in many of our modern chapels."

Of Matthew Sylvester, the founder of this society
and the colleague of Baxter, only few memorials survive. During youth, and while possessing only slender
means, he found himself thrown upon the world.
Some friendly assistance enabled him to prosecute
his studies at Cambridge University; but he left his
college sooner than he would have done had he possessed ampler means. Soon afterwards he was preferred to the living of Gunnerly, in Lincolnshire; and
was there silenced by the Act of Uniformity in 1662.
Sylvester was highly esteemed by his diocesan, Dr.
Sanderson, who strongly persuaded him to conform;
but "the unfeigned assent and consent that was required of him were two things that he much stuck

at." In the years immediately succeeding the Bartholomew secession, Sylvester led a life of ease with some distinguished Nottinghamshire families. He emerged from retirement, and settled in London while the City was suffering from the devastation of fire and plague; and with exemplary bravery espoused the cause of Nonconformity. It is gratifying to find that, while slighting personal danger, he never realised the miseries which were then so often the penalties of a conscientious procedure. The harmony characterising the united action of Sylvester and Baxter was no less honourable than remarkable. Indeed, the veneration of the former for his more gifted colleague almost exceeded allowable bounds; for notwithstanding his constitutional shrinking from death, Sylvester only desired to live and die with Baxter. He survived his friend, however, about seventeen years, having been suddenly taken to his reward in the year 1708. "He was," says Calamy, " an able divine, a good linguist, no mean scholar, an excellent casuist, an admirable textuary, and one of uncommon divine eloquence in pleading at the throne of grace." According to Calamy also, Sylvester was a genius whom defective elocution alone prevented from shining as one of the luminaries of his era.

The ancient borough of Kidderminster is situated one hundred and twenty-four miles north-west of London, and was called by the Saxons, Chiderminster—*i.e.*, a church on the hill-side with a stream at its foot. This town—so indissolubly associated

with the name and labours of Richard Baxter—
could boast of its prestige long ere the leaven of
Puritanism influenced English society. John Beau-
champ, domestic steward to Richard the First, was
rewarded for services rendered to that monarch by
the barony of Kidderminster. About the middle of
the seventeenth century the poet Waller, as lord of
the manor, disposed of his rights to discharge some
heavy political fines. In early times Kidderminster
returned its member to Parliament, but, by some
means unexplained, the burghers were deprived of a
privilege they re-inherited on the passing of the first
Reform Bill. A charter, granted by Charles the
First, exempted the town from local magisterial interference. Then there are certain local customs,
inherited from a ruder age—in themselves quaintly
interesting, but the perpetuation of which reflects
little credit on modern intelligence. Thus, on electing a bailiff in the olden time, the townsmen mustered in the streets and waged a war of cabbage-
stalks; but fortunately "the lawless hour" was re-
stricted to the prescribed limits. Heralded by music,
the newly-chosen official and his attendant officers
then marched to the residence of the out-going
bailiff, and during their progress the populace were
expected to pelt them with apples. In former days
the town was extremely unhealthy, a fact accounted
for by the confinement necessitated by its staple
trade; but, while fever and consumption were making unchecked ravages among the inhabitants, the

atmosphere was highly salubrious, as the more satisfactory condition of the suburban population plainly
proved. When Baxter flourished, the people harboured a deeply-rooted horror of witchcraft; and
this prompted them summarily to impose a horsepond discipline on the objects of their aversion.
The vicarage is now worth about £1,100 a-year,
but in the seventeenth century it had scarcely a fifth
of that amount attached to it.   The impetus given
by Baxter to religion and philanthropy would seem
to be yet benefiting the town—e.g., the number of
chapels, schools, and provident societies is far higher
than the average for a town of eighteen thousand
souls.

Baxter was born in the year 1615, or about the
time that that courtly sycophant, Edward Villiers,
was rising into political ascendancy. The elder
Baxter was a gentleman of Shropshire, whose debts
by some considerable amount exceeded his estate.
Richard first saw the light at the seat of his maternal
grandfather, Richard Adinery, of Rowton, with whom
he spent the first decade of his existence, after
which he was taken to his parents at Eaton Constantine, a place of small note in the vicinity of
Shrewsbury. " His schoolmasters were both lewd
and ignorant"—a fact sufficient to account for his
defective education. Indeed, but for the grateful
assistance of John Owen, of Wroxeter, the youthful
Baxter would have fared worse than he did; but
while Owen was serviceable in one direction, he

bears the blame of having deprived his *protégé* of an university training. His parents intended sending Richard to one of the great national colleges, till, diverted from their plan by the counsel of Owen, they placed him with a neighbouring minister, whose knowledge was stored upon his library shelves rather than in his head. To general incompetence this tutor added the sin of indolence, and Richard was consequently allowed to roam at will among the books, with neither assistance nor advice. But even thus early he was animated by that amazing industry which, in his case, was constitutional; and therefore, in spite of the difficulties of his situation, he visibly improved in learning during his stay of eighteen months. At this conjuncture Owen, because dying of consumption, had his place for a time filled by Baxter.

The insight into the moral and religious condition of England at this era which Baxter affords us, is shockingly interesting. Thus a description of a confirmation as then observed reveals some characteristics of Laud's ascendancy. Such young parishioners as were willing congregated in the churchyard, and the bishop, while hurriedly walking round, placed his hands on the head of each, muttering the while some indistinct sentences, which completed the ceremony. In rural districts even bad sermons were at a premium. In the parish where Baxter resided, the incumbent, being blind, was only competent to repeat the prayers from memory, and consequently a thatcher and a tailor were hired to read the Scriptures. The vicar of Kidderminster was an illiterate drunkard, whose income was partly derived " from the celebration of unlawful marriages." Patrons of livings became Simoniacs, and were not ashamed to lease such parishes as were in their gift. As numbers of the clergy were scarcely superior to their plebeian neighbours, they occasionally supplemented their stipends by such menial crafts as those of ropemaking and woodcutting.

The villages around Shrewsbury, as they existed in the time of Richard's boyhood, may be taken as fair samples of rural England in those days. Too often the clergy were no less degraded than their flocks, and the accounts of the condition to which certain parishes degenerated sounds incredible when related in modern ears. With some bright exceptions, the clergy only seldom practised preaching. In the place of study they unblushingly substituted gaming, drinking, and vicious sports ; and the only reverence shown for the Sabbath was manifested by their encouraging maypole dances, and sundry village games, instead of honouring those dictates of religion or even of morality in unison with the character of the day of rest. Thus tutored by precept and example, the populace for the most part progressed in debauchery till unable to appreciate the instructions of grave and sober ministers. At Eaton Constantine, where Baxter resided, a sermon was rarely heard in the parish church, " and the service was run over very cursorily and irreverently, and when that was done the rest of the Lord's-day was profanely spent in dancing under a maypole and a great tree." In the midst of such terrible surroundings, young Baxter was preserved from serious contamination ; although as a child he was addicted to lying and orchard-robbing. The means of his conversion, which soon after occurred, were the reading of Parson's *Resolutions*, and Sibbs's *Bruised Reed*.

The genius and industry of Baxter were sufficiently manifest in youth to attract the notice of some influential neighbours well qualified to promote his interests. Even at this conjuncture, that " crazy body " restrained his ardour to a degree which his spirit could scarcely endure. He was an indefatigable student, and studied philosophy under Richard Garbett, vicar of Wroxeter. Then came life's changes, many of them fraught with danger. During the domination of Laud, when the King was hoping to impose prelacy on Scotland, some siren charmers gained Baxter's inexperienced ear, and advised his aspiring to the equivocal honours of a courtier. His fond parents were allured by the bait and dazzled at the advantages the proposal promised. He was, therefore, summarily despatched to White-hall, to be handsomely received by his patron, Sir Henry Herbert ; and Sir Henry would probably have advanced his interests had not the glittering world to which fortune had introduced him, been at utter variance with Richard's predilections.

A month at court was a complete surfeit. He returned to Eaton Constantine to become "more indefatigable in the pursuit of knowledge than can
easily be imagined."

On attaining his majority, Baxter was suffering
from excessive weakness, rendered more alarming by
a strong cough and spitting of blood. That consumption would speedily cut down his fragile body appeared an absolute certainty. For two years he
remained afflicted by this extreme debility, which all
supposed to be but the precursor of death. Notwithstanding such painful drawbacks, the young
scholar's longings were still for the Church; and a
desire to be useful even in the smallest degree, led
him to apply for ordination to the bishop of Worcester. Thus did Baxter inaugurate his ministry.

Baxter's splendid career—for so it may be truly
designated—commenced at Dudley, a notoriously
wicked place, which his ministry slightly benefited.
At this stage he was a zealous conformist; but on
attending to the controversy between the Church of
England and the Puritans, some hitherto accepted
opinions were shaken, although he occasionally reproved Nonconformists for what he termed their
want of charity. After staying nine months at
Dudley, he settled under William Madstard, who,
it is gratifying to learn, was "a grave and severe
ancient divine." For a manse Baxter appropriated
the neighbouring vicarage of Oldbury, a parish which,
with some of its neighbours, enjoyed exemption from

18

prelatical interference, so that the ministers were at
liberty to honour just what *régime* their consciences
prescribed. The two pastors were zealous evangelists
among an "ignorant and dead-hearted multitude."
The staple trade of the town seems to have been represented by the numerous alehouses ; and therefore,
it affords no matter for surprise, if the chief obstacles
to the progress of good were "tippling and ill company."

Meantime the precursors of civil war were appearing thick and fast. By a resolution of Convocation
the bishops were required to impose the Etcœtera
oath, or to oblige the clergy to swear they would
never consent to the slightest alteration in the Rubric.
Next followed the imposition of prelacy upon Scotland, with its attendant train of troubles.   Then,
amid the prevailing discord, Ship-money became the
chief bone of contention; but the story of Ship-
money is too well known to need recapitulating here.
When the Long Parliament assembled in November,
1640, Baxter and Madstard were stationed at Bridgnorth.   We are afforded a few glimpses into the old
town, and see something of the local contentions of
those troublous days.   Let us take this example.
On a certain Saturday afternoon the Lord President
of the Welsh Marches, (the Earl of Bridgwater)
passed through Bridgnorth, *en route* for London.
Many of the meaner sort among the parishioners
embraced this opportunity of impeaching their
ministers on the basis of Nonconformity. Neither

of them, it was truthfully averred, would wear a surplice nor make the sign of the cross in baptism. They obstinately refused to pray and declaim against the Scots, as recently ordered by their diocesan. The wary Bridgwater listened with cautious attentiveness, he attended church, and even gave the petitioners some general advice; but when he found himself safely distant from the townsmen's importunity, he sent a message to declare that he had no jurisdiction in the matter.

Among the flagrant abuses which invited the attention of the Long Parliament, those of the Church Establishment were not the least flagitious. That Establishment was crowded with reverend time-servers, whose notorious licentiousness or literary incapacity bore testimony to their unfitness for the office they usurped. Feeling, therefore, that an era of freedom was inaugurated, numbers of parishes, petitioned to be relieved of pastors whose connection with the Church was a disgrace to the Christian profession. It was thus with Kidderminster; and, on account of the scandalous lives of the vicar and curate, their supercession was allowed. Baxter took possession of the parish, but the vicar retained his dwelling-house and a principal share of the stipend.

Baxter's marvellous experience at Kidderminster fills a page in the history of the Church as gladsome as it is encouraging. What he really accomplished is sufficiently wonderful, but its happy colours are set off to greater advantage by the dark ground of

18*

an unpromising beginning. His entrance on the
work of transforming the parish was resented by the
passionate hatred of a revengeful populace, and,
therefore, his herculean achievement of conquering
the dissolute habits of a town will proclaim to all
time that, his fragile body, which for half a century
people supposed was but stepping into the grave,
was inflamed by a zeal of enthusiasm having its
source in heaven. A programme of his pastoral
procedure has been bequeathed us. Besides the
heavy duties of each returning Sabbath, he held
week-day meetings for common instruction and
prayer, for the catechising of families, for discipline,
and for ministerial intercommunication. During his
connection with it, the church was enlarged by the
erection of five galleries; and, from being one of the
most irreligious, Kidderminster came to be one of
the most Christian of English towns. As such it
was the wonder of visitors and the delight of its
pastor.

The shock of civil war disquieted the old borough
soon after Baxter's settlement, he being " a mournful
spectator of the public confusions." Such, however,
as desire to study his extraordinary career at Kidderminster must peruse the narrative of Sylvester,
or its abridgment by Calamy. Understanding something of physic, the indefatigable pastor exercised
that art for the benefit of his poorer people, till he
deemed it prudent to abandon the practice in favour
of a regular practitioner. He truly delighted in

effecting good by any lawful means, no matter how great the self-denial. We find, for example, that the sixty or eighty pounds a-year, remitted him by the publishers of his books, were charitably distributed, as also were other gains not absolutely required for bare subsistence. His beneficence at one time would prompt the placing of a youth at the university, or anon, it distributed books among the poorer people ; and the latter class predominated at Kidderminster, for few, if any, of the inhabitants were wealthy. The leading manufacturers maintained their commercial state on forty pounds a-year, while the majority of master weavers lived as honest citizens on only half such a revenue. The people in general were extremely poor, and, to quote Baxter's own expression, "lived from hand to mouth."

On the raising of the standard of civil war persons suspected of Puritanical sympathies often risked imminent danger of outrage, even of life itself, from the "loyal" populace. Sometimes, while walking the streets, such as presumed to wear short hair would suddenly find themselves the objects of sudden and ferocious attack. Among the profane, "Puritan" was a contemptuous and reproachful term. Certain of the bishops rose into popularity by repressing too strict notions of morality, and by openly countenancing the Book of Sports. While extending their favour to the exhilarating pastime of Sabbath games, these ecclesiastics despised the monotony of afternoon lectures. When we analyse the constituent

parts of the forces arrayed on the Royalist side, our
admiration strengthens for those who discerned the
signs of the times, and risked life, property, and all
dear to them as freemen of England, rather than
succumb to the humiliation of seeing the iniquitous
cause of the King triumphant. In the City of London
men took their plate, and women their trinkets, to
the common treasury of the Parliament at Guildhall.
As a keen observer of his kind, Baxter noticed well
the elements which made up the contending parties.
The partisans of Charles were the upper classes and
their tenants; the defenders of the Parliament included the smaller gentry, with such as more highly
valued religion and morality. In the main, Baxter
himself sided with the Parliament; but the town
and vicinity of Kidderminster adhered to the Royalist
standard. Some adventures, encountered about this
time, are illustrative of the state of English society
in that era of ceaseless commotion. Once, while
riding through the city of Worcester, his grave-look-
ing mien and closely-cropped hair were noted by
certain passengers, who raised the usual cry of
"Down with the Roundheads!" but his fleet and
faithful steed helped Baxter out of this dilemma.
At Gloucester he enjoyed immunity from peril
because the town had gone over to the Parliament,
on which account, by contrasting with some neighbouring places, it appeared like another sphere. In
those eventful days our author's unsettled mode of
life was sufficiently diversified. At one time, while

the battle of Edgehill was raging, we find him preaching at Alcester, the church being shaken by the vibration of distant artillery. In the midst of such alarms he likewise preached a sermon at Bridgnorth on the death of Madstard, his former colleague. He boldly reproved the townspeople for so little profiting by their pastor's ministrations, on which account some judgment would surely visit their homesteads. This prophecy was strangely verified. Soon after, the forces of the King relentlessly destroyed both church and town, and by retiring behind the castle ramparts, they were enabled to defy their Parliamentary opponents. On peace being restored, and the town rebuilt, Baxter, on a memorable occasion, addressed the inhabitants, but the emotion affecting both hearers and preacher made the progress of the service a matter of difficulty.

Kidderminster was roughly shaken by the war, so that the pastor and a large portion of his flock were constrained to take refuge at Coventry. Among congenial society at Coventry, Baxter, who stayed about a year, and acted in the capacity of garrison chaplain, was lodged as a guest of Simon King, an hospitable burgher.

In the estimation of Royalist generals, Puritanism was the offence of offences, and the troopers, when able, were allowed to take sanguinary vengeance on such districts as sheltered so obnoxious a system or religion and morality. Thus, in common with others, the house of the elder Baxter was cleared of its goods, being left with "almost nothing but lumber." Numerous families left their Kidderminster homes to live a life of temporary exile, having for their chief means of support what movable property they could carry away. If too poor to command such a subsistence, the fugitives earned their bread by taking arms, choosing rather to serve as soldiers among freemen than to retain their hearths by violating conscience in obeying the call of a law-breaking monarch.

We can see something of Coventry as it really was during that year of tumult, 1643. England was shaken by civil and military discord, but Coventry was tranquil. News of Edgehill fight, of Cromwell's marches and manœuvres, or of Hampden's death, was peacefully carried into that quiet city, which is represented as having resembled a dry house unharmed by distant storms. This exemption from action, however, bred polemical contention; for the Presbyterians, headed by Baxter, gave particular heed to "An Anabaptist taylor," the result being a sharp controversy of small credit to the combatants. The Baptists put on a very determined front by sending to Bedford for Benjamin Cox, a renowned champion of their denomination, and known to his contemporaries as "An old Anabaptist, minister, a bishop's son, and no mean scholar." Other matters, nevertheless, demanded Baxter's attention. He travelled with a regiment to

Wem, a short distance from Shrewsbury, and was there made the happy instrument of releasing his father from prison.   After living for two months in the society of former friends and amid old associations, the pastor returned to Coventry. Such minutiæ may be accounted as trifles ; but let it be remembered that, they are trifles in the life of Baxter.

Partial as he was to a studious retirement, and loving as he did the functions of his sacred calling, Baxter's aversion to party politics and the excitement of war, would have prevented his enrolment among the army chaplains had not the higher consideration of duty overcome objections.   He consented to travel with the forces, and his adventures included a witnessing of the siege of Worcester, also that of Banbury Castle, and the important capture of Bridgwater. As we, at this distance of time, quietly note the action of men who won freedom for themselves and posterity, it strikes us as strange that such heroes could, in religious controversy, drown the terrors of war.   The soldiers, by their interminable wranglings concerning doctrine and practice, occasioned their chaplain serious inconvenience, for he would sometimes spend an entire day in promoting an amicable settlement of a vexed dispute.   The truth is, in those early years of the war the sects in general engrossed too much of Baxter's attention.   A well-meant opposition to Seekers, Ranters, and Quakers—who, he said, were "Ranters reversed"—occupied hours which he might have more profitably employed. But the middle of the seventeenth century, it is only fair to remember, was emphatically an age of disagreement, and of an undue prominence being awarded to minor matters. To illustrate this proposition, and show with what zest the populace divided into parties, it will be sufficient to mention that, on one memorable day, and before a crowded audience, Baxter and Toombs argued the baptismal controversy from nine in the morning till five in the evening. The decision of character shown by the former was not less apparent in politics than in religion. While strenuously opposing the policy of the Court, he could yet exert his great influence against the Covenant; and he prevented that famous instrument from being subscribed both in the town of Kidderminster and in the county of Worcester.

Although Baxter and others declined subscribing the Covenant, they refused in after times to pray for the success of Cromwell's Scottish campaign. Indeed, these Presbyterian divines acted unfairly in regard to Cromwell; for while benefiting by his wholesome rule, they regarded him as a mere usurper. We are, nevertheless, constrained to admire that straightforward honesty with which such men, under all skies and circumstances, uttered their sentiments. Thus, while preaching before the Protector and his retinue, Baxter denounced the sins of politicians who sought to promote their individual profit by taking advantage of the public distractions. On another occasion, he explained to Cromwell his political views in a conference of five hours' duration, and the purport of those views was, that Englishmen still prized their ancient monarchy. Like his too sanguine compeers, Baxter hailed the Restoration with many joyful anticipations, and, on the day preceding the King's recall—April 30th, 1660—preached before the Parliament.

At length the long-wished-for Restoration was consummated. The rude rejoicings of 1660 soon proved themselves the precursors of national trouble and of national humiliation. Baxter was speedily superseded by the sequestered vicar, and by the vigilence of his enemy, Sir Ralph Clare, was expelled the pulpit, notwithstanding that in the capacity of curate he would gladly have laboured unremunerated. By excluding Baxter from his diocese the Bishop of Worcester earned the censure of posterity. The parishioners of Kidderminster were not slow at expressing an admiration for their late pastor, and a corresponding disgust at the action of their diocesan. By violent invective from the parish pulpit, a trial was made to teach the people a more prelatical behaviour; but these spasmodic reformers could only evoke the derision of the townsmen. The people stayed away from their parish church—a procedure which prompted the rising party to resort to persecution. Recusants, on refusing to conform, fared very roughly; for while some were despoiled of their goods, others languished in the pestilent cells of the county gaol. The tactics of the episcopal party were characterised by neither principle nor honour. Imaginary plots were concocted to implicate the more conspicuous Dissenters. Thus letters would be forged purporting to be addressed by Baxter to certain others, specifying that arms would be provided at a given time and place. On such trumped-up charges many worthy citizens were imprisoned.

The autumn of 1661 saw the Nonconformists in a state of active vigilance. Venner's ill-timed and ill-fated plot—hatched at Limehouse, and acted out in the city streets—was yet affectionately remembered by certain "phanatiques," who now systematically opposed the re-introduction of the Common Prayer. The seamen of Plymouth " determined that the Common Prayer shall not come into Mr. Hughes's church;" and this action, so the populace were made to believe, originated with the Baptists and the Quakers. The most sanguine of the disaffected, however, entertained but a slender hope of securing toleration, and so wisely provided a vessel for the common use of such as preferred escaping to the Continent. By such means Hanserd Knollys retired into Holland, to avoid that official vengeance from which the Baptists so pre-eminently suffered. At a meeting in Southwark, convened by the latter denomination, the speakers referred to the King as " the beast ;" and so aggrieved did the Government consider themselves, that one of Cromwell's old lieutenants, of the name of Carter, was gravely charged with being "An Anabaptist costermonger." Intelligence reached

Whitehall of a coalition of Presbyterians and Baptists, who were fermenting sedition and preparing to
repress the Government by force of arms. In the
spring of 1663, the iron rule imposed on the nation
began to bear its legitimate fruit, for many, who
were prisoners for conscience' sake, died of disease
and of suffocation in the overcrowded prisons. Thus,
on the liberation of two hundred Quakers, twenty
were missing; that is to say, twenty lay dead in
their cells. The Presbyterians made some slight
show of conformity, but the spirit of resistance
animating the Quakers and Baptists was not to be
subdued by the most relentless cruelty. The
majority of those by whom the ejected clergy were
superseded were quite unworthy of any sacred
trust, as their disorderly lives and literary incompetence abundantly proved. Meanwhile, a bad
government, weakly administered, was disastrously
affecting trade. The mercantile world had no confidence in rulers, who simultaneously repressed Dissent and encouraged Popery. Taking advantage of
the times, the Dutch used every art to allure the
best of our English populace away. As regarded
the ejected pastors, " Some teach in schools, some
get into families; some cut tobacco and take up very
mean employments." Cornelius Burgess, a doctor
of divinity, whose income had been £1,000 a-year,
was among the number who begged their bread.

About this date Baxter and Calamy met with an
adventure which deserves recording. The two were

commanded to attend at Court. On proceeding to
Whitehall, they found the King in the best of
humours, and not inclined to spare his condolence.
With the true art of a royal dissembler, Charles
confessed his regret that such lights were not "pro-
testing against Popery." As the divines were passing
to the reception-room, many in assumed superiority
enquired, "What do these Presbyters here ?" When
the fact of the royal complaisance became known, however, this arrogance was superseded by " Your servant,
Dr. Calamy and Mr. Baxter." It is a curious discovery that, the more superstitious Dissenters as-
cribed their troubles to the adverse action of the
stars. Such persons conversed in mysterious tones
about "a strange conjuncture of the planets called
Trigon," which occurred in December, 1662.*

Bigotry and intolerance bore their fruit in the Act
of Uniformity. Baxter preached his farewell sermon in the Established Church on the last Sabbath
of May, 1662, and thus, for example's sake, adopted
the procedure of seceding three months prior to
Black Bartholomew. The Court seems to have been
really disturbed by the rumours of dissaffection
which the silencing of so great a number of faithful
ministers awakened among the religious sections.
When the coalition of the Presbyterians and other
Nonconformists was talked about, the City was re-

---

* See Calendars of State Papers, Domestic Series, Charles
II., 1662, &c.

presented as being the refuge of disloyalty. The King's uneasiness was increased by the return to London of disbanded troops, and by the "Multiplying of public and private lectures." The Conventicle Act, passed in the summer of 1663, was partly the offspring of these misgivings. While thus depressed on all hands, the Dissenters could not agree as to the lawfulness of attending parish churches; some advocated an occasional support to the established worship; others, demanding an entire separation, assumed a braver attitude.

What the social and political condition of the Dissenters actually was, immediately after Black Bartholomew, may be inferred from contemporary letters and documents among the State Papers. The Act of Uniformity was very rigorously enforced. Cared for by Providence and approved by conscience, still the excluded ministers, in their daily wanderings, were constrained to act with extreme caution, even in life's commonest affairs. Great numbers of pastors were crowded into the too narrow gaols; and, through being closely huddled together with common criminals, many were stifled by the pestilential atmosphere, or wasted by the ravages of prison fever. As before observed, the most determined stand taken against the intolerance of the ascendant party was that assumed by the Baptists and Quakers. It were idle to deny that, the ranks of Nonconformity in those days included many fanatics; but to assume that they differed in this respect from their opponents is

an ungenerous, because an unfair assumption.   Accounts are extant of the rumours which the oppressed
people industriously circulated ; *e.g.*, Providence was
appearing ; was even then avenging the wrongs of
the elect.   A certain clergyman had been smitten
by death after "Yielding to put on a surplice."
Another, while on his way to conform, had fallen
from his horse and died.   Such occurrences as these
were construed into the judgments of Heaven upon
faithless Amalekites.   On the other hand, the populace, intoxicated by loyalty, showed a supreme indifference to all religion ; and churches attached to
extensive cures only attracted from ten to forty
communicants.   In numberless instances, the clergy
were not only disgraced to their high profession, but
were a scandal to humanity.   Because they only
gave a desultory attention to their duties, such men
were unheeded by the vulgar, and despised by the
discerning.   Bands of devoted ones were found,
however, to perpetuate the principles and worship of
the Church.   Such, indeed, often took advantage
of the gloom of night ; and became indebted to damp
cellars in obscure thoroughfares, or to the rural seclusion of suburban barns ; but amid such adverse surroundings, they strengthened one another in Christ ;
and while dispensing the commemorative Cup and the
Broken Bread, adjured their fellows to be faithful
unto death.   To the Papists a far milder treatment
was meted out ; for they scarcely provoked any legal
interference.   When it actually occurred, the arrest

of Romanists was a mere subterfuge; and they were commonly released without further trouble. As had long been the case, the bishops were the uncompromising opponents of a tolerant policy. In the spring of 1663, for example, politicians were broaching the subject of relaxing the persecuting laws; but the prelates at once communicated with the commoners in the rural districts, and urged them to defeat so pernicious a measure. Their excessive grievances drove great numbers of Dissenters out of England; and their country's loss was the lasting gain of Holland and America.

It will scarcely amount to a digression, if, for insertion here, we select some particulars of the amiable Margaret Charlton, who eventually became Mistress Baxter. With exquisite gracefulness, her husband has delineated her character; and his picture is not tinted with overdrawn panegyric. The Charltons ranked among the county families of Worcestershire; and Margaret's father, who did not marry till his locks were grey, held the office of Justice of the Peace. On the breaking out of the civil war, the family became politically divided; Mrs. Charlton fortifying her mansion for the King, while her brother-in-law fought on the Parliamentary side. As will be imagined, feelings of ill-will and jealousy sprang up in the family; and these were aggravated by the fact, that Robert Charlton was next heir-at-law to the widow's only son. By connivance of the former, his sister's seat was stormed and taken by

19

the popular party.   After her son had settled in life,
Mrs. Charlton removed with her only daughter to
Kidderminster, the latter then being a handsome
maiden of the age of seventeen.   These ladies, by
their kindness and charity, soon won the esteem of
their neighbours the weavers ; for by what Baxter
calls a " Manly patience," the matron subdued her
constitutional infirmity of temper.

During the summer of 1662 Baxter was the subject of some curious enquiry and witty comment.
Like certain others of his class, he had, in an un-
guarded hour, extolled celibacy as a more convenient
state for Christian ministers than wedlock ; and like
those others, whose experience was identical, his
unnatural arguments were the prelude to taking a
wife.   The story is a pretty one ; and its beautiful
sequel pleasingly instructive.

Baxter may have been first drawn towards the
Charltons by their seconding his labours among the
parishioners of Kidderminster ; but in time, and by
almost imperceptible degrees, the sage found himself
in the power of a siren charmer, whose subtlety of
fascination he had hitherto little suspected.   He
chid himself, it would seem, on account of his natural
weakness, and resolved to exercise in future a more
becoming circumspection.   In such matters, as all
know, it is far easier to resolve than to act, especially when the fair object to be prudently avoided
appears week after week in the family pew with a
pensive pallor superseding her wonted rosiness.   It

so happened with Baxter and Margaret Charlton, till a mutual understanding was arranged which ended in a life union. The provisions of the marriage contract retained in her own power the whole of Margaret's fortune, which her lover would not deign to touch for fear men, by calling him a mercenary, should bring dishonour on the Gospel. They were married on September 10th, 1662, at St. Bennet-fink's Church, London. The few spectators who congregated on that autumn morning beheld a spectacle unique of its kind. The bridegroom was a poor clerk without a cure, with a prospect sufficiently dismal stretching before him, although his path of penury was a self-chosen path. The approval of conscience was above money value; and Margaret, with maidenly enthusiasm, admired that exalted piety and self-denial which had rejected the highest preferment for the sake of preserving an unsullied rectitude; and as a bride, was more than happy in possessing the means of succouring the man of her choice and veneration. Their after life was a strange experience of what may be termed joyous trouble. They were compelled frequently to remove from one situation to another, and on this account alone suffered much inconvenience amounting to real hardship. But wherever Margaret was there also was that lightsome cheerfulness only springing from unwavering faith. "I know not," says Baxter, "that she ever came to any place where she did not extraordinarily win the love of the inhabitants." Their

19*

first home was in Moorfields : thence they removed to Acton, and there successively occupied several houses. Margaret's chief temporal felicity consisted in promoting the welfare of others. Her liberal charities and gentle mien greatly endeared her to her poorer neighbours. Indeed, she so won the affection of the inhabitants that when she removed to a station ten miles distant the people of Acton attempted to restore their favourite by offering to subscribe the rent of a house. The presence of such a ministering angel lightened the heaviest burden: "She cheerfully went with me to prison," says her husband. "*She brought her best bed thither.*"

For a short time this happy couple lived at Totteridge. "The coal smoke so filled the room that we all day sat in that it was as a cloud "—words conveying a graphic insight into the everyday life of an ejected minister. At first it was Margaret's custom to dispense a tenth of her income to the poor; but at Baxter's suggestion the proportion was largely augmented. An extraordinary zeal in ministering to the poor occasionally exhausted her resources; but at such times she mortified her family pride by accepting from others what was necessary to sustain her beneficent action. She also derived great pleasure from seeing youths in training for the ministry, although none more heartily despised a student lacking " Good wits and parts."

Margaret died in June, 1681, at " a pleasant and convenient house in Southampton-square," a house she herself selected in her tender regard for her husband's health. On the departure into rest of this estimable woman the poor of Saint James's and Saint Martin's bewailed her loss as that of a guardian angel. With many tears did Baxter deposit her dear remains among the ruins of Christchurch; and probably he realised a keenness of suffering he had little imagined possible when he found himself separated for all time from the object of his purest love. How did he carry with him to the grave Margaret's dying words, "My mother is in heaven . . . . . and thou and I shall be in heaven." "The Lord gave, and the Lord hath taken away," exclaimed the stricken husband; "and he hath taken away, but that upon my desert, which he had given me undeservedly near nineteen years. Blessed be the name of the Lord. I am waiting to be next. The door is open. Death will quickly draw the veil, and make us see how near we were to God and one another, and did not (sufficiently) know it. Farewell, vain world, and welcome true everlasting life." *

To return to our more immediate subject, we find that Baxter on one occasion preached before Charles the Second, in the capacity of chaplain-in-ordinary and had conscience permitted, he might have transferred himself to the See of Hereford. As to other events in his life at this time, there are many letters

---

* Vide the closing paragraph of *A Breviate of the Life of Margaret . . . Wife of Richard Baxter.*

among the State papers containing allusions to him which deserve attention. According to the effusion of an informer, one Edmund Potter, the Dissenters boasted of their perfect acquaintance with Court proceedings; and derisively spoke of the Royal forces, which 50,000 patriots in London alone could annihilate. A Colonel Hunt is mentioned as a leader of the revolutionary party. Every Tuesday Hunt kept open house, and gave a "parson's ordinary" to the Nonconformists. Another mansion, seventeen miles down the Western-road, was a notorious Dissenting rendezvous, and the company often included Baxter, Manton, and their companions. The councils were strictly private, the women of the household being rigidly excluded. Such materials as these should be used by the historian with much discrimination, and the wheat carefully sifted from the chaff. For example, it is satisfactory to learn, even from such sources, that the Nonconformist leaders were occasionally entrusted with large sums of money, wherewith to succour their poorer brethren. We are informed, moreover, of the more prominent Dissenting stations. At the home of Hampden, in Buckinghamshire, Baxter often preached. Another refuge was the Countess of Exeter's mansion, in Little-Britain, where the most eminent Puritans were wont to officiate.

Then followed a time of anguish and of desolation, in which the irreligious populace were constrained to share. They were truly days of terrible

national trial. But equal to the crisis there
emerged from a hitherto enforced seclusion such
spirits as Janeway, Chester, Vincent, and others.
Like true spiritual heroes, these boldly entered the
stricken city to attend the sick, to console the
dying, and to preach the Gospel to flocks now forsaken by their affrighted pastors. Many sad
reminiscences might be collected of that fearful
ordeal through which England passed. On returning
to his Acton lodgings, Baxter found his friends of
the household still alive, but the churchyard
resembled a " Plow'd field with graves." Respecting
the Plague and the Fire, a few facts are obtainable
from our author's life. The citizens, we learn,
watched the flames with speechless misery, their
useless engines standing by the while. Then, in a
sudden and mysterious manner, the fire ceased its
ravages. The vaults of Old St. Paul's suggested
themselves to the stationers as a safe asylum for
those literary treasures with which the vicinity
abounded. But, alas! the books shared destruction
with the sanctuary. The King, attended by a staff
of nobles, rode about in great consternation, and as
impotent to check the relentless fire as was the
least important among the spectators. A more sig-
nificant fact was the appearance on the scene of the
Nonconformist leaders as already referred to. Taking
advantage of the confusion, they showed a magnanimous disregard of law, opened their meeting-houses,
and entered on pastoral work. Indeed, about this

time or soon after, the Dissenters' hopes were in the
ascendant by reason of the fall of Clarendon and the
rise of Buckingham.   The latter was influenced by
more liberal principles, and for the time religion
seems to have benefited by his accession to power.
Some were even sufficiently sanguine to talk of a
scheme of Comprehension.

During Baxter's residence at Acton he instituted
in his own home a meeting for Christian instruction.
The statutes against Dissent were so stringently
enforced that only a scanty assembly was attracted,
although his neighbours held their distinguished
townsman in high veneration, and correspondingly
valued his counsels.   When the laws for a season
were somewhat relaxed, however, Baxter was quite
overwhelmed with enquirers anxious to profit by his
able teachings.   The Vicar of Acton was a zealous
bigot, employing for a curate " a weak, dull young
man, that spent most of his time in alehouses."
Baxter attended church for example's sake, but was
no less on that account an eyesore to the worthless
clergy.   These "loyal" divines could little brook
the presence of their illustrious parishioner, and so
proceeded to concoct some heavy charges against
him, which were presented to the King.   Charles
never cared to have his pleasure interrupted by
clerical petitions; and at once rid himself of the
present intruders by referring them to the Bishop of
London—the sequel being that, as a Nonconformist
recusant, Baxter was committed to Clerkenwell Gaol.

All this occurred in 1670; but his imprisonment, it is pleasing to find, occasioned our author only slight inconvenience. He was respectfully and even considerately treated, and in addition to the use of a garden, enjoyed a comfortable apartment, while friends without plentifully supplied him with the necessaries of life. Infamous as were the times, the arrest of such a man drew down on the heads of those in power an inconvenient amount of odium. The efforts of friends at Court to obtain a release were seconded by Buckingham, who represented to Charles how such proceedings damaged his Majesty's reputation. Brought up by a writ of *habeas corpus*, the prisoner was acquitted by the Court of Common Pleas.

A short time after the above episode, Baxter lost a thousand pounds by the closing of the Exchequer; but a mere loss of wealth only slightly concerned him. In 1672 he took advantage of the Indulgence, and took out a preacher's licence. In that same year was founded the Merchants' Lecture; and who more fitting than Baxter to assist in inaugurating that famous institution, notwithstanding that the first sermon he preached in the course was denounced as Arminian by a certain faction of the citizens? He also served on another lecture in Fetter-lane; but in a sketch like the present it will be impossible completely to follow the thread of so diversified a career. When his heart and home were desolated by the removal of Margaret, his inward bitterness was supplemented by the persecution which about that time broke out with renewed virulence. Under the provisions of the Five Mile Act, he was once more suddenly arrested, and, as he had lately preached four times, the fines amounted to two hundred pounds. His strength was now reduced by age and disease ; yet he was only saved from the hardships peculiar to felons by the interposition of a friend, who publicly certified that the proceedings were endangering the pastor's life ; and such really being the case, Baxter was allowed to return to his bed. The King interfered in Baxter's favour, and the suit was abandoned ; but notwithstanding the royal influence, the latter lost the chief portion of his books and furniture—a loss which compelled him to relinquish housekeeping and to retire into lodgings.

We are assisted in forming an estimate of the state of public affairs at this date (1683) by many stray facts drawn from various sources. It was the year of the judicial murder of Russell and Sydney. Government informers were animated by a relentless industry ; for they even pounced on such mere youths and maidens as were found at Nonconformist meetings. In numerous instances very young persons were convicted of rioting on evidence no more satisfactory than that of having attended conventicles. Of these some were fined, some were imprisoned, and others were doomed to beat hemp at Bridewell. Other facts rise to the surface proving the un-

principled Government to have been as devoid of
honour as of charity. A certain clergyman, for
example, bequeathed six hundred pounds for distribution among sixty Bartholomew confessors, but the
Lord Chancellor ruled the bequest to be illegal, and
the money was not recovered until after the Revolution. A list was made of a thousand persons
suspected of dangerous practices; and in the estimation of the authors, such a galaxy necessarily included Baxter. On the appearance of a company
of officers to arrest him, our divine retired to his
study; and as locks could not be broken with impunity, his enemies determined to allow him neither
sleep nor refreshment; and to effect their design,
six men were stationed throughout the night at the
chamber door. After being arraigned three times
before the sessions, the old man was bound over in
heavy amounts to keep the peace. Pitiable to the
last degree must have been the condition of England,
and degraded indeed her Government, when the dangerous classes were made to include the devoted
and laborious Baxter.

Thus days and years flew on, and time brought
its wonted round of adventure. As regarded Richard
Baxter, the succeeding and iniquitous reign of James
the Second was destined to witness the perpetration of
a crowning piece of judicial folly. Jeffreys being now
in the ascendant, he proved himself a worthy agent
of a perfidious master. Immediately after the death
of Charles, Baxter was indicted for calumniating

the bishops in his paraphrase on the New Testament.
As all concerned knew perfectly well, the allusions
complained of referred to certain ancient pastors;
but the Government were glad of a lame excuse for
denouncing the book as " scandalous and seditious,"
since such a procedure promised to punish the
writer. The case came on in May, 1685, when
Baxter was in so weakly a condition that his counsel
endeavoured to get the trial postponed: " I will not
give another minute to save his life," roared Jeffreys.
" We have had to do with other sorts of persons;
but now we have a saint to deal with, and I know
how to deal with saints as well as sinners." Just
at that moment a neighbouring pillory was fittingly
occupied by Dr. Oates; and the wit of the judge
prompted a parallel between the plotter and the
divine: " He," cried his lordship, referring to the
lying informer, and pointing to the court-yard, " He
suffers for the truth; but if Baxter did but stand on
the other side of the pillory with him, I would say
two of the greatest rogues in the kingdom stood
there."

On the day of trial Baxter entered the court at
Guildhall, with a mien betokening serene com-
posure, such as a sense of innocence, and of the
injustice awarded him only could have engendered.
He was attended by Sir Henry Ashurst and Dr.
Bates; for now that dear ministering angel, whose
gentle heroism had so often encouraged him, was
aiding the joy of other spheres. On all sides

eminent persons thronged the court. Many conflicting sympathies were represented; but perhaps
none sanctioned that native insolence of the monster
who presided, and who disgraced in common both
his species and the bench of justice. The first case
of the day being concluded, the clerk proceeded to
call another, when he suddenly heard himself reproved in savage but familiar tones : " *You* BLOCK-
HEAD ; the next case is between Richard Baxter
and the King." Accordingly the differences between the divine and the Crown were entered into ;
and the obnoxious passages—the alleged reflections
on the English prelates—were read. The solicitude
of Sir Henry Ashurst had provided for the defence
the ablest counsel the town afforded, in the persons
of Wallop and Pollexfen ; * and one of these gentlemen now essayed to address the court : " My Lord,
I humbly conceive the bishops Mr. Baxter speaks of
were the plagues of the church and of the world."

* Pollexfen opened the defence. "When the trial came
on at Guildhall, a crowd of those who loved and honoured
Baxter filled the court. At his side stood Dr. William Bates,
one of the most eminent of the Nonconformist divines. Two
Whig barristers of great note Pollexfen and Wallop appeared
for the defendant. Pollexfen had scarcely begun his address
to the jury, when the Chief Justice broke forth, 'Pollexfen,
I know you well, I will set a mark on you. You are the
patron of the faction. This is an old rogue, a schismatical
knave, a hypocritical villain. He hates the Liturgy. He
would have nothing but long-winded cant without book :'
and then his Lordship turned up his eyes, clasped his hands,

" Mr. Wallop," screamed Jeffreys, " I observe you are in all these dirty causes, and were it not for you gentlemen of the long robe that hold up these factious knaves by the chin we should not be at the pass we are." " My Lord," returned Wallop, " I humbly conceive that the passages accused are natural deductions from the text." " You humbly conceive," Jeffreys again bellowed, " and I humbly conceive. Swear him. Swear him." Wallop however, was too accustomed to such legal routine to be readily cowed. " My Lord," he said, " I am counsel for the defendant, and if I understand either Latin or English the information now brought against Mr. Baxter upon such slight ground is a greater reflection upon the Church of England than anything contained in the book." But the lawyer was no match for his ferocious opponent. " Sometimes you humbly conceive," now cried the latter, " and sometimes you are very positive. You talk of your skill

and began to sing through his nose, in imitation of what he supposed to be Baxter's style of praying, ' Lord, we are thy people, thy dear people, thy peculiar people.'' Pollexfen gently reminded the Court that his late majesty had thought Baxter deserving of a bishopric. ' And what ailed the old blockhead then,' cried Jeffreys, ' that he did not take it?' His fury now almost rose to madness. He called Baxter a dog, and swore that it would be no more than justice to whip such a villain through the whole City.'"—*Macaulay's Hist. Eng.,* chap. iv. To Pollexfen the credit belongs of having given a smart repartee to the judge's indecent mimicry:—"*My Lord, some will think it hard measure to stop these men's mouths, and not let them speak through their noses.*"

in church history, and of your understanding Latin
and English. I think I understand something of
them as well as you; but in short, must tell you
that if you don't understand your duty better I
shall teach it you." Soon after Jeffreys was heard
denouncing Baxter "as an enemy to the name of
thing, the office and person of bishops." It was next
argued that in certain passages of the Paraphrase,
bishops were respectfully alluded to. Then Baxter
himself attempted to get a hearing. "My Lord, I
have been so moderate with respect to the church, that
I have incurred the censure of many of the Dissenters
on that account." "Baxter for bishops," retorted
the judge, "that's a merry conceit indeed; turn to
it; turn to it." An advocate immediately took the
volume and read : "Great respect is due to those
truly called to be bishops " — " Ay," interrupted
Jeffreys, with one of his savagest expressions, " Ay,
that's himself, and such rascals called to be bishops
of Kidderminster and other such places. Bishops
set apart by such factious, snivelling Presbyterians
as himself. A Kidderminster bishop he means,
according to the saying of a late learned author,
' every parish shall maintain a tithe-pig metropolitan.'"
Another endeavour on Baxter's part to make himself
heard provoked the well-known outburst, " Richard,
Richard, dost thou think we'll hear thee poison the
court ? Richard, thou art an old fellow, an old
knave. Thou hast written books enough to load a
cart, everyone as full of sedition (I might say

treason) as an egg is full of meat. . . . I know
thou hast a mighty party, and I see a great many
of the brotherhood in corners waiting to see what
will become of their mighty donne; but . . . I
will crush you all." On what was supposed to be
the conclusion of the evidence Baxter ventured to
ask, "Does your Lordship think any jury will
pretend to pass a verdict upon me after such a
trial?" "I'll warrant you, Mr. Baxter," was the
rejoinder; "don't you trouble yourself about that."
While walking from the court, accompanied by Sir
Henry Ashurst, the defendant turned on the wicked
judge and told him, that a predecessor of his would
have acted differently. "There is not an honest
man in England," was the reply, "but takes you for
a great rogue." When judgment was given, on a
future day, the author was ordered to forfeit five
hundred marks.

As Baxter had but recently lost a thousand
pounds by the closing of the Exchequer, the fine
was not discharged, and he was, therefore, imprisoned in the King's Bench as a defaulter.* Soon
after he was set at liberty and allowed to live in

* The sympathy Baxter's trials drew forth must have
greatly cheered him. At this date young Matthew Henry was
a student at Gray's Inn. The future commentator visited
the Puritan leader in his confinement, and gracefully offered
him a gift of money from Philip Henry; but, as the latter
was an ejected minister, Richard could not be prevailed upon
to accept the present by all the powers of persuasion the
youthful Matthew could command.

London, notwithstanding the provisions to the contrary of the Oxford Act. He now removed to Charterhouse-square, his last earthly home, and about the same time undertook to assist Matthew Sylvester at Rutland House. The depression of weakness and infirmity, however, told him that he had reached the last stage of his mortal pilgrimage, and he died on the 8th of November, 1691. His character has been so often delineated, that any attempt of the kind in this place would be superfluous. "The Industrious Invalid," "the Shakespeare and Demosthenes of English Theology," and "the Augustine of Nonconformity," are familiar terms to every Baxterian bibliographer.

Although linked with Kidderminster, Baxter's life and labours also pre-eminently belong to London, and are associated with many of the buildings yet remaining in the old city. At St. Margaret's, Westminster, we find traces of him as we fancy ourselves listening to his sermon before the Parliament, just prior to the Restoration. We can enter St. Dunstan's, Fleet-street, and there imagine ourselves witnessing a panic in the congregation, occasioned by an alarm that the building was falling down; and we may profit by the wise reproof and ready improvement which the preacher utters. At Oxenden-street we see him expelled from a chapel reared by the munificence of Mistress Margaret, but in which the devoted husband was only permitted to officiate once. At Swallow-street,

20

near at hand, and at Maid-lane, Southwark, we imagine ourselves to be a part of that great crowd of citizens who learned wisdom at the feet of this Puritan Demosthenes. At the Savoy, at Sion College, at St. Bride's, at St. Paul's, and at Whitehall, this same fragile form of Richard Baxter, even as a spectral child of fancy, rebukes us for so slightly improving life's fleeting hours, and for making so faint an impression for good on our generation. Noble Baxter! When compared with you, and with other like stars of the seventeenth century galaxy, what diminutive tapers do the majority of us appear! And how contemptibly poor and abject are they who live merely for earthly wealth and for earthly honour. ALMOST WELL, he replied, when at his death one asked him, " How are you ? " We take our leave of him at Charterhouse-square, unless, indeed, we follow his lifeless clay to its sepulchre in Christ-church, where it rests beside the body of his beloved Margaret. Noble Baxter! How plainly manifest is it to you now that, notwithstanding all its painful privations, your lot on earth was a blessed lot. We admiringly contemplate your work, but cannot describe your reward. To do so we should need your own, or even an angel's powers. *Our* incapacity to catch the light and music of sinless spheres is only equalled by the readiness with which *your* sanctified genius reflected the one and appropriated the other, to transfer them to the luminous pages of your immortal *Saints' Rest;* and the blessedness of your present condition you have yourself described in that greatest of all your writings :—*O, what a mighty change is this !* . . . *Farewell, sin and suffering.* . . . *Welcome, most holy heavenly nature.**

Connected with this important Society at Little Carter-lane at the time of his outset in life appears Edmund Calamy, the celebrated author of the Account of Ejected Ministers. His ministry under Matthew Sylvester lasted only four years; but a sketch of his life may with propriety be given in connection with the Society, since Calamy afterwards became a prominent leader of the Nonconformists. His family claimed a good descent, their ancestors having migrated from Guernsey, whither tradition says, they were driven in the days of persecution under Charles IX. of France. Amid the political and religious troubles of the Civil Wars

* The principal sources of information for the above have been the Calendars of State Papers, Domestic Series, Charles II.; the Life of Baxter, by himself, Sylvester's edition; and also Calamy's Abridgment; Bates' Sermon on the death of Richard Baxter; Baxter's Memoir of his Wife; several of his minor pieces, *e. g.*, The Quaker's Catechism, and his Letter to the People of Kidderminster; Wilson's Dissenting Churches, &c., &c. Baxter wrote between one and two hundred separate works, of which there are about one hundred in Dr. Williams's Library. An imperfect list by Calamy occupies twelve octavo pages. A selection from his political writings were publicly burned at Oxford on the day of Russell's death, in the summer of 1683.

the Doctor's grandfather enjoyed the powerful protection of the Earl of Essex while settled at Rochford, and on removing to London he succeeded Dr.
Stoughton at Aldermanbury, ·where ·he metamorphosed the rectory into a Puritan city rendezvous.
Calamy exercised a vast influence over the Presbyterians—a power he exerted in favour of the Restoration; so that for a season after the King's return
the divine was something thought of at Court. How
well the Government could remember such services
Calamy's subsequent arrest and imprisonment served
to testify.   On account of this injustice the conscience of Charles accused him, and he arranged to
hold an interview with the Puritan confessor, which
was made the occasion of proffering him the See of
Lichfield, on condition of his conforming.   The royal
offer was refused, and Calamy died soon after the
Fire of London.   His sons, James and Benjamin,
both conformed at the Restoration.   Edmund, the
eldest, was the silenced minister of Moreton, in
Essex, and the founder of the Nonconformist Society
in the Old Jewry.   Benjamin, as a *protégé* of Jeffreys,
became an uncompromising partisan of Episcopacy.
He published a treatise in defence of the last-named
regimen, and openly challenged a gainsaying of his
arguments.   Those arguments were refuted by
Delaune, whose moral courage and literary skill
cost him an imprisonment in Newgate for the
remainder of his life.   A notable inhabitant of
Calamy's father's parish was that victim of kingcraft,

Alderman Cornish. Young Calamy happened to be
walking up Milk-street on the day of the alderman's
execution, and he there encountered his uncle Benjamin, looking as though he would sink through the
pavement.

Edmund was judiciously trained during early life;
those liberal and tolerant principles being also carefully instilled into his mind, which in an age of
controversial violence characterised his sire. His
father was a staunch Nonconformist, who never
depreciated the Established Church. His wife was
a companion worthy of his amiable and gentle
nature. During his childhood she was to her son
an efficient tutor. She it was who taught him to
read, and when that art was fairly mastered, she
honoured a good old Presbyterian custom by sending
Edmund each Saturday afternoon to Dyers' Hall, so
that he might take his place among the catechumens
of pastor Lye.

A very pleasant and peaceful home was that of
the Calamys in Aldermanbury, and very profitable
was the social intercourse between divines of all denominations, which its ever-ailing master loved to
encourage. No higher fortune could have befallen a
youth like Edmund the younger than that of having
for daily examples those who were his home preceptors. But the time arrived when the boy needed
to benefit by a higher curriculum than his mother's
system embraced. In those days, as in ours, the
duties of curates were heavier than their stipends;

of this class was one Nelson—a resident of Aldermanbury—who fitted up, till it resembled a school-
house, the vestry of St. Alphage, and there in the
capacity of parish tutor supplemented a scanty income; his array of scholars, meanwhile, including
Edmund Calamy. As the latter made only little
progress under curate Nelson, he was ultimately
placed with "a kind of Fifth Monarchy man, called
Yewell, at Epsom;" but even at Epsom his physical
improvement became more apparent than his mental
progress. It must be mentioned to his honour,
however, that Yewell's crude opinions on religion and
politics sufficed not to conceal his genial disposition.
He evinced a tender concern for his boys, and even
incurred the expense of providing a London minister
to preach to them weekly. But as something more
than kindness and improved health was necessary,
young Edmund was recalled to London, there to
attend another academy in the neighbourhood of
Pinners' Hall. He now made satisfactory progress.
Morning and evening he crossed the City, and was
wont at times to encounter a citizen of so great an
age, that his lore included a story of his having
witnessed Elizabeth's entry into London, on her
accession to the throne, in 1558.

On that tumult subsiding which the alleged
popish plot awakened, the Court promoted a reaction of public feeling. The excuses offered for the
rigorous treatment of the Dissenters wore more of a
political than a religious complexion. The Non-

conformists are said to have resembled the crown
jewels, because pawned at pleasure to a vindictive
Parliament when supplies were needed, to be partially released on a dissolution. The year 1681
was a time of severe hardship to our Christian
fathers. Throughout England the Nonconformist
pulpits were vacant, not on account of faint-hearted
shrinkings from duty, but because the pastors
were languishing in county gaols. Calamy carried
with him to the verge of life many personal reminiscences of those never-to-be-forgotten days. Even
as early as his tenth year the sight of his child's
face often gladdened the solitude of such prisoners
as were confined for conscience' sake, or in other
words, he was frequently the almoner of persons
whose sympathy prompted them to relieve by such
an agency the men of whom England was then unworthy. From many such did young Edmund
Calamy receive a blessing. His father eluded imprisonment, and did so by a dexterous adroitness
with which the agents of the law were unable to
cope. He was continually being sought, but by now
assuming one disguise, and anon another, and by a
frequent change of residence, he escaped the vigilance of his enemies. They who convened the
Nonconformist meetings were constrained to act
with severest caution. As a mere child, Edmund
was often present at the proscribed assemblies, and
at such times he would ask himself the puzzling
question, Why could not men whose whole demeanour

was self-denying and peaceful, live on unmolested?
He was present on two occasions when military
intruders from Whitehall suddenly disturbed the
services.

Notwithstanding the roughness of the times,
Edmund received the best training his parents were
able to afford.   Thus, in addition to the educational
advantages already specified, he resided for a time
at Islington, in the house of Thomas Doolittle, and
was there in the society of youths who were destined
to achieve eminence in their several professions.
This school was broken up by the Government agents,
and Doolittle retired to Battersea.

Then came the winter of 1684, remarkable for
its severe frost.   The river Thames was completely
frozen; and, on account of the stalls and booths
erected on its surface, it more resembled a street
through a fair than its wonted familiar aspect.
Boats being superseded by coaches, the novelty of
the innovation attracted abundance of traffic.   Very
vividly did the scene impress itself upon young
Calamy's imagination; and he tells us of the multi-
farious sports—e.g., fox-hunting, bear and bull-
baiting, which the hundreds of booths and shopkeepers did their best to encourage.   There was, of
course, the roasted ox—the first thing suggested to
our fathers by such a scene as the frozen Thames.
For two months the citizens uninterruptedly enjoyed
their winter sports; and the events of that clear, dry
Christmas had only just become events of history,

when Charles the Second was no more. Young
Edmund stood in Wood-street, one dismal February
morning, to hear the heralds proclaim the accession
of James the Second to the throne of England. Bad
as he had been, the populace retained an affection
for the late monarch, and some tears were shed at
the mention of the name and title of the new King.
In this memorable spring of 1685, the elder Calamy
also died. His constitution had never been robust;
and, although treated by the most eminent phy-
sicians, he died of consumption at Totteridge, near
Barnet, whither he had gone for change of air. His
remains, on being brought to London, were deposited
in the church at Aldermanbury.

The now fatherless Edmund continued his education at Merchant Taylors' School, and subsequently
had several tutors, the most noteworthy of whom
was Samuel Cradock, the conductor of an academy
for university learning near Newmarket. Calamy
retained some pleasant reminiscences of the days he
passed in the home of Samuel Cradock. The latter
not only attended to his classes, but ministered to a
congregation at his own house on Sabbath days, and
did so without a stipend. After leaving this preceptor, Calamy returned to his former tutor, Thomas
Doolittle, whose meeting was in Monkwell-street,
but whose manse was overshadowed by the now
classical shrine of Sylvanus Urban, at Clerkenwell.
The young scholar formed many valuable acquaintances—*e.g.*, Shower, Howe, Taylor, and others, and

he acted on the advice of such able counsellors when he ultimately embarked for Holland to read theology at the Dutch universities.*

After going through his continental curriculum, Calamy returned home with some highly flattering testimonials from foreign professors. Prior to his settlement he travelled about England, and we are enabled to follow him in some of his wanderings.

* While Calamy was studying on the Continent he obtained some information of a certain Mrs. Schurman, who, besides her high literary attainments, possessed an exquisite skill in painting glass and china. One piece, in particular, on which she had only worked when in her best mood, was a specimen of consummate art. Her excessive pains did not go unrewarded; for many competent judges ventured an opinion that the glass in question was the finest thing of the kind extant. As the lady was well known, families of distinction, while passing through the district, usually made a point of inspecting her treasures, principal among which was the trifle referred to. Such callers were invariably very politely received. On one occasion, the visitor being a lady, the hostess pressed her to drink wine from the much-prized glass; and, accordingly, that article was handed over to a maid to be washed. In her nervous carefulness, the girl broke the cup, and, knowing too well the nature of the mischief she had done, she ran and hid herself. When obliged to restore the broken pieces, she exclaimed in terror, "I could not help it! indeed, madam, I could not help it!" Instead of upbraiding her maiden, this sage-like matron returned to her visitor to exclaim, in the language of truest wisdom: "I hope I shall learn from this passage to set more value upon my time for the future, than to throw away so much upon so brittle a trifle."

Another remarkable story of these times is supported by

He visited Oxford, and, while there, received an invitation to visit the people of Whitchurch, where the Nonconformists' pulpit was vacant. The messenger was accompanied by a horse, upon which Calamy returned, as desired. At Whitchurch a well-to-do tradesman of Andover was encountered, who, by way of addition to his compliments, requested that a young scholar bearing so eminent a name would also visit Andover. Accordingly, on

the testimony of Calamy. During the civil wars, a certain youth determined to join the Parliamentary ranks, and adhered to his resolution, although parents and friends dissuaded him from it. His resolve was so firmly rooted as to be proof against either entreaty or reason. His friends at last delighted him by giving their reluctant consent. In one of the sanguinary battles that followed, this youth was severely wounded; and, through neglect, mortification ensued. He progressed from bad to worse, until the surgeons decided on sacrificing the limb. The doctor, who attended the patient on the night preceding the day appointed for the amputation, carelessly left a bottle of dressing liquor and a flask of refreshing cordial standing together by the bedside. In the course of the night the invalid drank a large draught of the cauterising fluid, and his immediate sensations were those of being internally on fire. To all appearances he soon lapsed into a dying state, and on the following morning his body was in an intense heat, his eyes resembling balls of fire. Under circumstances so distressing, the surgeons decided on not proceeding with the amputation, but allowed their patient unlimited quantities of drink. The sequel was most extraordinary; for on examination, the injured limb was found to have recovered from the mortification, and in a brief space the youth was again abroad and in his usual health.

the Thursday following, Calamy and his host rode over to this hospitable merchant's house. A welcome not less abundant than the dinner which followed awaited them, and, during the progress of the meal, the host, in the course of his pleasant conversation, astonished his visitors by quietly remarking, " I have no doubt there will be a good congregation this evening." On finding himself thus fairly entrapped young Edmund experienced some chagrin; and his humour was not improved by the discovery that a messenger was abroad collecting an audience; for he "thought this sort of management pretty particular." The Andover of those days had its separate Nonconformist societies, but they had only a single meeting-house between them. The Presbyterians and Independents worked harmoniously together; and, at this conjuncture, the last-named section had lately lost their minister, Isaac Chauncy, the predecessor of Doctor Watts in London.

This visit to Andover of a young divine bearing so distinguished a name awakened unwonted excitement in the little republic. After concluding his sermon, Calamy was abruptly addressed by a dame wearing a high hat, and who was in all other respects, picturesquely attired. She invited the young orator to remain at Andover, whither, she declared, Providence had directed him. While nearly losing command over his countenance, Calamy replied that his youth would scarcely warrant the immediate acceptance of so important a charge, and, in addition to such considerations, he knew little of their disposition.   Because he had pleased them on a single occasion, it did not follow he should always succeed in doing so.   While proceeding to strengthen the position she had assumed, the ancient dame extolled the virtues of youthful Christians, at the expense of those of riper years.   "Come, come, mother," interrupted Calamy, "do not bear so hard on the old Christians among us."   He also embraced the opportunity of recommending the Presbyterian minister, whose duties were then inconveniently divided between Andover and Winchester: "Fix him wholly among you," cried he, "and ease him of going in his advanced age to preach at Winchester once a fortnight."   The old lady happened to be a relict of the extreme orthodox Puritan school; and her wrathful explosion now startled the company: "What, Mr. Sprint," she shrieked, "old Mr. Sprint?   Alas! he is a Baxterian!   He is a middle-way man!   He is an occasional conformist!   He is neither fish nor flesh, nor good red herring!"   Amid some glee, Calamy endeavoured to soothe the singular human phenomenon before him; but his words were to no purpose. "Sir," said the woman, as she stalked down the aisle, "I wish you a good night."

Calamy returned to Oxford, and in that neighbourhood inaugurated his ministry.   Soon after he removed to London, where he accepted numerous engagements.   His now seemingly prosperous path however, was not without its shades of sorrow; for about this time that bane of his kindred, consumption, cut short his sister's life. Meantime a settlement had not been decided on. Receiving a call from Bristol, he travelled thither to judge of the prospects presenting themselves. The stipend was £100 a year, with a house; but for the sake of his mother, who preferred remaining in London, this fair opening was declined. Immediately afterwards, by settling with Matthew Sylvester at Blackfriars, Calamy was honoured by next succeeding the immortal Baxter.

We get many glimpses into a young minister's diurnal experience in those distant days by attentively following our author's voluminous narrative. He lodged in Hoxton-square, and had Thomas Reynolds for a landlord and house companion. Their days glided happily on, for each was gladdened by the other's presence. Neither was rich. Reynolds was pastor at the Weigh-house; and as for Calamy, he received from Matthew Sylvester a quarterly allowance of ten pounds, the latter often retaining a smaller amount for himself. As an annual subscription of eighty pounds, however, was insufficient for the maintenance of two, a separation ensued, and Sylvester assumed the entire pastorate, while his colleague engaged himself to Dr. Williams, at Hand-alley, Bishopsgate. Calamy now gave attention to a matter of a tenderer nature. From the congregation of John Shower, in Jewin-street, he selected Mary Watts, to whom he was united in marriage in June, 1695. This happy union in no way interfered with the domestic arrangements at Hoxton, where the house was still shared by Thomas Reynolds.

Even in the days under review, several years after the Revolution, the Dissenters, for political reasons, avoided the ostentation of public ordinations; and made it their custom to hold such meetings in private. Calamy determined if possible to establish a more honourable precedent, and, with a view to that end, consulted several eminent divines. Singularly enough, both Bates and Howe shrank from encouraging the innovation, through fear of awakening Government suspicion. Nevertheless, others were found willing to conduct the solemnities of the occasion. The meeting was convened at Little St. Helen's, the service lasting eight hours, during which seven persons were ordained. On several accounts that longest summer day of 1694 was memorable in the annals of Nonconformity.

Calamy rapidly rose into popularity, and was elected to the Merchants' Lecture, at Salters' Hall, in 1702, shortly prior to his accession to the pulpit at Westminster. In this year he again visited Oxford, and became intensely interested in discovering that Clarendon's History of the Rebellion was passing through the University Press. Calamy was then engaged in preparing his Account of the Ejected Ministers, and a strong curiosity prompted him to obtain a sight of Clarendon's unpublished sheets. He went to the printers; but none of the employés dared to respond to so strange a request; and our author returned to his lodging is a disconsolate mood. Not despairing, he enquired of a certain tradesman, if any persons were engaged at the presses to whom a liberal donative would be acceptable. A being of the kind required—a poor Dutchman—was ultimately found; for he produced with alacrity what sheets were printed, and actually brought a portion of the manuscript also. By reading throughout the night, Calamy enjoyed his stolen booty. He was delighted by discovering that in regard to facts, Clarendon and himself were not materially at variance. This method of gaining his object cannot be commended as honourable. As regards Calamy's Account of the Bartholomew Confessors, its publication aroused the fierce resentment of the Anglican priesthood. Some opponents proposed condemning the book by a formal vote of Convention, but if such a design was ever seriously entertained, its execution was balked by a too eager appreciation of its probable effect on the sale of the book; for one of the publishers offered a purse of gold to any who would ensure the passing of the contemplated vote.

The first edition of Calamy's Abridgment of Baxter's Life was published in 1702. This work is a Defence of moderate Nonconformity; and as such became the spring-head of a controversy as it were, which in this place will not need any particular allusion.   Several books were issued by the contending parties. Calamy was arrayed against Hoadly, Ollyff, and Dorrington.   We must make due allowances for the temper of those times, and then the combatants will receive very high commendation, when we grant that they conducted their literary skirmish with a kindliness of spirit not at all characteristic of the Augustan age.

In 1708 the religious public was troubled by the appearance in England of the sect called French Prophets.   The leaders of these fanatics laid claim to inspiration, and were wont, besides, to go through some strange performances.   Calamy did his best to promote their discomfiture by publishing his Caveat against their doctrine and practice, for writing which he received the thanks of the Queen.   Our author's next adventure was a pleasant tour into Scotland; and of that journey he has left us ample details. On re-crossing the Border he carried with him the well-merited distinction of Doctor of Divinity.

His time was now occupied with many busy projects.   In 1713 he published a revised edition of his Account of Ejected Ministers, which the Nonconformists hailed as a seasonable memento of heroic suffering, but which continued to excite the less amiable attributes of the violent partisans of Church and State.   Of the latter party Dr. Walker assumed the championship, and volunteered to counteract what was deemed to be Calamy's pernicious in-

21

fluence. Circulars, containing a number of queries, were dispersed among the clergy. The questions principally related to those incumbents who were sequestered during the Commonwealth for alleged incompetence, ignorance, or immorality. The minutest particulars were eagerly sought after—*e.g.*, of the rudeness of Cromwell's Triers, and the violent behaviour of their abettors; and also of the successors of the superseded pastors, and of the school of fanaticism to which they specially belonged; of "their ridiculous praying or preaching, canting, formal or immoral practices; of the furious things they did and said" against the Government, the Church, and the State in general. The collectors of these historical materials were encouraged in their researches by the smoothest compliments and by the blandest assurances. Indeed, his grace the bishop and their reverences the archdeacons of the diocese highly approved the undertaking.

The above more particularly refers to the see of Exeter, where the clergy showed no indolence in doing as they were bidden, since the whole business was sanctioned by "the right reverend father in God, the lord bishop, and archdeacons of this diocese." It is true that the clergy encountered some obstacles and checks in their invidious enquiries. Thus, in a parish presided over by one of Dr. Walker's disciples, there lived a venerable dame, whose strength of body had declined, but whose wits were unimpaired by years. During the civil

wars her family espoused the Royalist side, and, on that account, severely suffered. Her father, it would seem, was superseded by those uncompromising advocates of pure religion and a grave deportment—Cromwell's Triers. With some glee the parson discovered in this old lady an agent competent to further his interest with Dr. Walker, and with "the reverend father in God, the lord bishop, and archdeacons of this diocese." Pocketing his sheet of queries, our parson hasted to the cottage, which he entered, and in the blandest of humours commenced some such dialogue as the following:—
"Well, my good mistress, it rejoices my heart to see you so blythe after all your family troubles and with your infirmities of age; but I hope yet to see some reparation made you for your losses in the late times of cant and fanaticism." "I am content, parson," she replied, "to let bygones be bygones, and go quietly to heaven." On the business assuming this unpromising aspect the chivalrous vicar chid "her simplicity, and told her he hoped she would be wiser than to let slip such an opportunity, and presently falls to asking her questions out of his paper concerning her father." The dame continued obstinate, and said such reminiscences "were better forgotten." At this stage the parson lost his temper; questions and arguments were superseded by invective, and he absolutely refused to stir without receiving a full account of the wrongs inflicted on the sequestered vicar, the dame's father. The revelation

21*

made, only bred further disappointment, and increased the clergyman's consternation, for the information "was not at all to his gust." Christian principle, in the person of his informer, proved superior to filial love. Vainly, by artful questions, did the parson endeavour to elicit admissions from which damaging conclusions could be drawn. He spoke at random some spiteful things about the minister installed by Cromwell's Triers, but his auditor's reply was a grateful acknowledgment of light received from that Puritan pastor. Chagrined at his final non-success, the parson "stormed and raged" with disappointment, till, finding all to no purpose, he rushed from the cottage, forgetting to pocket Dr. Walker's sheet of queries.

Circular letters were also dispatched into other dioceses; and shortly after the publication of Calamy's Account, Walker's folio was subscribed for by thirteen hundred persons. The sheer absurdity of certain details in the book excited some mirthful derision; but, on the other hand, the work was extolled as the Anglican Book of Martyrs. Churchmen, however, were not unanimous in admiring the monument raised by Walker, and one of their number contemptuously styled it "a farrago of false and senseless legends." Posterity can estimate the author's merit without being biassed by party rancour. Undoubtedly, the Doctor has done his best to palliate the odium of drunkenness, tavern-haunting, and swearing, so inseparably associated with the clergy of the Restoration; and any obstacles in the way of vindication he thought he annihilated by calling them " hackney imputations." Confusion of arrangement and mistakes in the text are also noteworthy features of Walker's book. Many of his "martyrs" could boast of attributes which degrade humanity below the nature of brutes, and, morally speaking, render man all that is contemptible.

Walker's task was at the best an invidious undertaking. He attempted to weaken his opponent's testimony by expressing suspicion that the Nonconformists' failings had been covered, or that at the least they had been extenuated. He portrays as worthy divines many whom Calamy in reply denounced as drunkards, profane swearers, rakes, mockers, or wanton liars—*e.g.*, one Bilton, of Mexburgh, in Yorkshire, " was infamous for his impudence and impiety." He was chairman of a society of rakes, and both by precept and example encouraged profanity and loose living. Another star of Walker's galaxy was " a drunken, profane wretch," who, not satisfied with practising buffoonery in general, must needs jest in his prayers. Another " worthy old gentleman "—who, in the war time, chose to refuse the sacrament to such as adhered to the Parliament —was fined for drunkenness. Charles Churchill, of Feniton, whom Walker eulogises as learned, pious, and loyal, was a mere jester on sacred themes, since his own wife confessed " he tells lies to make gentlemen laugh." Many other reverend examples

might be brought forward who were "famous for
nothing but vice." Many of these had been the
subjects of Cromwell's discipline, but they received
comfortable and considerable compensation. One
vicar is particularly mentioned, who had fifteen
livings in Oxfordshire, in addition to the parish in
which he chose to reside.

One episode in Calamy's life, belonging to these
times, deserves recording, as it reveals the art by
which authors sometimes introduced their wares to
the world in that unreading age. The Church was
then distracted by the question of subscription to
theological dogmas; and Calamy published an octavo
volume, in defence of the Trinity, which he hoped
would tend to promote peace among the disputants.
His book, he supposed, would attract a wider notice
if permission were granted of inscribing it to the
King; and, by the agency of Lord Townshend, leave
was obtained to present a copy to George the First
in person. This occasion gave the monarch an
opportunity of expressing his respect for the Three
Denominations; they were, he felt assured, his stead-
fast friends, and, as friends, he expected their
support in the forthcoming general election. At a
meeting of ministers, convened on the day following,
the honour of the royal confidence was acknowledged, and a message despatched to the palace to
assure his Majesty that his expectations would not
be disappointed. Copies of this volume—interesting on account of these historical minutiæ connected

with it—were presented to the Prince, the Princess of Wales, and to the three Princesses. Calamy received a government draft of the value of fifty pounds.

Having thus gone at some length into our author's career, it will not be advisable to extend our notice by giving full particulars of his latter days. During forty years he was an active London minister and a zealous advocate of the English Presbyterian order. His connections included a wide circle of distinguished friends, by whom he was honoured as the leader of the Nonconformists. Although his personal character needs no eulogy, it may just be mentioned that he was large-hearted, learned, pious, and amiable. He preached his last sermon on one of the opening Sabbaths of 1732, and died in the June following, in his sixty-second year, leaving a widow and six children. The number of his separate publications is thirty-nine. One of his sons, Andrew Calamy, ably assisted Edward Cave in the earliest days of the Gentleman's Magazine.*

Samuel Stephens, a young divine connected with this society, was cut down by fever in his twenty-

* For Dr. Calamy see The Historical Account of his own Life, edited by J. T. Rutt, 2 vols. 8vo.; Mayo's Funeral Sermon, 1732; Calamy's Church and the Dissenters Compared, &c.; Walker's Sufferings of the Clergy; Calamy's Account of Ejected Ministers; The Biographia Britannica, &c. Numberless references to the Doctor may also be found in the periodicals, pamphlets, and other works of his time.

eighth year. The sermon commemorating this sad event was Calamy's maiden publication: it is a quaint-looking quarto, "Printed for Abraham Chandler, at the Chyrurgeon's Arms, in Aldersgate-street."

Sylvester was followed by one destined to rise into high repute among the Dissenters—viz., Samuel Wright, with whose teaching the citizens were familiar, seeing he had already established a claim on their regard in the pulpit at Crosby Hall. Wright was born in 1682, at Ritford in Nottinghamshire, where his father held a good position in the Non-conformist ministry. His parents, who gave due attention to their son's early training, both died during Samuel's early childhood. It providentially happened that the orphan was well cared for, and placed in a school at Attercliffe, where he afterwards continued his studies under the famous Timothy Jollie. On young Wright's leaving the academy, his uncle admitted him to his own home in the capacity of family chaplain. Shortly after the uncle died, and the nephew removed to London, his ministerial experience as yet being extremely limited. At Saint Giles's he found a home in the household of Thomas Cotton, a Dissenting minister in that vicinity, who engaged Wright as lecturer. The latter's next remove was to Turnham-green, where he accepted a chaplaincy in the establishment of Lady Lat. A rising, and therefore, a more important step, was his settlement at Crosby Hall under Dr. Grosvenor.

Then on the death of Matthew Sylvester, in 1708, Wright succeeded at Blackfriars, and in doing so relinquished his other engagements, including a lecture in Southwark. At the time of his death Sylvester's church was in a most unprosperous condition, having suffered a gradual decline since the loss of Richard Baxter. The accession of a young and popular minister brought with it an immediate revival, and the scanty audience grew into one of the largest assemblies of the Presbyterians in London. In 1710 the importance of this station attracted the Sacheveral rioters, who destroyed the chapel—a loss, however, which the Government handsomely repaired. After this the pastor continued to extend his influence till his eminent services by tongue and pen were rewarded by the Scottish distinction of Doctor of Divinity. As an author, he was occasionally extremely popular, his piece on the New Birth having run through fifteen editions during its writer's lifetime. His works, characterised by Doddridge as being "candid, rational, and evangelical," are nearly fifty in number. But notwithstanding Wright's celebrity in that long since departed age, scarcely any particulars of his life are known beyond what has been related, and that he died at the age of sixty-four, in April, 1746. He had an assistant, Jeremiah Burroughs, who "Was reckoned a polite and fashionable preacher; but about the year 1717 he quitted the ministry, and obtained a more beneficial post under the Government." Another assistant was Thomas Newman, who finally succeeded his colleague, and continued in the pastorate forty years. His parents—citizens of London—after having judiciously trained their son, reaped the reward of seeing him rank among the more eminent of his contemporaries. He died in 1758. The sermon on his death, by Edward Pickard, contains nothing noteworthy concerning its subject.

Edward Pickard next follows. He remained at Carter-lane till his death in 1778. Born at Alcester, he was educated by successive tutors at Birmingham, Stratford-on-Avon, and London. He originally settled in the town of Shakspeare's birth. Thence he removed to Southwark, and thence again, in 1746, to Blackfriars, to take the lectureship under Thomas Newman, whom he eventually succeeded. Although he unfortunately embraced the tenets of Arius, he was much respected throughout the City.

Pickard was assisted by John Tailor, a former pupil of Doddridge at Northampton. After leaving his amiable tutor, Tailor settled at Rochford, and subsequently at Stowmarket. By the rural populace he was so highly appreciated, that they gave him the *nom de plume* of the Suffolk orator, but on removing to Carter-lane in 1760, he was unable to sustain this country-achieved fame. While failing to captivate the more polished ears of a City audience, " His presence in the pulpit was graceful, and his discourse

judicious." His theological tenets were of the lowest .
standard, which may be partly accounted for by his
having been the intimate friend of Priestley, for with
Priestley he sympathised both in " thought and sentiment on various topics of inquiry." Tailor died in
1766.

Thomas Taylor came after Edward Pickard, and
remained in the pastorate for nearly half a century.
He was reared at Kidderminster, and educated by
Caleb Ashworth, Doddridge's next successor. At
one time Taylor had a prospect of settling over the
Nonconformist congregation in his native town, but
certain obstacles preventing this, he removed to
Stoke Newington, where by accepting a chaplaincy
in the Abney family, he became styled " A second
Dr. Watts." He earned the respect of the Londoners, and rose to some eminence in the Merchants'
Lectureship at Salters' Hall; but he did not retain
that prosperity which the church enjoyed under his
predecessors. We can only just mention the names
of later ministers. Joseph Barrett, one of Dr.
Enfield's students at Warrington, served from 1811
to 1823, when infirmity compelled his retirement.
Next following came John Hoppus, who afterwards
accepted the professorship of logic and mental
philosophy in the University of Edinburgh. Other
names belonging to Carter-lane are those of John !
Fuller, George Lewis, George Watson, John Scott
Porter, James Yates, Dr. James Hutton, and Henry
Solly. The last was succeeded by Henry Ierson, ₁

who officiated at the last service held in the old meeting house, on Sunday, October the 13th, 1861.

After the death of Dr. Wright this society experienced a gradual decline of prosperity, still further promoted by the election of John Tailor, " The cordial friend of Dr. Priestley." Thus, by their looseness of procedure, the members opened a path for the humanitarianism of Yates and Hutton. This is a sad ending to a story like that belonging to Carter-lane, and only little more remains to be told. On the memorable day already mentioned, a large concourse was attracted by the novelty of a last sermon in a building of so many great and dear associations. " It was perfectly understood," says The Christian Reformer, in allusion to this occasion, " that the closing service would not be one of lamentation over decay." Let us venture to hope, notwithstanding, that to many present the season was one of mourning ; for, although a new chapel has arisen at Islington, the spectacle descried from *our* stand-point is that of a noble barque wrecked on the breakers of " unsound doctrine."

Chapter VIII.

THE KING'S WEIGH-HOUSE.

EAST-CHEAP has possessed attractions from time immemorial. These sprang in ancient days from a colony of cooks, the fame of whose dainty fare was extended to the provinces by persons famous among their fellows on account of having visited London. From an old ballad which portrays a countryman's progress through the city, we learn that the apprentices', " What d'ye lack," first drew attention to the finer materials of wearing apparel. Still progressing from the west, the traveller, in the vicinity of Cornhill, was tempted with old clothes ; but on reaching Eastcheap, the cries resounding on all hands, " Hot ribs of beef rosted ; pyes well baked, and other victuals," were sweet music to the hungry, and such were the delicious odours that even uncompromising vegetarians would almost have recanted at dinner-time. On a certain occasion, the sons of Henry the Fourth were drawn thither by savoury temptations. During one memorable night in 1410, the princes supped in Eastcheap, and on coming to high words with the neighbours, a riot ensued, which the Lord Mayor was called from his bed to suppress.

The King's Weigh-House originally stood in Cornhill, but after the great fire it occupied the site of the consumed church of Saint Andrew Hubbard. In early times the Weigh-House was an institution of considerable importance, and nothing prevented the chief Weigher from being a member of the Court of Aldermen. This personage employed four officials, and these superintended several subordinates, while the entire establishment was governed by the Grocers' Company. The business consisted of weighing and marking packages brought from vessels in the river. The fees varied from twopence to three shillings a draught, although for " A bagg of hopps " merchants paid the uniform charge of sixpence. Parliament passed many acts for regulating weights and measures. Foreigners disposing of merchandise in London were compelled to weigh their goods at the King's beam, and in the presence of sworn officials—men whose duties disqualified them for other business, and whose morality was guaranteed by any swervings from rectitude entailing an imprisonment of a year and a day. The custom of weighing was gradually relinquished, when varying standards were recognised in rural districts; and because the vulgar would not be trammelled by fixed rules, seventeenth century mathematicians provided their own measures. There are some quaint and ancient sayings which imagination at least attaches to the King's Weigh-House; sayings belonging to days when thirty-two grains of wheat were the legal weight of the English silver penny : *e.g.*, "A pint's a pound all the world round"—a popular fallacy now rectified into "A pint of pure water weighs a pound and a quarter." "Five score to the hundred of men, money, and pins; six score of all other things." *

The English Presbyterian society at the Weigh-House was founded by Samuel Slater and his supposed curate, Thomas Kentish, divines driven by the Act of Uniformity from Saint Katherine's-in-the-Tower. The Church as Nonconformists, assembled for a time in the same neighbourhood, but subsequently removed to Cannon-street and finally settled in East-cheap. It is to be regretted that so little is known of the first pastor, who died in 1670. Morally he was a very brave man. Throughout an industrious career considerations of ease or danger never led him into neglect of duty. During the dreadful plague visitation of 1625, which signalised the accession of Charles the First and annihilated a third part of the London population, Slater highly distinguished himself by faithfully and unflinchingly discharging every Christian office.

Slater was succeeded by Thomas Kentish, a son of the silenced minister of Middleton, in Durham. He studied at Cambridge University, and was ejected

* For further particulars see Stowe's Survey; and also Maitland's Seymour's and Pennant's Histories of London.

in 1662 from the parish of Overton, in Hampshire. At the hands of the government he experienced very rough treatment: while preaching for Janeway in Southwark, some officers suddenly dragged him from the pulpit and threw him into prison. He died in 1695. Of his private and public character Dr. Calamy entertained the highest opinion.*

Thomas Kentish had for an assistant John Knowles, who was born in the last year of the sixteenth century,† and educated at Cambridge University. Eventually he accepted a tutorship at Katherine Hall, and in the Commonwealth era twelve of his former students were simultaneously members of Parliament, while thirty others held eminent positions as Christian ministers. In 1635, Knowles left the University to become lecturer to the Corporation of Colchester, whither he found himself followed by Laud's persecuting enmity. An opportunity of prelatical spite occurred at the death of the grammar school-master, William Kempe, who had served the town since the reign of Elizabeth. When the mayor and his colleagues sought their lecturer's advice about appointing a successor,

* See Calamy's Account, and Continuation: Wilson's Dissenting Churches; Nonconformists' Memorial, &c.

† That is in 1600. "Cromwell was born in the spring of the last year of the sixteenth century," says Principal Tulloch, in his admirable essay on the Protector. According to this reckoning the sixteen centuries only contained 1599 years; for Cromwell was born on April 25th, 1599.

Knowles counselled them to choose a scholar of the name of Dugard, and a fellow of Sydney College. Accordingly, Dugard was installed in the situation, and the wisdom of this choice became amply demonstrated by the increased prosperity which the school enjoyed. Nevertheless this independent action excited the ire of Laud, who, coveting the place for a creature of his own nomination, with persevering malice obliged the master to resign. Knowles experienced intense disgust at these proceedings, and having already given offence in the affair of Dugard, he was not surprised at being sharply reprimanded for having slightly deviated from the Rubric. Taking warning, Knowles sailed for New England; and there, on one occasion, narrowly escaped being murdered by the Indians. When Cromwell restored order, the divine returned to his native land, and to a lectureship at Bristol Cathedral, an employment of which he was deprived at the Restoration. In Bristol he held a position of useful popularity; although to some of the sects, and to Quakers * especially, he proved himself an eyesore. The annoyances which came from certain "Friends" were chiefly

* Once a term of reproach; but never so used in this work. The Society of Friends has had too much to do with securing for England her present civil and religious liberties to be slightingly spoken of by any lover of his country. The allusions to E. Marshall, which follow, illustrate the spirit of those times. Such zealots were by no means confined to Quakers.

22

oral rebukes during public service, and never administered in an under key. In one instance the pastor's private door was fiercely assailed by an armed disciple of Fox, whose zeal apparently had annihilated his peaceful principles. Another Friend, Elizabeth Marshall, was strongly prompted by duty to visit "The Steeple House." The preacher's alleged heresy inflicted exquisite torture, compared with which the lodging in Newgate entailed by her temerity was felicity itself. On the orator's coming to his peroration, " She could not refrain no longer, (*sic*) but cried out, ' This is the word of God—the Lord to *thee*, Knowles; I warn thee to repent, and to mind the light of Christ on thy conscience.' " On leaving Bristol, Knowles settled in London, there to display heroic intrepidity in visiting during the horrors of the plague. It was about the era of the Indulgence of 1672, that Knowles connected himself in labour with Thomas Kentish. Both of these were very zealous evangelists, and excessive earnestness to propagate the faith became so apparent in the former, that he would occasionally sink exhausted upon the ground. When persecution again prevailed Knowles, undaunted, still pursued his way, openly declaring the while, how he preferred preaching the gospel in gaol to living luxuriously at home. He died in April, 1683.*

* Calamy's Account; Nonconformists' Memorial; the Annals of Nonconformity in Essex; Wilson's Dissenting Churches, &c.

At this conjuncture, and although the church showed a decline in prosperity, the members courageously invited to the pastorate Thomas Reynolds, the assistant of Howe. The Silver-street congregation embraced the *elite* of Nonconformity, and, consequently, to be called from an important sphere to a scanty gathering at Eastcheap was not likely to gain consideration. But Reynolds had proved himself to be no ordinary man. Neither promises of advancement nor friendly warnings sufficed to deter him from accepting the call. Once settled, he achieved immediate success, in consequence of which the old meeting room became inconveniently small, and necessitated the erection of a chapel over the King's Weigh-House.

Thomas Reynolds, as an elder son, was originally intended by his parents for the legal profession, and studied for some time at Oxford university. His withdrawment from college ensued because of some disagreement with his tutor; and returning to London, his native city, the student found the flame of persecution at its height, and the Dissenters' chapels closed by a tyrannical Government. His family pastor, John Howe, had already retired into Holland, many of his hearers, in the meantime, worshipping at Cripplegate church; and it was through attending divine service in that quaint sanctuary that young Reynolds was converted, and had his first desires awakened to enter the Christian ministry. His father, a pious and considerate man,

22 *

amid happier circumstances would have been delighted with those early predilections, but on realising
the desolation of the Dissenting interest, as seen in
the closed chapels, the exiled pastors, and the hatred
of the Court to all religion, he dissuaded his son
from venturing so hazardous an enterprise. But no
anticipation of hardships nor of difficulties can
subdue the ardour of youthful minds when enthusiasm springs from higher sources than earthly considerations. Thomas was now placed with Charles
Morton, an eminent scholar, who in those unsettled
times maintained an academy at Newington-green.
When the times grew yet rougher, young Reynolds
and others embarked for Germany, there to complete
their education. At Geneva he attended the lectures of Dr. Turretine, but ultimately removed to
Utrecht. We find that during the days of his preparatory study, Reynolds's life was clouded by sorrow
and dark spiritual visions, and these drove him on
to the border land of despair. Providence, however,
dispelled the gloom of doubt and misgiving.

Reynolds returned to London, and on commencing
to officiate in neighbouring pulpits, his superior
powers were quickly appreciated. Then came the
Revolution to inaugurate happier times, and to
attract back to their native land numbers of refugees
then in Holland. The rising fame of this young
divine brought him under the notice of Howe and
the Silver-street congregation. These well-to-do
admirers had not long prevailed on Reynolds to

settle among them when there came a pressing call from the destitute people of the late Thomas Kentish. But all things seemed to unite to detain the lecturer in his first-chosen and more comfortable sphere. He had not arrived at the age of experience. An influential and polite society allowed him a handsome salary. His own family opposed a removal; and what appeared a still greater objection was the smallness of the proposed charge, their church members only amounting to seventeen. Reynolds, however, decided to remove, and the wisdom of his procedure was evinced by the abundant prosperity which immediately attended him. Although not acquainted with many particulars either of his pastoral or private life, we esteem his memory, for he was one who pre-eminently answered the demands of the Christian ministry. "His thoughts were clothed in a plain and manly dress; he avoided the extreme of an uncouth rusticity and a gaudy eloquence."

During the period of eight years, ranging from 1699 to 1707, the assistant at the Weigh-House was Jabez Earle, who ultimately resigned in favour of Hanover-street, Long-acre, where he continued for sixty years. A young man, by name James Read, being next appointed lecturer, he discharged that office satisfactorily till the Dissenters became divided by the unseemly disputes at Exeter and Salter's Hall in 1719. During that memorable crisis Read gave high offence by dividing with the non-subscribers. The majority of his people voted for his supercession, while the minority were clamorous in his defence. In the angry controversy which ensued, the coffee-house loungers took an active share. Read's admirers even presented him with a silver medal. After suffering considerably on account of supposed heterodoxy, he became assistant to Dr. Evans, of Petty France, and, on succeeding his colleague, remained there till his own death, in 1755.

This unhappy episode in the life of Thomas Reynolds acted disastrously on his health and spirits, and for a season threatened to be fatal. Unfortunately, four years later, he was assailed by that formidable opponent, Simon Browne, of the Old Jewry, who revived the quarrel of the subscribers and non-subscribers. For years prior to his death Reynolds suffered from the weakness of an impaired constitution—a result of excessive application to literary pursuits, and a somewhat hard usage from his brethren. He died in the summer of 1727, one of his last acts consisting in the offering of a prayer for the weal of the Weigh-House society. During his days of health and strength he had feared the hour of death, but when overtaken by the last great foe he declared that he was going to heaven on a bed of roses.*

* Wood's Sermon on the death of T. Reynolds; a letter to the Rev. T. Reynolds by S. Browne; An Answer to the Rev. S. Browne, &c., &c.

It may be mentioned here that the eighteenth century brought with it a controversy about publicly singing the praises of the Deity; and the Weigh-House ministers were early pledged to defend the use of psalmody. A Friday evening lecture was established partly for this special purpose. In the year 1708 a volume of the sermons on this subject was published "At the Golden Candlestick, at the lower end of Cheapside." To this work * we are indebted for information respecting those strange objections with which the preachers found it necessary to deal.

Although constituting a digression, they will scarcely be out of place, if, in connection with this sketch of the Weigh-House meeting, are given some reminiscences of Nonconformity during the fifty years following the Revolution, our authorities being the contemporary literature of the era and later histories.

The Revolution itself had hardly been possible but for the Dissenters' influence. By their coalescence with the moderate party in the Church of England against King James the Second and Popery, the Nonconformists at the least saved their neighbours of the Establishment from a humiliating persecution, if from nothing worse. It was a singular

---

* This was entitled Practical Discourses on Singing, and it was followed by three companion volumes, one on Prayer, 1711; one on Hearing the Word, 1713; and one on Reading the Scriptures, 1717.

spectacle, and as interesting as its issues were important, when the Romanist chief of a Protestant Church, by unkingly manœuvres, sought to deliver over to the common foe a hierarchy he had sworn to protect; and the noble ingenuousness characteristic of our fathers during the nation's ordeal, and their resistance of temptations to taste the sweets of revenge, showed more conclusively than their oral teachings that, their action partook of the spirit of Christ. With the Dissenters lay the balance of power; and high and eager were the bids offered for their influence by the Crown and by the Church. With few exceptions, Dissent evinced to the world that purity of faith was not to be sacrificed for retaliation; and even they, who servilely addressed the King on his illegal indulgence, were victims of mistaken policy rather than of bad intentions. The day of danger came and went, but the Church, which in her extremity had earnestly craved the alliance of all Protestant sects, showed no desire to continue the acquaintance after the enemy retired. The sagacious William, it is true, with a wisdom and liberality superior to his age, and incomprehensible to his advisers, would have conceded justice to Nonconformists had not his efforts and wishes been frustrated or overruled by Parliament. The King, who under Providence became the political saviour of England, and whose reign was one long struggle for freedom against European despotism, could obtain nothing from his senators more worthy of the times than the Act of Toleration—a measure only extending its privileges to such as subscribed the theological articles of the Anglican Church.

Indeed, the Whigs at the Revolution became so intoxicated with their triumph, that they failed for the time to see what Hume afterwards perceived and honestly confessed, that Puritanism had a principal hand in preserving intact our English liberties. Had the national Church embraced all the people, a monarch of absolutist predilections would easily have overborne opposition and extinguished liberty of conscience. But the far-seeing politicians of the Revolution did not fail to understand the crisis; and from this realisation of their true position sprang the Whigs' opposition to Comprehension. What could be more suicidal than embracing in one establishment those forces, which apart counteracted one another's evil tendencies, but the alliance of which would ensure the annihilation of the last check to arbitrary power, and open a smooth way for the triumph of absolutism? By opposing Comprehension, Anglicanism frittered away a golden opportunity of extending its empire; by an identical policy certain of the Liberal party sought to preserve intact the legitimate influence of Nonconformity.

The clergy as a class were the least satisfied with the Revolution. According to Burnet, a large proportion of the parish ministers, as Jacobitical agitators, desired to rob Dissent of its newly-won privileges, because Dissent had become a formidable obstacle to the cherished scheme of reinstating the exiled Stuarts. But obscure rural clerks—the nobodies of their regimen—were not the only enemies of freedom. Several ecclesiastical dignitaries, some of them men of supposed moderation and of sterling character, were favourable to the suppression of Nonconformist academies. But all were kept in subjection by the good sense of William himself, so that the time of his death was not only a gloomy season for England, but a day of evil forboding for the future of her free Churches.

When the grave closed over the remains of King William the dominant class in Church and State became more encroaching. They turned the accession of a female Stuart into an opportunity for renewing their attack on Dissenters' liberties. Thus originated the Occasional Conformity Bill and the Schism Bill, the agitation connected with which continued through many successive years—years of uncertainty, wherein the peers won our fathers' gratitude, and that of all lovers of constitutional government, by the policy of continually rejecting the former, and so postponing its passing till its apparent triumph came too late to be effective. In the meantime, in remote districts, persons found it difficult, if not impossible, to secure a righteous administration of the laws. In some instances Nonconformists were subjected to the violence of party mobs and the injustice of party "justices."

The controversy on the above-named Jacobitical measures was not entirely fruitless. Jacobitism exposed its deformity till it ensured ultimate defeat by sowing the seeds of its own ruin. In their rabid earnestness to crush opponents, the friends of Charles Edward were aided by scurrilous scribes, whose violent diatribes clearly showed that toleration belonged not to the Stuarts' royal principles; and those professing such Utopian principles were likely to be obnoxious to the State under the proposed new order of things. Places in the State of trust and emolument were as much a Dissenter's birthright as any other Englishman's; but if their price were to become a mortgaging of conscience, then let them go as trifles in comparison. The Dissenters themselves regarded with disfavour those of their brethren who communed in the Establishment for official reasons. " 'Tis a novelty an abuse," observed one, "crept in among us, and we are glad to have it condemned by authority." The discussion yielded a full harvest of libellous pamphlets. One day would bring forth a furious farrago on The Wolf stript of his Clothing; on another day would appear an exposure of the interior of Dissenting academies.

The Sacheverel riots exercised a wide-spread and pernicious influence on the nation. Toryism strengthened its hold on popular affection, and so dismayed the Whigs that their abandonment of the Dissenters was the price paid for the Earl of Nottingham's apostasy from his party—a condition of

the coalition being the cessation of opposition to the
Occasional Conformity Bill. This was a remarkable instance of principle being sacrificed to party
interest.

But perhaps the gravest crisis of those times—
a crisis imparting peculiar interest to the closing
months of Anne's eventful reign—was the passing
of the Schism Bill, a measure which legally came
into force on the day of the Queen's decease. An
unholy phalanx of bishops, infidels, and renegades
promoted the fleeting triumph of this piece of intolerance. Dissenting schools and colleges were to
be closed; and parents were to be deprived of the
right to educate their offspring according to conscience.

As the High Church or Jacobitical leaders grew
more sanguine of success, they would seem to have
imagined that things in general were delivered into
their keeping; and the reign of Anne did not close
without witnessing scenes of violence enacted at their
instigation. Many principal towns were shaken by
anti-Nonconformist riots; and at Oxford the Presbyterian meeting-house was destroyed. Then, ere
many weeks were passed, a retribution in various
forms overtook the religious zealots of that ill-timed
revolution. A Tyburn crowd enjoyed the rare treat
of seeing a clergyman hanged in full canonicals.
Of divers members of Oxford University, the
Government made severe examples. The Pretender
and his adherents at least proved to the world that

the blows aimed at Nonconformity were really designed to prostrate the supporters of the Hanoverian
Succession.

The Dissenters of Queen Anne's day had not
entirely discarded a predilection for Puritan customs, then fast growing obsolete, since the fathers
who adopted them had nearly all passed from the
mortal stage. On the question of keeping Christmas, for example, there existed great diversity of
opinion.* The strictest of the Dissenters objected
to the observance of the 25th of December as a
festival. Their prejudice against the Common
Prayer was aggravated by the consideration that a
popish feast was associated with the nativity of
Christ. The Churches of Scotland and of New
England supplied arguments to strengthen the
position they assumed. If the Anglican, in reply,
ventured on adducing the example of Lutherans, his
opponent objected to having semi-papists introduced
in argument. No particular day, the Nonconformist urged, should commemorate an event belonging to the universe and to all time. It could
not be proved that the Apostles ever honoured
Christmas, and the excesses of successive years
became crowning objections to its observance,
Others were moved by far stronger antipathy. They
saw in Christmas a continuation of those heathen

---

* Dissenters generally, if not universally, objected to the
religious observance of Christmas Day, and had no service in
their chapels on that festival.

Saturnalia, "those mad feasts in honour of Saturn kept at the same time by the heathen as the Christians." They discovered 'Carol' to be derived from 'Ceres,' and 'Yule' from 'Aulos'—a hymn sung at an idol's festival. Nevertheless, that extreme aversion to keeping Christmas, evinced by former generations, had to a large extent died out with the Puritans, and the above remarks only apply to their strictest descendants.

Among the denominations, the Baptists were least inclined to honour the festive season, but the Quakers being unanimous in contemptuously rejecting a religious obligation imposed by authority, openly followed their common pursuits amid the national rejoicings. Between Quakers and other Dissenters little sympathy existed, for in a dialogue spoken by an Anglican and a Nonconformist, we find Friends referred to by the latter as "A wild and enthusiastical sect, which had discarded the badges of Christianity." Certain Presbyterians and Independents, who attempted the innovation of preaching on Christmas Day, did so without reward. In one instance there was a large falling off in pew-rents, and in another the people refused to attend. Even such as were partially successful, observed a discreet silence about any connection between the day and Christ's nativity. Some there were who preached on Christmas Day, as if to make an occasion of declaiming against its observance.

When at length George the First was triumphantly

installed, the Jacobitical clergy continued to do their utmost to further the cause of treason, and the Pretender. Bolingbroke, who hated all religion, but the religion of Dissent in particular, was shocked "for at least two minutes" when dismissed from office, and thus tried by wit to hide his chagrin. Damaging reports were circulated concerning the royal family. Preachers, in hundreds of parish pulpits, unblushingly insulted the King, while many a rural clergyman rivalled the squire in the gust with which he drank the Pretender's health. "They (the clergy)," says a contemporary, "show themselves his most violent enemies . . . with an enmity not only particular and personal, but intemperate to the last degree."

Considering that the Church was the sanctuarium of political renegades, it is scarcely strange that the accession of George the First should have been signalised by the publication of numerous seditious pamphlets, the itinerant vendors of which were subjected to a wholesome prison discipline, while the authors were rebuked by Addison in his Tory Creed. How consistent were Jacobitical professions, when the professors were not avowed papists, is well known to the student of history. Men zealously bigoted to the Thirty-nine Articles, sacrificed wealth and honour to enthrone a monarch whose principles were subversive of the established religion.

The question, What were the customs of our fathers as regards their religious services, if not of paramount importance, yet possesses considerable interest. On Sabbath mornings the meeting-houses opened at nine. The singing of the 100th psalm or some similar piece commenced the service. Three prayers, reading, expounding, and a sermon an hour long followed, the whole probably occupying about double the time of its modern counterpart. The morning order was repeated in the afternoon; evening worship being superseded by catechetical exercises in the family. It became common for masters of households to repeat such portions of the sermon as memory or note-book supplied, and frequently a pastor himself passed pleasant Sabbath evenings in the manse parlour, in company of those neighbours who chose to attend.

In 1717 the Bangorian controversy irritated the religious world—a dispute not so bare of fruit as disputes in general, since it led to the curtailment of the powers of Convocation. Benjamin Hoadley, bishop of Bangor, although clear-headed in politics, favoured the low Arminians in theology. He published a sermon on The Kingdom of Christ, the political sentiments of which were what most would now accept as in unison with Christianity, but sentiments now regarded as reasonable and scriptural, in the days of George the First sufficed to awaken Tory denunciations, since Tories could little brook the idea that their own party was not created to hold others in subjection. Words ran high. The press yielded a harvest of pamphlets. The King ordered a prorogation of the ecclesiastical parliament, and it has never since regained its power.

As a matter of course the old Dissenters were occasionally scandalised by renegades and black sheep. Let one example suffice, the episode having been reported by Mr. Urban in the first year of his literary life, or in 1731. The minister of Nayland, in Suffolk, resolved on conforming, since by a friendly agency he found an opportunity of being introduced to the bishop of the diocese. This Dissenting pastor's wits may not have been of the brightest, nor his learning the most correct, and because the bishop gave him no such encouragement as the convert supposed his heroism merited, he retired in disappointment. A man of resolution, however, is not cowed by one failure. Another bishop was sought, who happening to be from home, the would-be convert concluded that fortune was against him. He abandoned his design, returned in repentant mood to Nayland, and as an auditor, with abashed face, took his place in the meeting on the following Sabbath morning. Ultimately he retired, to continue his humble vocation as a Nonconformist, in a remote corner of England.

As years rolled on without bringing relief, intelligent Dissenters keenly realised that the Revolution had left them shackled. Thus, on Lord Mayor's Day, 1732, the then recently founded Nonconformist rendezvous, Dr. Williams's Library, sheltered a meeting convened to discuss the expe-

diency of taking active measures for agitating the
repeal of the Test and Corporation Acts. A larger
meeting in Silver-street Chapel followed, at which
conflicting sentiments were freely vented. Some
even apprehended a breach of the peace if the proposed action were adopted, and the most sanguine
did not anticipate success. It would be both tedious
and out of keeping with this cursory sketch, were
the attempt made of furnishing a digest of our fore-
fathers' debates on this great question. The subject
is mentioned here merely because at Christmas,
1732, Nonconformist grievances commanded a large
share of public attention, as a reference to the literature of the day will discover. One class of writers
warned Dissenters to beware of heeding Jacobitical
bids for their influence. Let reforms come slowly,
they argued in effect, since the worthiest Churchmen desired a repeal of the obnoxious statutes.
Liberal concession would strengthen the throne by
uniting various sections of the best affected Englishmen in one invincible Protestant phalanx. The
grievance complained of, it was confessed, had
originated under the Stuarts, as the fruit of Jacobitical machinations to weaken the Dissenters by
creating divisions. Newswriters complimented the
Three Denominations on account of a self-denial
which prompted the bearing of a burden of wrong
rather than succumb to the common enemy. One
chronicler supposed injustice was perpetuated because, that through the corruption of human nature,

persecution is inherent in Established Churches. ✕
On the contrary, other journalists declared that the
agitators would not rest until possessed of all the
churches in the empire.

On the rise of Methodism its leaders became the
subjects of a widely-spread jealousy. Members of the
Establishment turned from them as from a species of
Dissenters. Dissenters generally looked with suspicion on the new sect, because regarding Wesley's
regime as unfavourable to independence.

In the meantime, from the rigid exaction of tithes
there sprang much bitter feeling and opposition to
the State Church, if not to Christianity itself. Occasionally the peace of a district would be endangered by the rigorous enforcing of the law on the
part of clergymen; and Quakers, as hereditary opponents, were oftentimes very shamefully used, their
treatment being the more notoriously disgraceful
because they readily allowed themselves to be dis-
trained on for the amounts claimed. Many vindictive incumbents were not satisfied with a procedure
which would have insured them their legal dues.
Intense hatred of the Quakers' enlightened politics
carried many a case into the ecclesiastical courts.
Eight hundred pounds, in one instance, were taken
from ten persons whose tithe in the aggregate
amounted to fifteen pounds. But some experienced
worse things than pecuniary loss; they languished
away their months in prison or even died in noisome
cells. In such business the Established Church was

23 *

commonly the persecutor, for when a bill providing for Friends' relief passed the Commons, prelatical influence prevented its passage through the Lords. Indignation engendered by unearthing these facts is slightly solaced by the counter discovery that, the tables were sometimes turned. When a Quaker farmer had to be dealt with, tithes were more easily set down on paper than realised in substance. Certain sturdy agriculturists would render no account, while showing equal determination in refusing to compound. Parsons were left to garner their dues as best able, and were made to smart for any illegal action.

We receive a more correct acquaintance with the social condition and religious usages of byegone times by searching for what general historians pass lightly over. When, for example, we learn that England abounded with "innumerable alehouses," and that even many religious professors habitually gave their evenings to the seductions of village hostelries, we have a sad revelation of social delinquency, though a profitable study, if by comparing such days with our own, we learn gratitude, and discover how the world progresses towards the goal of Good. Such customs were largely the result of a dearth of wholesome literature ; for all the information many received was what they got in tavern parlours. A curious incident in the history of the Gloucester Journal shows how uncultured they were who read at all, and such were very visibly superior to the masses who had not taken the first steps in knowledge.

The Gloucester Journal was one of the most widely circulated papers of the early Georgian era. Messengers regularly appointed, carried it into neighbouring counties and also into the Principality. On the occasion of some riots occurring in Wiltshire the editors made them a text for a leading article, and proposed to establish the innovation by giving from time to time other pieces by able writers on contemporary events. It speedily transpired that the large constituency of the journal failed to appreciate anything so intellectual. Protests were uttered by a crowd of readers, by whom the change was regarded as but an editorial device to deprive them of their customary news; and, in consequence, prudence dictated the abandoning of the "leader" scheme. The dense ignorance of the people pained the more zealous of the Nonconformists; and from these times many of our schools date their origin.

During the years under notice the stipends of ministers were low; but in numbers of instances, and in towns especially, their duties may have been comparatively light, as co-pastors were more common than at present, or at least they were so in London and in great towns. At one time we find the opinion gaining ground against allowing pastors stated salaries—a fallacy ably combatted by Keach in his lifetime. But this degression is already too lengthy.*
It is time we returned to the King's Weigh-House.

* For the facts embodied in the above I am indebted to a number of contemporary pamphlets, such as the Lawfulness

During the four years from 1732 to 1736, the assistant lecturer was Samuel Sanderson, whose life-work is commemorated in a sermon by Palmer, editor of the Nonconformists' Memorial. Born at Sheffield in 1702, Sanderson enjoyed the tutorship of Timothy Jollie, of Attercliffe, and John Eames, of London. Having completed his college course, he accepted a chaplaincy in a family of distinction, and preached as opportunities offered in the vicinity of the metropolis. He settled at the Weigh-House as lecturer, and ultimately relinquished that office in favour of Bedford, where throughout the rest of his life he remained in connection with John Bunyan's chapel. Sanderson and Ebenezer Chandler—the allegorist's next successor—achieved a success in the town well merited by the harmony which cha-racterised their labours. Their pastoral industry and amiable character won the sympathy of all parties, while their own church enjoyed uninter-rupted prosperity. Sanderson preached regularly three times a week, besides devoting Saturday after-noons to catechising young persons. He assiduously aimed at fulfilling his duty with credit to himself, profit to others, and, above all, he sought to honour his Master. His mortal illness—a nervous fever—

and Right Manner of Keeping Christmas, 1710. The danger of Disobliging the Clergy, &c., &c. Also to the earlier volumes of The Gentleman's Magazine; Bogue and Bennett's History of Dissent; Wilson's Dissenting Churches, Appen-dix, &c.

only disabled him for a single Sabbath.   The pastor
likewise laudably exerted himself in assisting ministerial candidates, many of whom he instructed in
grammar learning, besides collecting funds to aid
their future progress.   A life so earnest and useful
doubtless abounded with events of interest fraught
with profitable instruction, but the details were suppressed in accordance with Sanderson's own desire.
Dying rather suddenly, in January, 1766, his remains
were interred in the graveyard adjoining John Bunyan's chapel at Bedford. *

On the resignation of Samuel Sanderson, Dr.
William Langford, of Silver-street, became assistant
lecturer.   Educated at Glasgow University, he first
settled in the ministry at Gravesend, but resigned
his rural charge in order to become co-pastor of the
church which had been under the charge of John
Howe in London.   He engaged himself to the
Weigh-House Society in 1736, eventually to assume
the pastorate.   The Doctor ably discharged his office
till his seventieth year, when many infirmities inci-
dental to nature disabled him.   Death quickly succeeded, to find him happy in Christian assurance.
In the spring of 1775, on a Saturday afternoon, he
went to Croydon on a visit to a friend, intending to
reap benefit by change of air; but at six o'clock on
the following morning he died.   His last recorded
words issued from a well-spring of comfort within,

* See the Theological and Biblical Magazine, April, 1806;
Palmer's Sermon on the Death of Samuel Sanderson, &c.

" I have been in pain through unbelief, but now all is removed by faith." He published eleven single sermons. *

Dr. Langford had an assistant in Samuel Palmer, of Hackney—a name familiar to many through his editing the Nonconformists' Memorial. Being a native of Bedford, Palmer in his youthful days enjoyed the privilege of attending Sanderson's ministry, and subsequently of studying under Dr. Ashworth at Daventry Academy, whence he removed to Hackney. On the decease of his colleague, in 1766, Palmer succeeded him, resigned his office at the Weigh-House, and spent his remaining days in a sphere in which Bates and Henry had already laboured. He died in 1813, and his remains lie in the graveyard adjoining St. Thomas's-square Chapel, Hackney. Another Weigh-House lecturer, and a son-in-law of Dr. Langford, was Edward Vennor, who removed to Ware, and laboured in that town for a great number of years.

Dr. Langford was succeeded by Samuel Wilton, a native of London ; and, although only in his thirtieth year, a doctor of divinity—an American honour he specially prized on account of his being an enthusiastic apologist for the War of Independence. This divine, who spent his early years at Hackney, was

* Gibbons's Sermon on the Death of Dr. Langford; Wilson's Dissenting Churches, &c.

✝ Thomas Toller's Sermon on the Death of Samuel Palmer, &c.

educated at Christ's Hospital, whence he removed
into Hoxton College to study under Drs. Kippis,
Savage, and Rees.   Even in youth, Wilton's amiable
manners and literary culture rendered him a general
favourite with the accomplished society entertained
at his father's house.   When he inaugurated his
ministry by settling at Tooting, the widow of his
predecessor celebrated the event by rebuilding the
chapel at her sole expense.   The Doctor remained
at Tooting about nine years, happy, industrious, and
successful.   Although his private means were ample,
he studied frugality so that more of his substance
might succour the needy; and, in addition to this ,
flow of charity, his genial nature made him delight
to entertain at his board his Nonconformist brethren,
the majority of whom were poorer than himself.
Evening service was then comparatively rare; but,
in the case of Dr. Wilton, zeal in the work of evangelisation prompted the establishment of a Sabbath-
evening lecture at Mortlake.   A man like Wilton
lived to nurture Nonconformity, and to advance the
cause of liberty; but, while he would strenuously
defend his denominational principles, he valued many
friends within the Anglican pale.   On removing
to London he preferred a rural manse at Hackney
to the house in Rood-lane, which had sheltered his
predecessor Reynolds, for Hackney contained his
best friends and earliest acquaintances.   Under Dr.
Wilton's ministry its former prosperity was restored
to the Church; and his labours were bearing abun-

dant fruit when death cut down the labourer in April, 1778.   He preached his last sermon in Mare-street meeting-house, and died a few days after of a fever caught while visiting a family in the district. Having immediately before his departure sent for Samuel Palmer, the latter exclaimed, as he ap-proached his dying friend, " This is the most painful meeting we have had."   " We shall soon meet again," replied Wilton cheerfully.   His spirit fled just as the hour-hand pointed to midnight, on April the 3rd, 1778.

The fact deserves honourable mention that, al-though he studied under some Arian professors,* Dr. Wilton during life consistently adhered to the orthodox standard.   He preferred the Independent to the Presbyterian system.   His method of study and his pulpit habits were peculiar.   A rapid utterance, evincing a great command of language, early engen-dered contempt for written discourses.   His deli-very was not controlled by any oratorical art; for the preacher usually stood in the pulpit quite motion-less, and with his eyes riveted on the bare Bible, as though he were closely perusing a manuscript. In his study were found numbers of sermons clearly written, from which his surviving relatives would have published a selection, but for the author's express directions to the contrary.   Dr. Wilton ob-served two fasts in every year—one on his ordina-

* This remark only refers to Drs. Rees and Kippis. Dr. Savage, the theological tutor, remained sound.

tion day, the other in commemoration of his providential escape from death by drowning on an occasion ¹ when his horse plunged into some deep water while . travelling near Tooting.*

At this stage an unsuccessful endeavour was made to induce Robert Gentleman, of Shrewsbury, to accept the pastorate.   Subsequently, John Clayton

* Samuel Palmer's Sermon on the death of Dr. Wilton; Wilson's Dissenting Churches. See also The Theological Magazine for 1801, and The Protestant Dissenters' Magazine, vol. vi. The following is taken from the appendix to Orton's Letters to Dissenting Ministers: " He (Dr. Wilton) had the fullest claim to their esteem and love, for he was most exemplary for his assiduity and attainments, for a respectful attention to his tutors, and for his courteousness and unaffected kindness to his fellow-pupils. One trait, in particular, of his disposition towards them is worthy of being recorded. His ardour in the persuit of knowledge, and of every qualification for the important work to which he had consecrated himself, was entirely free from jealousy and selfishness.   He was solicitous to excite and cherish the same ardour in his associates.   He was at that early period of his life, modestly communicative, and a zealous premoter of useful conversation. At his father's house, and at the apartments of his fellow students, he would join with them in reading the classics, and in pursuing other branches of literature; and though a reciprocal communication was the idea under which he represented the design of those meetings, his liberality in imparting information was equal to his superior abilities and furniture.   On such occasions, too, and at every suitable opportunity, he would, in the most amiable and unoffending manner possible, suggest hints respecting the spirit, conduct, and views, which became those who were under a course of education for the Christian ministry.

was chosen in October, 1779, being then in the twenty-fifth year of his age.

The venerable form of John Clayton is still remembered by many. There is no reason to doubt that, by his teaching he permanently benefited the church at the Weigh-House during his pastorate, although occasionally his teachings, as in the case of his sermon on the Birmingham riots, were the opposite of judicious. To go back to the days of Clayton's youth carries us far into the last century, when people lived and worked much as their fathers had done before them for more than one generation. In the middle of the century there lived at a place called West End Farm, in the county of Lancashire, a cotton bleacher, whose life of sober industry won the esteem of the neighbours. The family was large, and John, our present subject, being the only son of his parents, became somewhat over-indulged by his mother.

John Clayton's education commenced at a grammar-school in the neighbourhood of his home, where he and his companions enlivened the monotony of a village curriculum by dividing into religious and political parties; and, because fitted both by nature and prejudice for the office, the embryo divine assumed the championship of the Protestant party. His family not being Dissenters, John was reared within the pale of the Establishment; but although he appears to have been serious, he possessed but little genuine knowledge of Christianity at confirmation,

and he was not really converted until circumstances:
brought him under the ministry of Romaine.

Intending John for a chemist, his parents apprenticed him to that profession ; and although his.
after life became different from the course planned,
much useful knowledge of practical value was gained,
under the pharmaceutist. This employment he suddenly forsook, disposed of a borrowed gun, and ap--
peared in London, much to the surprise and annoyance of his then more sober relatives. This exploit,.
bad in itself, had one good result—it became the
indirect means of introducing young Clayton to the-
Countess of Huntingdon; and his entrance into her·
ladyship's college at Trevecca influenced the whole
course of his life. The patronage of the estimable·
Countess was an honour which one of superior rank·
and intellectual strength to John Clayton might have·
coveted. Her widowhood of forty-six years she
employed in ceaseless endéavours to disseminate the·
Gospel. The theological institution at Trevecca she··
established at great personal sacrifice, and there, as.
the foundress, she delighted to be found employing
herself promoting the comfort of the students with a
mother's solicitude. Because her ladyship for the··
most part was her own secretary, several hours·
a-day were occasionally occupied in attending to a.
large correspondence. She evinced excessive anxiety
for the welfare of her fellow-creatures, and well
would it be were her example of self-denial oftener·
exhibited. In the hospitable Welsh academy, the-

students enjoyed every requisite which conduces to mental progress and domestic comfort. Able professors and a good library were provided. Each student had a private study and a separate garden ; besides conveniences for bathing and recreation, with all other necessaries. The visible solicitude of the Countess for the eternal weal of man would deeply affect both tutors and students, and during family prayer the group were frequently found in tears. So remarkable was her earnestness that one who commemorated her life in a funeral sermon declared that, she would have derived more pleasure from benefiting one soul than from the sudden inheritance of a large fortune. The blessing of heaven rested upon the college till it became a centre of Gospel influence—a source of life to the Church during the retrogressive Georgian era. The flaming zeal of the matron infected the inmates till sometimes they devoted half the night to earnestly praying for the conversion of mankind. No higher fortune could have befallen John Clayton than to find such a training-school, and to have for a counsellor the inestimable Countess of Huntingdon. He had the additional fortune to rise into high favour with his patroness, as she proved by many motherly actions. At one time, because he gave symptoms of weakness she sent him to Tunbridge Wells ; and her ladyship's letters of 1777 show the anxiety she experienced on account of Clayton's health.

A large proportion of the discipline at Trevecca

was actual preaching. So heavily did the work press on young Clayton that we find him complaining that his too-frequent preachings left him but little time for the self-culture so necessary for securing future usefulness. Then, moreover, preaching students in the reign of George the Third traversed a rough path, as can be demonstrated by an anecdote illustrative of Clayton's early ministry. Once he conducted an outdoor service in the neighbourhood of Christchurch, news of which coming to the ears of certain lovers of sport, a lad of their number spent a morning in collecting rotten eggs wherewith to pelt the preacher and entertain the crowd. As the service proceeded Clayton presented an appearance as strikingly odd to spectators as disagreeable to himself; but circumstances did not prevent his praying for these pitiable assailants. The episode passed away not to be remembered as anything extraordinary until thirty-six years after, when a gentleman called the occurrence to remembrance by craving the forgiveness of the Weigh-House pastor for having been ringleader in the Christchurch outrage.

During his stay with the Countess of Huntingdon, Clayton had no idea of one day gracing the Nonconformist ministry, for it is doubtful if he would ever have been a Dissenter had not the Bishops of Llandaff and Lincoln acted as the instruments of breaking off his affection from the Establishment. In those days Lady Huntingdon's Connexion was particularly obnoxious to those easy-living churchmen, who combined Tory politics with Arminian theology. The quibbles of one bishop were echoed by another, until Clayton resolved to make no further effort to enter the Church of England; and happening, about the same time, to read Towgood's Letters on Dissent, his Nonconformist principles became finally settled. This unexpected turn in the tide of events disappointed the Countess, and she expressed her disapproval of Nonconformity in a lengthy letter.

While itinerating for Lady Huntingdon, Clayton became acquainted with a young man of ancient family — the notorious Sir H. Trelawney. As their friendship strengthened, the Nonconformist principles of the student may have influenced the baronet till he decided on treading a like path of self-denial. However that may have been, the ordination of Sir Harry at Southampton was long remembered as one of the most strikingly pompous services ever known among Dissenters. Passing months seemed only to knit together in yet closer friendship the student and his titled companion, and for a time they lived together at the ancestral seat of the Trelawneys at Looe. They were also one in labour, striving to dispel that gross spiritual darkness which then, in a greater degree than now, overhung the county of Cornwall. Their combined action in evangelisation won the applause of philanthropic people no less than the gratitude of those whom they benefited.

The life-story of Sir H. Trelawney abounds with sad passages. While proving himself a man of honour, he lacked that strength of character so indispensable to men of rank who set their face against the follies of fashion. But as he belongs not to the Weigh-House, he may be dismissed with an anecdote concerning his marriage, which occurred in 1778. For his bride he took a beautiful girl, who, apparently without her lover's knowledge, annulled a prior engagement in order to please her parents by securing for herself a more splendid station. The spectacle was a gay one, when, after their honeymoon, Sir Harry and his wife returned to his seat at Looe, to be welcomed home by his friend Clayton and the servants of the establishment. The young baronet proceeded to open a number of letters, and during the perusal of one in particular his countenance changed, betokening some shock sustained by his nervous system. Evening wore into night, but he would neither eat nor converse. At length he confessed to Clayton that he had received an affecting expostulation from his wife's former lover, who had written, while ignorant of the marriage, calling on Trelawney as a gentleman to withdraw his claims on the lady's affections. This affair is supposed to have influenced Sir Harry more or less till the end of his days, although his married life continued to flow on happily. He became very changeable, and joined the "Rational" party. He and Clayton soon after separated, and do not appear to have corresponded during the last forty years of their lives.

John Clayton's introduction to the Weigh-House was effected by means of a gentleman who encountered the young preacher in Cornwall. The Church voted unanimously for his settlement, with the exception of a lady who refused to vote, and she afterwards became Mrs. Clayton. The ordination took place on the 25th of November, 1778. Fostered by his ministry, the Church by an increased prosperity showed that her interests were in competent hands. The pastor's rising popularity prompted the Lady Glenorchy to invite him to Edinburgh, under her ladyship's patronage—an offer he respectfully declined. One result of these changes at the Weigh-House was the diversion of all collections from the Presbyterian Fund, on account of the low doctrine into which many of its members had lapsed. From this date the society has ranked with the Independents.

On settling in London, Clayton persevered till he achieved a respectable reputation in his profession. He exercised considerable influence in his own limited sphere, which might have been wider, had not his crude political creed prevented his becoming a representative Nonconformist, although by some in power he appears to have been mistaken for such a person. In his sermon on the Birmingham riots, sentiments were advanced which hitherto had been strange to the Dissenting pulpit, but the numerous contemptuous replies testify to this day that, the Three Denominations disowned the performance as presumptuous and insulting. But consolation was not wanting, for " Mr. Clayton's weak and malignant invectives," as Robert Hall styled his arguments, drew from the greatest pulpit orator of his time that masterly work, Christianity Consistent with a Love of Freedom. The Weigh-House pastor could coolly confess he had never read this remarkable treatise ! Remarkable as is the book, this admission of John Clayton is even more remarkable.

John Clayton's marriage was in all respects a happy union. He showed sufficient worldly wisdom to select a wealthy bride—Miss Flower, the daughter of a city merchant. Although the sequel proved highly satisfactory to all concerned, the family at first regarded the reverend suitor with ill-concealed aversion; the mother, in particular, contemptuously spoke of him as " a penniless parson."

The pastor was elected a member of the Eclectic Society, and he accepted the Merchants' Lectureship at New Broad-street, and also another in Fetter-lane. As regards his life-work in London, to describe one week will be to describe the whole, for he succeeded, more than any other quotable example, in rendering every seven days a panorama of his entire career. Usually he chose his texts on Monday; Tuesday was devoted to pastoral visiting, and principally in the City; Wednesday and Thursday were study days; on Friday visitors were received; and on Saturday

24*

he enjoyed some recreation, such as walking or driving, giving the evening to prayer and meditation. His punctuality could not have been more marked had his movements been regulated by clockwork. At eight each morning he took his place at family prayer, and he is not supposed to have been two minutes out of time during a space of forty years. This excessive love of order, as a second nature, characterised all he did; but whether the habit of working with the regularity of a machine is worthy of imitation or admiration, we will not venture an opinion, for most people will not attempt an impossible discipline. It is admirable to see men, and especially divines, penurious of their fleeting hours, but many have excelled in redeeming time without making their life a monotonous round. What John Clayton may have found a profitable procedure, others would feel to be an unnecessary burden.

As a pastor, John Clayton may have had his faults, but he laboriously and conscientiously discharged his duties. As a public man, in a political sense, he only represented a single household in Highbury-place, for his political opinions were not worthy of being identified with Nonconformity. In the family he enforced so strict a discipline that the wonder is he did not spoil his children and dependents by too much of a good thing. Assuredly the picture given us of this painfully neat divine as he ruled in his household excites our awe if it does not command our love. Such callers as entered the pastor's study would probably feel ill at ease, lest by stepping on the carpet, or by sitting in a chair, they should disturb the reigning order, for the very dust seemed to keep off the shelves, and the well-swept fire-place appeared as though it directly sympathised with the scrupulously clean secretaire and its tidily-arranged drawers. One piece of furniture in this sanctuarium would now suffice to shock our notions of parental kindness, although its mention is quite necessary to complete a true portrait of what John Clayton was at home. This was " The silver-headed monitor," otherwise a heavy whip, hanging over his study door. Indeed, the pastor's stern nature would seem to have resembled the nature of those heroes of the civil wars who quoted Scripture over the opponents they chastised, for whenever the young Claytons earned a horsewhipping it was heralded by a reading and an expounding—an unlovely pro-cedure, calculated rather to breed contempt for the Bible than respect for the flogging. Punishment was likewise deferred, to show that it emanated from principle. Most young persons if subjected to such a discipline would probably recognise the " prin-ciple " which corrected them, without discovering the existence of parental feeling.

The public ministrations of John Clayton are thus alluded to by his biographer: " His preaching was characterised by the compass and variety of his subjects; by its adaptation to passing events and occurrences; by accurate discrimination of the states and characters of his hearers; by warm affection, tender sympathy, and impassioned expostulation, and by an obvious concern to give to all classes their portion in due season. His manner was grave, but not dull; familiar, but not colloquial; plain, but never coarse; pointed, without being personal, and in no instance that can be remembered, anecdotal, or approaching to wit or drollery."*

Thus did John Clayton pursue a prosperous course. Robert Hall spoke of him as "The most favoured man I ever saw, or ever heard of." In the year 1821, symptoms of failing strength were manifest; and an assistant—E. Parsons—was engaged. Five years later the pastor resigned, and the people showed their appreciation of his worth by presenting him with a testimonial of the value of £228. He retired to Gaines, near Upminster, and there he died, at the age of eighty-nine, in September, 1843.†

John Clayton's successor, Thomas Binney, has just closed a pastorate of forty years' duration.‡ But it is foreign to our purpose to write about

* Memorials of the Clayton Family.

† For a more ample account of John Clayton see Memorials of the Clayton Family; many facts concerning the Countess of Huntingdon will be found in the Sermons preached on the occasion of her funeral by various divines.

‡ See Mr. Binney's Sermon at the King's Weigh-House; A Forty Years' Review, &c.

living divines. It will suffice to say, that, under Providence, the Pastor's life-work has greatly benefited those intelligent classes with whom his peculiar talents have brought him in contact. His pastorate has certainly proved the most auspicious of any connected with the Weigh-House Church, and probably has not been surpassed in usefulness by any divine who, since the Puritan era, has laboured in London.

Chapter IX.

THE Worshipful Company of Salters of London enjoys the distinction of being ranked among those twelve ancient livery fraternities of the City which pride themselves in their royally-granted privileges and abundant wealth, a due proportion of which is dispensed in charity. From various English monarchs, ranging from Edward the Third to James the First, this guild received eight charters. Elizabeth, on ascending the throne, fully confirmed their possession of certain privileges, and since that date the Salters have been an incorporated company of the metropolis. At consecutive periods they have occupied five halls. The original building stood in Bread-street, and was erected in the middle of the fifteenth century. From the reign of the Sixth to that of the Eighth Henry, this hall continued in use, and after existing a century, was damaged by fire, rebuilt, and had an addition made to it of several almshouses for the use of such reduced members as might need accommodation. In 1598 the premises,

were again destroyed by the flames, and the Company subsequently purchased a noble mansion near.
London-Stone, known as Oxford House, which, however, shared with its neighbours the common desolation of 1666. A large room of this house was
frequently the scene of political discussion during.
the sitting of the Long Parliament. In the seventeenth century, likewise, two Salters, who were raised.
to the mayoralty, celebrated on this spot their term
of office. The structure which succeeded the great
fire had attached to it large and luxuriant pleasure-
grounds, highly valued by the citizens, because·
adorning the centre of the City. The famous.
meeting-house, rented from the Salters by the Dis-·
senters, was a portion of the same estate. The·
commercial prosperity early enjoyed by this honourable brotherhood, encouraged them, it would seem,,
to achieve a prestige for hospitality. A bill of fare,,
dated 1506, contains a list of viands then sufficing
to feast fifty persons, and although the Salters of.
old times may not by eating have endeavoured to.
encourage their traffic, yet the proofs, in the docu-·
ment referred to, are abundant that they inherited.
prodigious appetites. In the summer of 1821 the
hall was taken down, and the present magnificent,
structure completed six years later.

The Church, which for so long made " Salters'. ·
Hall " familiar as " household words " in Dissenters'
ears, was gathered at the era of the Restoration, and
originally assembled at Buckingham House, College-

hill—a mansion deriving its name from its profligate
owner, George Villiers.   It is unknown who first
marshalled this Nonconformist band, but Richard
Mayo, who died in 1695, was the first minister
about whom any particulars have descended.   The
chief source of information respecting this old Presbyterian, is a funeral sermon printed in small
quarto, and " Sold at the Three Legs, over against the
Stocks' Market." Mayo was born in or about the year
1631. He pursued his preparatory studies in London
under John Singleton, a celebrated scholar, by whom
he was thoroughly grounded in general knowledge,
and in those great principles of religious and moral
rectitude from which in after-life he never deviated.
When, during the Commonwealth, Presbyterianism
and Independency were in the ascendant, Mayo was
preferred to the living of Kingston-upon-Thames,
although he may have occupied another sphere in
previous years.   In addition to his duties at Kingston, the pastor sustained a weekly lecture in Whitechapel.   He achieved such singular popularity as
could only have sprung from burning zeal and rare
oratorical power.   On the occasion of each visit
the interior of the church was closely packed by
the overflowing audience which pressed into the
too limited area, and every position, where a glimpse
of the lecturer could be obtained, or a note of his
voice heard, was eagerly occupied.   The windows
even were frequently darkened by the numbers of
persons who clung about their vicinity.   This mani-

fest anxiety of the multitude to hear the Word apparently inspired the preacher by imparting fresh animation, till as though pulpit and pew were united by an electric current, orators and hearers glowed with a common enthusiasm. On seceding with the two thousand confessors of 1662, Mayo was in due course elected to the pastorate at College-hill.

In the happier days of William the Third, the Church erected the meeting-house at Salters' Hall, but the pastor's after career proved only a brief one. Till the end of his days, Mayo was esteemed a man of eminent piety, to which he joined a rare amiability of disposition and a diligent performance of his duties. He rose habitually at five on Sabbath mornings, so that he might devote the day's earliest hours to prayer and meditation. Several of his sermons are extant, from which a tolerably correct estimate of their author's mental calibre may be formed. A contemporary described his preaching as " methodical, clear, and generally derived from his text, like ripe and fair fruit that drops from the bough whereon it naturally grew."

In the year 1688, Nathaniel Taylor was chosen assistant lecturer, and he remained with the people until his death in 1702. In later years he suffered very severely from bodily affliction, having been occasionally necessitated to enter the pulpit upon his knees. Taylor was trained by the indefatigable Edward Veale, at whose house he had John Shower for a fellow student. Those young scholars were in the habit of walking from Wapping to Bishopsgate, in order to attend the lectures of Charnocke, in Crosby Hall. A brief insight is obtained into that eminent Puritan's genial nature, by discovering what interest he took in the progress of the young men. He gave them his valuable advice, and for their benefit, critically listened to their early sermons. It is remarkable that each *protégé* of so distinguished a patron, occupied in succeeding life a foremost place in his denomination—the one having been stationed in Salters' Hall, and the other at the Old Jewry. Taylor displayed superior talents ; yet, during the opening years of his ministry, he only appears to have served some country congregation; and, eventually when he removed to London, he did so to succeed his college companion, John Shower, as lecturer at Westminster, under Vincent Alsop. He held this position for, or about, five years, and was at last driven into Holland by the prevailing perse-secution. On returning from the Continent in quieter times, he was engaged as lecturer at College-hill. Hard study impaired his constitution and brought on premature decay. Added to personal suffering was the affliction of an invalided wife, whose death preceded that of her husband's about a year. Taylor's severe suffering probably awakened a feeling of sympathy for him throughout the City, and increasingly endeared him to his own people. The pastor earned the general esteem of his contemporaries, who revered him as an accomplished

Christian scholar. He excelled in a knowledge of several sciences; and after a lengthened and laborious investigation of the basis of a Christian's belief, Taylor was wont to teach his hearers, that no better reason for accepting a tenet can be given than that of finding it in the Bible. While vigour lasted he possessed a fine voice and a bright imagination, and was, in consequence, a powerful expounder of sacred truth. He manifested much fondness for little children—a pleasing trait in a good man's character. Anxiety for the welfare of youth taught him to give special attention to catechising, and he fulfilled his office so winningly and affectionately as to render himself extremely popular among an unusually large number of the youth of London, whom he led in regular order over the Assembly's Catechism. Taylor's course was at length unexpectedly terminated in rather a sudden manner; but his happy departure was a befitting sequel to the career he had run.* "He was a man," says Matthew Henry, "of great wit, worth, and courage; not much older than myself." "The Dissenting South," wrote Doddridge, "There is vast wit and great strength of expression in all he wrote. His language is remarkably proper and beautiful."†

* Funeral Sermons by John Shower and John Newman on the death of Nathaniel Taylor; Calamy's Continuation; Wilson's History of the Dissenting Churches.

† "He (Thomas Taylor) was the father of Mr. Nathaniel Taylor of Salters' Hall, who was so well known and so much

Sixteen hundred and sixty-two threw its shade into many succeeding years, and over many manly hearts, aching by reason of domestic desolation, and re-wounded by witnessing the hardship which tender women were constrained to bear for conscience' sake. Ministers whose natal day occurred about the time of this great crisis, usually referred to the fact with complacent satisfaction, and regarded their advent into the world at that particular period, as traceable to Providence. It was thus with Matthew Henry, and also with William Tong, the commentator's excellent biographer. The last-named, in the year following Taylor's decease, succeeded at Salters' Hall. The family to which he belonged had formerly settled at Eccles, in Yorkshire. He was very early deprived of his father's counsel by death; but he possessed a mother equal to the task of starting him in life. She was a noble specimen of the old stock of Puritans, then fast diminishing; and was, moreover, an uncompromising Nonconformist. To this superior woman's watchfulness and prudence,

esteemed in this City. He gave him the name of Nathaniel out of his great respect for the honourable Nathaniel Fiennes, Esq., of Newton Tony; who, though he himself lived not to be Viscount Say and Sele, yet was the son, the brother, and the father of those who bore that title. This noble gentleman, and after his death, his religious lady, were very kind to several Nonconformists in this county, and particularly to Mr. Taylor, who without such generous help, would very difficultly have been able to support, or bring up a numerous family."—*Calamy's Continuation*, p. 867, *ed.* 1727.

Tong became immensely indebted, and whenever he afterwards referred to his mother's character, he naturally did so with sincerest veneration. To her, under Providence, it was mainly owing that he entered the ministry, his early predilections having leaned towards the legal profession. During the years immediately preceding the death of Charles the Second, a celebrated Presbyterian professor read lectures before a small cluster of youths, whose studies he directed, and who shared his quiet home at Natland, in Westmoreland. Under this tutor, Richard Frankland,* Tong pursued his academical studies, having already enjoyed the advantage of a superior preliminary education. A somewhat correct estimate of the noble lessons inculcated at Frankland's retreat, may be drawn from the fact that, William Tong, on finishing his course, went forth to preach about the country, although such a practice entailed serious personal danger. The young scholar's heroic action, however, failed to involve him in any of the then penalties of moral bravery.

When at length Tong commenced his regular ministry in the neighbourhood of Chester, he at once rose into a popular preacher, and could have accepted a station in the Establishment had he chosen to conform, but he was proof against such temptations. He, nevertheless, in his younger days, used portions of the Common Prayer, and had thereby

* Frankland educated three hundred youths, most of whom became ministers.

greatly shocked a certain parson, who complained
to his diocesan, and so occasioned Tong to abandon
the practice for ever after. When, in 1687, by
reason of the Indulgence, the Nonconformists reopened their meeting-houses, this young divine was
occupying the pulpit at Chester, to which Matthew
Henry immediately succeeded. During his stay
in that quaint town, Tong found a valuable friend in
Anthony Henthorne, a gentleman of fortune, who
prior to presenting the congregation with a chapel,
opened his own mansion for religious services, and
sustained the minister as a member of his own
family. The various denominations then assembling
in Chester, worked harmoniously together for the
common good. Settled in the town were two
Anglican divines, whose ministrations were so highly
appreciated, that the townspeople attended the
Churches during canonical hours, and, between those
hours, gathered in crowds at the Nonconformist
meetings.

While engaged in working so delightful a field of
Christian labour, Tong became afflicted with what
his friends judged to be a decline, till he unexpectedly recovered. On account of not being permanently settled at Chester, he listened to a call
from the principal inhabitants of Knutsford to plant
a Nonconformist interest in that town. The late
clergyman of the parish the people had esteemed as
a pattern of rarest sanctity. Throughout the district
the pastor had won so high a reputation for holiness

that even the Dissenters thought themselves privileged
to attend his ministry. On this good man's removal,
however, a strong party desired for their rector one
who would advocate a less rigid discipline, and whose
general views of religion would sanction a wider
license in worldly matters. The inhabitants inherited the legal right of choice, and therefore the
High Church party ultimately prevailed in electing
a minister of their own school. As a result, the
more conscientious church people allied themselves
with Dissent for the purpose of planting a church of
the Presbyterian order, and of calling Tong to the
pastorate. This programme succeeding months saw
fully accomplished, although about two years after,
the pastor removed to a more extensive sphere of
usefulness at Coventry; and it is interesting to
know that many free churches of the surrounding
country were originally the preaching-stations of
William Tong. In subsequent times, when the
eighteenth century had far advanced, old persons
were often encountered who remembered, and loved
to speak of the Presbyterian pastor's indefatigable
labours, for, in addition to other things, he maintained an academy for ministerial students.

On the decease of Nathaniel Taylor, in 1702,
Tong succeeded at Salters' Hall. This step added
to his reputation, and, by placing him in a station
of wider influence, enabled him directly and indirectly
to act as a benefactor to his poorer compeers in the
distance. Tong was properly an English Presby-

terian, but his sympathies were divided between his own people and Independency. He freely mixed with the sister denomination till his death in the spring of 1727. During his twenty-four years' term of office a large and prosperous congregation was maintained. In London, as elsewhere, he engaged in many works apart from his stated duties. As an author he was highly esteemed, much that he wrote being still valued, as, for example, The Notes on Hebrews and the Revelation in Matthew Henry's Commentary. He has likewise bequeathed us memoirs both of the commentator and of John Shower, of the Old Jewry. As a writer all may judge of him; and as to the rest, Newman in his funeral sermon has styled him " the prince of preachers." Tong merited this high distinction in consequence of the ready facility with which he illustrated Gospel truth by striking ideas, while clothing the whole in the common Saxon of the English people. He betrayed in later years a slight decline of intellectual vigour; and when he departed into rest it was abundantly manifest to surviving friends that Tong's mortal frame had gone to the grave worn out with ceaseless labour. His charity to the poor, it may be mentioned, often necessitated something stricter than charity nearer home.*

English Presbyterianism has in some respects a melancholy history, for Arianism was early imbibed

* Newman's Sermon on the Death of William Tong; Wilson's History of the Dissenting Churches.

by large numbers of that great denomination; and
the defection proved to be a prelude to Socinianism.
At first the enemy's stealthy encroachments remained
unobserved, or his gradual advances were not regarded with sufficient concern to attract any serious
notice. But soon after the Brunswick family acceded
to the English crown, the friends of Nonconformity
realised with some alarm the grave nature of the
situation. The facts about the disputes at Salters'
Hall, in 1719, respecting subscription to articles of
faith are not sufficiently known to render superfluous
a brief recital of an unfortunate quarrel. Upon the
city of Exeter the odium is attached of having
originated the ferment. In the summer of 1718
several ministers of the West observed with much
concern, that strange doctrines were making progress
among them. They convened a meeting, at which
they conferred about the means likely to arrest the
progress of the evil. In the first instance the one
best plan to adopt, they imagined, would be to allow
the new notions to burn themselves out, or to let
them die of exhaustion. Any hopes founded on
such a basis ere long turned out illusory, for the
abettors of Arianism continued industriously to propagate their tenets, and to accompany their endeavours with profuse avowals of liberalism and charity.
The London ministers, so these itinerants assured the
country people, held and taught opinions identical
with their own. The effect of such efforts among
the people was only too soon apparent. On all

25 *

hands vulgar and illiterate disputants quarrelled about Christian doctrine till Exeter was scandalised by the unseemly liberty such debaters took with truths at once sacred and momentous. Meanwhile the defection deepened its roots and widened the area of its influence. While thus strengthening in growth among the vulgar, the boldness of the infected party visibly increased, as first one pastor and anon others following, were found to declare for Arianism. Such preachers commonly perplexed their hearers by rejecting this text or that as no part of the canonical Bible. The controversy thus hotly maintained in meeting-houses, the streets, and market-places, penetrated even to the judicial bench, for while country women carried home in their baskets on Saturday afternoons, tracts overflowing with incomprehensible opinions retailed from Emlyn and Whiston, a judge on his circuit publicly rebuked the abounding errors. The Anglican clergy exerted all their power to make capital out of the crisis, and their pulpits, from the cathedral downwards, rang with denunciations and urgent warnings against contracting contamination from Nonconformists, who—the preachers averred—had denied their Lord, and by the press were sowing broadcast their blasphemies respecting Him. A conclave in the town passed resolutions which invited the pastors in general to declare from their pulpits against the obnoxious tenets. Among the four Presbyterian leaders who then presided over three congregations

in Exeter, James Pierce stood forth as the champion.
With much assurance Pierce reduced the Doxology
down to the standard of his own belief. Alarmed
at the turn affairs were taking, several ministers met
together and dispatched a message to London for
advice. This letter elicited a reply from the metropolitan pastors, which included some general Christian counsel and protestations against the innovating
doctrines. This, however, sufficed not to soothe
men's passions, and the warfare in consequence proceeded apace.

In those days the Western Presbyterians held
both spring and autumn gatherings. In the September meeting of 1718, the disputed dogmas furnished a text for a most intemperate debate, in the
course of which the pastors present were required
to express their doctrinal belief. Many gladly testified to their continued attachment to the pure old
gospel; others wavered, or embodied their answers
in uninterpreted scriptural phrases. Many, however,
boldly avowed the Arian tenets. The vote taken
showed that some leading men were with the latter
party—the younger ministers being especially affected. The time-honoured custom was, for a united
service to precede and follow those half-yearly
synods. In the present instance the several gatherings in the town were attended by much excitement.
Pamphlets swarmed from the presses of the opposing
sections. Some writers fiercely assailed old opinions,
and tried every manœuvre which promised to ad-

vance their cause. Their publications were distributed through the post-office, or were gratuitously
supplied to the farmers who frequented Exeter
Market. The housemaids and apprentices, who, as
usual, rose at sunrise on those autumnal mornings,
were wont to find in shutter chinks, or underneath
doors, treatises on the TRINITY, or the mysteries
centring around the Person of Christ. By such
agencies the controversy reached the humblest members of the denominations. Many of the pamphlets
emanated from mere wanton scribblers of neither
ability nor reputation, but others proceeded from
eminent authors. At this stage of the dispute, the
Churches of Exeter sought the advice of five leading London divines. Overwhelmed and perplexed by
what was really a grave emergency, the ministers
referred to, decided on calling a synod of the Three
Denominations at Salters' Hall, to meet on February
the 19th, 1719.

Meanwhile, intelligence arrived from Exeter that
the orthodox ministers had passed resolutions respecting errors to be withstood at any hazard ; and
denial of the divinity of Christ was classed among
defections which warranted a Church in refusing a
pastor's ministrations. But by this time the con-
tagion had reached the metropolis, and examples
might be adduced of the Western principles having
been carried out, whether as respects ministers
ejected, or members expelled. The Stoke Newington
minister, Martin Tompkins, was visited by the first-

named discipline, and on retiring to Hackney to live as a private gentleman, he injudiciously published a tedious narration of his trials.

The object of the celebrated Synod of 1719 was primarily to adopt some plan for restoring peace. The meetings opened on Monday, February the 19th, on which day the discussion was adjourned till the Friday following. The postponed debate had its progress interrupted by a proposal from Thomas Bradbury, of New-court, to annex a declaration on the doctrine of the TRINITY to the contemplated advices for the Western Churches. This drew forth the most determined opposition. Mark Key, of Devonshire-square, and his colleague, both attended, but neither they nor their brethren of corresponding faith could assay to speak without being contemptuously snubbed as "Anabaptist teachers." From all parts of the room there came hisses for Bradbury, to which the old Independent rejoined with stinging sarcasm. From this stage the proceedings were unexampled on account of the strange rudeness and insult with which opposing sections assailed each other. On a show of hands being taken, Bradbury's party claimed a majority, but their opponents demanded a legal division. Accordingly the Non-subscribers retired to the gallery, calling out the while, " You that are against persecution, come upstairs; " to which Bradbury himself replied, " You that are for declaring your faith in the doctrine of the Trinity, stay below." The Subscribers were fifty-three, their opponents were fifty-seven; thus, by what was called a "scandalous majority" of' four, the Synod decided not to interpret theological articles. Some minor facts connected with the conference are amusing—*e.g.*, Pastor Nesbitt, of Hare-court, and his assistant, John Conder, both attended. The former voted with the Subscribers, but even grave Presbyterians grew merry, and the outer world laughed derisively at the pastor's eccentric colleague, who naively severed the gordian knot by signing for subscription, and dividing with its opponents. One aged pastor inadvertently signed the Subscribers' roll, and produced a marked effect by repairing his error with tearful congratulations on the noble stand then taken for liberty of conscience.

Meanwhile, exaggerated reports were current, which lost nothing by being retailed about the town by coffee-house loungers. The late majority soon tasted the results of their action. On the next day of meeting, March the 3rd, they loudly complained of being charged with having relinquished the orthodox tenets. One other endeavour was made to persuade them to subscribe the first of the Thirty-nine Articles, but on this proposal being rejected, the party from which it emanated walked away in a body, and at a subsequent conference, affixed their signatures, to the number of sixty, to the first article of the Anglican Church. Although the fifty ministers now remaining constituted a minority, they proceeded to draw up advices for the Exeter Churches. Dr. Oldfield, the moderator, requested the Subscribers to return, and at the same time desired to be informed if they intended remaining separate. The answer returned by the seceders was, that they were completing some business on hand, and, having subscribed to the first Article of the Anglican Church, and the fifth answer of the Assembly's Catechism, they invited their brethren to follow the example. Dr. Oldfield again rejoined, that no notice could be taken of what was done privately, but he once more desired the seceders to return to their places. A brief interval having elapsed, the Subscribers replied: they had done in private what they had declared in public, and furthermore they regarded themselves as the Body of London ministers. The assembly was now split into opposing sections, each of which complained of the other's want of order. Each party held their procedure to be legal, and each remitted advices to Exeter.

The non-subscribers were chiefly Presbyterians, and did for the most part conscientiously adhere to the orthodox tenets. They strongly protested against any endeavours to fasten upon them the odium of heterodoxy. The action they adopted was, nevertheless, sincerely regretted by many on account of its supposed disastrous influence on the Dissenting interest. Numbers imagined that had the whole body of ministers at Salters' Hall boldly subscribed what they already believed, a most salutary check would have been administered to

Arianism. The congregations of the West anxiously awaited the result of the London Conference. Their worst fears were realised. The Non-subscribers repelled with indignation the slightest imputation of heresy. A number among them could refer both to oral and written denunciations of Arian opinions. Tenets of Divine origin, they argued, human testimony could not strengthen, nor could a ministerial reputation be heightened by subscription; for persons already classed among Arians would be designated hypocrites on attempting to remove the stigma. In the advices despatched to Exeter by these divines, there is little, if anything, to which exception can be taken. The document differs from that of the other party chiefly in this, that there is an absence of any declaration respecting our Lord's divinity. The accompanying letter is written in a strain of unexceptionable orthodoxy. The combatants maintained a war of pamphlets through many subsequent years, and the controvertists have bequeathed us some literary curiosities. One writer on the non-subscribers' side averred himself to be inspired by Dr. Calamy, who had lately arrived from the moon. This class of writers were headed by Pierce, and refused even to subscribe to the fact that three and two make five. Spiritual creeds, they declared, were mental fetters, no more to be imposed on the conscience than irons on the body. The orthodox party are represented as standing in high favour among lunar circles. Creed-makers, who upon earth merely infested the Church, enjoyed in the moon a grateful retreat amid congenial spirits. The locality appropriated by this fraternity had been strangely mistaken by astronomers for a volcanic crater, whereas it now revealed itself to be a distinct colony, with a celestial convocation house—a lunar Salters' Hall. A chemist in the satellite had discovered a drug called *Potestas Sacerdotis*—an extract from papal bulls, Assembly's Catechisms, Lessons, and Homilies. When skilfully mixed, this essence was extremely potent—a drop taken at bed-time freeing the mind in a few hours from all rational moderation. Such authors reproached the subscribers with charges of bigotry and retrogression, and so endeavoured to repay insinuations of heresy from which they themselves had suffered. Bradbury, however, repelled the enemy as though he regarded them as very small fry. They were a set of scribblers in ambuscade, whose ravings and despisings he regarded as a favourable omen that alarm existed in darker regions.

As misrepresentations became more numerous, each party hastened to publish a version of the quarrel. In the heat of controversy, it may be feared, all concerned, acted unfairly. While the matter was thus progressing in London, the Dissenters of Exeter, by locking their chapel-doors, ejected three of their ministers. The indefatigable Pierce published several pamphlets, and detailed the hardships borne by himself and brethren. He was replied to by a work called Arius Detected and Refuted, which, with the rejoinder it provoked, Plain Christianity Defended, created additional bickerings. Another important work on the TRINITY, emanating from the subscribing section, was written by Tong, of Salters' Hall; Robinson, of Little St. Helens; Smith, of Silver Street; and Reynolds, of the Weigh-House. In connection with the disputes the names of Calamy, Watts, and a number more, do not appear. They are reported to have walked from the meeting at an early stage of the proceedings.

At the sign of The Bible and Crown, in the Poultry, was found the common literary store-house of both parties. John Clarke, the publisher, dealt largely with Nonconformist authors. From his house, small works, wherein the vexed question was viewed from various standpoints, issued forth in shoals. The pamphlets abound with scandal and counter scandal; with hard hits aimed at opponents, as payment in kind. Indeed, Clark printed so many books for nonconforming clients, that the Anglicans had their spleen excited, and attached to him the reputation of being a two-faced oracle. The publisher's procedure made the imputations on his honesty appear apparently reasonable. Among the Salters' Hall collection is a printed letter, circulated to expose Clark's unfairness. His offence in our day would scarce rank as a breach of literary etiquette. The above is an outline of a quarrel, the effects of which extended through a long course of subsequent years.[*]

Joint pastor at Salters' Hall with William Tong, and one of the subscribing ministers, was John Newman, who was born in or about the year 1676. In common with so many of his contemporaries, Newman studied in youth under working pastors, his first tutor having been Samuel Chapman, the ejected vicar of Yoxford. The embryo divine early appeared by that fondness which Newman manifested for catechising his schoolfellows. He afterwards made further progress under John Woodhouse, a Leicestershire scholar. Such was his proficiency, that he was judged competent to engage in public duties before he attained his twentieth year. On settling in London, he accepted a lectureship under Joseph Read, of Bloomsbury. While at this station Newman proved his possession of superior abilities, so that on the death of Richard Mayo, he succeeded to the lectureship at Salters' Hall. At this early date the young divine was only little known in the Metropolis, and accordingly, an Alderman of

[*] Case of the ministers ejected at Oxon ; A Defence of the Case, &c.; A True Relation of some Proceedings at Salters' Hall ; A Vindication of the Subscribing Ministers ; Plain and Faithful Narrative of the Differences among the Dissenters at Exeter ; Anatomy of the Heretical Synod at Salters' Hall ; An Account of the late Proceedings, &c.; An Authentic Account, with resons for not Subscribing ; The Doctrine of the Ever-blessed Trinity Stated, &c.

the congregation introduced him to his new friends, and this civic patronage influenced the members in their choice. The connection of pastor and people through many succeeding years, became a source of common satisfaction. Being well served by a powerful memory, Newman from the first practised extemporaneous preaching. He achieved such high excellence that during the closing years of William's reign he was as much esteemeed as any London minister. His term of service extended over a period of nearly half a century, his death having occurred on Saturday, July 25th, 1741. Dr. Doddridge being then in London, attended the funeral in Bunhill Fields, and delivered a graceful oration at the grave.*

Six years prior to his own departure, Newman experienced a great sorrow in the loss of his son Samuel, a promising preacher, who died in the midst of work and usefulness, in his thirtieth year, on the last day of May, 1735. Having been born and educated in the City, he belonged pre-eminently to Salters' Hall; for there the sabbaths of his youth were spent. As a boy he scarcely went for his education beyond the bound of the Lord Mayor's jurisdiction, those two eminent scholars, Eames and Ridgely, having then flourished in close proximity to the Newmans' home. By paternal care, Samuel was

---

* Barker's Funeral Sermon for John Newman; Wilson's Dissenting Churches.

shielded from worldly contamination, and escaped
those vices of large towns to which many are too
openly exposed. He was thus well trained for the
duties of life, and showed his appreciation of the
advantages enjoyed by manifesting predilections for
the course his friends desired him to pursue. On
being, while yet young, honourably passed by the
examining mininisters, he became assistant to his
father at Salters' Hall, but after seven years he died,
to the great grief of his friends and congregation.
The vacancy was filled by Jeremiah Tidcomb, of
Radcliffe; but his decease occurring shortly before that of the elder Newman, the pulpit became
entirely vacant when the latter was taken.

The death of Matthew Henry, while journeying
homewards in June, 1714, occasioned the settlement
at Hackney of one destined to assume in after years
a high position among the Presbyterians, and to become closely connected with Salters' Hall. While
seeking a successor to their late pastor, the Hackney
Dissenters found John Barker, then an assistant of
Dr. Grosvenor at Crosby Hall. The early years of
this eminent man's life are veiled in obscurity, little
or nothing being known of his birthplace or of his
parents. A Matthew Barker was the ejected minister of St. Leonard, Eastcheap, and he, it is imagined,
may have been related to our present subject. At
that date conflicting theological opinions found a
home in Hackney, and in the year of Henry's death,
his people were unsettled. The high prestige of the

commentator sufficed to keep the threatening symptons in abeyance; but after his death the question of choosing a successor split the congregation into rival parties, whose collision was sufficiently alarming to threaten a breach of the peace. When, eventually, a majority elected Barker to the pastorate, their decision awakened a climax of disorder; and the chagrin of the minority so roughly vented itself, that a temporary guard about the chapel became a necessity. These unpleasant and unseemly occurrences only subsided when one party withdrew to establish elsewhere a rival pulpit. By this secession was originated the Old Gravel Pit Chapel, and the separatists are still represented by the Unitarian Society in Paradise Fields. Those of the members who remained pursued their way in undiminished strength and influence after this division. The pastor grew in popularity till he achieved a foremost place among his evangelical contemporaries; and when five years later, the Western disputes culminated in the London Synod, he not only divided with the Subscribers at Salters' Hall, but in common with many others, made strenuous endeavours to confirm his people in the orthodox tenets. Through fifteen years Barker sustained the pastorate unaided, an unusual procedure in those days among the larger Presbyterian Churches. In 1729 he found a colleague in Phillip Gibbs, who after staying eight years at Hackney, resigned on account of changing his belief. Ultimately Barker himself acted on this example by relinquishing his charge. He deviated, it would seem, from the strict letter of Calvinism, though he probably lapsed no lower than the Baxterian standard. In 1738 he retired, and sought at Epsom the seclusion he loved. During many years following he only preached occasionally; but the death of John Newman in 1741, terminated his rural leisure, for Barker received an earnest call to the pastorate at Salters' Hall. He shrank from assuming so onerous a responsibility; yet earnest anxiety for the welfare of others prompted his using every means to serve the bereaved church, whether by public ministrations or by private visiting. He likewise consented to fill the vacancy of the Merchants' Lectureship at Salters' Hall. It is pleasing to discover, that, between two such spirits as Barker and Doddridge, the closest friendship was maintained. In the collected correspondence of the Northampton sage are some letters from Barker, which discover the writer's anxiety for Salters' Hall, and his desire to secure a suitable pastor. Regarding the tie of affection between Doddridge and Barker, one affecting incident may be related. The former, while on his last journey, received at Shrewsbury a letter from the London pastor, wherein he so forcibly expressed his Christian solicitude, that the invalid was overcome by emotion till apprehensions were actually felt of fatal consequences. Barker only survived the amiable doctor about twelve years. He retired to Walthamstow, and

26

ultimately to Clapham, and there devoted his evening of life to the preparation of several pieces for publication, such as selections from his sermons, which the readers of those days well appreciated. In later years. Barker manifested considerable concern at the Unitarian invasion of Nonconformity. He comforted himself that the people were not so far gone as their leaders; and if such a calamity should ever be realised, he thought the Dissenting interest would cease to be worth being anxious about. He used every influence to discourage those teachers who already were sufficiently advanced to leave out Christ in their discourses. He was wont to look fondly back on times when Dissenters were wellnigh universally famed for warmth of love and abundant faith. John Barker lived out a course of eighty years, and died in May, 1762.*

Francis Spilsbury, whose connection with Salters' Hall dates from 1742, belonged to a family justly renowned in the annals of Dissent. His grandfather had been the ejected minister of Bromsgrove, Worcestershire, and the old man carried with him to the grave some marks of that treatment which his adherence to principle entailed. This old Puritan wedded a sister of Bishop Hall, and left an only son, who inherited his father's virtue. That son was

* Our information respecting John Barker is very slender. A sketch of his life and labours will be found in Wilson; and several of his letters are included in the Doddridge correspondence.

John Spilsbury, who settled at Kidderminster, in days when the effects of Baxter's labours were not effaced from the town by time. Here, in 1706, Francis first saw the light. As his predilections sympathised with his father's desire, he in due course entered on the work of the ministry. He studied for four years under Dr. Latham, of Findern, Derbyshire. Thence he removed to Glasgow University in preference to that of Leydon, on account of the bad moral repute to which the Dutch schools had then attained. On completing his academical course, Spilsbury returned to a desolate home, his father and two sisters having departed ere he could reach their dying chambers. He then accepted a lectureship under Matthew Bradshaw, of Kidderminster, whence after a short stay he removed to Bromsgrove, and from Bromsgrove he went to Worcester, there to labour during seven years. At each station the pastor enjoyed the happy consciousness of having achieved success. He was subjected to strong temptations to conform, principle on one occasion having compelled his refusing the living of Ashby-de-la-Zouch.

Spilsbury's introduction to the people at Salters' Hall was effected in a very remarkable manner. During the summer of 1741 he visited London, hoping to enjoy some brief relaxation from labour, and a season of friendly intercourse with his venerable brother, John Newman. On arriving in town, Spilsbury was shocked at finding his host not

26*

only seriously ill, but actually dying. Of necessity
the visitor supplied the pulpit on the two succeeding
sabbaths. Dr. Harris, of Crutched-friars, it appears,
had some time previously, advised the people respecting Spilsbury—"Choose him, for he will wear well."
As circumstances favoured a settlement, he accepted
an invitation to assume the pastorate, and through
the succeeding twenty years worked conjointly with
John Barker. The last-named resigned in 1762.
Our divine maintained his reputation and usefulness
through forty years in London, his life having been
that of a laborious and painstaking student. His
theological sentiments were Baxterian, while his
natural disposition was of the most amiable type,
seeing that one who knew him has testified to Spil-
bury's inability to be harsh or unkind. He never
achieved what is commonly understood by popularity, although he ably sustained an important
position, and by a careful discharge of duties apart
from the pulpit, as visiting the sick and needy, he
gained and merited a large share of popular affection. He was called to rest on the communion
Sabbath morning of March, 1782.*

Another eminent man, once associated with
Salters' Hall, was Hugh Farmer, who, although of
the independent order, sustained the afternoon lectureship from 1761 to 1772. Farmer was born in
the neighbourhood of Shrewsbury, in 1714. His

* Worthington's Sermon on the Death of Francis
Spilsbury; Wilson's Dissenting Churches, &c.

maternal grandfather, Hugh Owen, was the ejected
minister of Bronyclydwr.   The parents of the
younger Hugh set him apart at an early age for the
Nonconformist ministry, and carefully prepared him
for that work by first placing him in an academy at
Llanegrin, and subsequently at Warrington, under
Dr. Charles Owen.   The far-famed tutor, however, to whom Farmer became especially indebted,
was Philip Doddridge, who about this time founded
a college at Northampton, having for a first student
this afterwards celebrated divine. Imagination readily
transfers us to that bygone age, and into the shoemaking metropolis, where the good doctor, happy
among his scholars, with quick eye perceived in
young Farmer those manifestations of genius which
his ready judgment pronounced the precursors of
fame.   The interior of this academy, as it was when
Hugh removed from Warrington, affords an interesting glimpse of student life in the days when Bolingbroke wrote for the Craftsman, and when Sylvanus
Urban was settling down in his "Strong Tower" at
Clerkenwell.   At Northampton, Farmer, in common
with his fellows, paid sixteen pounds a-year for
board, and four pounds for tuition.   Although wash-
ing was done from home, bed-linen entailed an additional charge of a guinea per annum.   Another
guinea went for the rent of a study, and yet another
was expected for the library fund.   Such as gave
any attention to experimental philosophy subscribed
towards the expense of the apparatus.   This curri-

culum, which sufficed for so many eminent ministers
of the last century, cost about thirty pounds a-year.
Nevertheless, it does not appear to have been very
eagerly taken advantage of, for we learn on the
authority of the Doctor himself that, in 1739, there
were vacancies for "two or three more." Farmer
left Northampton to settle at Walthamstow as chaplain to the eccentric Mr. Coward. This patron, as
a leading Nonconformist of those times, erected a
chapel, in which his *protégé* preached, the congregation enjoying the repute of being one of the most
wealthy and genteel societies of any then assembling
around the metropolis. As many as forty carriages,
we are told, were commonly counted at the meeting-
house doors after morning service. On account of
certain odd things he practised, joined to extreme
opinions concerning trifles, the gentleman with
whom the pastor resided enjoyed a widely-spread
celebrity among the country people. The household *regime*—most rigorously carried out—included
the bolting and locking of doors and fastening of
windows at six o'clock in the evening, an extra hour
being allowed during the summer months. But,
whether in June or December, after the specified
time, no person's ingress or exit was under any circumstances tolerated. No statute of the Medes and
Persians was ever more irrevocable than the bye-
laws of this domestic autocrat; for had his own lady
appeared at the outer gate a minute later than the
fatal chime, she would probably have found her

spouse as inexorable as his favourite locks and bars.
Certain is it that, on a particular occasion, the
pastor and chaplain imprudently stayed out until
after the clock had struck, say, seven in the evening.
As he may possibly have anticipated, Farmer's case
presented an aspect sufficiently gloomy. The only
way out of the dilemma was to seek a lodging at
the home of a less scrupulous family. The pastor
accordingly called at a mansion inhabited by a then
eminent solicitor of the name of Snell. The sequel
was pleasing, and coincided with the experience of
Dr. Watts in another instance. Instead of remaining
only a single night, Farmer remained during thirty
years, and in elegant retirement produced the works
on which his literary reputation is based. While
strength remained he busily pursued a course of
authorship—his exposition of Demonology and
Miracles, meantime, creating some sharp controversy.
Although so fully engrossed by other matters, he
sustained unaided the pastorate at Walthamstow
until 1761, when the engagement at Salters' Hall
necessitated the appointment of an assistant. During
those ten years of City labour Farmer attracted the
largest afternoon congregation of any among the
Presbyterians of London. Besides his numerous
other occupations, he preached in turn the Merchants' Lecture at Salters' Hall, and also served on
Dr. Williams's Trust. His several appointments
were one by one relinquished on account of the
advances of age and weakness. In 1785 he became

nearly deprived of sight, and two years subsequently he died, having attained to the seventy-third year of his age. According to the strict directions of his will, a quantity of valuable manuscripts were ruthlessly destroyed, and the editors of the Biographia Britannica had their reasonable vexation awakened by the scrupulous rigour with which the executors obeyed their injunction.*

Hugh Farmer was succeeded in the afternoon lectureship by Hugh Worthington, who eventually assumed the pastorate at the date of Spilsbury's decease. After serving the Church through a period of forty years, he died in July, 1813. He was a native of Leicester, where his father officiated as the Presbyterian minister for more than half a century. This old divine presided over the congregation assembling in the old meeting-house, as the townspeople called it, situated at Butt's Close, Saint Margaret's, Leicester. This society had been gathered in the year 1680, but the chapel was erected twenty-eight years later, with seat accommodation for eight hundred persons. For a lengthened term the society enjoyed the reputation of being the most important and influential body of Christians in the district, not excepting the Establishment. The pastor, who died in the autumn of 1797, lived to be eighty-six, his tenure of office having extended from his thirtieth year. His circle of friends included

* Biographia Britannica; Nichols's Literary Anecdotes of the Eighteenth Century.

the best families of the neighbourhood, by whom he was regarded as a man of amiable and benevolent disposition, joined to respectable abilities.

Amid such scenes the younger Hugh was reared, while he found in his father an able preceptor. He ultimately removed to Daventry Academy, there to study under Dr. Ashworth. The young scholar had scarcely completed his teens ere his principal enlisted his assistance in the work of tuition. In his twenty-second year Worthington visited London, and on one occasion preached at Salters' Hall, and so edified the people that they invited him to accept the recently vacated lecturship. During his lengthened connection with the old meeting-house the pastor earned the respect of a large proportion of the citizens, while many of his more private friends bore eminent names in the republic of letters. It was Worthington's original intention to have resigned his office on completing a term of forty years' service. It strangely happened that, on the day preceding his death he was employed in preparing a discourse which he intended should celebrate his relinquishment of active duty. Death, however, suddenly carried him hence on Monday, July 25th, 1813, and after he had attended at Salters' Hall the day before. He died in the sixty-first year of his age. He was eulogised by the Gentleman's Magazine as "A man of sound understanding, considerable learning, eloquent in his delivery, happy in his choice of language, and clear and perspicuous

in his elucidations." To what degree he advanced
in those "rational" sentiments which so disastrously
affected his denomination, it would be difficult to
determine. It may, nevertheless, be mentioned that,
James Lindsey, who preached Worthington's funeral
sermon, awakened his hearers' indignation by remarking *en passant* that, he and his late friend had
been agreed so far as Gospel doctrine was concerned. Such a fact tells favourably in Worthington's
favour. He may possibly have been a high Arian,
but if so he deviated from the faith of his predecessors, none of whom lapsed lower than the Baxterian
standard.*

Worthington was successively assisted by several
lecturers. In 1782 he had Robert Jacomb, who,
after eight years' service, resigned in favour of
Wellingborough. Thence he removed to Leicester,
and acted as the colleague of the elder Worthington,
whom he succeeded in the pastorate. He finally
retired to Bath without any charge. Robert Winter,
of Hammersmith, likewise assisted at Salters' Hall,
as did also John Saville, of Homerton Academy.
But by this time the glory of the old sanctuary had
departed, and ere long it was forsaken by its ancient
occupants, the Presbyterians. Some people now
obtained possession of the premises, who styled the

* Lindsey's Sermon on the Death of Hugh Worthington;
Rees' Encyclopædia; Wilson's History of the Dissenting
Churches; Gentleman's Magazine, vol. lxxxiii; Nichols's
Literary Anecdotes of the Eighteenth Century.

hall The Acopagus, and themselves The Christian Evidence Society. This experiment in fanaticism proved an unsuccessful adventure, and its champion sank into bankruptcy. The Baptists next entered on the field in 1827, to re-open the hall in the presence of a noble band of celebrities. Within the last few years the meeting-house has disappeared. The society has removed to a northern suburb, and now meet in a newly-erected chapel worthy of bearing the name it retains of SALTERS' HALL. The pastor may be congratulated on inheriting a pulpit so closely linked with our old City history and its Nonconformist associations.

Chapter X.

FOOTPRINTS OF THE BAPTISTS IN OLD LONDON.

THE reflection is certainly fraught with sadness, calculated to stir up mournful emotions, that Christian Churches after once planting, should fail to reflect the Saviour's glory by ceasing to disseminate, the news of the Cross. Numberless sanctuaries of Old London have passed away before the remorseless encroachments of commerce. The last traces of many ancient chapels are now completely effaced by capacious ware-rooms, cranes, and counting-houses. Concerning this subject, divers questions crowd into the mind, and there remain unanswered. What occasioned the extinction of these Christian institutions? Was their life-vigour forfeited like that of the barren fig-tree, because of fruitlessness? Did their light burn lower and lower with the roll of years, for lack of sustaining faith? Did slothful pastors encourage lukewarmness in the flock, or did the cause of decay lie beyond the remedial reach of either? What man can tell? Nevertheless, if the old landmarks have been removed, their sites retain an interest and a sacredness which no modern surroundings are able to dispel.

One of these spots is Crutched-friars. A visit to the neighbourhood awakens memories of an era of gloomy superstition, when England was darkened by the shades of ignorance. In those days the brothers, from whom the nomenclature is derived, were wont to emerge from this sombre haunt into the City thoroughfares, each betokening his order by displaying a blood-red cross upon his habit, and by carrying in his hand a crucifix of iron or of silver. The monastery *régime* included the daily invocation of blessings upon the capital. As it came to pass in the majority of instances, so did it happen in Crutched-friars—increase of wealth fostered corruption, till the scandal of the monks' dissolute lives hastened the confiscation of their patrimony. Henry the Eighth conferred the estate on Sir Thomas Wyatt, who made it a site for his town mansion. In after years the premises were metamorphosed into a glass manufactory, which was destroyed by fire in the days of Elizabeth.

Some few years after the accession of the Stuarts, one of the earliest distinct societies of Baptists possessed a meeting-house in Crutched-friars. The chapel was opened by the separatists from Lathop's congregation of "Independents"—the most celebrated seceder being William Kiffen. Second only to the hero of Devonshire-square was Paul Hobson, who took a leading share in establishing the Baptists as a denomination. He "joined with Mr. Green and Captain Spencer," says the trustworthy Crosby, "who raised a Baptist Church in Crutched-friars." The persons referred to were at that time the leaders of their brethren in London. Hobson assumed the honours and duties of the pastorate, and, on the outbreak of civil war, his functions as a divine in no way interfered with his seizing a sword to fight as a captain in the Parliamentary army. None understood better than did Paul Hobson how to shout defiance at cavaliers, and to frown withering contempt upon servants of Baal. The fury with which in the field he sought the annihilation of malignants, corresponded with those other attributes of the religious zealot which he manifested while preaching or disputing. His perseverance in denouncing other sects, allied to a violent abuse of the Commons, became at length an excuse for lodging Hobson in Newport Pagnell gaol, the agent being Sir Samuel Luke, *alias* Sir HUDIBRAS. Hobson returned to London in custody, but, through the aid of influential connections, his incarceration soon became a thing of history. On regaining his liberty, this military divine resumed preaching, "to the great mortification of his persecutors," and formidable either in soldierly or polemical art, he for a time sustained a meeting in Moorfields. Subsequently he accepted the chaplaincy of Eton School, whence he was ejected at the Restoration.

The neighbourhood of Mark Lane is rich in Non-conformist associations. Here that poet of the Universal Church—Isaac Watts—inaugurated his London ministry. In the parlour of a private citizen, wherein his congregation assembled, we may fairly suppose that many of Watts's hymns were first introduced to the Christian world.[*] In Rood-lane—close at hand—in the olden time, the Weigh-House pastor was content to own a manse. Not far distant —in Philpot-lane—there formerly stood one of those old halls, which, belonging to the City guilds, so frequently served as Dissenting Chapels. The building now particularly alluded to, but long since demolished, was the property of the Worshipful Company of Turners. Like the Stationers, who of old possessed a hall in this vicinity, the Turners provided more sumptuous premises elsewhere. The building in Philpot-lane had a very chequered history. In the Revolution year the Baptists were its tenants. Then the Quakers came into possession. The Quakers were succeeded by the Independents;

---

[*] Just to show what popular admiration this great and amiable man commanded, the verse below is taken from a poem, on Nonconformity in London, which appeared in the Gentleman's Magazine for July, 1736, and written, as some suppose, by Richard Savage:—

> " . . . The gentle Watts, in him we find
> The fairest picture of an humble mind ;
> In him the softest, meekest virtues dwell—
> As mild as light, as soft as evening gale."

then came the Baptists again ; and finally, the Independents were its last inhabitants.

In the revolution era, a controversy regarding the Imposition of Hands divided the London Baptists. The Arminian section strongly advocated the custom, scarcely rating its importance below any Christian ordinance. A society of this strict class established themselves in the locality in question, the chapel being situated in White's-alley. These people separated from their pastor, Richard Allen, when he relinquished their favourite tenet—a division originating the Church in Turners' Hall.

If he did not correspond with what would now be called a popular preacher, Richard Allen sustained a fair reputation, besides earning the merited esteem of contemporary Nonconformists. He owed neither literary acquirements nor means of usefulness to any academical institution; but such disadvantages the indomitable perseverance of maturer years fully repaired; and he lived to rival the ablest of his compeers, either in general knowledge or in philological lore. In the days of Charles the Second, Allen manfully resisted the forces of persecution till few excelled him in moral bravery. His everyday experience included the roughest discipline. He knew what it was to be interrupted, even in a week-night service; and to be carried thence to prison by military intruders. Other events of his history graphically illustrate London pastoral life two hundred years ago. For an example take the following:—Allen

and his people have assembled for worship at five
o'clock on a Sabbath morning. With apparent
reason the worshippers expect, that at so early an
hour they will enjoy immunity from legal interference. They are destined to suffer grievous disappointment. While the service progresses, soldiers
rush into the apartment, and their inhuman roughness
and coarse speeches strangely contrast with the
reverential mien of the preacher, who placidly sees
the military rabble tear down the galleries and
abuse the people. Anon, a certain son of Mars
seizes a form, sends it whirling across the chapel,
and although, by taking a false aim, he misses the
Pastor's head, he unmistakably demonstrates to the
spectators that his arms are stronger than his wits.
What injury was done to the people on this occasion
does not transpire. The meeting-house was damaged
to the value of fifty pounds.

While composed of General Baptists, the Church
in Turners' Hall scarcely differed in faith from the
sister societies professing Particular Redemption; for
the people's religion being of an evangelical type
their pastor freely associated with divines of the
Calvinistic school. This Church was one of the
earliest to introduce singing into public worship;
but a lively controversy was sustained through many
years ere the prejudices of the stricter sort could be
overcome. After the Revolution, when the "Augustan
age" had set in, and when every clique possessed
its public haunt, the ministers of the Baptist denomi-

27

nation met weekly at the Hanover Coffee House, Finch-lane. Of this club Allen became a leading member, and as such won the high esteem of the sedate conclave, and in 1704, he and his followers were admitted into the London Association of Baptist Churches. When the pastor died in February, 1707, he left a large congregation.

Turners' Hall being vacated in 1695, the people removed to Barbican, and their old quarters were now used for less honourable purposes. One George Keith attracted a number of hearers, who assembling here, accepted as spiritual fare, his eccentric harangues. · He boasted of being a " reformed Quaker;" such reformation consisting in uniting the faith of Bunyan to the eccentricities of Penn. The " Church " was attacked by a writer, who shielded by his *non de plume* of Calvin Philanax, made the congregation a laughing-stock by exposing their fantasies. Keith appears to be identical with the George Keith, of whom Noble gives a sketch in the continuation of Granger's Biographical History; if so, he ultimately found a home in the Fleet, while there to be excommunicated by his diocesan, on account of profligate effrontery.

A man who completely outstripped all predecessors in singularity now occupied Turners' Hall. This was Joseph Jacob. Reared a Quaker and a linen-draper, neither the religion nor the trade of his fathers discovered to him a sphere worthy of his genius and tasteful to his eccentric predilections.

Therefore he sought other avenues wherein to exercise his abilities. It is satisfactory to find, however, that Jacob was sufficiently patriotic to gallop westward, in 1688, for the purpose of sharing the national greeting to William the Third. Beginning as a preacher in a meeting-house in Thames-street, Jacob ere long offended his audience by the severity with which he condemned the actions of persons eminent in station and influence. His congregation included a member of Parliament, Shallet by name; and by Shallet's exertion, Jacob was finally ejected from the pulpit. On retiring from this sphere of labour, Jacob manifested a contempt for his enemies by literally shaking the dust from his shoes.

After leaving Thames-street, Jacob provided a chapel in Southwark, where he continued his ministrations to the " Reformed Church." The society rejoiced in a straitlaced discipline; and candidates for admission to communion were required to conform to the articles of government, and to affix their signatures as pledges of honour. Of what the pastor's vagaries consisted it were useless to explain. Although an enthusiast, he may not be charged with any endeavours to anticipate either the dreams of Swedenborg or many other heresies which are flaunted in these later times. Nevertheless, Jacob exercised a jurisdiction over his flock which to us appears sufficiently singular. Certainly a similar reformer would occasion considerable con-

27 *

sternation among the too-fashionably-apparelled Christians of to-day.

Nevertheless, posterity has partly sanctioned the innovations conceived in the fertile brain of Jacob —*e.g.*, standing during the singing of praise, and the cultivation of "whiskers upon the upper lip," both of which he rigidly enforced. A salutary code was also prepared for the becoming control of female attire; but none will regret that the custom of so onerous an oversight died with its originator. The "reformed" people never worshipped with others of a different order; and they engaged not to marry without the pale of their society—Joseph Jacob only being competent to tie the hymenial knot. Notwithstanding the benefits attached to the discipline described, it proved a weariness to the flesh. The congregation gradually dwindled away; but still undaunted, Jacob removed into the City to settle in Turners' Hall. He laboured on a few years longer, till in 1722, the "reformed church" died with its pastor—the remains of the latter finding a resting-place in the old graveyard of Bunhill-fields.

In 1704 the Baptists again made a home of this time-honoured meeting-place. In Spitalfields there existed an old society which had just lost its pastor, William Collins. The members resolved on migrating Citywards for the purpose of amalgamating with others of corresponding faith who met in Lorimers' Hall. The majority decided on introducing psalmody, while the minority protested against the innovation, and retired into Turners' Hall. They found a pastor in Ebenezer Wilson, son-in-law to the heroic Fownes, of Broadmead, Bristol, and father of the well-known Samuel Wilson. Ebenezer, who died in 1714, was an able divine and a reputable scholar. He never achieved popularity, but many of his hearers being wealthy, he was handsomely provided for.

Wilson's successor, Thomas Dewhurst—about whom scarcely anything is known—was a native of North Britain. Following, in 1725, came the learned physician, Dr. Rudd, but having already given particulars of this divine, any further reference is rendered superfluous. He and his people removed to Devonshire-square in 1727, when the entire premises were delivered up to them; consequently the congregation at Devonshire-square Chapel are lineal descendants of the church in Turners' Hall. After the Baptists had finally forsaken this last-named place, some persons calling themselves Independents entered into possession; they do not appear to have been recognised by that denomination.

One day, in September, 1739, John Wesley preached in Turners' Hall; and, during the service, the beams supporting the floor, having their strength overtaxed by the weight of two thousand auditors, suddenly gave way, to the consternation of everybody present. Fortunately, however, the cellars beneath had recently been stored with casks of tobacco, and these supporting the sinking floor, the people were rejoiced at finding themselves more alarmed than injured. As it was, says Wesley, the boards sank "a foot or two, and I went on without interruption."

The efforts our fathers put forth to meet the religious necessities of the era they lived in, if not so energetic as they should have been, were not so disproportionate to their abilities as we, in these happier days of improved opportunities, may imagine. Londoners of the seventeenth century supposed themselves to be living in a city as populous as the modern metropolis. The intelligent portion of the Christian community, through indulging such a delusion, must have been deeply impressed by the little progress that religion, and more especially religion as represented by Nonconformity, made among such imagined crowds. The notions of our ancestors respecting the magnitude of London fitly corresponded with their calculations regarding the City's future growth. In the time of Charles the Second, Sir W. Petty, as a member of the Royal Society, published some carefully-compiled tables relating to the population. His ingenious reasonings tended more towards alarming than edifying his hearers when he explained what London would expand to in their own time; equally fitted to awaken consternation was Sir W. Petty's portrayal of London as it would be. In the year 1800, the inhabitants would number five millions three hundred and fifty-nine thousand. In 1840—so exact was Sir W. Petty that he reckoned to ten souls—the number would increase to ten millions seven hundred and eighteen thousand eight hundred and eighty. Vast, therefore, as is our present capital, it has little more than a quarter of the importance to which our Puritan ancestors supposed it would attain.

Such trifles are merely by the way. We proceed onward to Gracechurch-street, there to find some legible footprints of the Puritan Baptists. If the exact site of their settlement cannot be pointed out, the fact is owing to the historian's remissness, for Crosby is addicted to the vice of breaking off his narrative just when and where his readers would know more. The case of Gracechurch-street is no exception to his wonted procedure.

A meeting-house once existed in Gracechurch-street, and in Puritan times it was associated with an able physician and Baptist minister, Dr. Carolus Maria Du Veil. His conversion from Judaism to Christianity excited the revengeful passions of Jewish connexions—an experience analogous to what others have suffered under similar circumstances. The elder Du Veil manifested his abhorrence of the Christian tenets by attacking his converted son with a sword. On first receiving the Gospel, Carolus could only grope his way into the shades of Roman Catholicism. With their usual readiness at making all events, if possible, redound to the extension of their system, his new allies sought to use the abilities of so able a convert against the Huguenots. The researches entailed by the allotted task brought other truths to light, which making an immediate impression on the unbiassed student's heart, led him to relinquish popery for the purer communion of Anglicanism. On coming to England he made friends of Tillotson, Stillingfleet, and a number of others. He took holy orders, accepted a chaplaincy in a nobleman's family, and lived among the best society.

This last change in Du Veil's life occurred in 1677. Amid his new surroundings, his chief business was the study of English; but he never sufficiently mastered the pronunciation of our language to acquire a fluency in public speaking. He closely applied himself to the study of English literature; and in the library of Bishop Compton, of London, he perused for the first time the publications of the Baptists. These books more than interested him—they bred desire for an interview with the denominational leaders. There was then living in the household of Dr. Tillotson a maid-servant who communed with a neighbouring Baptist society, and whose faith drew forth many banterings from her fellow-workers. Du Veil expressed to this girl the longing he had for an interview with Hanserd Knollys. The sequel was, that the two eventually met at the mansion of a nobleman in the vicinity where Knollys was occasionally entertained. The latter, after this, introduced his newly-made acquaintance to the noble galaxy of his compeers—Kiffen, Keach, Gosnold, and others—who were fathers in their denomination. Delighted with his new associates, Du Veil began diligently to examine the differences separating such men from other Christian bodies, the result being his acceptance of the tenet of Believers' Baptism. The thorough honesty of the man's convictions and motives cannot be doubted, for the immediate temporal loss his conversion occasioned him, constituted little less than pecuniary ruin. If we except the amiable Tillotson, Du Veil was forsaken by his friends, and therefore he now divided his time between literary pursuits and the practice of physic. At or about this time the Baptists in Gracechurch-street lost their pastor. In an evil hour he quailed before the persecution of the Restoration, and through fear had given place to the enemy by relinquishing his belief. This action occasioned remorse so intense that the unhappy subject of it, by taking his own life, escaped from a world where each day was but a round of horror. The afflicted congregation invited Du Veil to take them in charge, and he consented. Because only able to speak English very brokenly, his immense acquirements never won the pastor any lasting popularity; and the church ceased to exist as a separate society at the pastor's death, or at the close of the seventeenth century. Du Veil's writings are chiefly commentaries on various books of the Bible. He wrote with correctness in Latin and English. May this recutting of his almost forgotten name not prove altogether unprofitable labour.

Hitherto the labour of portraying the customs,

sufferings, and victories of the Nonconformists in old London, has proved a task of pleasure, and the hope is entertained that these histories and word-pictures have not overtaxed the reader's patience. Each spot connected with these reminiscences has many memories hanging around it—welcome treasures to a Dissenting archæologist. Such must experience a pensive pleasure in holding up to the light of modern times the sayings and actions of men by whose precepts and example our fathers were instructed, and by whom they were directed to a better inheritance. Where now is that great motley crowd which of yore enlivened these identical streets? Where, alas!

" For them no more the blazing hearth shall burn,
   Or busy housewife ply her evening care;
No children run to lisp their sire's return,
   Or climb his knee, the envied kiss to share."

Their lives have been stereotyped by the hand of time, and as the trees have fallen, so do they lie. What should prompt the eschewing of evil more than this awful fact: our words and actions are impressed on the days in which they were spoken or performed? While scrutinising the lives of workers who preceded us, let this truth exercise its legitimate influence, that as regards ourselves also, father Time will prove himself to be an unflinching and impartial witness.

Rightly to understand what a sacrifice Du Veil voluntarily made by embracing Nonconformity, it is necessary to know something of party warfare, or more properly of religious warfare, in the Puritan era. Numbers of the lampoons on Dissenting leaders are either too absurd or too indecent for quotation. Such pamphlets, usually emanating from foes to all religion, will not repay attention; but the literary offspring of various party zealots, oftentimes written in strains of ferocious satire, is more interesting.

In 1681 a poetical broadside, purporting to be a faithful description of the Dissenting preachers, was circulated in London. It belonged to a department in our literature now happily extinct, but which was vigorously maintained in those never-to-be-forgotten times, when the political horizon grew darker daily, when Episcopacy was at last apparently triumphant, when Liberty was driven from her natural home, and when Nonconformists could under no circumstances safely assemble. The spectacle of England's humiliation, to High Church bigots, to Court trimmers, to believers in the divine right of kings, was a landscape tinged with paradisaical hues. The voice of mourning from closed meeting-houses, and the despair of homeless ejected ministers, were replied to by our poet:

> " What! shall a glorious nation be o'erthrown
> By troops of sneaking rascals of our own?"

He also describes the Nonconformist preacher:—

> " He's one that scarcely can be called a man,
> And yet's a pious holy Christian,
> He's big with saving faith (he says), yet he
> Has not one spark of common charity."

Dissenters, it plainly appeared, were despisers of reason—a fact which accounted for their rejecting Episcopacy, and for their refusal to honour bishops. All, however, was easily comprehended; Reason discountenanced their dark designs. Nonconformist preachers are portrayed as immoral livers, and their prayers as insults to the Deity. As for their sermons,

> " You'll quickly find sedition is hid there."

Then follows a descriptive touch of the Three Denominations :—

> " They all mankind except themselves despise ;
> Chiefly the great, for being good and wise.
> Some subtle have, and some have giddy souls ;
> Some fools, some knaves, and some are knaves and fools.
> These vermin would even the best things command,
> And suck up all the sweetness of the land."

At the Revolution, poetasters of another school reached down their lyres from the willows, and Church and State was roughly handled in the sheets of doggrel they scattered among the people. One author deals some telling blows at the enemy, The High Church Bully, in a sheet of that name, *e.g.*:—

> " Rome, whose footsteps you so closely tread,
> Great Rome ! thy mother Church and darling head."

Then follows a graphic description of an Anglican's sermon. If heated by the fumes of his own political or theological diatribes, the pulpit creaks by reason of blows received from the fists of its sub-

stantial orator. His fiery nonsense echoes down the
ancient aisles till the auditors imagine themselves
overtaken by a tempest of thunder and lightning.
The excellence of arbitrary laws is insisted on,
while moderation is proved no less unscriptural
than the Hanoverian succession. Throughout, the
harangue

"Mightily extols all High Church ranters,
Now lashes all false brethren and Dissenters."

On the proclamation of the Indulgence of 1687, the
Nonconformist press once more worked unrestricted.
An anonymous author in a quarto pamphlet detailed
the Dissenters' sufferings. Although written some
years previously, the manuscript had been laid aside
in consequence of the danger attending the dissemination of such publications. One minister (Delaune)
had died in Newgate for the offence of having composed a similar treatise. Many others who may not
have actually died in their cells were scarcely less
fortunate, since they failed to leave their loathsome confinement until the germs of mortal diseases
were sown in their constitutions. Only by a strong
mental effort can we realise the sufferings of these
confessors. Their personal pains were a heavy
cross, but to bodily anguish were often added many
agonising reflections—that a wife was sinking under
hardship; that daughters were exposed to privation;
or that sons, on whom the father had fondly centred
his hopes, were constrained to earn a pittance by
wheeling a barrow, or by driving a cart.

The curious pedestrian, whose antiquarian tastes may occasionally prompt an exploration of our old City's secluded nooks, will be well aware of the archæological attractions attached to St. Helen's, Bishopsgate. The rural dress of the graveyard surrounding the quaintly-interesting church, pleasantly contrasts with the neighbouring crowded thoroughfare. St. Helen's is one of the few city churches which escaped the fire of 1666. On its erection in the twelfth century, its pious founders dedicated their work to the mother of Constantine, and secured for the foundation some important privileges. The sanctuary was inherited by the neighbouring priory, the nuns assembling for prayers in a portion of the present building, then separated by a partition from the portion allotted for public service. The partition was removed on the dissolution of the nunnery in the reign of Henry the Eighth.

No less a person than Hanserd Knollys preached in Great St. Helen's. Possessing a chapel of very respectable dimensions, he attracted a thousand hearers. Hitherto Knollys had officiatad in parish churches whenever facilities for so doing occurred. His most lively enemies were the Presbyterians, and probably at their instigation the landlord of the meeting-house refused to allow the Baptists to continue in possession. Moreover, a committee of divines, who sat during the Commonwealth, evinced an effrontery quite uncharacteristic of their modern representatives, by ordering Knollys to preach no more—an injunction he was scarcely the kind of being to honour with attention. The pastor, how-ever, removed with his followers to Newgate-street. The chapel in Great St. Helen's disappeared, and regarding either its site or fate, history is silent.

East-cheap was the cooks' quarter in ancient London. Through a long period there flourished here a leading society of the Baptist denomination. Doubtless the spot has a narrative belonging to it, abounding with interesting histories, could the records be recovered. Baptists have certainly been remiss in the matter of bequeathing history to posterity, and accordingly but few particulars of Great East-cheap are now obtainable. Wilson supposes, that after Du Veil's removal, his people were ab-sorbed by a congregation which met in Tallow-chandlers' Hall, Dowgate-hill. This united body eventually removed to Maidenhead-court, Great East-cheap, but when the lease of this chapel ex-pired in 1760, the members dispersed themselves among various societies. In this old meeting-house a Wednesday-evening lecture was established, which Dr. Gill sustained for thirty years. This sermon was continued at Cripplegate, Little St. Helen's, and Devonshire-square.

The first pastor, John Noble, was born about the time of the Restoration. Some particulars of his life are preserved in a funeral discourse, the quaint title of which is emblazoned with a death's head, a skeleton's limbs, and the implements of grave-digging. The sermon, by Edward Wallin, was preached on the longest day of 1730.

During his early years Noble tasted a full share of the prevailing persecution. A common experience made his parents and their children familiar with the routine of prison discipline—a discipline, however, which never sufficed to suppress their courage, nor to annihilate their determination to persevere in righteousness. While in captivity, the prison cell served young Noble as a study, and on regaining his liberty he set up a school, and laboured as a Gospel minister. He was sufficiently successful in the country for news of his fame to reach the capital. Two London Churches simultaneously invited him to take them in charge, and of that both might enjoy his ministry, they united. As a theologian, Noble prominently expounded certain favourite tenets, till many accused him of teaching Antinomianism. However this may have been, he was "A man of learning and excellent parts." In circles outside his immediate connection the pastor was regarded as a man of uncharitable proclivities and harsh demeanour. Crosby thinks these failings were more apparent than real, or, even if real, were only manifested at Eastcheap. When presiding at the monthly assembly of denominational representatives, Noble's moderation of speech and becoming mien excited the surprise of observers familiar with their brother's more disagreeable attributes. A memorable illustration of this occurred at John

Gill's ordination in 1719. Noble vehemently opposed the custom of laying on of hands, but he preached the sermon on the day in question, although the obnoxious custom was observed. He died in June, 1730, to the intense grief of his people, who interred his remains in Southwark Park.

This period in the history of the denomination, and of England, appears to have been one of those calms which sometimes, in the national as in individual life, or in the political no less than in the natural world, precede and follow change and commotion. Sir Robert Walpole controlled public affairs. The country was quietly enjoying a term of peace. The contemporary press represents the nation as having reached a height of happiness above the average, which sprang from a full tide of commercial prosperity. If such pictures of England as she existed a century and a half ago, are slightly exaggerated, the colouring has tinges of truthfulness. Fifteen years had flown since the Pretender's ill-fated adventure; and while his English supporters were growing fewer, his adherents on the Continent were dying in exile. Old-fashioned opponents of the Hanoverian succession were fast diminishing. The Tories, or Jacobites, by a salutary experience, were being taught something of reason. Trade being good and money abundant, the consumption of articles of luxury by the common people was daily increasing. In this era, moreover, a new page was turned in English literature, for a nota-

28

bility rose whose celebrity is even yet sustained, although his career has far extended into the second century of its duration. Our allusion is to Sylvanus Urbon, who now took possession of St. John's Gate, Clerkenwell, and published Number One, price sixpence, of the Gentleman's Magazine.

Noble's assistants were Samuel Wilson, who removed to Goodman's Fields, and Peter Davenport, the probable founder of the Church at Liverpool, but about whom little only is known. The immediate successor of John Noble was Samuel Dew, a native of Michel Dean, in Gloucestershire. Of an humble origin, his parents destined him for nothing more pretentious than the stone-cutting craft. While earning his bread by this latter occupation, Dean's leisure hours were devoted to learning —a course in which he persevered until his ministrations became acceptable to a body of Christians in his native town, and this led to his settlement according to the Nonconformist order. His accession to the pulpit at East-cheap occurred in 1731. As a country pastor, Dew pursued a course of usefulness and popularity, but to the more cultivated members of a City audience his homely discourses were not so acceptable, so that his followers were chiefly partisans of the extreme Calvinistic school. In 1760 the congregation had sufficiently declined to render unadvisable a renewal of the lease of the chapel. The members dissolved their union, and while some settled under Dr. Gill, others retired to Devonshire-square.

The old meeting-house then passed through a few more stages—ominous of approaching demolition. Among those who successively held possession were the Swedenborgians and the German-Lutherans. About seventy years ago the building was removed; not even a trace of the site it occupied is now discoverable amid the surrounding commercial activity.

Tallow-chandlers' Hall has some reminiscences belonging to it separate from those already alluded to. Elias, a son of Benjamin Keach, gathered a congregation at Wapping, and after their pastor's death, the people removed into the City and assembled in the Tallow-melters' Hall. Thence they migrated to Angel-alley, Whitechapel.

To turn aside into Thames-street is again to find ourselves standing upon interesting historical ground. Prior to the erection either of the Tower or London Bridge, a battlemented wall protected the southern boundary of the river—a fortification which remained intact till the encroaching waters undermined its foundations. In the reign of Henry the Sixth the Warwick family possessed a mansion in Thames-street—the Earl having, as is supposed, wrested the property from its rightful owner.

Here, in the olden time, and in the hall of the Joiners' Company, a fraternity of Baptists congregated. During its prosperity this society was one

28*

of the wealthiest in the denomination, but unfortunately its history cannot be traced to its original planting. The first pastor of whom any accounts survive, is John Harris, who died in 1691, and who was simultaneously assisted by two colleagues ; a fact in itself testifying to the importance of the station. This trio are found to have signed the Confession of Faith of 1689.

Joseph Maisters, a native of Kingsdown, Somerset, appears as a preaching elder of this society. He was born in the memorable November of 1640. In his sixteenth year he entered Magdalen College, but when at the Restoration, practices were introduced among the Fellows which Maisters deemed objectionable, he took up his quarters in Magdalen Hall. As a penalty for Nonconformity, he was refused his degree of Bachelor of Arts, although he had fairly won that distinction. Disappointed, though adhering to principle, he allied himself to the Dissenters, and in 1667, was ordained pastor over a people both few and small, at Theobalds, in Hertfordshire. The times were gloomy and disheartening. Numberless annoyances and difficulties springing from persecution had necessarily to be endured and overcome. None but candidates of the truest Christian type were then found seeking admission to Nonconformist communion. Very strong, therefore, was the uniting tie which bound a persecuted pastor to a persecuted people ; the Church at Theobalds being no singular example of the truth of this remark. When Maisters became invited by the rich and influential company in Thames-street to settle in London, no persuasives could make him entirely forsake his rural followers. His country hearers were received into communion at Joiners' Hall, and on removing thither, the pastor reserved one Sabbath in every month to minister to his Hertfordshire flock. The church soon after removed into Pinners' Hall, and by permission of the Independents—the lease-holders—held their services on Sabbath afternoons. As a preacher, Maisters enjoyed a fair reputation; but he never ventured on publishing a single piece. He died in 1717, and lies in Bunhill-fields. Jeremiah Hunt, the Independent minister at Pinners' Hall, celebrated the pastor's memory and Christian attainments in an appropriate funeral discourse. Maisters was a Calvinist; his eulogist was an Arian. Notwithstanding so awkward a discrepancy, Crosby's complaisance designates the latter "a shining light."

In the days of Thomas Richardson, 1718-30, who next succeeded, the Church removed to Devon-shire-square. The last minister, Clendon Dawkes, a native of Wellingborough, was a divine of considerable learning, and of respectable powers. He continued his pastorate until 1751, when, on account of diminished numerical strength, this once prosperous society voluntarily dissolved its union, and Dawkes settled at Hemel Hempstead, where, seven years later, he died.

One other reminiscence of Thames-street may be here introduced. In Elizabeth's reign the vicinity was remarkable for its brewhouse, whence the citizens chiefly derived their supplies of beer. This institution stood at Broken Wharf. Near at hand was an "ancient great hall," belonging to the City Water Works of the sixteenth century. This estate had formerly been the site of the Duke of Norfolk's town mansion. Some footprints of the Baptists are found here, for here preached Hanserd Knollys. In 1691, he and his congregation left the meeting-house to settle in Newgate-street, and afterwards to find a home in Curriers' Hall.

When, after the Bartholomew massacre of 1572, the Huguenot subjects of that royal assassin, Charles the Ninth of France, sought an asylum in England, a number of them settled in London, when the citzens gave their colony the expressive *sobriquet* of Petty France. This neighbourhood, the aspect of which has been entirely changed by the formation of new streets, occupied the area between Bishopsgate and Moorfields. The thoroughfares of Petty France were interesting by reason of many sacred associations. They contained the homes of many whom duty had required to encounter the Papacy in the full vigour of its treacherous power: that apostate church, whose abettors, through being too meanly subtle to risk honest controversy, or honourable war, have been wont to promote their iniquitous designs by political dissembling, assassination and priestcraft.

On some uncertain site in Petty France stood a meeting-house of the Baptist denomination. The Church thus situated in the heart of the City, found itself fully exposed to the persecution of the Restoration. It formed one of the more conspicuous butts whereat the Government aimed their vengeful shafts, while manifesting their infallibility and hatred of Dissent. The worshippers, who, in those dreary days, attended meetings in Petty France, could never calculate whether it would be their fortune peaceably to separate, or whether they would be maimed, and carried away to prison. Their services were often interrupted by military intruders, Charles the Second's soldiers being experienced adepts in the valorous exploits of destroying pews and of frightening women. Apparently the accounts of the earlier pastors in this district have perished; for the "very learned and judicious" William Collins is the first of the list whom the somewhat capricious Crosby deigns to mention. That honest historian manifested predilections by no means singular, when he preferred giving unreadable dissertations rather than history; for John Piggott, in a funeral sermon, professed to give an account of Collins; and, in doing so, has taken considerable pains to multiply words without knowledge, carefully omitting to mention either the time or place of his subject's birth. Some facts, however, are given by Crosby— who always interests us when he ceases arguing —from which we infer that Collins was a scion of

some considerable family.   After receiving a superior
education, he set off on his travels; and in those
days, for a student to make a tour through Europe
the sequel to his college course, was quite uncommon.   While enjoying these perambulations, neither
theology nor general literature was neglected ; and in
philology and medical science his attainments were more
than respectable.   From some of his high connections
there came alluring proffers of Anglican preferment;
but such temptations were manfully repelled.   On
returning to England, Collins entered the ranks of
Nonconformity.   Difficulties vexed him as they
vexed others under similar circumstances.   Now
his way is clouded by perplexity until the path of
duty is not clearly discoverable.   One whole day is
set apart for seeking divine direction with fasting
and prayer.   These exercises are scarcely concluded,
when there arrives what Collins's simple faith accepts
as an answer to his heart's request—a call to settle
in London from " The baptised Church in Petty
France."   Only little besides the above is known
about this divine.   Here he laboured, and here he
died.   In addition to being an excellent philologist,
he inherited a natural capacity for extempore
preaching ; a practice which from time immemorial
has found high favour among the English Baptists.
His humility and moderation were generally admired.
Then at length, when his labours were closing, and
the going down of his earthly sun was the earnest
of approaching repose, the good hope became beauti-

fully manifest as the crowning triumph of his Christian life. In September, 1702, Collins lies languishing upon his dying couch; a friend steps to his side, and, in reverential tones befitting the occasion, enquires, "Sir, I hope you are not afraid to die?" "I bless God," rejoins the pastor, "I have not been afraid to die these forty years."

The "learned and judicious" Nehemiah Cox assisted Collins at Petty France; and, whether we regard him as a shoemaker or as a doctor of divinity, he is an interesting member of the Baptist galaxy of Old London. One of his supposed ancestors—a bishop under Queen Elizabeth—had been roughly handled for promulgating unepiscopal views concerning infant baptism. Nehemiah was born and reared at Bedford, where his family went with the Dissenters, and where young Cox, during his youth, benefited by the counsel and friendship of Bunyan. He was, doubtless, advised by the latter, when he bravely volunteered, in the midst of prevailing persecution, to enter the lists as an evangelist, in 1671. Like a sincere worker, who realised the importance of his message, Cox persevered in a rough and difficult path, wherein he encountered his share of Government opposition. On one occasion and before his brethren, he penitentially confessed to some miscarriages; but probably these were nothing more heinous than some unpalatable censures of Church officers, which, on consideration, were manfully retracted as uncharitable. Prior to removing to London, in 1675, Cox was settled at Cranfield—a sphere where he necessarily supplemented a scanty stipend by working at the shoemaking craft. Eventually, the doctor was arraigned before the judges at Bedford assizes; and, throughout his defence, which he conducted himself and unassisted, he occasioned the lawyers unusual and extreme inconvenience, by arguing, as inclination prompted, or perhaps, as it suited the subject, at one time in Greek, and at another time in Hebrew. The presiding judge listened in some amazement, while again inspecting the indictment to get assured, if possible, that neither eyes nor ears were playing deceit. The prisoner legally claimed the right of pleading in such tongues as suited his humour, notwithstanding that none were competent to reply to the strange sounds he uttered. Mr. Justice promoted the popular merriment by remarking to his bewigged and chagrined satellites, the counsel for the crown, "Well, gentleman, the cordwainer has wound you all up." Necessarily, the prisoner got sent about his business; for in that era, a preaching shoemaker, whose harangues in the dead languages were unintelligible to benchers and members of Inns of Court, was similar to a more modern example, when one of our magistrates lately released a prisoner because "too contemptible for punishment." Dr. Cox died in the same year as his preceptor, Bunyan—that year of liberty, 1688.

Mention is made of Thomas Harrison, another

assistant of William Collins, who ultimately removed to Lorimers' Hall, to be cut off, while yet young, in the midst of his usefulness. In 1701, on 'the meeting-house in Petty France being forsaken in favour of a chapel in Artillery-street, the people retired from a spot closely associated with the heroic period of their history. With the various phases which that heroism assumed we can never be acquainted. They had frequently been illtreated with savage ferocity, and once had had their premises taken from them. They could now afford voluntarily to resign, beneath the benign rule of William, what, during the ascendancy of the perfidious Stuarts, they had clung to with the tenacity of life.

In the days we are speaking of, the City attracted crowds of Sabbath worshippers from neighbouring districts, and in many instances the London societies became the parents of suburban churches. A chapel in Hart-street, Bow-street, was an example of this outgrowth. Between 1691 and 1729 the General Baptists were stationed in this vicinity. The sanctuary—long since removed—stood, as usual, secluded from the notice of casual passengers. Its records have perished, what little we know having descended through the parent Church in White's-alley, Philpot-lane. The society in Hart-street was formed for the convenience of those strict disciples of western London, who refused to commune with professors honouring a less rigorous *régime*. The tenet they held in peculiar estimation was the Im-

position of Hands upon newly-received members.
Manifesting an excessive reverence for this custom,
the people walked long distances to worship, in preference to attending a ministry where the practice
was dishonoured. The old General Baptists, however, who retained their purity of faith, were zealous
promoters of Christianity. They were animated by
the purest motives, and honestly endeavoured to accomplish their sacred mission, but this Hart-street
scion of so honourable a house grew weary of the
control of its City parent and early preceptors.
Disagreement and consequent disorder completed
the extinction of the society about forty years after
its inauguration.

The Commonwealth days were remarkable for a
prolific harvest of controversial tracts, and many of
these, directed against the Baptists, are written in
strains of virulent contempt. Some were serious,
another class were satirical, and others, by reason of
their quaint and obsolete style, cannot fail to prove
to modern readers a well-spring of facetiæ. One
set of authors showed strong predilections for ac-
cumulating offensive details connected with the
pranks and heresies of certain fanatics, who, arising
in Germany, were called Anabaptists, because to
their mad vagaries and practices, they added adult
baptism by immersion. To the satisfaction of large
numbers of readers, Baptists in general were proved
to be dangerous theologically, politically, and morally.
In the spring of 1649 there appeared a pamphlet

entitled, England's New Chains Discovered. In the opinion of the House of Commons, the author had committed a grave offence, and they ominously expressed their indignation. Some fanatical partisans were looking on who sought to turn this irritation of Parliament to their own advantage. Efforts were made to throw upon the Baptist denomination the odium of having produced this political squib—a manœuvre partially successful, because the paper had been publicly read by its zealous abettors in several of the London chapels. Perceiving what injury their principles were likely to sustain in the estimation of spectators, Kiffen, supported by others, prepared a petition for presentation to the Commons. On Monday, April the 2nd, the petitioners appeared at Westminster, and, among other things, complained that, "Through the injustice of historians, or the headiness of some unruly men formerly in Germany, called Anabaptists, our righteous profession heretofore hath been, and now may be made odious, as if it were the fountain source of all disobedience, presumption, self-will, contempt of rulers, dignities, and civil government whatsoever." The deputation disclaimed having aided the circulation of the offensive paper. While the clerk read their loyal address, Kiffen and his companions waited without the Parliamentary chamber. On being called to the bar of the Commons, the Fisher's-folly pastor, as the mouth-piece of his brethren in London, made a graceful oration, the exact words of which have descended to posterity.* The Speaker, in handsome terms, acknowledged both speech and petition. The Baptist galaxy were assured that Parliament accepted their loyal sentiments as no less Christian than reasonable. In return for the satisfaction their petition had afforded, the petitioners were permitted to print their paper, and they departed with the assurance that their rights of conscience would be guaranteed. The satire and opposition which Puritanism provoked and encountered, mainly sprang from the hatred of our fallen nature to the severe morality which the Puritan discipline alone sanctioned. Doubtless the Puritans themselves too frequently erred on the side of eccentricity; nevertheless, it is not easy to understand why, what at the worst, was only religious carefulness, in every way commendable, should have awakened contemptuous aversion so widely spread. That this was the case, however, is well-known. How Puritanism was misrepresented and villified by licentious writers may be learned

---

* Kiffen spoke as follows: "Mr Speaker, we have not troubled this honourable House with any petition, nor had done it now, had we not been necessitated thereto by a late paper called England's Second Chains, brought to our congregations, and publiquely read in some of our publique meetings, without our consent or approbation, being there openly opposed by us; and we could do no less, in conscience of our duty to God and you, than discover it and disavow it."

Vide *The Humble Petition and Representation of several Churches of God in London, commonly (though falsely) called Anabaptists. London, April 3, 1649.*

from the multitude of tracts, composed by authors,
who supposed their thoughts on religious matters
to be of sufficient importance for bequeathment to
posterity. "Envy will merit as its shade pursue."
The aphorism is peculiarly applicable to the era of
Owen and Baxter.*

Rhyme was a favourite medium among all classes
for the conveyance of sentiment. Many whose
mental weakness prevented their concocting rhyth-
mical prose, found it comparatively easy to produce
any number of doggrel couplets, which the class for
whom they were written read with admiration. On
the breaking out of the civil wars this kind of

---

* In 1647 there appeared a satire on Puritanism called the
Brownist's Conventicle. This black-letter pamphlet is a
dish of delectables. Among other things, there are printed
specimens of graces before and after meat in the alleged
Puritan fashion. The modern reader will scarcely complete
the perusal of this squib without coming to the irresistible
conclusion that, after all, it was manifestly the luxuriant
parterre in which onr sturdy fathers thrived which excited
the envious spleen of their opponents. In witness we give
this extract—and *only* an extract—from the grace before
dinner, delivered, of course, with a nasal twang and turned-
up eyes:—"I beseech thee good Father make us thankfull
for all these thy bountiful blessings upon our boord. Let
this dish of chickens put us in mind of our Saviour, who
would have gathered Hierusalem together as an hen gathereth
her chickens, but she would not; but let us praise God for
these chickens being six in number. Let this leg of mutton
call us to remembrance that King David was once a shepherd.
. . . Here is an excellent loyne of veale, let it prompt us

literature was dispersed among the troops. In "A Spiritual Song of Comfort or Incouragement to the Souldiers that are gone forth in the Cause of Christ," we read :—

> " Though some in horses put their trust,
> And others in chariots take delight,
> 'Tis not *their* might, nor with *their* power,
> But with His spirit we doe fight."

At or about the time of the assembling of the Long Parliament, in 1640, a more pretentious poetaster obliged the world with The Lofty Bishop, The Lazie Brownist, and The Loyal Author. Each

to remember the parable of prodigall child, whom to welcome home, the father caused the calfe to be killed, which I thinke could not yeeld a better rump and kidney than is now before our eyes. . . . By this cramm'd and well-fed capon, let us be mindfull of the cock which crowed three times. . . . . What see I there? A potato pye and a sallad of sparagus. . . . When that Westphalia bacon comes to be cut up, let us think of the herd of swine. . . . Make us thankfull for thy bounty sent us from the sea; and first for this jole of sturgeon, and let it so far edifie us, as to think, how great that whale's head was which swallowed up the prophet Jonas. And, though those lobsters seeme to be in red coats like cardinals, having clawes like usurers, and more bones than the Beast of Rome. . . Yet, having taken off their papesticall capes and cases, let us freely feed upon what is within. . . . I conclude with the fruit. . . . These pippins may put us in mind of the forbidden tree. . . . . Had she not, wild wretch, eaten ye forbidden apple, all our crabs had been very good pippins, and all our thistles very good harti-

member of the trio is supposed to sing his speech, and the Churchman begins : —

> " What would yee lazie Brownists have ?
>   You rage and run away,
> And cry us downe, our Church and eke,
>   And forme therein we pray.
> Oh, monsters great ! abortive sonnes,
>   Your mothers to forsake.
> To church you doe restrain to come
>   Your prayers there to make."

The bishop's song occupies thirty-two lines. The Brownist sings an identical number in response :—

> " Your lofty Lordshipp tearmes us lazie,
>   And runagadoes too ;
> But I could wish you bishops would
>   But labour as we do.
> The apostles of our Saviour Christ
>   You plead you doe succeed,
> And yet would starve those soules which they
>   Did labour for to feed.

Meanwhile, the author, in censorious mood, has weighed the demerits of either side. At length he also speaks, and in words which representatives of

choaks. . . Thus as briefly as I can I have gone through every dish on the boord. Let us fall to and feed exceedingly, that after a full repast we may the better prophesie." In the grace after dinner mention is made of some distinguished Puritan names. One is a button maker, and another a felt worker ; but more important than all is Master How the cobbler.

29

his class of to-day would designate "withering satire," exclaims :—

> " The Brownists' noses want a ring
>   (To draw them with a rope),
> . The prelates' wings do cutting need,
>   (Lest they fly to the Pope)."

Such fantasies of the seventeenth century will always retain their freshness of interest for historical students. Any moderate acquaintance with the literature of the Cromwellian era must tend to heighten our contentment with these happier times. It will do something besides. It will convince us that the history of the age in question has yet to be written.

If we credit the City chroniclers, we shall believe that the nomenclature of Houndsditch is derived from an open sewer which formerly ran in that direction. This ditch was one of the pestilence breeders of ancient London. Its contents included the miscellaneous refuse of the neighbourhood—a neighbourhood, it may be well to remember, celebrated for its dead dogs. The street, by its name, even yet commemorates the fate of these unfortunate *hounds*. In the sixteenth century the nuisance was partially compensated for by some neighbouring recreation grounds, the pleasant area of which covered several acres. Prior to Henry the Eighth's seizure of it, this estate surrounded the monastery of the Holy Trinity. After dispersing the brotherhood,

Henry bestowed their patrimony on Sir Thomas Audley. At a former period, the beneficence of a certain prior found exercise in erecting several cottages for invalids near at hand, and in laying out their little gardens. Usually the inhabitants of this hospitable refuge were persons hopelessly bed-ridden. In keeping with the founder's wishes, the custom was for these poor people to open their case-ments on Friday mornings, not forgetting to exhibit white napkins on their window-sills. Then it hap-pened, that the charitable and pious who walked that way remembered the poor by laying down their alms as they passed.

In Houndsditch or its immediate vicinity a con-gregation of Baptists formerly assembled. At or about the era of the Restoration the pastor was the distinguished Henry Danvers—a political and theo-logical celebrity whose character his contemporaries extolled as belonging to an able divine and a dis-cerning controvertist, whose private worth corres-ponded with an unspotted public career. Modern times have seen the old Baptist's character depre-ciated. According to a great historian, Danvers was a reckless but cowardly bravado, whose spirit sufficed to carry him to the brink of action, but whose craven heart always prompted a retreat. A man whose cowardice made him forsake his friends when dangers threatened, and whose want of courage only exempted him from the scaffold upon which many of those friends expired. "Danvers was . . . . hot-headed,

29 *

but faint-hearted," we are told; "constantly urged to the brink of danger by enthusiasm, and constantly stopped on that brink by cowardice. . . . . In every age the vilest specimens of human nature are to be found among demagogues." Presently we will examine the basis on which these aspersions rest. Another historian—our old friend Crosby—calls " Henry Danvers a worthy man, of an unspotted life and conversation."

It is a matter for regret that Crosby has only left us a very meagre and confused account of this singular person—singular, if we merely consider him as the author of some thousand pages in defence of Believers' Baptism, thereby provoking the opposition of a Pædobaptist galaxy, of which Baxter was the leader. In the truest sense was Danvers a remarkable man. His congregation was supposed by Wilson to have been identical with the one in Crutchedfriars; if so, he had a predecessor in the redoubtable Paul Hobson.

At one period during the unsettled times of the civil wars Danvers was governor of Stafford. At Stafford he appears to have embraced some of the less harmless tenets of the Fifth Monarchists, although he never sanctioned the fantasies of the extreme fanatics. As a provincial governor, he enjoyed all the advantages springing from the hereditary prestige of a good family. The common people are no despicable judges of character in high places; and by the common people Danvers was esteemed as one devoted to his duty, and a man not to be corrupted by bribes. As it happened with so many of his compeers, so fair a reputation availed him nothing after the Restoration. He belonged to a party of too-enlightened politics, and professed a theology too self-denying, to find favour with king or parasite in that "golden age of the coward, the bigot, and the slave." Danvers's religious sympathies and his extraordinary zeal in defending a distinguishing tenet of his denomination drew upon him considerable odium. Numbers of enthusiasts, because slightly differing from him in belief, regarded the Baptist with spiteful enmity. Time-serving cavaliers laughed in derision. At length Danvers's enemies, by conspiring together, contrived to get him imprisoned in the Tower; but his wife, a lady of position, possessed considerable influence at Court, and so obtained her husband's liberation. This favourable turn of events sadly disconcerted a host of opponents of various parties, for Danvers's political patriotism was only equalled by his evangelistic earnestness. He heartily sympathised with Monmouth's ill-fated enterprise, and in consequence of having shared that hazardous business was compelled to take refuge in Holland. In that asylum he died in 1686.

The meeting-house in London wherein Danvers officiated was pointed at by Edwards in the third part of Gangræna. That unamiable Presbyterian called his readers' attention to the fanaticism of the congregation. Hanserd Knollys and others had presumed to anoint a blind woman's eyes, and to accompany the action with prayers for her restoration.

Danvers was a very industrious author. His writings, which for the most part are controversial, chiefly relate to that distinguishing tenet of his denomination, Believers' Baptism. His pamphlets awakened a vindictive opposition of more than average violence, even in an age when polemics of every school indulged in unseemly personalities. Happily for this more enlightened era, the literary freedoms of the seventeenth century have for ever passed out of fashion. The opposition encountered by Danvers, however, Crosby describes as "haughty, bitter, wrathful, and provoking." The historian's language is no exaggeration; yet we shall not do well if we allow such expressions to depreciate the able men who entered the arena as the author's opponents. All parties in those days adopted a rude address, as though uncouthness imparted argumentative strength. It would be too much to expect that the pamphlets of the indefatigable Danvers were free from the common disfigurement. Nevertheless they were partially successful, if success may be measured by the able answers they provoked. One of the combatants raised a cry of dishonesty. Danvers, he declared, misquoted authorities and garbled extracts. This charge of literary dishonesty was closely pressed, till the denominational leaders in London testified in a printed paper to the spotless character and valuable writings of their uncompromising champion. Yet not only in such polemical fencing did Danvers exercise his skill and prowess; he has left fruits of other accomplishments than those belonging to the mere disputant. For example, he arranged "Solomon's Proverbs in English and Latin, alphabetically . . . for the help of memory"—a little performance well deserving of a reprint in *fac simile*.*

Englishmen in these days will scarcely allow that a man's character is necessarily forfeited, because, while opposing a government and family, whose crimes provoked a revolution, he took some extra precautions to preserve his life. That Danvers was

* This work was published in 1676, and its ingenious editor intended it to serve as an educational text-book. The English and Latin are upon opposite pages in each opening. The metrical introduction is in the quaint Puritan style— *e. g.* many less instructive delineations of folly have been drawn by more ambitious poets than these lines:—

> " Or what's a fool that is with riches graced ?
> A swine in whose foul snout a gem is placed.
> Or what's a fool on whom honour doth wait ?
> A long-ear'd ass, sitting in a chair of state.
> The miser's a fool, and so is he
> That spends his wealth in prodigality :
> Whom, if they went to wisdom, she would show
> A fair and middle path wherein to go.
> And art thou great ? be not a fool ;
> For thou thou'lt make thy folly more conspicuous.
> Acquaint thyself with wisdom, wait upon her,
> And she will add true glory to thine honour.
> By her king's reign ; and princes do decree,
> By her advice, justice and equity.

a political plotter none will venture on denying. William Russell and Algernon Sydney were also political plotters, and the heart of Danvers beat with theirs when they sought to check the encroachments of kingcraft. He was arraigned for an alleged share in the Rye House Plot,* and, as we learn from Spratt's True (?) Account, he was only released on bail. At that conjuncture the English seemed bent on spilling the best of English blood; and,

> A fool, that is in honour, doth but show
> Himself to be a fool in folio.
> Justly might wisdom then preferred be
> By Solomon, 'bove wealth and dignity.
> A sacred flame it is which no'er shall die,
> But ev'n now burns for us to warm us by.
> A flame that gives not only heat but light,
> Not only warms the heart, but guides the sight."

* Danvers is several times mentioned in the account prepared by Lord Grey for the use of James the Second; and his name occurs in a manner which shows him to have been an important conspirator in Monmouth's insurrection. Danvers, it appears, had to exert all his influence to prevent a rising in the City on the occasion of James's coronation— e. g., "Mr. Smith came to us from England, the exact time I know not; but I remember he gave us a particular account of your Majesty's coronation, and said if it had not been for the great industry of Colonel Danvers, and others of our friends in the City, there had been a rising at that time, which was designed by some hot-headed men in London, who had drawn many of their friends from Hertfordshire and Essex to London to the number of 500, with intention to oppose your Majesty's coronation." We read again: "Four men came to us from our friends in London. . . . Their

therefore, when a prisoner was discharged by the craven judges, it amounted to an admission of innocence. Shortly after this adventure, Danvers retired into seclusion, "on account," says Lord Macaulay, " of a grossly calumnious paper, of which the government had discovered him to be the author."

This " calumnious " tract is styled " a malicious libel," by that courtly trimmer, Bishop Sprat, of Rochester. The historians in general avoid describing the purport of this pamphlet, or even mentioning its title.* It belonged to a class of political squibs then not uncommon, but to circulate which was to entail considerable danger. This one, in particular, attempted to prove the Earl of Essex to have been guiltless of suicide, and to have been foully dealt with by his enemies. On finding themselves thus openly accused of an execrable assassination, the King and his ministers were greatly

business was to acquaint the Duke of Monmouth that several thousands were enlisted in London, and were to be under the command of Colonel Danvers, unless his Grace appointed another head." Monmouth replied, " That as for Colonel Danvers, he thought him a proper person to command them."—*Grey's Secret History of the Rye House Plot, etc.*

* The title reads thus : " Murder will out ; or, a clear and full discovery that the Earl of Essex did not feloniously murder himself, but was barbarously murdered by others, both by undeniable circumstances and positive proofs." This curious piece was published immediately after the Revolution. On the title-page the author is styled "Henry Danvers, Esq."

enraged. Possibly some humilating remembrances mingled with and embittered their chagrin, while they recalled the doings of that dark Friday in July, 1683, when, as Russell's trial proceeded, London was suddenly horror-stricken by intelligence of the Earl's untimely fate. Whatever may have been their feelings in the matter, those in authority made strenuous endeavours to trace the writer of the obnoxious missile. Success only attended them to the discovery of his name. A reward of one hundred pounds was immediately offered for Danvers' apprehension, and he was advertised for in the London Gazette.*

Now as regards this paper, the Government may

* The advertisement is as follows:—"Whitehall, Jan. 4. Whereas, Henry Danvers, commonly called Colonel Danvers, late of Newington, in the county of Middlesex, stands accused upon oath of several treasonable and traitorous practices against his Majesty, and is fled from justice. His Majesty has commanded notice to be given, that whosoever shall apprehend the said Henry Danvers, and cause him to be delivered into safe custody, that he may be proceeded against according to law, shall receive a reward of one hundred pounds, which his Majesty hath ordered to be forthwith paid by the Lords Commissioners of the Treasury."—*London Gazette, Monday, January 5*, 1684-5.

The above was repeated in the issue of the Thursday following. In the number of the paper for July 27th there was a royal proclamation, calling on Danvers and others to surrender within twenty-one days. Our divine, it is needless to say, had not sufficient politeness to prompt compliance with the King's commands.

be excused for having experienced some chagrin at so venomous an attack on their honour and humanity. So likewise must Danvers be exonerated from the odium attached to dishonest motives; for that he really believed Essex owed his death to treachery cannot fairly be doubted. Nor, indeed, did he stand alone in entertaining that opinion. Calamy quotes a passage from Rapin, wherein that historian says, Essex left a son, who always believed his father to have been murdered. Although posterity has arrived at different conclusions, it would not be difficult to show. that Danvers merely circulated a version of a catastrophe which numbers regarded as the offspring of Romish machinations.*

An examination of the authorities whence a low estimation of Danver's character is drawn, will prove their united testimony to be of only little value. First, and most pretentious, comes Archdeacon Echard. During the reign of George the First, Echard achieved enviable success in history writing; but those modern readers lose but little who seldom disturb his long since forgotten volumes. Being himself a comfortable pluralist, Echard pleaded for the interest of Church and State by expounding that policy which execrates "The Grand Rebellion,"

---

* See Calamy's Autobigraphy, I., 110. Essex had a French servant, who attended him during his imprisonment in the Tower. This man's sudden disappearance immediately after the Earl's death awakened many suspicions.

or the days when Hanserd Knollys could officiate in Bow Church. From this writer's pages we learn that Cromwell was a dissembler, a hypocrite, and a cunning schemer. On the eve of the battle of Worcester, this monster of Independency made a contract with the powers of darkness, the Enemy of Man, being described by the witness, supplying the information, as " a grave, elderly gentleman, with a roll of parchment in his hand." A writer who, under whatever circumstances, and with whatever qualifications, could venture on intruding such rubbish as this into a history of his country, scarcely deserves that contempt usually awarded to literary pettifoggers. But Echard was apologist in general to the enemies of English liberty. Thus the cruel and mean-spirited Laud is glorified as " the greatest benefactor to all public designs of piety and charity." The Scottish nation, the Nonconformists, and the patriots Russell and Sydney, are maligned in common. The author professedly rejoiced in the Revolution, but gave what prominence he dared to Jacobitical politics, and the doctrine of passive obedience.

Such a writer, among Dissenters at any rate, will not rank highly as a trustworthy historian. A century and a half ago, our fathers complained of his facts and misrepresentations. To others, his awkward manner of citing authorities occasioned constant perplexity. Even learned readers found it difficult to separate what was

Echard's own from what belonged to somebody else. *

Now, the chief authority which historians can adduce in substantiation of aspersions on the fame

* In 1718 Dr. Calamy published "A Letter to Archdeacon Echard upon the occasion of his History of England, wherein the principles of the Revolution are defended, the Whigs and Dissenters vindicated, several persons of distinction cleared from aspersion, and a number of historical mistakes rectified." This piece is a pamphlet of 128 pages. Calamy allows to Echard the possession of that necessary genius for writing history; and a good work of the kind had long been a desideratum. Echard's labours in ecclesiastical research, however, had already been too extravagantly lauded. The English history in consequence met with a generous acceptance; and the Dissenters deemed it an imperative duty to refute its errors and to expose its calumnies. Calamy volunteered to complete this uncongenial task. Echard manifested a strong dislike for Puritans of every party, and accordingly most bearing that name are maligned as soon as they appear upon the scene. Nonconformists and Jesuits are placed on a level as common foes to that polity which allowed Echard to write books at his ease, while growing rich by the revenues of distant cures. One old clergyman rebuked this slander by showing the vital difference between Nonconformists who would merely put aside the surplice, &c., and Jesuits who would suppress the Bible. With an able hand, Calamy dissects his opponent's shortcomings. Echard is plainly told, "Many of the authors cited by you have so little credit in the world as to be far from giving sufficient warrant to justify your inserting things from them into a history." The archdeacon excluded or made use of matter as it suited his capriciousness or the temper of the intolerant party to which he belonged.

of Henry Danvers, is a manuscript quoted by
Echard, and written by the notorious Robert
Ferguson—a political recusant, whose memory all
parties in common agree to execrate. Whether
Ferguson be regarded as a trimmer, a turncoat, a
liar, or a knave in general, his character will show
itself to have been as repulsive as his personal
appearance.* Echard himself entertained the lowest
opinion of this audacious pedant, to whom he was
indebted for the filling of a few columns. Ferguson
strove hard but successfully, to earn the well-merited
contempt of every religious and political section.
While probably thriving on guineas transmitted from
Whitehall, apparently he promoted the Revolution.
That sturdy exponent of Whiggism, and hero of the
Dunciad, Oldmoxon, denounces Ferguson as an
arch-traitor and a villain. Burnet believed him to
be simply a knave. Even the opinion of Lord
Macaulay is not less decisive, for in the fifth chapter of the History of England, Ferguson is portrayed as "a cast-out Presbyterian and a mere
swindler. He lived among libellers and false
witnesses." He was also "violent, malignant,
. . . . delighting in intrigue, in tumult, in mis-

---

* Ferguson is thus described:—"A tall lean man, dark
brown hair, a great Roman nose, thin jaw'd, heat in face,
speaks in the Scotch tone, a sharp, piercing eye, stoops a
little in the shoulders; he hath a shuffling gait, that differs
from all men, wears his perriwig almost over his eyes, about
forty-five years of age."—*Echard, Hist. Eng.* 1064.

chief for its own sake." This Ferguson was born a plotter. He plotted against James during James's ascendancy; but plotted for James when James became an exile. After having aided the Revolution, he espoused the opposite extreme, and even conspired against the peace of Queen Anne. A political renegade by profession, was it wonderful, when such a creature experienced pleasure in concocting and circulating falsehoods about such former associates as, unfortunately for themselves, had been parties to his unprincipled machinations? ‡

It was necessary thus far to detail the character of Robert Ferguson, because our present complaint is that, on the authority of such an outcast, sanctioned by such an historian as Echard, the reputation of an old Nonconformist military hero is made to suffer. With a prescience uncharacteristic of honest writers, Ferguson prefaced his farrago by affirming "There stands nothing in it but what is exactly true." Among the phenomena of social life we occasionally find that slanderous trifles are veraciously introduced. Upright persons expect their

* Ferguson went over to the Jacobites in 1690, on which circumstance Macaulay observes:—"For his apostacy he could not plead even the miserable excuse that he had been neglected. The ignominious services which he had formerly rendered to his party as a spy, a raiser of riots, a dispenser of bribes, a writer of libels, a prompter of false witnesses, had been rewarded only too prodigally for the honour of the new government."—*Hist. Eng., chap.* xxv.

word to be taken without such introductions. Ferguson, on the contrary, was strongly suspicious that posterity would refuse him a hearing.*

Seeing, then, that the aspersions cast by Lord Macaulay on the fame of Danvers are only supported by a witness whom the inimitable historian himself denounces as a worthless libeller, exception to them may fairly be taken. Regard for truth, and English love of fair-play, will not sanction our taking it for granted that, this Baptist minister and parliamentary colonel was either " hotheaded " or " craven-hearted," nor that he was one of those viler curiosities of humanity " usually found among demagogues."

If these things cannot be proved, neither can another assertion of Lord Macaulay : Danvers " had drawn on himself the severe censures of the most respectable Puritans by attempting to palliate the crimes of Matthias and John of Leyden." Any slight examination of the accused man's writings will clearly prove that, he never did attempt to

* It may not be generally known that Ferguson was the ejected minister of Godmersham, Kent. In London he was a predecessor of Dr. Watts. He gave the most ferocious counsels to his brother conspirators of the Rye-House plot. Not only were the King and Duke to be assassinated ; malignant judges and sheriffs—had Ferguson's advice been acted on—would have had their skins hung up in Westminster Hall. At another time he advised the blowing-up of a theatre, with its entire audience, when Charles and hi brother should be present.

excuse the enormities said to have been committed by the fanatics named. He did doubt, however, whether the outrageous wickedness had been enacted as alleged. To doubt the correctness of certain relations very widely differs from a palliation of the crimes such accounts may include. Then again, "the censure of the most respectable Puritans" really emanated from Obadiah Wills, a fierce partisan writer, who laboured to identify the principle of Danvers's denomination with the atrocities of German enthusiasts.*

Now, so far is the assertion from truth of Danvers having provoked a general Puritan censure, that a number of leading Puritans voluntarily signed a paper drawn up for the express purpose of clearing their compeer from Wills's unfounded calumnies. Wills accused his opponent of literary dishonesty, and appealed to the Baptists in general to say if the charge could be disproved. On being appointed to

---

* According to Wills, Baptists were animated by "principles of darkness upon which many black characters are writ." The crimes alluded to by this writer, and associated with the siege of Munster in 1535, Danvers, like all reasonable men, held in abhorrence. He "supposed there was cause to doubt of the truth of those monstrous villanyes acted in their communities in the latter part of the siege as mentioned by their malitious enemies the Papists, and many of their inveterate enemies the Protestants." Our author's opinion was strengthened by things quite as odious having been circulated about Calvin and Luther.—Vide *Innocency and Truth Vindicated*, chap. iv.

30

examine this matter, such judges as Knollys and Kiffen exonerated their brother from all discreditable action. Crosby was in a position to write with some authority, and Crosby declares the old contro-vertist to have been " a worthy man, of an unspotted life and conversation." Probably only few will question Crosby's historical integrity.

Therefore it naturally follows, while no worthy evidence can be adduced to warrant our forming a degrading estimate of Danvers's mien and profession, we have strong reasons for supposing him not to have been worse than what Crosby describes. His con-troversial writings survive to testify to their author's abilities. Echard and Ferguson may be dismissed as untrustworthy witnesses, and Obadiah Wills as a blinded partisan whose zeal exceeded his justice. The testimony of more charitable men remains—testimony sustaining the inference, that after living a patriot's life, his zeal for the Liberties of England brought Danvers to an exile's grave.

Having enjoyed under Cromwell abundant pros-perity, the Baptists bitterly realised the calamities of the Restoration. In 1660 the London churches ad-dressed Charles the Second in a paper purporting to give an humble account of their situation and grievances, and printed copies were circulated among the various congregations. Apology is offered for not addressing the monarch by those titles of honour usually awarded—an omission not springing from any lack of loyalty and respect. This petition bore the signatures of twenty-six denominational elders. A perusal shows us how unpopular were the anti-pædobaptists during that summer of mad loyalty. Church-members were frequently arrested even while attending their daily business. Vexed on the one hand by the iniquitous government of a profligate ruler, on the other hand, Dissenters' lives were endangered by the boisterous and ignorant king-worship of the streets.

A few weeks prior to Charles's installation there appeared a squib called The Anabaptists' Recantation. The denominational chiefs are made to confess having hitherto been " a seduced and misled people . . . a wretched and confused multitude." Kiffen is a "sweet preacher upon Solomon's Canticles," and Parliament is besought to grant him "liberty to make his recantation in his own synagogue." Kiffen's able colleague, Thomas Patient, is " our orthodox preaching taylor." Then follow confessions of desperate endeavours to undermine the foundations of Church and State, of futile efforts to frustrate the Restoration by privately " seizing the honourable City of London." The petitioners are made to assume a show of penitence for having planned the burning of churches, and the suppression of preaching by the " conceited doctrine " of their own tenets. How such equivocal compliments were appreciated, and how ably they were answered, another squib, The Asse's Complaint against Balaam, will help us to judge. The fol-

30*

lowing couplets have reference to the Anglican
clergy :—

> " For we are burdened with our old Sir Johns,
> Who, when we ask for bread, do give us stones ;
> And only cant a homily or two,
> Which daws and parrots may be taught to doe.
> Drunkards cannonicall, unhallow'd bears,
> That name God oftener in their oaths than prayers."

In the neighbourhood of St. John's Gate—a rare,
quaint, and interesting mediæval relic, and a shrine
around which was once supposed to flit an airy
shape (the shade of Sylvanus Urban)—are discoverable some faint traces of the Puritan Baptists. The
gate, erected many centuries ago, but still so completely preserved, was of old the southern entrance
to the chief monastery of the military monks of St.
John of Jerusalem. In after-times these fighting
churchmen became possessed of an enormous inheritance; but their glory faded and their wealth
departed amid the happier light of the Reformation.
The materials of its magnificent chapel were taken
to the Strand to be used in the erection of old
Somerset House. Towards the close of the last
century, and while the workmen were digging the
foundations of the present St. John's Church, was
discovered the coffin of William Weston, the last
prior, who died in 1540.

Near this spot, so rich in religious and literary
reminiscences, there stood in olden times an ancient
mansion, built of wood and stone, and belonging to

the priory of Sempringham, Lincolnshire. Shortly after the Restoration, the Nonconformists took possession of these premises ; and to John Yoxley, the ejected minister of Kibworth, the credit belongs of having here gathered a congregation of Independents, who became extinct about the end of the same century. The vacated apartment was next occupied by the Baptists, who removed from another station. Their minister was Dr. William Russel, an able physician and member of Cambridge University. To Russel the chief delight of existence was controversy. He loved to exert the powers of his strong intellect in conducting oral and written disputations. We read of a grand debate on baptism which was held at Portsmouth, according to royal license, in 1699, Russel being a leading combatant. On separating after their unprofitable encounter, each polemical warrior claimed the victory, which really belonged to none of them. Russel wrote prodigiously on Believers' Baptism, and other subjects. Among the " Friends " he was exceedingly unpopular; and a treatise he published—Quakerism is Paganism —may have blighted the last hopes of reconciliation. Although both he and his books are forgotten, the pastor did not live in vain; and Crosby wrote less like a partisan than a lover of justice when he supplied materials whence we infer, that Russel was a scholar, an orator, and a Christian.

The Old Jewry is a spot abounding in Jewish and Christian associations. Prior to their banish-

ment from England, in the days of Henry the Third,
this was the Hebrews' chosen quarter in London.
How severely these old inhabitants suffered from
the fanaticism of a superstitious populace, and from
the dishonest exactions of a nominally Christian
government, will not need to be explained. During
the eighteenth century the Old Jewry possessed the
attraction of the famous meeting-house elsewhere
described. In this interesting vicinity the Baptists
established themselves in Puritan times, having for
a pastor Jeremiah Ives, about whom we can learn
but little. Neither of predecessor, nor of successor,
if such there was, can any particulars be related.
Ives himself was earnest, able, and industrious, but
evinced a lively abhorrence of both Quakers and
Papists. His polemical taste keenly relished a baptismal combat with Presbyterians, for in such encounters
he seems to have proved himself the Achilles of the
capital. On the fame of Jeremiah's prowess reaching
Whitehall, Charles sought to diversify the monotony
of a royal life by witnessing an argumentative con-
test between an ordained Romanist and pastor Ives,
" disguised in the habit of a clergyman." The merriment of the distinguished audience reached its
height when a singular turn in the proceedings suddenly terminated the discussion. The skilful disputants were fencing over the question of apostolical
succession. With an air of triumph, the priest avers
that Ives' reasonings weigh as heavily against infant
baptism as against the tenet in hand, but the readi-

ness with which the truth of this proposition is allowed opens the eyes of the sharp-witted papist. Sorely is he chagrined at finding he has argued, not with an Anglican vicar, as imagined, but with a veritable Baptist minister—brimming over with satisfaction at the discomfiture his subtlety has occasioned to a cub of the Beast of Babylon.

Not many paces from the Old Jewry is Basinghall-street, formerly containing the hall of the Worshipful Company of Lorimers. Connected with this place belong several Nonconformist histories, unfortunately for the most part wanting. The General Baptists, who came into possession in 1699, seceded from a neighbouring society which had excluded their pastor, Joseph Taylor. Taylor embraced the tenets of Calvinism, an example his followers quickly followed. Joseph Harrison, Taylor's successor, was still a young man when removed by death immediately after his settlement in 1702, and during that year the people left the hall and migrated to Spitalfields. The sanctuary was next taken possession of by the Independents. Neal, the historian of the Puritans, it may be mentioned *en passant*, was ordained at Lorimers' Hall. In after years, the Wesleyans, and the Countess of Huntingdon's connection, successively used the time-honoured building which has long since passed away.

We should evince an unbecoming and reprehensible lack of complaisance did we visit Red Cross-street without paying our compliments at

DR. WILLIAMS'S LIBRARY. But, alas! to the sore
inconvenience of its studious visitors, the old institution has been swept away to clear an area for
the very unornamental tunnels of the Metropolitan Railway; and, if report speaks truly, the
compensation has been unworthy of the havoc
occasioned.

The nucleus of the present fine collection of books
and pictures in the Library was formed from a three-
fold source. First were the literary treasures belonging to the founder himself; secondly, there was the
library of Dr. Bates, who died at Hackney in 1699.
To these were added the collection of Dr. Harris,
who, in the first part of the last century, was the
Presbyterian minister at Crutched-friars. The
original catalogue of 1727 appeared two years
prior to the opening of the library. A new list
of the books came out in 1801. That in present
use was published forty years later. The annual
surplus yielded by the Trust estates, is devoted to
the enriching of the collection, which now is deposited in a private house in Queen-square, and the
facilities for study and reference enjoyed by the
visitors cannot be too highly commended.

Nearly opposite the library—in Meeting-house-
alley—stood an old chapel, which descended from
the Independents to the Baptists, in 1760. The
minister, Thomas Craner, had previously profited by
a pastoral experience in Bedfordshire. His rural
followers were wont to honour a custom—happily

peculiar to themselves—of *as*senting and *dis*senting ¡
to the orally-expressed sentiments of their pastor by
remaining silent, or by stamping on the floor, the
latter being the sign of disapprobation. One aged
member, in particular, enjoyed a widely-spread
notoriety on account of the strength animating his
legs in spite of many tokens of declining vigour.
Very naturally, divers perplexities crowded into the
pastor's mind while he sought some honest method
of checking the weekly annoyance ; and the course
ultimately adopted illustrated the working of an ingenious mind, sufficiently amusing, although the
precedent may prove comparatively valueless in this
peace-loving era. On a certain Sabbath, the disaffected mustered strongly, and proved more than
ordinarily troublesome. But salutary surprise
awaited the congregation. The venerable offender
already alluded to was suddenly and effectually
cowed by being given publicly to understand, that
only considerable amendments in his behaviour
would exempt his nasal organ from an infliction
not sanctioned by the laws of Nonconformity, but
which he could see referred to in Proverbs thirty
and thirty-third. In other words, Craner assured
his noisy auditor, that unless he improved in manners
he would find himself the object of pastoral discipline,
and be led by the nose from his pew to the street.
The divine escaped from these disagreeable people in ¹
1756, and settled in London, where he died in 1773.
He has been depicted as "a drawling, inanimate

preacher, very high in his notions upon some doctrinal points."

A man of singular temperament, by name Augustus Clarke, succeeded Craner. Having received ordination at the hands of a Greek bishop, he claimed the right of officiating in the English Establishment. Eventually he relinquished Pædobaptism, and settled at Redcross-street, his election meanwhile dividing the congregation. By actively sharing in the anti-Romanist riots of 1780, Clarke further estranged his people; and when, shortly after, he resigned, the church was dissolved. The old chapel was successively occupied by Scotch seceders, Independents, and Baptist Sandemanians.

There was another chapel in Redcross-street, built by a Mrs. Masters, and in that lady's lifetime occupied by John Stevens, the expelled pastor of Devonshire-square. After the death of Stevens, his office remained vacant till 1781, when Thomas Mabbott, of Digby, in Lincolnshire, succeeded. Born in 1742, he suffered all the disadvantages springing from poverty and an ill-training. At length he was diverted from a plebeian career by one of Wesley's preachers, and one of Bunyan's books. Religion created a thirst for learning, and after some perseverance in study he commenced preaching. He settled in Redcross-street, but removed to Hoddesdon in 1791. When depressed by the weakness of declining years, Mabbott could only ascend the pulpit slowly and painfully. Nevertheless, his sermons were delivered with a strong and earnest utterance. He died in December, 1800.

From Redcross-street to Aldermanbury is only a few paces, and Aldermanbury is a classical spot in the annals of Nonconformity. Here, in bygone centuries, was situated the ancient hall wherein the Guilds assembled for the transaction of civic business. The street is also associated with two other events, as widely different as two extremes, but each retaining its peculiar interest—the ejectment from the living in 1662, of Edmund Calamy; and the mysterious tragedy of Elizabeth Canning, in 1753—the simple housemaid, whose alleged adventures rivalled the stories of chivalry, enchained public attention, and produced numbers of pamphlets on either side of a dispute, the mystery of which, time has failed to solve. The fine old Saxon church destroyed in the great fire, had attached to it several Puritan memories. In Aldermanbury a son of the rector just alluded to, and himself an ejected minister, by inviting divers Christians to meet for worship in his parlour, formed the nucleus of the celebrated Presbyterian Church in the Old Jewry, as already shown. Also, in Aldermanbury, some dim traces are found of the seventeenth-century Baptists. Where their station was, or who ministered to them, history does not inform us. Near this place, moreover, the Baptists had another congregation whose records are unfortunately wanting. These people met in Brewers'

Hall, Addle-street, in the days of George the Second.*

In the meantime our peregrinations about these noisy streets have taught us this cheering lesson: The *silence* of history is its better portion. The progress of merely human events, or the working of the kingdom of darkness, is heralded by ostentatious parade. Heaven's achievements are effected more quietly. It happens, therefore, that although Good proceeds so noiselessy, it is yet making greater conquests than we oftentimes dare to hope. We are dazzled by false glitter; deceived by shouts of mock victories: and our mundane nature is fascinated by the triumphal arches which brazen-faced wickedness erects, till even our religion becomes earthy, and the truth is forgotten, that the Kingdom of God cometh not with observation. What crowds of Christian workers have lived, laboured, and died in London! While unable in so many instances, even to point out the sites of their chapels, much less their place of sepulture, who would dare to

* Here is a quaint scrap belonging to Brewers' Hall:—
"The annual feast for the natives of the parish of St. Giles's, Cripplegate, will be held at Brewers' Hall, Addle-street, on Monday the 3rd of August next. Those gentlemen who are natives of that parish may be furnished with tickets by John Pine, clerk of the above said parish, living within three doors of the parish church, and are desired to indorse their names and places of abode on the backsides of their tickets for the better sending to them for the future."—*London Gazette, Thursday, July* 16, 1685.

estimate the importance of their humble endeavours to promote the Gospel of Christ! While the histories of such remain unwritten, what pains have been taken to chronicle regal banquets and imposing processions! But God will remember His servants. The forgetfulness of man can never diminish their reward. How abundantly will this be proved on the morning of that Day of days, when the darkest secrets of time shall be revealed to assembled worlds.

YATES & ALEXANDER
7, SYMONDS INN
CHANCERY LANE.
PRINTERS

AND AT CHURCH PASSAGE, CHANCERY LANE.

NONCONFORMITY IN SOUTHWARK.

IN PREPARATION,

Uniform with "ANCIENT MEETING-HOUSES,"

THE

METROPOLITAN TABERNACLE;

OR,

AN HISTORICAL ACCOUNT OF THE SOCIETY FROM ITS FIRST PLANTING IN THE PURITAN ERA TO THE PRESENT TIME,

WITH OTHER SKETCHES RELATING TO THE RISE, GROWTH, AND CUSTOMS OF NONCONFORMITY IN SOUTHWARK.

BY

GODFREY HOLDEN PIKE.

WITH AN INTRODUCTION BY

THE REV. C. H. SPURGEON.

.

www.ingramcontent.com/pod-product-compliance
Lightning Source LLC
Chambersburg PA
CBHW031808270326
41932CB00008B/343

*9 7 8 3 3 3 7 1 5 0 6 3 1 *